Hezbollah: The Story
of the Party of God

THE MIDDLE EAST IN FOCUS

The Middle East has become simultaneously the world's most controversial, crisis-ridden, and yet least-understood region. Taking new perspectives on the area that has undergone the most dramatic changes, the Middle East in Focus series, edited by Barry Rubin, seeks to bring the best, most accurate expertise to bear for understanding the area's countries, issues, and problems. The resulting books are designed to be balanced, accurate, and comprehensive compendiums of both facts and analysis presented clearly for both experts and the general reader.

Series Editor: Barry Rubin

Director, Global Research International Affairs (GLORIA)
Center Editor, *Middle East Review of International Affairs* (MERIA)
Journal Editor, *Turkish Studies*

Turkish Dynamics: Bridge across Troubled Lands
By Ersin Kalaycıoğlu

Eternal Iran: Continuity and Chaos
By Patrick Clawson and Michael Rubin

Hybrid Sovereignty in the Arab Middle East: The Cases of Kuwait, Jordan, and Iraq
By Gokhan Bacik

The Politics of Intelligence and American Wars with Iraq
By Ofira Seliktar

Hezbollah: The Story of the Party of God: From Revolution to Institutionalization
By Eitan Azani

Lebanon: Liberation, Conflict, and Crisis
Edited by Barry Rubin

The Muslim Brotherhood: The Organization and Policies of a Global Islamist Movement
Edited by Barry Rubin

Nabih Berri and Lebanese Politics
By Omri Nir

Hezbollah: The Story of the Party of God

From Revolution to Institutionalization

Eitan Azani

HEZBOLLAH: THE STORY OF THE PARTY OF GOD
Copyright © Eitan Azani, 2009, 2011

First published in hardcover in 2009 by PALGRAVE MACMILLAN® in the
United States – a division of St. Martin's Press LLC, 175 Fifth Avenue,
New York, NY 10010.

Where this book is distributed in the UK, Europe and the rest of the world, this
is by Palgrave Macmillan, a division of Macmillan Publishers Limited, registered
in England, company number 785998, of Houndmills, Basingstoke, Hampshire
RG21 6XS.

Palgrave Macmillan is the global academic imprint of the above companies and
has companies and representatives throughout the world.

Palgrave® and Macmillan® are registered trademarks in the United States, the
United Kingdom, Europe and other countries.

ISBN: 978-0-230-10872-1

Library of Congress Cataloging-in-Publication Data

Azani, Eitan.
  Hezbollah: the story of the party of God: from Revolution to
institutionalization / Eitan Azani.
      p. cm.—(Middle East in focus)
  Includes bibliographical references and index.
  ISBN 0–230–60588–5
  1. Hizballah (Lebanon) 2. Lebanon—Politics and government—1975–1990.
  3. Lebanon—Politics and government—1990–4.
Shiites—Lebanon—Politics and government. 5. Islam and politics—Lebanon.
  6. Geopolitics—Middle East. I. Title.

  JQ1828.A98H6225 2008
  324.25692'082—dc22   2008029179

A catalogue record of the book is available from the British Library.

Design by MPS Limited (a Macmillan Company)

First Palgrave Macmillan paperback edition: January 2011

10 9 8 7 6 5 4 3 2 1

Printed in the United States of America.

Contents

Preface

The last three decades of the twentieth century showed signs of the rise of the Islamic movements in the Middle East as they became a leading power factor in the resistance to the existent social and political order. The Islamic wave is prominent in its scope and strength and placed in the radical margins owing to its violence. Movements such as Hezbollah and Hamas are clear examples of this phenomenon. The growth of revolutionary movements has employed and still employs many researchers and regimes. The nature and characteristics of these movements differ across societies and eras. They are influenced by the relations between the state and the society; by the social, economic, and political conditions within a country; by the regional system; and by the international arrangement. These movements uphold internal dynamics characterized by a transition from spontaneous and informal patterns of activity toward a structure of institutions and organization based on formal norms and rules.

The background, the conditions, and the procedures that allowed for the development of Hezbollah are similar, in certain aspects, to those that influenced the directions of development of other revolutionary movements. Altogether, the model that developed in Lebanon is unique and different due to the Lebanese ethnic sectarian structure, Lebanon's unique geopolitical condition, and the movement's Shiite Islamic nature. Hezbollah was established at the peak of a crisis in the Lebanese system. It was clearly a product of internal Lebanese social and political as well as regional procedures from the 1970s onward—they all prepared the groundwork on which the radical elements of the Shiite sect began to flourish.

In late 1982, Iran's delegates in Lebanon succeeded in helping those radical groups get organized under the umbrella of Hezbollah (God's party) around the pan-Islamic vision and harnessed them for violent activity against the West in general and against Israel in particular.

The movement broke into international awareness in 1983, after a series of terrorist attacks against the multinational forces (MNFs) and the Israeli Defense Force (IDF) in Lebanon, and remained there for about a decade due to terroristic activities such as kidnapping Western citizens in Lebanon, hijacking airplanes, and organizing terrorist attacks abroad. These attacks were characterized by innovation and extreme violence. They caused the withdrawal of the MNFs from Beirut (February 1984), the withdrawal of the IDF into the Security Zone (May 1985), and the "succumbing" of the Western governments to the demands of the Iranians in the negotiations for the release of the hostages.

During the 1990s Hezbollah handled three significant challenges: first, the end of the civil war and the strengthening of the Lebanese regime; second, the establishment of Syrian hegemony in Lebanon; and third, the peace process in the Middle East. A sharpening of the tension between the Lebanese identity, which the movement wished to promote, and its Jihadist identity occurred during those years. The movement adopted a pragmatic Lebanese policy and diminished its revolutionary characteristics and pan-Islamic approach. Decisions were translated into activities. The movement's delegates were elected to the 1992 parliament and from 2005 even served in the Lebanese government.

They acted in order to promote the resistance and the movement's interests. The revolutionary elements were removed from the movement and its institutions. The movement's leaders and spokesmen conducted a campaign in order to settle for its crowd of followers the tension that was created between the movement's objectives, as they appeared in its platform and its pragmatic approach, which obviously contradicted these goals. With the entry of its candidates into the parliament in the election of 1992, a new era in the history of Hezbollah commenced, ensuring it, as far as it could see, better chances of survival as a political movement, even if peace agreements with Israel were signed and it were to be disarmed.

The IDF's withdrawal from Lebanon in May 2000 opened a new chapter in the reciprocal relation between the players of the regional and the Lebanese system and new opportunities for the movement in the political and the operative arenas. The occurrence of significant procedures and events in the international arena at the beginning of the current century influenced the ongoing in the regional arena.

The September 11 terrorist attacks spurred an American retaliation and entry into Iraq, alongside a reexamination of the international policy facing the terrorist organizations and terror-supporting countries, such as Iran. During this time, Hezbollah managed to survive and expand its activity in Lebanon while rejecting the demand for disarmament. The death of Hafez al-Assad and the policy of his successor, Bashar al-Assad, toward Hezbollah only benefited the movement. Hezbollah was equipped with advanced means of warfare and with the professional knowledge required for their operation; the movement constructed a significant military array in southern Lebanon and positioned itself as the "defender of Lebanon" against possible Israeli aggression. Even the Second Lebanon War (July 2006) couldn't create a process that would lead to its disarmament. The manifesto of the Second Unity Government of Lebanon (November 2009) aptly expresses how Hezbollah is coming closer to achieving its goal of taking over the Lebanese political system from within, as a preliminary step to the Islamization of Lebanon in the long run.[1] Iran and Syria's substantial support with weapons and funding – which are helping to turn Hezbollah into a military force and a strong economic player in Lebanon – enabled the movement to leverage this power into political power.

The basic assumption of this study is that Hezbollah is a revolutionary Lebanese social movement that has been through procedures of change from a pan-Islamic revolutionary movement to a pragmatic Lebanese movement, which uses a combination of open activity within the Lebanese political system and confidential, violent terroristic activity outside this system. Hezbollah operates in the environment of three different systems: the Lebanese, the regional, and the international. These systems uphold complex and dynamic reciprocal relations between themselves that influenced and still influence the movement's directions of development.

The Lebanese system is divided into three subsystems. The interorganizational system (relating to the movement) includes the movement's leadership and its activists. The sectarian system includes within it the members of the Shia sect living in Lebanon and abroad. The Lebanese political system, this goes for the framework of the Lebanese state , suffers from shocks and instability since its inception.

The changes in the strength, status, and characteristics of the Lebanese system, through the years, have influenced the patterns of activity as well as the direction of development of the internal Lebanese forces and the activity traits of the regional players.

The second system is the regional system, which includes within it four players, each of which has directly and indirectly influenced the procedures of change within the Hezbollah movement. Each player's level of influence upon the changes in the movement is derived from the nature and the quality of the relations between the player and the movement and from the stage of development that it is at (establishment, consolidation, expansion, or institutionalization). The regional system is composed of two subsystems: the "Israeli system," meaning the state of Israel, and the "Arab regional system," which includes Syria, Lebanon, and Hezbollah (as a nonstate player). Iran was included in the Arab regional system due to the fact that it is a player with influence upon the system in general and upon Hezbollah in particular. The common denominator for all the above-mentioned players is the struggle against Israel. Iran and Hezbollah share between them an additional common denominator: a Shia-Islamic one.

The struggle between these two subsystems of the regional system takes place on two axes: the axis of the Arab-Israeli conflict and the axis of the Shiite-Islamic conflict. The Hezbollah movement, which operates as a player on both the axes, took advantage of its connections with Syria and Iran in order to expand its activity and become established as a weighty regional and internal Lebanese player. At the same time, it exploited its relations with Iran in order to decrease Syrian pressures or to thwart Syrian moves that jeopardized its status.

The third system is the international system, whose involvement in the Middle Eastern arena is influenced by regional and international restraints and limitations that make it difficult to minimize or restrain Hezbollah's power.

In the absence of basic consent over defining Hezbollah as a terrorist organization, the influence of the international system upon the Hezbollah is very minor.

This study is based on a great deal of diversified information from primary sources, with an emphasis on the Arab and the Lebanese media. It includes statements, speeches, and interviews (published in local newspapers or broadcast over the radio or television channels) of Lebanese officials and Hezbollah and Israeli leaders. The primary sources further include manuscripts and articles by senior officials of Hezbollah and influential Shia clerics in Lebanon. The study is also based on my nonmediated, in-depth familiarity with the Lebanese experience derived from many years of service in Lebanon and from many conversations, meetings, and discussions that I have had with numerous Lebanese figures from all sects. In order to get a complete picture and also clarifications in this field, I have interviewed rehabilitated ex-South Lebanon Army soldiers who have been absorbed in the Israeli society.

1

Social Protest Movements—
Theoretical Framework

Introduction

The emergence of social movements is not a new phenomenon; it has occupied and still occupies researchers and numerous governments. Social movements and revolutions are complex social phenomena that do not work according to one model. Their nature and characteristics differ across societies and eras. They are influenced by the relationship between the state and the society; by the social, economic, and inner political situation; and by the international system. The inner dynamics of these movements are characterized by a transition from spontaneous and informal action patterns, usually based on the charisma of the leader or group, to an established structure and organization based on formal norms and rules.

A social movement is defined as a social framework that is usually organized—acting outside the established system, possessing characteristics of collective action, and making use of certain levels of organization and action that create continuity—for the sake of promoting or preventing changes in the existing social order.[1]

J. McCarthy and M. N. Zald defined social movements as an accumulation of views and beliefs within the population that represent priorities for changing some of the elements of social structure or of the distribution of social welfare.[2]

This definition, like most definitions that relate to social movements, contains elements of collective action, structural characteristics (continuity, basic organization), objectives, organization, and action outside the establishment. Social movements generally bear a social message. They differ from one another in the nature of the message and in its power. Neil Smelser (1962) claimed that there are two main kinds of messages: normative and ideological. Movements with a normative message are generally aimed at making limited and specific changes (social reforms) within the existing social order (such as changing the laws regarding the employment of children, outlawing drugs, etc.). In contrast, movements bearing an ideological message intend to create deep, fundamental changes in the existing social order to the point of destroying it and building a new social order by means of a revolutionary act.[3]

These movements are a product of social protest and operate outside of the existing system. Some conspicuous examples are the movements that led the

French and Russian revolutions, fundamentalist revolutionary movements, and militant movements for the attainment of civil rights.

In the fundamentalist movements carrying an ideological message, the individual is the key to social change; therefore, their actions are centered, first and foremost, on the formation and rebuilding of the individual's world of beliefs and values as a basis for changing the existing social structure and establishing a new social order. Social movements differ from one another in their objectives, in the nature of their actions, and in the public that supports them. With this, similar characteristics can be found that associate certain types of social movements with one another. All movements operate to advance the interests of the groups that comprise them.

Social Movements and Their Target Audiences

A social movement operates within an environment of various target audiences; its actions, the direction of its development, and its messages are derived from the reciprocal relationships and influences between and within them. As a generalization, these target audiences can be divided into three groups: those who support the movement and its actions (supporters), those who oppose it (opponents), and those who avoid taking a stand of any kind, the indifferent ones (bystanders).

The movement supporters comprise the main target audience upon which every social movement is based. This audience includes a number of groups that are differentiated from each other by the extent of the connection and by their activity within the framework of the movement. All of them support the movement in one way or another, or their interests are represented by it. These groups have reciprocal connections, and individuals move between the groups. The intensity of the connection between the group and the movement determines its place in relation to the other groups as follows:

A. *Movement activists*: This is a label given to the group of people found in the first circle of movement supporters. They belong to the core group of every social protest movement. This group is made up of groups of activists possessing a common identity, shared goals, and a readiness to sacrifice for the sake of advancing the aims of the movement. This group is the motivating force of the movement, and from within it emerges the charismatic leadership.

B. *Adherents of the movement*: This is a label given to the group of people found in the second circle of movement supporters. They are found in close proximity to the core of the movement. They support the key ideologies and the goals of the movement and occasionally join collective actions carried out by the movement, but they are not active members within its framework.

C. *The constituency*: This is a label given to the group of people found in the third circle of movement supporters. They support the movement and its messages, but avoid joining it actively. This group comprises a manpower pool for both the adherents of the movement and the activist core group and therefore constitutes an important layer for enlistment activity.

D.   *The passively interested*: They constitute the fourth circle. This label is given to the group of people who have a clear interest in the accomplishment of the movement's goals, since they will benefit from it, but do not take any active steps within the framework of the movement.

Opponents of the social movement are derived from its aims and character (revolutionary or reform). When it challenges the government institutions, the opponent is the state. Revolutionary movements embody, by their nature, a high level of potential danger for their opponents, since they are uncompromising and tend to work through violence (usually against an existing established system). Therefore, one of the clear signs of a conflict between a revolutionary movement and its principal opponent (government, foreign conqueror, competing movement) is extreme violence. In this connection, it is fitting to emphasize that the rise of a social protest movement encourages the appearance of opposing movements that resist either the nature of its activity or some of its aims or both and work to neutralize its power.

Bystanders are included in the category of those who are indifferent both to the movement and its goals, as well as to the responses and actions of its opponents. This group stands on the sidelines as long as its basic interests are not harmed. Hurting these interests may cause the members of this group to take a stand and join one of the two sides.[4]

There is a continual system of dynamic reciprocity and influence between these three groups (supporters, opponents, indifferent bystanders). This system is central in influencing the nature of dialogue between the groups and within them, the level of support or lack of support of the movement, its traits, and the pace of its development. Every movement draws its strength from its size in relation to its opponents and competitors. The greater the number of people who are mobilized to join the movement, the more the legitimacy of the opponent is brought into question.[5]

The Principal Theoretical Approaches

In the research literature, there are four main theoretical approaches that explain the formation and action of the phenomenon of social movements. They differ by identification and in accounting for the causes of the social movements' development, and mainly in the weight ascribed to the influence of one of the various factors in the process, owning to differences in the point of view of the researchers. Adherents of the psychological discipline consider psychological traits and changes at the individual and general level as the principal explanation for the formation of movements. In contrast, researchers from the social-economic school claim that the social position and the distribution of resources are the primary explanations for the shaping and activity of social revolutionary movements.

The *theory of relative discrimination* is based on psychological approaches and maintains that individuals will establish protest movements or will join them when they feel deprived in relation to other groups in the population. For them, joining a movement constitutes a means of improving social status and restoring justice to its rightful place.[6]

Critics of this theory argue that this is only a partial explanation for the establishment of social movements. In their opinion, discriminatory condition is neither a mandatory nor a sufficient stipulation for founding a movement. This theory does not deal in any way with the contribution of social resources and processes causing the formation of a protest movement.

According to the *mass society theory,* social movements appear following a process of societal disintegration. They comprise people who are socially and personally disconnected and feel worthless as individuals. Joining a social movement provides a sense of belonging and social affinity. According to this approach, people with a strong social connection will less frequently join social protest movements.

Critics of this theory argue that it ascribes an exaggerated importance to the influence and weight of the psychological aspect on the micro level (individual) to the point of absurdity. From this, it can be deduced that social movements are a product of defective people and not of a defective society. Furthermore, the research findings of Doug McAdam, John James Whalen, and Richard Flacks, who analyzed the personal profiles of those who joined social movements in the United States during the 1960s, clearly contradict the social isolation approach that supports the theory. They found that people who entered social movements had, in fact, a strong social and political affinity.[7]

The *theory of structural tension* was developed in the 1960s by a researcher named Smelser. It emphasizes the social dimension and its influence on the development of movements. According to this approach, six factors encourage the growth of movements: a high level of social tension, a sense of relative discrimination, the presence of agitating factors, the development of leadership and organizational structure, readiness to join collective action, and the way the governmental system reacts. Critics of this theory argue that it ignores the role and the value of resources in the explanation of the formation of movements.[8]

Resource management theory adds a central dimension to the explanation of the formation of movements. It maintains that the success of movements does not depend merely on the sense of frustration ensuing from relative discrimination, but also on the presence of resources. The existence of resources such as money, manpower, means of recruitment and distribution, and accessibility to communication media is essential for the emergence of movements. A movement must enlist internal or external resources to finance its activities, which is particularly critical in the initial stages. At this point, supporters of this theory emphasize the important factors in the development of a movement: the availability of resources and the existence of a formal organizational infrastructure.[9]

The Conditions for the Development of a Social Movement

Demographic and social changes were and continue to be among the central factors in the emergence of social protest movements. Rapid demographic changes cause two main processes to occur: one, accelerated urbanization, and two, the development of new administrative and professional elites, proletarization, new social stratification, and alternation in the structure of social identities.

The processes of urbanization and industrialization have influenced social structures, particularly community structure. In developing nations, they generated the transition from a rural society to an industrialized society and have caused far-reaching changes in the traditional social structure.[10] These processes were characterized by competition, struggle, and bureaucratic relationships that stood in complete contradiction to the qualities of the traditional community and those of close interpersonal relationships. The city became a political and economic center, drawing to it youth from the peripheries who were seeking work and economic opportunities. In most places across the world, and particularly in developing nations, the accelerated urbanization process was faster than the governmental systems' ability to provide basic and vital services for these populations. As a result, slums and refugee camps grew on the peripheries of the large cities, offering fertile ground for the growth of feelings of frustration and alienation and for the emergence of protest movements.

This combination of an economic crisis on the one hand and the development of an inner social conflict on the other, alongside the rise in importance and influence of ideologies (especially religious ones—symbolizing a return to the old clear and known dictates), caused the undermining of the existing social order and the development of various social protest movements.[11]

Political Opportunities

The concept of "political opportunities" is directly connected to the governmental system and its ability to govern the country's affairs. The nature of this system's inner structure, its strength and coherence, and the relationships among the elites are factors that influence the formation of political opportunities. Political and social conditions influence, to a great extent, the birth and success of a social movement while providing an explanation for the causes of the appearance and nature of its actions.

As early as the 1970s, researchers of political movements defined the term "the structure of political opportunities" as a situation in which a certain group decides to act and challenge the existing political system. It follows that a weak governmental system will provide more political opportunities for the growth of protest movements, which will operate to exploit the weakness of the system, build themselves at its expense, or even capture authority or rule. The Lebanese and Palestinian cases (the rise of the Hamas movement) are clear proof of the existence of this phenomenon. A particularly weak governmental system facilitates the growth of local militias on the basis of a common factor (familial, communal, or local). These local militias struggle among themselves for the existing public good, for control of cellular areas, and for political power. The actions of the Lebanese militias during the 1980s or the actions of the Palestinian militias in a number of areas in Gaza, Judea, and Samaria (2003–2008) in the "twilight period" of the Palestinian Authority can be seen as examples.

A number of social revolution researchers have sought the reasons for revolutions in the processes that preceded them, in the character of the groups that made up the society, and in the state of the ruling institutions (bureaucratic and military).[12] The notion that political and social structural changes are among the central causes in the weakening of the governmental system and simultaneously accelerate the development of social movements is commonly held by many researchers.[13] With this, it is fitting to emphasize that political opportunities do not create social movements; rather they enable their establishment. As a result of political processes, conditions develop allowing the emergence of new groups. Broadening struggle among the elites or a decrease in the state's capacity to suppress resistance, or alterations in the structure of political power, all comprise opportunities for new groups to break into the public awareness and actualize the goals defined for themselves.[14]

Organizational Conditions

One of the foundational conditions for the formation of social movements is the existence of a basic core group. A core of this type leans on the infrastructure of existing social institutions or on social networks possessing a common basic structure (familial, tribal, communal, religious, professional, sectorial, ethnic, etc.). The presence of an organizational infrastructure, such as this, enables the exploitation of political opportunities for the formation of a social protest movement.[15]

Theoreticians (Herbert Blumer, Ralph H. Turner, Lewis M. Killian, and Neil J. Smelser) who have analyzed the collective behavior of protest movements argue that social movements are essentially different from institutionalized systems. They are spontaneous, lacking organizational structure, and their members are considered as irrational, acting beyond boundaries and normative constraints. They also claim that the organizational structure and the institutions are cultivated as the movement continues on its way.[16]

In contrast, and in complete contradiction of their position, the researchers of the "Administration-resources" school (Gamson 1975, Zald and McCarthy 1973, Anthony Oberschall 1973, Tilly 1978) claim that social movements act rationally; moreover, they behave and develop in a way that is similar to that of established systems. These movements are based on a premovement social structure that includes movement organizations, institutions, and social networks. This structure provides them with the organizational resources and the framework critical for "collective action" and for the formation of the movement. "Collective action" is defined in this regard as the action of protest groups for promoting shared goals and is executed by rational players for the sake of achieving the movement's goals.[17]

Accordingly, the nature of a social movement, the arena of its activity, and its action strategies are a consequence of the character, scope, size, and placement of the groups and social organizations that constitute it. Included in social organizations and groups of the type aforesaid are different social and community establishments such as religious institutions, educational institutions, charitable foundations, and associations, friendly societies of different sorts and assemblies.

Premovement social structure plays a central role in the development of movement organization. Social groups, establishments, and unions of different kinds, as well as circumstances or crises, cause the formation of a unifying common ground. They comprise the framework required for the development of an organizational movement core on the one hand, and on the other, they supply organizational resources such as the manpower, financial resources, communication networks, leadership, and ideology required for it.

These premovement structures respond to changes in social circumstances and to crises. Their social and political positions change, and they develop action patterns on two levels. On the internal plane (within the group), they deal with defining goals, forming the decision-making process, consolidating action strategies, and building an embryonic organizational structure. On the external plane (facing the target audience and opponents), actions are centered on actualizing strategies, broadening enlistment efforts, and shared protest activity.

Naturally, centers of power and local organization come into being around local leadership or centers. These constitute part of a broad system, based on cooperative connections between establishments belonging to the same category (religious organizations, educational institutions, charitable institutions) and between the organizations and people from different categories. This system enables congruity of action and delivers information, messages, and instructions for action between institutions and people.[18]

The importance of the movement's inner organization derives from its capacity to shape action strategies that can be assimilated by the activists, to translate them into joint action, and, with time, to be flexible enough to change them according to a shifting reality. The organization's ability to execute these is dependent, among other things, on the way the movement centers are placed, on the inner communication network, and on the strength of the connection within the national leadership. The task of the movement's organization is particularly difficult during the initial stages of the movement, when its structures are still in their embryonic stages.[19]

From here, we learn that the growth of the movement is enabled when both internal and external conditions (political opportunities) are present simultaneously. Regarding the internal conditions, it seems that the combination of organized groups, establishments, and organizations with a common affinity along with leadership possessing a vision and internal and external organizational resources is likely to serve as a sound basis to set in motion a common action and the establishment of a movement. The formation of suitable internal and external conditions creates the framework that enables rapid movement expansion.

The manner and pace of interior movement growth are influenced by the size and disposition of its potential target audience (sectorial, common interest, communal, religious, discriminated against), the development of a coalition between various groups or community establishments, religious entities, the union of different organizations into a common organizational framework (generally, this is a reorganization of small organizations) and as a consequence of the acceleration of the processes during the course of joint driving action.

Explications for Recruitment to Protest Movements

Before dealing with the issue of recruitment, it is fitting to explain the term "recruitment" (mobilization) in the public-civic sense. According to Smelser, it is a process that propels people, influenced by a public policy of a certain nature, to act for the sake of advancing their personal interests. The emphasis is on the phase in which the individual wakes up and decides to take action.[20] Karl Wolfgang Deutsch defines mobilization as the process in which groups and new mechanisms of control are created due to the rise of new social issues or the aggravation of old ones.[21] William A. Gamson sees in mobilization a process aiming to augment the presence of the individual in collective action while tightening the connection and loyalty between the individual and the organization or the leadership layer.[22]

All three of the aforementioned researchers defined the term "mobilization" in the context of the organizational phase of the entity. On the other hand, Charles Tilly sees it as one of the components of collective action. He emphasized that movement mobilization is the process in which the group gains collective control of resources that serve its operation. As the process of the mobilization reaches its finalization, a collection of passive individuals turns into a group of activists participating in public life.[23]

From the integration of these definitions, it appears that the recruitment process is one that arouses individuals into action and organizes them in a group framework for the purpose of advancing common interests and making an impact. The ideas embodied and interwoven in the aforementioned social process are the activation and creation of commitment. In groups where individuals have a certain extent of obligation to act, the "initiators-recruiters" invest effort in motivating these individuals to act. On the other hand, with an unorganized assortment of individuals, the "initiators-recruiters" must devote effort in shifting the people from a general low willingness to act to a high eagerness to act in a collective manner.

The initial premovement group is created from the desire of people possessing an identical social background. Their preliminary goal is to activate other people by means of heightening awareness about an existing problem and a recommended solution. All these are intended to influence the way the governing system allocates resources. The main quandary that such a group faces is how to motivate individuals to join collective activity.[24]

It is not unintentional that one of the essential queries in the research of protest movements touches on the subject of enlistment to the movement. To other questions concerning the motivation to join a social protest movement— why does a different level of involvement exist in the same movement, why does enlistment to divergent protest movements differ, and why is one individual involved in social protest activity and another is not?—there are no clear, unequivocal answers. Two research approaches attempt to offer an explanation for the phenomenon: the psychological approach and the structural approach.

Those who support the psychological approach find explanations in the individual's personality structure, based on psychological theories dealing with the correlation between frustration and aggression. According to them, an individual's frustration finds its release by means of activism or violence. These theoreticians claim that the level of frustration is related, in one way or another, to the individual's personality structure and emanates either from unresolved inner conflicts or from his positioning on the margins of the society or as a result of relative deprivation. This level of frustration causes psychological tension within an individual, who discharges it by means of joining a protest movement.[25]

Conversely, supporters of the structural approach maintain that the enlistment of an individual to a social movement is influenced by his societal positioning and by the nature of his links with a forming movement organization. This approach does not negate the importance of individual personality traits, but does argue that they do not clarify his motives to join the movement. According to this approach, the most important source of enlistment is the social network. Empirical studies show that most of those enlisted in movements arrived through family ties or via friendly connections. This demonstrates that the likelihood of those who were connected to premovement social network to enlist to movement is higher then the rest. [26]

Social connections, by their nature, are an expression of interpersonal communication and interaction. In it, they advance solidarity, encourage the individual to enlist in shared activity, and influence his decision to join the movement.[27] This enlistment is not a result of the individual's momentary decision; rather it is a consequence of a decision-making process. The first phase of the process is found in the movement's field. The individual will join shared activity only when an existing apparatus will cause him to do so. This apparatus is usually an organizational one. It is that which initiates the appeal to the individual, directly or indirectly, and offers him to join the ranks of the movement and participating in shared activity. The task of the movement, at this point, is to create a common ground, broad enough to enable the individual to identify with it (i.e., religion, race, or sex).

In the second part of the process, the individual examines the advantages and disadvantages that may stem from his decision to join, for himself and for his close social environment. The decision will be influenced, according to the advocates of the structural approach, first and foremost by the social environment of the potential enlistee and by his network of connections with movement activists.

On the other hand, the advocates of the psychological approach conjecture that joining a movement is an outcome of the personality structure of the individual, from the fabrication of feelings of frustration and from the possibility of discharging frustration by means of violence within the movement framework.[28]

The recruiting process must be examined, therefore, from two intertwined points of view: the standpoint of the movement and that of the individual. The movement's target audience (as aforementioned) is made up of a number of divergent populations, groups and individuals. This structure obligates the movement to use varied methods of action and sophisticated effort for the purpose of maximizing the number of enlistees to the movement. Dirk Oegema and Bert Klandermans found that sympathy for the goals of the movement does not ensure the enlistment of the individual to the ranks of the movement, as the readiness of the individual for collective activity does not necessarily lead to participation in such an activity. Furthermore, even participation in one "shared activity" does not promise participation in another one.[29]

From the movement's point of view, the individual's commitment to its ranks is an outcome of a gradual process on his part, which entails several stages.

At every stage, the movement is required to "convince" the individual to pass to the next phase. The ultimate objective of the movement is, therefore, to translate the individual's or group's willingness into concerted activity within its framework. The first step in achieving this goal is a direct or indirect appeal to the target audience using a variety of channels and methods. The intent of this appeal is to create the required recruitment motivation by means of defining a common denominator and emphasizing mutual identity. Creating motivation enables the movement to proceed to the next phase of the recruitment, which is removing potential interfering barriers. In this case, the most significant obstruction is the "expected cost" as against the "expected benefit." When the individual discerns that the price he is required to pay for joining the movement is higher than the benefit he can expect from it, he will not join. Thus, the movement works to emphasize the considerable benefit of joining its ranks on the one hand, and on the other, minimizes the required cost.[30]

Such being the case, joining the movement is influenced by factors linked both to the individual and to the movement. At the individual level, his enlistment is influenced by his personality structure, by his sense of deprivation and frustration, and by his place in the social composition. At the movement level, the success of enlistment is dependent on the following factors: the scope of movement social networks and the nature of their displacement, the level of sophistication and suitability of "the enlistment operation" to the target audience, the character of the shared activity and its influence on changing the "price of joining" against the expected benefit, the development of public discussion, the reciprocal system between the movement, its supporters, and opponents, and the existing political circumstances.

The Policy of Repression as Encouraging or Curtailing Enlistment

From the individual's point of view, enlisting in a movement is conditional, as mentioned earlier, on the level of the demanded price tag. Therefore, the policy of repression is influence the individual's decision to join or to avoid joining the movement. Repression, according to Tilly, is all action taken by the challenged group that raises the price for joining collective action. In contrast to repression, facilitation is action that lowers the price. In his claim, repression limits collective action by one of two methods: first, by raising the price of joining, and second, by repressing the activity itself.[31]

Researchers have offered various explanations regarding the extent of the influence of repression on the individual's decision. Researchers of the "psychological persuasion" see in repression policy a factor in the formation of feelings of anger, which result in the development of a protest movement. In their view, repression is an element that radicalizes the position of all the players.[32]

Researchers of the "administration of resources school" are divided in their opinions concerning the influence of repression. There are those who see in it an element that prevents and delays the emergence of a protest movement.[33] This approach supports the notion that repression decreases the enlistment of people in a protest movement. The reason, in their judgment, is that repression, from the standpoint of collective action theory and from the individual's point of view, raises the price he can expect to pay in case he decides to join the movement.[34] In contrast, there are those who maintain that repression actually speeds up the development of protest movements. It enables a gain of broad sympathy and public support.[35]

Contradictory explanations raise the question of whether, when, and under what circumstances repression causes people to join a protest movement and when it prevents it. The answer is not unequivocal, since there are several levels of repression (beginning with legal sanctions and ending with the execution of opponents), and it has both direct and indirect influences on the character of the protest. Repression does not always achieve the desired effect, and since it is aimed directly against the protest, two results are possible: intimidation or radicalization.

Repression, by its nature, arouses psychological reactions in the hurt individual and his close environment. Arousing a feeling of frustration is perceived as illegitimate and immoral action on the part of the ruling entity. Denial of the legitimacy of the government, alienation, and anger are also associated reactions. These feelings, combined with the belief that there is a possibility to alter existing social conditions by means of protest activity, including violence, lead to the development of a protest movement. Violence in opposing perceived immoral repression can be justified in the individual's view. If that is the situation, it can be deduced that the development of a protest movement, as a consequence of a policy of repression, depends on several probable components. These include individuals who see repression as illegitimate and illegal, understanding the potential for change in their actions. The level and scope of social networks, activity for advancing collective protest, and the capacity to create sympathetic public opinion favoring advancement of the protest may also result in the formation of a protest movement. When the conclusion is reached on the part of individuals that their mobilization can bring the requisite change, they will join the movement, in spite of the high price. In the absence of these conditions, it is more likely that repression will cause intimidation due to the high price that those who join the protest are expected to pay.[36]

The Ideological Framework as an Instrument for Recruiting and Broadening the Movement Foundation

It is said that the key to understanding the individual's motivations for joining a protest movement is found in the process of defining and building a conceptual framework, which is done at the outset. The individual sees the movement as an agent of change acting to create new meanings for events that took place in the past as well as for the processes taking place in the present. This approach to the ideological conceptual framework and to its importance lays down three basic assumptions: [37]

A. The likelihood that the individual will join a protest movement is higher when its conceptual framework matches that of the individual.

B. The conceptual framework is dynamic and changing and is reevaluated and reformulated both because of the influence of developing reciprocal relationships between the groups and individuals and because of the events themselves.

C. The movement core is responsible for the formation and consolidation of the ideological conceptual framework and its propagation.

This observation of the reasons for recruitment presumes that the conceptual-ideological framework bears certain importance in the process of formation of social movements. Feelings of discrimination, alienation, and accessibility of resources are very important conditions, but they are not enough to motivate the individual to join in action within the movement framework. For this purpose, a mechanism is required that knows how to translate feelings and resources into action for the sake of common goals. This mechanism is the movement core that works simultaneously both for the attainment of resources and for the definition of a conceptual framework and the formation of strategic action. These tools, particularly the latter two, enable the movement organization to find the formula that unites the feelings of individuals in a broad common denominator and to define a frame of action that is directed to encourage individuals to join the activity within the movement framework. Since social action is dynamic in nature, a core organizational leadership is required to continually regenerate and to be ever one step ahead of the opponent; if not, it will be destroyed (conceptually or physically) in *statu nascendi* (during his formation).

In light of this, movement cores use all existing means at their disposal or within their capacity to directly or indirectly reach the most numerous and varied target audiences possible and to enlist it in its activity within the movement framework. In this framework, they invest effort in communicating and cooperating with groups or organizations that are working in the same area for the purpose of producing conditions for joint action under the same organizational framework or even under a new organizational entity framework. Another highly important means for the movement organization is the media. Use is made of manipulative means (usually violent) that will intensify the exposure of the movement in the mass media (radio, television, the Internet, tapes), alongside a continual use of mailings and the transmission of various kinds of messages. Direct contact with potential enlistees is also a recruitment tool for extending their ranks.[38]

Movement organizations that are conscious of the need for renewal act to create the broadest common denominator possible between different groups in the population (movement activists, supporters, and bystanders) by means of translating events that touch their daily lives into common symbols while using mobilizing rhetoric. This is done by identifying values, beliefs, interests, and the cultural codes shared by individuals or groups toward which the movement is directed and by creating affinity or congruence between them and its values. This common denominator is intended to pave the way for joining these individuals or groups with the movement. It is worth emphasizing that the conceptual-ideological framework is intended also for preserving the existing situation as well as for tightening the connection between the movement and its activists.[39]

The dynamics created in the social environment change, influencing the pace of process development, the frequency and traits of events in the field, the character and scope of the enlistees to the movement (individuals, groups), and the quality of the common denominator. These, on the other hand, give rise to the formation of new values, cause the weakening of former understandings and beliefs, and put in question the suitability of the existing conceptual framework. This is usually the phase in which a rational movement is required to develop new insights and to form a conceptual framework that suits the new circumstances. The purpose of this framework is to encourage the enlistment of new people to the movement and to deepen the affinity between the movement and its activists. The more flexible and adaptable the framework is, the greater will be the number of people who join.[40]

"Public Discussion" and Protest Movements

In every social system, a constant social polemic public discussion takes place to one extent or another within the existing social institutions, between groups and organizations, and within the political system. The public discussion actually shapes the conceptual framework and the shared activity. The formulators of public discussion—whether they are those with power, ruling by means of the media, or those that challenge them—can generate events with great public repercussions compelling a reaction or reference from the opposing side.

The purpose of the public discussion, from the point of view of a protest movement, is to assist in accomplishing its goals, forming sympathetic public opinion, and challenging its opponents. The success of the "opposing public discussion" is dependent to a great extent on the rhetoric capacity of its forgers and their ability to give it current significance that suits the emotional state of the target audience. It can be assumed that the stronger the identification individuals feel with the principles of the movement, as they are expressed in the public discussion, the greater is the probability of their actively joining the framework.

Rhetoric comprises one of the main tools of expression of a social protest movement. It not only influences events, but is also influenced by them. The movement uses it to enlist individuals and groups to its common activity, and leaders use it to form the world of concepts for its activists and to justify their actions. The struggle of the movement over a place in the public discussion is not an insignificant matter. Control over the mass media is found, usually, in the hands of its opponents, and they, from their perspective, will not hurry to allow the movement to take control of these resources. The movement is usually found on the fringes and must "conquer" a place in the public discussion for itself, change its focus, and reorganize itself while advancing the subjects it is interested in dealing with, which is generally a confrontation with existing established values.

Significant events in the life of a society such as war, calamities, decisions that touch the life of individuals and their activity, or prolonged repression are examples that are likely to motivate social protest processes among groups, unite them, and form a "framework" possessing a shared identity and purpose.

This framework will express the protest both in the public discussion and on the operative plane. In these cases, the shapers of public discussion from among the protest movement translate the sense of frustration of individuals into a consensus of common beliefs by creating a framework of new implications and new symbols and linking them to historic events and symbols possessing deep significance in the life of the society.[41]

Dramatic events, by their very nature, cause deep changes in awareness in individuals and groups and generally in society. The challenge facing a protest movement is how to exploit the events for the attainment of maximum exposure for the movement's ideas and how to strengthen enlistment and the responsiveness of the passive public to the movement's challenge and its alternative message. The means for this is the "public discussion." The success of a movement rhetoric in taking over the "public discussion" in these cases is dependent, to a great extent, on the might of the opponent and on its situation in relation to it, on the strategy taken by its spokesmen, on their personal level, on the way they turn to the different target audiences, on their capacity to create delegitimization of the regime and, at the same time, provide moral validation and legitimacy for the movement's actions. This alone is not enough. The movement's spokesmen are required to link between the stakes and the beliefs of the different target audiences and to create a broad enough common denominator that will allow, on the one hand, the joining of individuals and groups and, on the other hand, the expansion of its resources. The purpose of protest movements is to convince the public, by means of the public discussion, that its opponents do not provide the solutions to the problems the society faces and that, therefore, their replacement is inevitable.

The relationship between the movers and operative activity is a dialectic one. On the one hand, operational activity is influenced by the tension and escalation in the public discussion; on the other hand, the events in the field, whether intended or inadvertent, are likely to influence the tendency to radicalization in the public discussion. Those that shape the public discussion within protest movements make use of a combination of two tools, public discussion and operational activity, in attaining their goals. The reciprocal system between the operative activity and the public discussion begins with the appearance of social problems. These cause the development of social tendencies that express their protest both on the plane of public discussion and on the operative plane. In cases where the sides do not reach an agreement, spiraling escalation is generated both in the attributes of the public discussion and in the operative activity in the field.

Operational activity feeds the public discussion and supports its direction; concurrently, it can also lead the public discussion into new directions with the following consequences: the dismantling of existing coalitions and the establishment of new ones, the rising and falling of power centers, the disassembling of existing organizational frameworks and the foundation of new movement framings, and a change in the level of movement legitimacy or of its opponents and in the support base. The fastest pace of change will usually take place in the phases of the movement's formation due to the conflict existing in this phase. In this period, subjects related to the existing social order are redefined, old beliefs and ideologies are challenged and refuted, and the public discussion undergoes a rapid process of evolution.[42]

The struggle for the "conquest" of the public discussion requires shapers of public discussion of protest movements to develop strategic skills and tools that will allow them wide exposure in the media. One way is making use of independent and alternative communication channels and circulation that are in the movement's control or accessible to it. In general, they are posters, independent newspapers, sermons in mosques, tapes and pirate television, radio stations, and mainly the Internet. The second way is making use of distribution means belonging to bodies or organizations closely related to the movement and even those of the opponent.

The Influence of Reciprocal Relations between Protest Movements and Their Opponents on the Direction of Their Development

Protest movements develop outside the established system, and for the most part, they constitute opposition to the existing government. They keep away from activity in the regular political channels because they do not want to assimilate into establishments and organizations that are stronger than they. They work in existing systems, are influenced by them, and influence them. In these systems, there are central players and players in supporting roles. The three central players are the movement, the state, and the opposing groups, and alongside them play the three supporting actors: the media, the nonestablishment elites (external resource support), and the public. Between these actors and among them, complex reciprocal relationships develop that, to a great extent, determine the direction of the movement's development, the nature of the conflict, and the scope of those involved in it.[43]

The movement: The existence and expansion of protest movements depend, to a great extent, on their capacity to invent new tactics and to be several steps ahead of their opponents. The innovative tactic is created out of a conflict between the movement and its adversaries. This gives birth to waves of protest. Throughout their course, a new social and cultural structure is stabilized that is based on a system of symbols, ideological frameworks, and new insights. These are intended to justify collective action, to support it, and to expand the circle of participants. At the peak of a protest wave, new tools develop that become part of the coming waves of protest.[44] Among the famous ones are groups using violence during the course of a protest wave attain not only wider exposure, but also no less antiviolent reactions.[45]

The state/opponents: The state is the principal adversary of the protest movement and is usually the strongest. It cannot endure injury to the law and public order or threat to the legitimacy of the regime. Thus, violence compels the state to take steps to repress it. The rejoinder to violent action is based on two central action strategies: repression and facilitation (containment). The strategy of repression is aimed at eliminating the protest activity and at deterring potential recruits. It is activated by means of the different judicial and security systems, including actions such as making it illegal, making arrests, impinging on the leaders, and conducting special and clandestine operations. The strategy of facilitating (containing) is intended to cause a split in the movement by means of strengthening the moderate components and isolating the radical groups. The purpose in this strategy is to annex the movement to the existing political system to the point of assimilation. There are countries that use both these strategies simultaneously, but in different doses, and there are those who use one of them, usually the strategy of repression. In this case, one of two things happens. Either the recruitment to the movement is brought down because of the rise in the expected cost of joining it or, alternatively, there is a growth in the number of recruits because of a rising sense of frustration and alienation among the groups and individuals who are exposed to the repression.[46] It is worthy of mention that steps of repression taken by the state in certain cases create public and media sympathy toward the protest movement, thus advancing its concerns.

The public: The public is an important objective for every body that works on the social plane. It is clear to all the players that public opinion is a tool possessing great value in pressuring decision makers. They form their policies, usually in accordance with the mood prevalent among the voting public.[47]

Nonestablished elites: They comprise a players of great importance because of their ability to provide vital external resources for the development of the movement such as funding, leadership, and connections. In addition, they constitute pressure groups on decision makers.[48]

The media: It has a special status in the system detailed above. It influences the formation of public opinion and comprises a powerful instrument, bestowing predominance on whoever holds it or is credited with public exposure through it. The stance of the media is derived from the type of regime it works within. In democratic governments, the media enjoys great freedom of action and independence in determining its positions in covering controversial subjects. On the other hand, in nondemocratic regimes and in developing countries, control of the media is usually in the hands of the regime. In one way or another, the leaders of protest movements act to increase their exposure in the media as leverage for the advancement of their interests. In places where possible, they invest effort in setting up independent communication channels.

Interaction and reciprocal relationships develop between these players The system that include the players compels them to develop strategies and tactics for action that will give them an actual advantage and will be, from their point of view, leverage for the perpetuation of development. Therefore, protest movements strive to translate their first move into political power or, to the extent that this is not possible, to continue in protest outside the established system while seeking new tactics for action (innovation) as a basis for attaining an advantage over the adversary (surprise) and, in it, to disrupt its capacity to neutralize the tactic innovation, which is the ultimate means for attaining this goal. It enables bridging the gap of power between the movement and the existing governing entities in places where conflict develops. This innovation often appears as a consequence of the activation of violence.[49]

We witness three approaches illuminating, each one from a different standpoint, the causes and processes influencing the direction of the movement's development and the nature of its activity. All the approaches see eye to eye with the contention that radicalism and institutionalization are consequences of protest waves and that the combination of both processes is the reason for the waning of these protest waves.

The first approach (Karstedt Henke) analyzed the counter strategies of Germany in its action to eliminate the phenomenon of waves of terrorism in the country. This approach maintains that the outbreak of protest usually surprises the country. Thus, in the absence of exact information and out of a desire to quickly eliminate the phenomenon, it reacts aggressively in the first phase while using repressive strategies in an ineffective and unfocused way. Such kind of activity sometimes attains an inverse result. It intensifies the alienation and encourages groups and/or individuals to join collective action. In the second phase, as part of a learning process, drawing conclusions and more exact information, the country takes measures of combined strategic action (repression and facilitation/containment), whose purpose is to cause a split in the movement, to isolate the radical groups, and to diminish their influence. Knowledgeable policy, even if mistakes occur in the identification of the different groups, succeeds in stirring a development of inner conflict within the movement and between the pragmatists and the extremists and, in certain cases, even in causing a schism in the movement. In this case, the country has more legitimization to set in motion extreme repressive means against radical groups. As a consequence, the number of radical activists will decrease, they will be compelled to go underground, their activity will be curbed and protest waves will grow smaller. This model perceives forces, external to the movement, in this case the state, as a central influence in determining the directions of the protest and the movement.[50]

The second approach, by Sidney G. Tarrow, argues that the development of a movement stems from inner processes that generate competition within the movement organizations as well as between them and political organizations. According to his approach, political opportunities such as weak central governments, the presence of supportive allies, divided elites are all basis for the emergence of new protest movements. Once they are molded, interaction takes place within them as well as competition between groups and individuals, determining the level and the pace of innovative tactic development, the character of protest waves, and the operation strategy. Two assumptions are assimilated at the base of this approach: one, when competition between internal movement organizations is strong, the nature of the protest will be more violent, and two, protests in which movement organizations are involved will be more effective than those that are unorganized.[51] Movement organizations that join for shared activity compete with one another for exposure and mass support. For this reason, they make use of violence. This leads to an intensification of the conflict, to the rise in cost of joining the movement, and to a diminishing of the target audience that is willing to join at this price. As a result, the scope of protest waves grows smaller and two different directions develop, pragmatic and radical, that draw apart from each other. The reason for this, according to Tarrow, is the essential existence of the competition between the organizations and within them.[52]

The third approach, that of Ruud Kooperman, maintains that the direction of a movement is influenced simultaneously by factors and processes outside the movement as well as by internal processes that take place within the movement organizations and between them. According to this approach, impelling competition develops during the first phase between the movement organizations and within them for the use of violence as a means of attaining the support of the masses. In an environment such as this, relatively moderate groups are also dragged into using violent action. From the moment a wave of protest erupts, it is influenced by the way the state reacts; in other words, it is influenced by the correlation between the activity with repressive characteristics and activity with facilitating characteristics (containment). In general, it can be said that, in spite of the great disparity existing in the characteristics of protest activity in different types of regimes and in different cultural contexts, the action strategies of the state and the way they are implemented, in the right measure and timing, have a significant impact on the character of the protest, its scope, and the orientation of its development.[53]

Alongside this, another influence presents, emanating from the internal competition of the organization. This influences the appearance of new movement organizations and the disappearance of others. At the very peak of the protest, the movement organization changes in importance. There is a need to translate the accomplishments of the protest into political power, which compensates for the loss of innovation. According to Koopmans Ruud, the movement organization will labor to join an existing political player, a different movement organization, or external initiators. Cooperation with these elements is usually accompanied by the adoption of pragmatic strategic action characterized by a leaning toward moderation and the production of discord with radical factors in the organization. The latter will intensify the struggle to the point of turning to extreme violence and terrorism in order to be heard. Paradoxically, this course strengthens the standing of the pragmatic movement organizations, since it improves their situation in conducting negotiations with possible partners and encourages support for them as a balance against the extremists.[54]

According to this approach, the decrease of a protest wave lessens the likelihood of the movement's success, and it becomes less attractive to join. Actually, the longer the wave of protest lasts, the more the chances that its initiators will succeed crumble. The greatest chance is at the beginning of the wave in which optimal conditions exist for success (divided elites, a weak government, and mass support). This is one of the reasons why protest movements define short-term goals that can be achieved. The attainment of these goals constitutes leverage for the continuation of action and encourages enlistment in the movement. Lack of success or a series of failures exacerbates the tension between moderates and extremists and intensifies the internal debate and the struggle within the movement, which ultimately weakens it and intensifies violent action. [55]

In conclusion, this approach asserts that the development of protest movements is a result of reciprocal systems and the influences between external movement and internal movement factors. To a great extent, the interaction between them determines and molds the character of the movement, the constitution of the movement organizations, and the odds between the moderates and the extremists within it.

Protest Movements, Religion, and Ethnicity

The religious aspect: For many years, social movement researchers have underrated the importance of religion as an important factor in the development of a protest movement. In the age of social theories based on rationality, religion was, as far as they were concerned, a factor of marginal value in the development of movements. Many saw in religion an irrational social system of values, based on faith in a higher power and an eternal truth, and essentially cut off from the guiding principles of secular ideologies.[56] Christian Smith, who researched the religious aspect of protest movements, asserts that, in contrast to the opinion of many researchers of social movements, the religious value system is found in all levels of private life and in public matters; therefore, it is appropriate to include it as one of the weighty components in the development of a protest movement. Sometimes, social religious faith, political standing, and social status go hand in hand as in the case of Ireland, for example. The importance of religion in social movements is embedded in its capacity to ground the feelings of frustration and alienation and to provide a framework and a very broad common denominator, indeed. This is because religion is assimilated into all the social layers, accompanies individuals from the time of their birth, and is easy to connect to in times of distress. Furthermore, religion provides exclusive solutions for the preservation of commitment to a collective purpose and to family identity (also in situations in which the price of joining rises because of a policy of repression) by means of applying symbols and meanings from the distant past to current reality and supplying the emotional resources for the preservation of activism over time.[57]

In fundamentalist sects, protest activity is defined in terms of holy war "Jihad", the will of God, terms that are recognized by and obligate all who are counted in or connected to a religious system. In many social systems, religion constitutes the only source of moral standards, and for this reason, it encourages or supports actions that are intended to change the existing social state and to implement social justice on the basis of religious moral verification; for example, the notion of enforcing the Shariah. In developing and traditional societies, religion is integrated into all areas of life. In these societies, the community stands at the center. The individual grows up in a societal reality in which a system of beliefs exists regarding the obligations of the individual toward the community he belongs to, in which he is required to act in accordance with the existing societal code and to do all he is able to do to advance the objectives of the community. In contrast, in modern capitalistic societies, the individual is in the center and he operates, first and foremost, in the advancement of his personal welfare and objectives.

The religious system comprises a source for recruitment of individuals or groups. It has the tools to convince its recruits to sacrifice their welfare and even their lives for the sake of shared purposes. There is great importance, indeed, to this mechanism that produces activists who are willing to rise above their own personal interests to the point of self-sacrifice for the sake of advancing the objectives of the movement. It defines the intensity of the movement in relation to its adversaries and lessens the value of repressive strategies and facilitation (containment) that are taken in opposition to the movement and its actions.[58]

The religious system has the tools to provide organizational resources that are likely to be critical in the various stages of protest. It is well equipped to provide leadership, supporters, finances, communication networks, social networks, and distribution mechanisms. In the centers of religious ceremony, regular gatherings take place in which information can be conveyed, public opinion shaped, listeners incited to common action, and the connection strengthened between the movement and its activists. The heads of the system are linked to one another with a hierarchical network of connections that enables the rapid transmission of information, ideas, and instructions for action. Therefore, the involvement of organizations or religious systems in protest activity has a significant influence on the mode and pace of its development, both because of the position of religion as a central factor in the lives of individuals and the public and also because of the ability of the religious systems to provide vital resources for the growth and success of the movement.[59] Religion in fundamentalist societies also serves as a central tool in building, founding, and preserving a shared identity. This identity improves the strength of the movement to form its objectives, to define the framework for action, and to found social solidarity. Its structure on a religious basis sharpens the differences even more between the movement and its environment; it creates a stronger affinity between the individuals and the movement and intensifies the motivation of activist groups to carry out shared actions.[60]

The ethnic aspect: Susan Olzak and Joan Nagel define ethnicity as a term that expresses ethnic boundaries, or ethnic emphases, expressed in similar traits such as skin color, language, or religion.[61] In the last decades, the phenomenon of ethnicity has broadened, in spite of the efforts of nations of people to mold a shared national identity. In Nagel's view, ethnicity is a consequence of a rise in nationalism and the expansion of the state's internal political action. The action taken by the state to form a national identity contradicts and competes with the identities of ethnic groups. The states' control of the distribution of resources causes competition between the groups in the population. These arguments, alongside the international recognition of the legitimacy of ethnicity as a basis for competition over resources, advance the development of ethnic movements. Ethnic demands serve today as a basis both for the appearance of political organizations and for the emergence of ethnic protest movements.[62]

Behavioral theoretical models concerning the subject of "ethnic competition" maintain that modernization and its expressions, such as industrialization, urbanization, bureaucracy and new political game rules, encourage common activity that is based on ethnic identity. According to this approach, established systems in modern society lean on a very broad societal base composed of groups with common identity and interests. Therefore, only large groups can challenge established systems. In the opinion of these theoreticians, this argument explains why shared identities of a low level such as family, tribe, or village integrate into groups possessing a higher level of shared identity such as ethnic, racial, sexual, or religious identity.[63] Ethnic groups will turn in the direction of protest only when they feel intended deprivation and discrimination in relation to other groups (relative discrimination theory). The paradox is that, for this purpose, they need to be rich enough in resources and means or at least having the capacity to recruit them to be capable of challenging the established system (resource management theory) and to advance their interests.

The Development of Protest Movements

The literature deals, rather extensively, with the explanation for the phenomenon of the appearance of social protest movements from the 1960s in the twentieth century and onward. Theoreticians from the fields of psychology and social sciences have offered models that explain the phenomenon, on the level of both the individual and the movement. However, theoretical literature has not dealt sufficiently with the phenomenon of fundamentalist (religious) and ethnic movements or in shaping a theoretical model of principles that characterize the phases and the development of protest movements in general and fundamentalist protest movements in particular. It is worthwhile to point out that the diversity of types of protest movements, their areas of occupation, and their character make the development of a characteristic theoretical framework difficult. Therefore, the existing model developed by the researchers of the 1970s identifies four principal stages in the life of a social protest movement.[64]

The first stage is the establishment, in which a movement originates when external and internal conditions exist for it.

The second stage, consolidation, is adjacent to its origin. The movement must define objectives, lines of action, and policy to decide on tactics of action and to market itself to the public. At this stage, the movement works to expand its ranks by conducting collective action, drawing the attention of the media, forming public opinion, and creating the conditions of cooperation and alliance with other organizations/groups for the purpose of attaining essential resources.

The third stage, bureaucratization, is the passage from action patterns that rely on a charismatic leader to action patterns that rely on organizations, professional staff, and bureaucratic traits. Not all movements go through the process successfully. Some of them disappear even before they begin it. Some lose the supporting audience during the process because of its significance, the relinquishment of the revolutionary fire that characterizes a movement in its initial stages. Research that deals with revolutionary movements points to their tendency in the first stages to form around the charismatic leadership of an individual or group. The trademarks of this pattern are the existence of a special and revolutionary ardent moral spirit among the members of the movement, the absence of a fixed organizational system, and a strong inclination to destroy existing institutions.

The transition to the institutional action pattern is a consequence both of internal processes and of external constraints. It issues from the need to preserve the accomplishments attained up to that time, to protect the movement from external threats, and to enable it to exist and to operate in a changing environment and for a prolonged period of time. The passage to institutionalized action patterns points to the adaptability and pragmatism that exist in the movement.[65]

The fourth stage is decline. As in every dynamic life cycle, the stage of decline arrives, and thus, it occurs in the development of a protest movement also. The sociologist Frederik Miller enumerates four possible reasons for the decline of a movement: first, successful attainment of the objectives of the movement; second, internal struggles and the dwindling of resources; third, obstruction of the leaders of the movement from achieving its objectives by taking facilitation strategies (containment) and by giving benefits (money, prestige, and personal status); and fourth, the success of repressive action taken by the government.

To summarize, social protest movements and revolutions can be a complex social phenomenon that does not work according to a unique model. They appear subsequent to political opportunities and are influenced by relationships between the state and society; by the internal social, economic, and cultural state of affairs; and by regional and international systems. In these movements, an internal dynamic exists, characterized by a transition from spontaneous, informal action patterns, based usually on the charisma of the leader or group as well as on revolutionary zeal, to a structure of establishments and organization based on formal norms and rules that blunt the revolutionary fervor and are characterized by pragmatism and a system of checks and balances. It is adequate emphasizing that, in spite of the existing dissimilitude between cultures, there are many similarities between protest movements that have emerged in different places.

2

Development of Social Movements in Muslim Society: The Phenomenon and Its Characteristics

The Idea of "Umma" and the Means to Realize It: Dawa and Jihad

The vision common to all Islamic movements is based on the idea of "Umma"—the establishing of the Islamic community of believers that will unite all Muslims of the world and restore Islam's status as the leading factor in the world. The tools for the realization of this vision are Jihad ("holy struggle") and Dawa ("invitation," "propagation," or "call"). Both are drawn from the concepts of the classic Islam and express a yearning for the days of Islam's glory. The world, from an Islamic theological point of view, is divided into two parts. The first part, Dar al-Islam, includes territories under Islam's control; the second part, Dar al-Harb, is under the heretics' control, and the fighting for its subjugation to Islam is still not complete. The two instruments, Dawa and Jihad, support and complement each other. However, while Dawa is based on nonviolent measures designed to rectify Muslim society through the systems of education, indoctrination, and social solidarity, Jihad, at its origin, strives to achieve this goal through violent measures.[1]

Much has been written about the concept of Jihad in classic and modern Islamic literature, and it has numerous aspects. Some, including the Islamists, interpret Jihad as a concept that includes various types of activity: Jihad of the heart, Jihad of action, domestic Jihad inside Islamic states against heretical rulers (a primary goal for many of the Islamic movements), external Jihad, offensive Jihad, defensive Jihad, and economic Jihad.

Not all the aforementioned types of Jihad employ physical violence.[2] The radical Islamic trend, influenced by the writings of Qutb, disseminates the opinion that only Jihad of the violent kind might decide the campaign against the pro-Western Muslim regimes and create the conditions for the foundation of an Islamic theocracy.[3]

Jihad is a central tool in the service of the Islamists. In his book *Knights under the Prophet's Banner: The al-Qaeda Manifesto (Fursan Taht Rayah Al-Nabi)*, Ayman al-Zawahiri (Bin Laden's deputy) extensively refers to this topic. He argues that, with the appearance of the Islamists, a new perception started to crystallize among Muslims interested in the victory of Islam : there is no solution except Jihad. This Jihad should be based on acts of sacrifice, must be particularly violent, and should terrify and cause as many casualties as possible to the enemy.[4]

In July 2003, a conference of Islamic sages from the Muslim world took place in Stockholm. It was chaired by Sheik Yusuf el-Qardawi, one of the senior leaders of the Muslim Brothers. The conference dealt with the topic "Jihad and the Denial of Its Relation to Terror." At this conference, Qardawi presented his research, justifying Jihad against Israel with the argument that it is a Jihad of necessity. He explained that, inter alia, from the standpoint of religious law, the blood and property of a resident of Dar al-Harb are not protected because of his actions and violence toward Muslims.[5] In the Shia tradition, Jihad in its offensive sense is considered to be an optional commandment until the moment when the lands of Islam are conquered by foreigners. From that moment on, Jihad becomes a commandment, applying personally to every Shiite believer.[6]

The duty of implementing the commandment of Jihad was, and still is, a central issue under debate between those wishing to hold sole authority to declare war (ruling elites and the state) and those challenging the state and its institutions by turning to this facility of personally binding Jihad. Applying this measure apparently makes it possible to circumvent the authority of the state. The issue sharpens even more when the question of the duty of implementing personal Jihad is discussed.[7]

To summarize, Jihad has many faces, and the Islamic interpretation makes use of it according to its needs. The Islamists utilize the concept of Jihad to justify their violence on the one hand and to expand their circle of supporters on the other hand, by portraying their violent activity as a moral imperative and a religious duty against the heretics and enemies of Islam.

Research Approaches in the Analysis of the Phenomenon of Radical Islam

The research on the development of Islamic social movements grew following the emergence of the Islamic phenomenon as an influential factor in national, regional, and international systems.[8] The Iranian revolution of 1979 was the first significant expression of that. This phenomenon, especially its radical margins, also challenges the existing social order in Muslim countries; it is, directly and indirectly, connected to violence and terror. In the study of the phenomenon of radical Islam, three schools of thought, differing in their way of treatment of the phenomenon, can be distinguished:

1.   The first discipline regards the Islamic phenomenon as an exceptional social fact, unique to Muslim societies. Therefore, as far as the supporters of this discipline are concerned, the Western social theories are not suitable and do not contribute to the understanding of the Islamic phenomenon and the reasons for its rise. They argue that Islam is not just a religion, but also a comprehensive framework for life, which is composed of a system of specific and unalterable principles and rules. As such, it outrightly rejects all that characterizes modernity in its present form

(secularity, democracy, and nationality). At this point, the similarity between the researchers of this discipline ends, and they are divided into three subgroups, differentiated in their political and cultural worldview and in the proximity/distance of the researchers to the phenomenon. The first subgroup comprises the Islamists themselves. It contains researchers, intellectuals, theologians, and religious figures from the first or second circle of the leadership groups of Islamic movements. They establish the Islamic discourse and shape the ideology and the required conceptual frameworks for the advancement of the goals they set for themselves.[9] The second subgroup contains researchers and intellectuals with a cultural affinity to Islam, who identify with the phenomenon. They emphasize the positive aspects of the phenomenon and the trends reflecting the progression of Islamic society toward democracy. This democracy, in their opinion, is different in its characteristics from Western democracy, but nevertheless contains firm democratic foundations. This group underrates the threat of radical Islam and strives to change the West's hostile attitude toward Islam.[10] The third subgroup holds a completely opposite opinion. According to it, Islamic fundamentalism is the consequence of the repression and dictatorship that have characterized Islamic culture and history from time immemorial. Therefore, Islam in general and the fundamentalist kind in particular constitute an extremely significant threat to the West and to the stability of the pro-Western regimes in Egypt, Jordan, and Saudi Arabia.[11]

2.   The second discipline regards the Islamic phenomenon as part of a worldwide phenomenon that characterized the last decades of the twentieth century and whose essence is a return to religion's origins as an answer and a solution to the hardships of the individual. These researchers base themselves on the theoretical groundwork already existing in the social sciences, dealing with social movements.[12] Their studies are comparative in nature and try to isolate the variables applying to fundamentalist social movements. They regard the phenomenon as a threat to democracy in its wider context, including the rights of the individual, secularism, and scientific and technological progress. The most comprehensive and broadest research, best representing this approach, was conducted during the 1990s and led by the University of Chicago. Within its framework, the phenomenon of fundamentalism and the forms of its expression in the various cultures were investigated over a wide gamut of aspects.[13]

3.   The third discipline holds the opinion that fundamentalist Islam is a product of social processes and class power struggles within Muslim societies, aimed at acquiring political power for the advancement of ideological interests. This phenomenon is similar to other negative populist movements in history such as Fascism and Nazism. The approach of these investigators is based on existing social theories and argues that fundamentalist Islam is a product of reciprocal connections between the social structure, interclass struggle, ideology, and the nature of the regimes in Muslim countries. The followers of this approach see this phenomenon as a significant threat to democracy and the future of Islam.[14]

The existence of these three disciplines of research attests to what extent this topic is complex and controversial. The discussion on Islamic movements is affected by the viewpoint of the research (social, religious, philosophical, or defensive), the time of the research, the cultural attribution, the myths created around the issue, and the affinity of the researcher to the phenomenon. At the basic level, there are disputes regarding the question of whether the Islamic movements are social or political in nature; those who research the phenomenon in its social context seek explanations as to the evolution of fundamentalist movements, how they developed, and what types of movements evolve in different Muslim societies. On the other hand, research dealing with the political context focuses on the influence of Islamic discourse and philosophy in the development of Islamic fundamentalism in various political and economic situations across the Muslim world.[15]

The sentiment, in the West, toward the research of the phenomenon is influenced by the negative image Islam has acquired as a result of the violent and terrorist activities of Islamic movements and the damage they have caused to Western interests. Moreover, the hostile attitude of fundamentalist Islam toward the West makes it difficult for Western researchers to study the phenomenon in an objective and impartial manner. To balance the picture, it should be emphasized that the Muslim mainstream, which dominates most Muslim states— "institutionalized Islam," tends toward modernity, has a moderate and pragmatic Islamic orientation, and usually is not in conflict with Western culture. Notwithstanding, the Muslim world is immersed in a deep internal cultural struggle between the mainstream and the radical Islamist stream, and here lies the potential for threat. This struggle will determine the future character and form of Muslim states and the nature of their relations with the West.

The radical movements strive to instigate change using a revolutionary act, as epitomized by the Iranian model. For that purpose, they employ action strategies combined with violence and terror on the one hand and education, propaganda, and welfare on the other hand. The goal of these movements is to replace the secular regimes in Muslim states with Islamic regimes, to establish new Islamic states in places where Islamic groups fight other state entities, and to continue the fight against Western culture along their mutual frontiers. The outlook on the conflict with other cultures is assimilated in Islamic thought and philosophy from time immemorial, according to which the world is divided into Dar al-Islam and Dar al-Harb.

The primary goal of the social movements in the Muslim world, be they radical or reformist, is to change (by revolutionary or gradual means) the state governmental system and establish an Islamic theocratic state. The appearance and expansion of the Islamic wave, especially the radical one, in the late twentieth century was the result of four factors and historical events: first, the Iranian revolution, which marked the first significant victory of Islam over the West; second, the power of Arab oil from the 1970s on, which was used by the Persian Gulf states (mostly by Saudi Arabia) to finance Islamic activities across the Muslim world and outside it, beginning with building Islamic centers and ending with funding the Mujahideen (Islamic Jihad fighters) in various conflict areas in the world; third, the victory of the Mujahideen over the USSR in Afghanistan, also perceived as an ideological and cultural victory of the spirit of Islam over the might of the superpowers; and fourth, the disintegration of the Soviet bloc and the collapse of communist ideology. The vacuum that was created provided an opportunity for the marketing of the Islamic alternative as a holistic solution, capable of succeeding where the great Western ideologies, represented by the secular regimes in the Muslim states, had failed.[16]

As a rule, Islamic social movements are not essentially different from other protest movements in their qualities and the trends of their evolution. The aspect that differentiates them, however, is the environment of their operation, expressed by unique codes of behavior and the existing tension between their attitude toward the modern state and the idea of the pan-Islamic nation. This tension, saturated with contrasts and contradictions, causes clashes and social and political struggles on the one hand, and on the other hand, it creates dynamic patterns of behavior that are based on mechanisms of mediation, compromise, and tension adjustment. The practical manifestation of this is evident in the approach of the Islamic movements that adopt an activity style of "walking the edge" in their relations with the establishment. These movements labor to realize the goal of applying Islamic law onto the state in stages, while employing strategies that combine an Islamic religious approach and political realism.[17]

Islamic social movements are not a new phenomenon in Islamic society; they have characterized it from time immemorial. However, in the last three decades of the twentieth century a significant change occurred in their disposition and goals. They led the resistance to the political order existing in Muslim societies and acted toward the founding of a new political and social order based on Islam. This change is a product of social and political processes that transpired in these societies in the 1950s, causing the creation of social groups frustrated with the policies of the Muslim states, the failure of Western ideologies, and modernity and its consequences.[18] The social hardships and the feelings of frustration among these groups paved the way for the development of the Islamic social approaches, which regarded Islam as the only solution for changing the situation.

The character of Islamic movements, as that of all other protest groups, differs across countries. Some use violence to achieve political goals. This willingness to employ violence is not just a function of the ideological framework of these movements, but is also, largely, a reflection of the political culture of that country and a consequence of the level of repression followed by the state. Some Islamic movements appeared after many years of premovement activity in social networks and communal institutions, and some appeared with the rise of the Islamic wave.[19]

In any case, in its current state, this is a new phenomenon that appeared after the rise of the modern state. The Islamic movements learned to acknowledge, some the hard way (e.g., the case of the Muslim Brothers in Syria), not only the power of the state and the regional and international systems, but also their own limitations. They acted, and still do, within a framework of constraints and political opportunities to promote their interests. The status of Islam in popular culture helps these movements expand their influence among considerable portions of the population, with an emphasis on the lower classes (the middle-low and low classes), and secures them long-term survivability even in places where suppressive policies are employed.[20]

The scope of the Islamic phenomenon in Muslim countries and the potential for threat that is latent within it cause the rulers of these countries to lose much sleep. Each of them employs his own methods to reduce its proportions and minimize its political potency: some using a bear hug (inclusion strategies), some applying a stranglehold (suppression strategies), and some combining both strategies. Even in the regional and international arenas, there is a mounting apprehension about the capability of radical Islamic groups and regimes to induce "culture wars" to conflagrate and threaten the foundations of the social and international order, the democratic values of the West, and vital Western interests. The success of Muslim fanatics in seizing power in Iran in 1979, in Sudan in 1989 (with the help of the military), and in Afghanistan in 1996 (beginning the reign of the Taliban) only deepened these apprehensions. Muslim fanatics succeeded in influencing the governments and societies even in places where they were not successful in seizing reign, such as in Saudi Arabia, Egypt, Jordan, and the Gulf Emirates. The problem that the international systems in general and the Middle Eastern ones in particular have to confront is the ever-increasing use of extreme terrorism by Islamic movements. It should be added that, although they constitute a marginal minority in Muslim societies, they gain extensive resonance and media coverage due to the nature of their violent activities and the level of potential threat they embody.[21]

Fundamentalist Islam is, therefore, part of a global phenomenon whose principles are a return to the foundations of religion as a solution to the hardships of the individual and society. Here is the rationale to examine this phenomenon with experimental tools based on existing social theories. Notwithstanding, there is a uniqueness to the Islamic phenomenon that does not exist in other non-Muslim societies. It crosses the boundaries of the state both in philosophy and in practice (the idea of the Islamic nation). This difference obligates the design of additional theoretical tools to explain this phenomenon, the reasons for its growth, and the processes of its evolution.

Explanations for the Emergence of Islamic Social Movements

The emergence of Islamic social movements is a common and periodical phenomenon in the history of Islam. These movements usually appear following crises, as is the case with other social movements. The current wave started in the second half of the twentieth century and is characterized by the rise of reformist and revolutionary Islamic protest movements that hold a similar common denominator: the demand to apply Islamic law upon the state. These movements were transformed, in the course of time, from a marginal element in Muslim society to a leading social and political element having widespread influence and control over the members of the low and middle classes in society, as far as posing a direct and indirect threat to existing governmental systems, regional systems, and international interests. The intensity of the phenomenon stems from the fact that it combines within it social and political protest. Some suppose that this phenomenon (with religious revival as its driving force) is defensive in essence, resembling a desperate reaction of the weak against everything that represents the West (power, modernity, and secularity).[22]

In light of this argument, some questions, around which the following discussion will revolve, are asked: What are the causes and the explanations for the development of the Islamic social protest? Is it similar in its qualities to protest movements in other cultures? How were Islamic protest movements transformed from a marginal element in society to a widespread phenomenon that threatens the stability of regimes? What is the weight of Islam as a motivating element for the appearance and evolution of protest movements in Islamic societies?

The reasons and explanations offered for the development of the Islamic phenomenon are many and varied. From amongst the explanations for the phenomenon, the following should be mentioned:

1. *The general social explanation*: It can be generalized that social protest movements are the product of social and demographic processes. The extent of their success depends on the existence of suitable preliminary organizational conditions and political opportunities. In times of crisis, the processes of their emergence and evolution are accelerated. This generalization holds true for the Islamic case as well.[23] The return to Islam is the first step in the birth of an Islamic protest movement, the basis upon which it grows. The values of the religion make it possible to shape the behavioral model on the basis of a religious common denominator, upon which the religious fanaticism grows. This fanaticism is translated, in this case, into revolutionary activism.[24]

2. *The theological-social explanation*: Since the beginning in the mid-1970s, a discussion is being held in the Islamic world. This discussion revolves around two main topics: the first pertains to the reasons for the weakening of Islam in front of the West, and the second pertains to the changes that the Muslims need to make to transform this situation. Many participants in this discourse are of the opinion that Islam is weak and inferior in relation to the might and superiority of the West and that there is a need to take steps to change the situation before it is too late. The main disagreements in this view revolve around the severity of the situation, the level of required urgency to change it, and the nature of the required action (revolutionary/reformist). The analysis of the state of Islam, as reflected in the writings of the participants, reveals that, in many Muslim states, it was pushed to the margins and in its place the phenomenon of secularity and modernity, imported from the West, spread, was embraced by the elites, and disseminated to the entire the population. Moreover, the existing regimes invested in the assimilation of the idea of nationality as a basis for social solidarity and loyalty to the regime, while pushing aside the social solidarity based on Islam. The religious establishment, as the radical writers point out, not only refrained from stepping into the breach before the increasing secularity, but also cooperated and invoked rationales and interpretation from the scriptures and tradition to justify the actions of the regimes, upon which it was completely dependent.[25] Radical intellectuals and Islamic theologians described the state of Islam somberly, using symbols, expressions, and terms of deep religious and pessimistic meaning, in order to mobilize their listeners and their readers into collective

action. The fourteenth century of the Islamic calendar (ending in the 1970s) was described as the century of Islamic decline. The current situation was defined as the era of "new Jahaliya," whose very existence obligates the launch of a Jihad.[26]

3. *The social identity crisis explanation*: Since the nineteenth century, Muslim societies have been experiencing processes of social change that are in continuous conflict with Western culture and its influences. In the beginning, it was the struggle against colonialism. Later, it became a struggle against Arab regimes that were established on the basis of the Western model, which contradicts the Islamic approach in essence. The failure of the new nation-states to deliver the goods they promised (economic prosperity and security), in addition to the series of defeats they suffered in their wars against Israel, created identity crises in Muslim societies, leading them to seek an appropriate alternative to the existing regimes.[27] The identity crisis is not a self-contained entity; it creates feelings of discontent, frustration, and alienation that grow stronger in places where individuals or groups are exposed to varying levels of repression. All these cause the development of the crisis of legitimacy. When this happens, it is utilized well by leaders of protest movements to create delegitimization of the regime and to expand recruitment for activity within the movement.[28] The appearance of fundamentalist Islam from the 1970s on resulted from, inter alia, the collapse of the theory that had dominated the Muslim states since the 1950s, according to which the assimilation of Western models, ideologies, and technologies would bring about economic and technological blossoming. In the early 1970s, it became clear that the expectations held by the masses from modernity had not been realized. The promises made by the states to their citizens were not fulfilled; the conditions of many individuals and groups in the population worsened compared with small groups enjoying economic prosperity. Added to this, the defeat of the Arab states in 1967 intensified Islam's weakness before the West and deepened the feelings of hopelessness, loss of identity, and pessimism that became prevalent among the populations of these states. These feelings made the populations more attentive to the Islamic message emanating from the seminaries of the Islamists. They argued that the defeats in the wars against Israel were "defeats of regimes that did not wave the flag of Islam. They waved any flag but the flag of Islam . . . ."[29]

4. *The demographic explanation*: The Islamic phenomenon is urban in its roots—the product of the accelerated urbanization processes and the emigration of millions of people from the country to the city, taking place in many developing countries/societies, including the Arab states, starting from the 1950s. In a Muslim city, people of all classes live in the same city but with considerable differences between them: elites opposite members of the lower class; veteran residents opposite newcomers. The pace of urbanization and emigration in the Muslim countries is much faster than the rate of expansion of the cities. As a result, massive pressure is created on the job market, housing, and services in many of the cities in the Muslim states, and the circle of unemployment expands. The first casualties of

these processes were the immigrants from the country to the city, usually lower-class people. They resided in the slums surrounding the cities in crowded and destitute conditions, cut off from their familial roots and from their new surroundings, and suffered from the lack of basic social services, bureaucratic slowness, and various repressive government apparatuses. The neglect, the lack of services, and the loss of the feeling of belonging supported the development of religious fanaticism that, in essence, is the expression of difficult reality and the loss of hope among the youth.[30] Their location at the bottom of the social ladder and their inability to change or improve their position, caused the germination of feelings of frustration and alienation among these youths, who were seeking a supportive framework. To them, the Islamic movements provided not only a supportive framework, but also a feeling of belonging, clear goals and purpose, and a hope for the improvement of their condition. The second group hurt by the rate of urbanization was that of the middle-class youths, students and their families, who regarded the acquiring of education as a key to improve their socioeconomic status and social mobility. The hundreds of thousands of university graduates found it very difficult to find appropriate employment due to the incompatibility between the education system and the economic system. The latter was not constructed to absorb the graduates of the education system and the universities, who were thus forced to settle for jobs that did not suit their education and did not meet their expectations for economic improvement. These graduates also experienced the results of the economic liberalization that was introduced in a few Arab countries during the 1970s. The results included an eruption of high inflation that corroded their wages, the creation of a "nouveau riche" class that adopted ostentatious Western behavior patterns, and the spread of a Western-style consumer culture.[31] The processes of accelerated urbanization and liberalization did not fit with a third world reality and with the ability to appropriate resources and the sources to support them and were like a boomerang for the regimes in Muslim countries. The high expectations for economic change did not hold the test of time. Their collapse contributed to the development of feelings of alienation against the existing social-political order and the injustice inherent in the nature of the modern state, mostly to the antagonism toward modernity and its expressions among groups and individuals of the middle and lower classes, including the graduates of the academia. For them, return to the bosom of Islam was an appropriate response to everything that modernity represented. The polarization of the rich and the poor served as fertile ground for the activity of Islamic and opposition movements who were waging a joint struggle against the established economic policy, regarded by them as unequal and unjust. No wonder, therefore, that although the Islamic solution, which called for doing social justice through the redistribution of wealth, seemed utopian and unattainable, it was still adopted by the members of the middle class, who were frustrated by their condition and preferred the promise latent in it over the existing reality.[32]

Exploitation of Political Opportunities

Beyond the aforementioned reasons and explanations, the leaders of the Islamic trend were wise in exploiting political opportunities while revealing political realism and a sound understanding of the reality in which they operated. Islamic movements exploit political opportunities as a leverage for breaking through into the public consciousness and as a basis for expansion. Their success is influenced, inter alia, by a correct analysis of political opportunities and their translation for gains in the field. Examining the sociopolitical background that preceded the emergence of pan-Islamic movements in the Arab states reinforces the aforementioned postulation. For example, the Egyptian Muslim Brotherhood movement, one of the first Islamic movements in modern times, was founded in Egypt in the late 1920s due to increasing agitation against colonialism. Since then, it has traveled a long way, navigating between pragmatism and radicalism, according to the development of the nature of its interaction with the authorities and in reaction to the appearance or disappearance of political opportunities. Another example can be found in the appearance of the Egyptian Islamic movements Al-Gama'a al-Islamiyya, Al Takfir Wal Hijra, and Al-Jihad al-Islami in the late 1970s and later in the 1990s following social crises and the feelings of alienation and frustration with the regime, which erupted with full force after the defeat of the Egyptian Army in the Six Day War (1967).[33]

Another clear example of the importance of identifying political opportunities for the existence of a movement was provided by the Muslim Brothers movement in Syria. This movement, founded in the 1940s, operated at varying levels of recognition, reciprocation, and cooperation with the governmental system in Syria, and within the framework of the accepted rules of the game, for about twenty years. The situation changed in the 1960s with the rise to power of the Ba'ath party. The movement metamorphosed into a violent struggle against the regime, reaching its peak in 1982. In response, the Syrian president, Hafez al-Assad, employed particularly severe means of repression. The movement was badly damaged, and its infrastructure in Syria was almost entirely destroyed. In this case, the leadership of the movement was not wise enough to understand the limits of its power, and especially, the fact that a political "window of opportunity," which would justify crossing over to a violent route as far as declaring an uprising, had not been created. The case of the Muslim Brothers movement in Syria constituted a clear example of the failure to determine whether a political opportunity existed.[34] However, correct analyses of reality and the exploitation of internal and external political opportunities took place during the 1980s. Examples include the emergence of the Islamic Jihad movement, the Hamas movement (exploited the eruption of the Intifada to establish the movement in 1987), and the Hezbollah movement in Lebanon, at the conclusion of Israel's, "Peace for Galilee" war (1982).

Islamic Movements—Typology and Main Similarities

Islamic movements have been operating in Muslim societies from as early as the first few decades of the twentieth century. Since the 1970s, the phenomenon has expanded, reflected by the appearance of new movements, in the nature of Islamic discourse, and in the scope of the quest of the Arab regimes and the international system to understand the phenomenon and find ways to halt it. A review of the phenomenon shows the existence of similarities and characteristics common to many of the Islamic movements. However, there is a difficulty in outlining a theoretical model that could predict when, and under what circumstances, an Islamic movement might arise and what kind of movement it would become. A multitude of influential circumstances, including internal social processes, the nature of the political culture within the state, and the existence of regional and international influences, has given birth to various types of Islamic movements, as well as to the different types of relationships between them and the state. These relationships, in the opinion of John Voll and John Esposito, are the product of three influential elements. The first is the status of the movement when it was being established (legal/illegal) and the changes to this status over time. The second is the level of activism/ revolutionism of the movement and the nature of the threat it poses to the regime. The third is the attitude of the regime toward the Islamic movements and the blend of action strategies it applies to them (repression/ inclusion).[35]

This framework of relations dictates the behavior patterns of the movements. Some of them operate in the open, and some follow semi clandestine or fully clandestine modus operandi. The nature of the clandestine activity and the deliberate disinformation tactic employed by these movements, in addition to the fact that many of them operate in states where free press is nonexistent, make the study of this phenomenon difficult. Accurate and reliable information on the number of movements and their characteristics, size, and deployment is not available. In spite of this, processes and conspicuous characteristics can be identified with a reasonable level of accuracy from the existing information.

A comparative study conducted on Islamic movements pointed to the existence of similarities and duplications in their basic characteristics, including their names, the use they make of Islamic symbols and expressions, their goals, their types (reformist or revolutionary), their size, and the characteristics of their activity.[36] The findings of this study indicate that there is a marked connection between the parameters of young (initial stages of development), small (between ten and a thousand activists) movements, high militancy, clandestine characteristics, and a charismatic leadership. There is a similarly strong and clear connection between the parameters of a movement that is mature, large, has a low level of militancy and overt public activity, and a bureaucratic leadership.[37] These findings fit the theoretical models dealing with the passage of movements from a model of charismatic leadership to the institutional model.

Trailing the activity of Islamic movements reveals that, similar to social protest movements in other countries, in this case as well, there are mutual connections between the level of activism of the movement and the stage of its growth (young or mature) in relation to the system in which it operates (chaotic, government repression, real centralist regime, or divided elites). The activity of Islamic movements is simultaneously conducted at two levels: the first is external, against opponents, and the second is internal, toward supporters. The movements are influenced by the target audience they aim for and oscillate between the extremes of violent action versus pragmatism and deep communal social involvement versus total detachment.

The external activity against opponents mainly involves the use of violence. Notwithstanding, in certain countries (such as Egypt, Jordan, and Lebanon) conditions were created that made it possible to maintain dialogue, ties of cooperation, and understanding between the movements and the governmental system, as far as integrating the pragmatic majority of these movements into the existing political system. In such cases, the movements take advantage of the public stage and their ability to influence the allocation of resources to establish their influence among their audiences and to expand it to additional classes of the population. It should be emphasized that the reciprocal relationship created between the movements and their opponents influences the levels of violence and pragmatism that both sides apply.

At the internal level, the Islamic movements greatly emphasize community activity and a connection with the basic family unit. This activity is based on the tradition of solidarity inherent in Islam, and it is well used by the movements to advance their goals. They invest considerable resources in providing community and social services, including health care, welfare to needy families, solutions for the housing shortages, and, especially emphasized, religious and educational services starting from infancy. The purpose of this investment is to induce a deep commitment among the community members toward joint activity within the framework of the movement. Through this community activity, the Islamic movements strengthen their connections with, and grip over, the members of the lower class and the middle-lower class, to whom most governmental systems existing in Muslim countries fail to provide services.

Opposite the approach of activity within the Muslim societies, there is a more extreme approach of total withdrawal (Hijrah) from society. The proponents of this approach choose a way of life of seclusion from existing society, which they regard as Jahalic (heretical), while adopting a lifestyle that characterizes the ideal society (the era of Muhammad) in their opinion, as a preceding act for the revolutionary change. The disengagement from society, characterizing these movements is, inter alia, a way to protect themselves from the influences of the regime and the heretical society and reflects a will to create a pure model of an ideal society, disconnected from the influences of the modern secular society.[38]

To summarize, there are dynamic reciprocal relationships between the movements, their supporters, and their opponents at the level of public discourse and at the operative level. These influence the level of discourse, its topics, and the cooperation between the various publics. The rapprochement or estrangement between Islamic movements and the establishment will influence the nature of public discourse and the level of cooperation between reformists and revolutionaries. Examples for this can be seen in the reciprocal relationship between the Muslim Brothers in Jordan and the Jordanian authorities, as well as in the relationship between the Muslim Brothers in Egypt and the Egyptian authorities.[39]

The researchers of political Islam identify two types of Muslim movements: reformist and revolutionary.[40] The reformist movements represent the mainstream and generally tend to adopt nonviolent action strategies. Since the 1920s, and until the end of the 1970s, these movements focused on action in the areas of education, welfare, and mutual aid as a leverage to advance processes of return to religion and to strengthen their status among the public. When their influence broadened, particularly from the 1980s, they started to integrate themselves into the political process in their countries. For that purpose, they established political institutions and bodies and sent representatives to participate in election campaigns as independent parties or in joint rosters with non-Islamic parties, aiming to create the process of change from within. The reciprocal relationships between these movements and the establishment systems are complex and dynamic.[41]

According to the reformist-pragmatic approach, the establishing of the Islamic state will only be possible at the end of a gradual and prolonged bottom-to-top process. The instrument for that is the Dawa, whose purpose is education, indoctrination, and pleasant propaganda. This approach does not rule out integration into the political system and the acceptance of the political rules of the game, as long as these make it possible to take advantage of the situation to create the desired change from within the system. Its proponents work to exploit political opportunities, to establish/expand religion-based social movements (ensuring high odds of survival against repressive policies), to create public pressure on the authorities, to demand changes to the political system, and to acquire sources and resources. Notwithstanding, it should be emphasized that participation in the political games obligates concessions, even those made for outward appearance's sake. The solution, unique to these movements, is holding the rope on both ends. They did not relinquish their vision (application of Sharia), but due to pragmatic considerations and the preference for achieving immediate goals, they were less vociferous about the issue. This approach is an expression of a sober outlook on reality, combined with the understanding that, at this stage, a decisive conclusion cannot be attained through revolutionary acts against the existing regimes. Therefore, they adopted a gradual approach involving temporary compromises. Moreover, these movements comprehended the meaning of the might of the modern state and, in addition, the opportunities latent in this might to further their goals.[42] Among the obvious examples that should be mentioned is the Muslim Brothers movement in Syria and Jordan.[43] Oliver Roy, a researcher of fundamentalist Islam, calls this phenomenon "neo-fundamentalism."[44]

The revolutionary movements, on the other hand, wrote on their shield the application of Islamic law upon the state through the use of violence, outside the institutionalized system. The revolutionary approach gained momentum following the Islamic revolution in Iran and developed in parallel in both of Islam's main branches: the Sunni and the Shiite. In the Shiite branch, revolutionary movements developed on the basis of the philosophy of Ayatollah Khomeini. The most noticeable point in Shiite revolutionism is actually the sharp and swift transition of the members of the community from political passivity, which had characterized them for centuries, to radical activism, as an instrument for the application of Islamic rule. The Sunni revolutionary branch is different from the Shiite branch on a few parameters, but it strives to achieve the same aims.

The Sunni revolutionary leaders are not religious figures, unlike the leaders of the Shiite movements. The Sunni revolutionary leadership is disengaged from the Sunni religious establishment. Its members are usually educated people, academic graduates from the fields of science, and autodidacts in matters of religion, who are influenced by radical Islamic religious scholars. In their eyes, the regimes, and partly the religious establishment as well, are responsible for Islam's serious condition. As far as they are concerned, the solution is clear: the destruction of the existing social order, which is based on the mainstays of the modern Western secular culture, and the reestablishment of Islamic culture while relying on Islam as the basis for the new social order. The way to reach this objective is through Jihad against the corrupt regime within the Muslim states.[45] In this category, worthy of mention, are the messianic Islamic movements operating from outside Muslim society to achieve the change through Jihad.

The Islamic Discourse

Discourse, in a social context, is an instrument of social construction that gives frequently renewed meaning to the existing reality.[46] The public Islamic discourse is polemic and dynamic in nature, influenced by events and influences them. It is aimed at creating processes that will motivate the listeners to take action, or at the very least, to have an opinion. This discourse has defined directions and goals; it undergoes processes of change as a consequence of reciprocal relations and interactions between its originators, its listeners, and the people it challenges, both at the level of discourse and at the level of action. In times when tension is low or when the players' interests coincide for a while, the discourse is conducted within a clear and agreed-upon framework, and all sides restrict themselves within its boundaries. On the other hand, in times when tension escalates, or conflict of interest emerges, discourse becomes poignant and aggressive and accordingly the operative activity accompanying it. These characteristics appear in the discourse of protest movements and establishment systems in all cultures, including Islamic culture.

An analysis of the characteristics of Islamic discourse in the last century reveals that the discourse takes place in Muslim societies at varying levels of verbal moderation/violence, starting with a moderate and pragmatic discourse within a known or agreed-upon framework and ending with a polemic, emotional, and aggressive discourse. The characteristics of the discourse are influenced by the nature of the reciprocal relationships between the sides participating in it: Islamic movements and establishment systems. The goal of the generators of Islamic discourse is the establishment of an Islamic state. The discourse is shaped to achieve this goal by motivating individuals, and groups within the population, toward joint action within the movement. This is hardly a simple task, due to the complex relationship between the religious mentality and the political act in Muslim countries. Religious mentality and political action are reconciled through the Islamic discourse. It makes extensive use of Islamic symbols, holding deep religious meaning, while giving them a contemporary interpretation. These symbols are integrated into the messages of the movements in order to create the widest possible common denominator as a basis for an Islamic identity, collectiveness, solidarity, and a unified goal. The discourse that creates these processes provides legitimacy, inspiration, and confidence in the righteousness of the social and political struggle. The Islamic movements use Islamic symbols to create a common identity. The obvious example is the Iranian revolution, in which rhetoric, Islamic symbols, charismatic leadership, and political action were intertwined.[47]

An example is also provided by the Shiite community in Lebanon, where extensive use was made of Islamic symbols to create social mobilization and willingness for sacrifice through the presentation of contemporary interpretation of historical events, such as the one given to the rituals of the "day of Ashura."[48] The style of discourse and the shaping of its messages are derived from the types of movements, the action strategies they employ, and the nature of the reciprocal relationships between them and the existing regimes (political pressures, repression, or, alternatively, freedom of expression). Discourse is influenced by the personal standard, the status, and the inclinations of its generators and the nature of the popular culture. The radicals adopt the vociferous radical style, calling for the overthrow of the regime in a violent revolutionary act, in contrast with the pragmatists, who tend to adopt a polemic style at various levels, suited to the reality and the times in which the movement operates and in accordance with the various constraints existing in its sphere of operation.[49]

The historical events of the twentieth century left their mark on the Islamic discourse and influenced the trends of its evolution and emphases. From the beginning of the twentieth century until the late 1940s, the generators of discourse acted to recruit the masses for an active resistance against the West and its influences by using religious motifs and the traditions found in popular culture, as a leverage to create the change. During the fourth decade, the Islamic discourse focused on trying to create a dynamic that would bring about the replacement of the weak and "corrupt" pro-Western regimes by strong Islamic regimes. The secular Western culture and modernity were perceived by the Islamists as key causes for the corruption of society.[50] The intellectuals whose writings mainly influenced discourse in that period were Sayid Jamal al-Din, aka al-Afghani (1838–1897), Hassan al-Banna, the founder of the Muslim Brothers movement in Egypt (1906–1949), and Sawafi, the founder of the Faithful of Islam movement in Iran (1923–1956).[51] The 1950s and the 1960s witnessed dramatic changes in Islamic thought. In their beginning, aggressive military regimes appeared in the Arab states, incorporating the secular pan-Arabic message, guided by Nasser. These regimes made efficient and wise use of the governmental power at their disposal to expand their control over the population and to suppress any initiative opposing the regime. The activity of the Islamic movements was outlawed and suppressed by the authorities, and the movements' leaders were placed under arrest. The collapse of pan-Arabism in 1961, the failure of the military regimes to provide economic welfare, and especially the defeat of the Arab states in the June 1967 Six Day War severely hurt the prestige of the military regimes and, even more, the Arabs' self-image. The process of secularization that characterized Muslim society until that time stopped, and in its stead, a mass return to Islam began.[52] During this period, the Islamic discourse developed in two channels: radical and pragmatic. The radical discourse was shaped into a set doctrine in the mid-1960s by the most important radical thinker of that time, the Egyptian Sayyid Qutb (1906–1966). While imprisoned in Egypt, Qutb analyzed the bleak state of Islam and the causes for it. On the basis of his analysis, Qutb crystallized a new conceptual-ideological framework that included a whole set of justifications and interpretations taken from the Islamic universe and tradition, which provided the needed ratification for acts against the existing regimes. Qutb determined that the existing regimes were illegitimate (the concept of new Jahaliya) and called for the waging of a violent struggle aimed at toppling them in a revolutionary act, combined with Dawa activity by an avant-garde nucleus, the vanguard marching before the corps. The new radical discourse outrightly rejected the existing political culture that embraced the ideas of nationality, Arab socialism, and pan-Arabism, arguing that they were imported from the culture of the West and that they should not be assimilated into Islamic culture.[53] The pragmatic (and the seemingly moderate) discourse was shaped by pragmatic leadership in the Islamic movements, influenced by the combination of strategies (repression and inclusion) adopted by the regimes to tactically change, perhaps ostensibly, the qualities of the discourse and to dampen its messages. Its generators preferred activity within the rules of the political game of the existing systems. They agreed with the radicals that modernity was equivalent to the new Jahaliya, but in their opinion Islam had not reached a situation where all was lost and, therefore, there was no need to take extreme steps, as Qutb's doctrine suggests. The pragmatic line in that period supported the struggle to overthrow the existing regimes, while strictly observing a setting of legal activity and adhering to the conventional rules of the political game. It strove to use the powerful instruments of the state (the media, parliamentary podium, and various forums of decision making) for advancing the goals of Islam. In parallel, it promoted activities of Dawa to prepare the ground for a return to Islam.

From the 1970s on, the Islamic phenomenon expanded as a result of a number of processes at the economic level, which caused feelings of frustration and discrimination among broad segments in the Muslim societies, alongside some significant events at the military-political level. Among the prominent events influencing the shaping of the Islamic discourse at that time were the following: in the 1970s, the October war of 1973 and the peace process between Israel and Egypt and the 1979 Islamic revolution in Iran; in the 1980s, the development of an Islamic Jihad arena in Afghanistan, the Iran-Iraq War, the assassination of Anwar al-Sadat, the suppression of the Muslim Brothers in Syria, the "Peace for Galilee" War, the emergence of Hezbollah, and the rise of an Islamic regime in Sudan; and in the 1990s, the fall of communism, the Gulf War, and the emergence of al Qaeda.

The process of return to Islam, starting in the late 1960s, gained momentum in the 1970s as a result of the crises of shattered expectations and the expansion of repressive actions in Muslim states. The prominent discourse in these decades was the radical discourse, which took shape in the 1960s in Egypt and Iran and gained followers in many Muslim countries from the 1970s on. This discourse emphasized the pressing need to combine revolutionary violence and education using "segregated communities." It suggested a comprehensive solution that appealed to many middle- and lower-class groups in the population.[54]

The centrality of the Islamic discourse in those decades was perfectly evident by the expansion and number of Islamic publications, the construction of new mosques on a grand scale, an increase in the circulation of religious tape recordings, and a change in the styles of clothing and appearance of many youths. Most of the prominent Islamic intellectuals from the 1970s on were influenced by Qutb's philosophy. Among them were Said Hawa—the ideologue of the Muslim Brothers in Syria, Fathi Yakan—general secretary of the Lebanese Muslim Brothers, Muhammad Abd al-Salam Faraj—the ideologue of Sadat's assassins, Abdullah Azam—from the founders of a theological framework for defensive Jihad, and Ayman al-Zawahiri—the leader of the Egyptian Jihad and the deputy of Osama Bin Laden. Among the most prominent Shiite intellectuals of the 1960s and the 1970s were Khomeini—the first to succeed in implementing his philosophy and leading an Islamic revolution, Imam Sayyed Moussa as-Sadr—the founder and leader of the Amal movement, and Sayyed Mohammad Hussein Fadlallah—the spiritual leader of the Hezbollah movement in its initial years.

By and large, it can be said that even though the radical discourse did not define the topics on the public agenda in terms of issues of religion and society in Muslim countries in the last few years, it nevertheless greatly influenced them directly and indirectly. In the context of the pragmatic discourse it should be emphasized that leaderships of Islamic movements that formulated new action strategies assimilated them into their congregations through the discourse while relying on seemingly religious interpretation, with the goal of justifying, and mostly legitimizing, decisions that strayed from the declared ideology.[55] In any case, the Islamic discourse is a very powerful medium in Muslim societies and countries in the political-religious and social arenas.

Islamic Thought—Central Motifs, Directions, and Trends of Evolution

Islamic thought comprised the basis for Islamic discourse, and, as Islamic discourse did, it developed in two channels: radical and pragmatic. Intellectuals from both channels regard Islam as the comprehensive solution and agree on the need for action that will bring Islam into power again. The debate centered on the means that should be adopted to achieve the goal. Every channel had an ideological infrastructure based on the philosophy of a leading intellectual, such as Sunni Qutb and Shiite Khomeini in the radical channel or Hassan al-Banna and al-Hudaybi in the pragmatic channel. Notwithstanding, Islamic thought is dynamic and is influenced by, inter alia, the reciprocal relations evolving between various political systems and the movements, with their followers and opponents.[56] One of the foundations upon which Islamic thought is based is the motif of hatred for the West. The abomination of the West has motivated and still motivates Islamists to carry out actions against Western objectives, while taking high levels of risk and going as far as self-sacrifice. A few examples of these actions are the launching of Hezbollah suicide attacks against the multinational forces in Lebanon and the Israel Defense Force (IDF), the phenomenon of the Palestinian suicide attacks, the September 11 attacks, and the operations on global Jihad arenas, such as the one occurring in Iraq.

Alongside the hatred for the West, Islamic discourse led the hatred to the culture of the West. According to both pragmatic and radical Islamic thinkers, the fourteenth century of the Islamic numeration, ending in 1979, was signaled by Islamic decline, the recognizable expressions of which were the technological, economic, and spiritual weaknesses of the countries of Islam, in contrast with the undeniable might of the Western states. The radicals in the group were extremely pessimistic in their diagnosis of the state of Islam. The discourse emanating from their seminaries was clear and unequivocal. It called for immediate and revolutionary activity to change the existing social and political orders. This discourse was saturated with poignant expressions against the West and its culture: heretics and members of "the party of Satan," in Qutb's version, or "big Satan" in Khomeini's version.[57] Its arrows were aimed primarily against modernity and its main expressions: secularity, individualism, and a Western political culture. These values, according to the Islamist thinkers, stood in complete contradiction to Islam and, therefore, had to be completely uprooted. In the same breath, additional ideas such as nationalism and Arab socialism were rejected.

Khomeini—the Father of Shiite Radicalism

The radical thought in the Shiite world was crystallized in the 1960s by Khomeini, who is considered to be the father of Shiite radicalism. He was influenced by the idea of the Islamist state of Abul Ala al-Mawdudi. Khomeini was the first Islamic thinker to lead an Islamic movement to victory over a pro-Western regime in a revolutionary act.

His philosophy is based on the world of Shiite concepts and symbols, but it contains quite a few similarities to the Sunni radical thought. He, too, had reached the conclusion that Islamic society is severely ill, and that a radical act is needed to rescue it from the existing situation. According to him, religious figures, and only them, are necessary and qualified to lead the nation. His book titled *Wilayat-e Faqih*, or *Hukumat-e Islami* (Islamic government) in a later edition, is based on the Islamic approach, regarding divine law as the source of authority. However, Khomeini developed this idea much beyond that. He argued that every other governmental approach that is not based on divine law is heresy. In his opinion, the fundamental condition required from the ruler is proficiency and understanding of the divine law and the ability to interpret it. This ability, in his opinion, exists only in figures of religious authority and, therefore, Khomeini's conclusion was that at the leadership of the state must be the religious men with the skills suitable to govern it according to Islamic law.[58] Khomeini redesigned central concepts from the Shiite existence and culture and made wide use of them for the dissemination of his messages and for the mobilization of people for collective action. The two most prominent concepts he developed and perfected were the willingness for sacrifice (Istishahad) and xenophobia.[59]

The sacrifice motif was embraced by the Lebanese Hezbollah movement and was shaped to suit Lebanon's needs. It became an anchor in the Islamic discourse in Lebanon and a cornerstone in the plan for the establishing of the "resisting population" that Hezbollah strove to establish in Lebanon. In an interview dedicated mostly to the issue of sacrifice, conducted with Hezbollah deputy secretary general Sheik Naim Qassem on November 1995, he said that the justification for the sacrificial operations is anchored in the Koran and in the Islamic tradition and is subservient to the rulings of the teachers of dogma. The motives for the sacrificial operations are purely religious, even though they intend to achieve political goals as well. These operations, in his opinion, would yield great gains.[60]

Khomeini's strategy, which many Islamists tried to emulate, but largely unsuccessfully, from the 1970s on, included four main components. The first is the founding and establishing of an Islamic movement. The second component is the delegitimization of the regime and those heading it, by denouncing them as traitors and Jahali (heretics). Khomeini did so by inflaming hatred of the West and of Israel and directing it against the Shah and his regime, which were completely identified with the West. The third component is the basing of sources of authority alternative to the establishment. This is accomplished by setting up Islamic committees, while calling for the restriction of connections with the establishment to the necessary minimum. The fourth component is the presentation of a credible alternative to the existing regime, an issue that Khomeini postponed until the last stage of the revolution. When that stage arrived, he published his perception regarding the rule of the religious leaders.[61]

Khomeini made extensive use of rhetoric and violence. His ideas were summarized and broken down into simple, basic, and easy-to-remember slogans, and were integrated countless times into his speeches, which were carried out in a simple language taken from the popular sphere of concepts and culture. The violence in his teachings was the fuel driving the wheels of the revolution. Khomeini chose the Ashura rituals as favored occasions for the organization of waves of violence (a formula successfully implemented in Lebanon as well). Correspondingly, he ordered the organization of special units dedicated to damage the symbols of government and Western culture, such as cinemas, banks, and houses of entertainment across the country, with the aim of causing unrest and the expansion of violence to the national level.

Khomeini's revolution, according to his outlook, was an Islamic revolution meant to outline the road for the whole of the Muslim community. Therefore, Iran started to "export the revolution" and assist the radical Islamic movements around the world, including extreme Sunni movements operating in the Middle East and Africa. The success of the revolution created a monumental Islamic awakening, whose waves reached all the Muslim countries and communities worldwide.[62]

Islamic Movements in Processes of Change

Islamic social movements undergo processes of adjustment. These processes of change are expressed by a shift from revolutionism to pragmatism and from operating in the wide pan-Islamic circle to operating in the arena of the national state (the internal sphere). These changes are the outcome of processes of development and reciprocal relations between the systems (the internal, regional, and international), the environments in which the movements operate, and the movements themselves. The reciprocal relations and the mutual influences between these systems define/mark, to a large degree, the path on which movements will evolve. The degree of influence of these systems on the path of a movement depends on the nature of the reciprocal relations between the various entities and the particular stage of the movements' lives.

The central question in this context is, therefore, what explains the adjustments in the path of an Islamic movement, and what is the relative weight and degree of influence of the players in the various systems on the nature and direction of the changes taking place in the direction of a movement.

For that purpose, a theoretical model should be outlined, linking the milestones and the stages of development of the movement, and the environments and theatres of operation of that movement. The model I am suggesting will henceforth be called "A model of evolution of fundamentalist movements" ("the five stage model"). The transition from one stage to the next in the suggested model is not obvious. It is conditioned on the development of processes and on the reciprocal relationships between them in three circles: the first is the movement-community, the second is the national, and the third is the regional and the international. The five stages that I found proper to define as central in the process of fundamentalist movements' evolution are foundation; consolidation; expansion; institutionalizing; and the last stage, should conditions enable, seizing the reign or assimilation or disappearance.

1. *Foundation*: This is the first and critical stage in a movement's career. The main process taking place in this stage is social, religious, and political mobilization of groups and individuals, led by charismatic leaders. The explanations for the foundation of a movement should be looked for in the processes that took place in the period preceding it. Generally, a movement is based on groups in society that developed a sense of relative discrimination, alienation toward the regime, and frustration. These groups are more open to receive the revolutionary, antiestablishment message and to join collective action to change their status. However, this is not sufficient. Religious and social mobilization can occur in societies where the governmental system is weak, which means political opportunities are created to the development of a movement and, in parallel, the willingness of frustrated groups to take violent action grows. This is the first test point for the abilities of a charismatic leadership. It should simultaneously overcome two high hurdles. The first is the definition of a sufficiently wide common denominator and of common goals and visions that will cause individuals to want to join collective action. In this case, the Islamic common denominator, found at various levels of society, particularly in popular culture and the vision of establishing an Islamic state, is embodied in the slogan "Islam is the solution." This provides the necessary glue. The second hurdle is the motivation of individuals to take violent action against the ruler in countries where this goes against the political culture. The approach that was adopted by most of these movements was the delegitimization of the regime and those who head it. Not unintentionally, this matter of delegitimizing the ruler occupied considerable importance in Qutb's thought and in Khomeini's activity to overthrow the Shah. Once a movement rises, organized as it may be, it lacks mechanisms of central direction and control. At this stage, its standing is unsound, and it is

based on nuclei of fanatic activists who are organized in secret cells, compartmentalized from each other. The action strategies characterizing movements at the founding stage are strategies of extreme violence, without central control, a fact that stems from the lack of control mechanisms on the one hand and on the other hand the importance of violence in the eyes of the leadership as an instrument to increase exposure and resonance and to recruit support. This violence outlines, to a large extent, the issues of public discourse.

2. *Consolidation*: This is the second stage in the career of a movement. It is very important for the continuation of a movement's path because, during this stage, the groundwork shaping the nature of the movement and its activity is laid. In this stage, the ideological framework is crystallized and brought to the attention of the movement's members and to the potential target audiences. This framework provides the basis for the definition of the aims of the movement, its goals, and its activity policy. This is the stage where the movement starts to recruit additional followers and train them for violent or civil action, according to its needs. This activity obligates the establishment of organizational apparatuses. This is the stage where sprouts of organizational structure start to appear in the infrastructure of the institutions, or premovement organizations and groups that joined it. The activity of the movement, at this stage, is possible only when the systems surrounding it make its continued existence possible. It depends upon the continuation of the existence of the political, internal, and regional window of opportunity that made its foundation possible and upon a facile and supportive community environment for it to continue and evolve. However, this is not sufficient. The continuation of activity requires funding sources. These can be internal or external. Usually, at these stages, the sources for funding are external, arriving from elements or entities that have interest in the continuation of the movement's activity. At later stages of their lives, the movements strive to decrease their dependence on external funding sources and to expand their income basis through independent funding, including violent and illegal activities (robbery, smuggling, drugs, forgery, etc.). At this stage, the line of action aimed at delegitimizing the regime continues. The operative activity continues based on the clandestine infrastructure and has characteristics of extreme violence, but with a small difference—sprouts of central guidance start to appear. At this stage of the movement's life conditions are not yet ripe for the establishment of institutions and the leadership continues to act along the same action patterns that characterized its activity during the foundation period.

3. *Expansion*: Fundamentalist movements will reach this stage in their lives only when the conditions that led to their foundation have not changed significantly, their opponents were not wise enough to take action strategies to stop them, and the reciprocal relations between them and their surrounding systems make their continued growth possible. At this stage, a number of processes occur, sustaining each other. The first process is the expansion of recruitment activities and an expansion to additional

territories (in terms of both ground and additional levels of society). This is accompanied by the expansion of the civilian activity of the movement. The second is the consolidation of embryonic social, military, and political institutional structures. Within them, an organizational culture characterizing the institutional model takes shape. This is the stage where institutional checks and balances start to be created and to be applied to the charismatic leadership, making it less independent in its decisions than before. The third process is the development of sensitivity to internal and regional occurrences. This sensitivity originates from the aforementioned processes and from the fear of losing the achievements gained so far. This is the stage where the action strategies employed by the movement are also influenced by cost-benefit considerations. The appearance of an embryonic military organizational system makes it possible to direct the violent activity and to match it to the current action policy of the movement. At this stage, usually, the dialogue between the movement and the governmental system begins. This dialogue is the result of either the success of the government's strategies (repression and inclusion) in "driving a wedge" between the pragmatists and the extremists of the movement, or the insight of the movement that its goals can be promoted even from within the existing political system, and following its rules of the game. This is also the point at which the differences of opinion emerge between the extreme margins, which continue to act toward the violent overthrow of the regime from outside the institutionalized system, and the pragmatists, prefer to reach partial contemporary achievements, and to seize rule gradually, using its institutions.

4. *Institutionalizing*: This occurs when the environments of activity change. The political window of opportunity that made it possible for fundamentalist movements to grow rapidly is reduced, and the action strategies of the opponents become perfected. The movements have a firsthand experience of the might of the state. These occurrences influence the proximate environment of the movement, and its scopes of recruitment grow smaller, as a result of either the exhaustion of its current potential or following its opponents' counter activities or both. This stage is characterized by the development of new reciprocal relations between the movement and its surroundings. It is more sensitive to changes and processes in its surrounding systems. Therefore, it tightens control over its military and civilian activities. At this stage, manifestations of pragmatism are observable in the processes of decision making and cost-benefit considerations become primary. The institutions are expanded, and the emphasis goes from a charismatic action pattern to an institutional action pattern, resulting in an increase in the institutions' influence and a restriction in the leader's freedom of action. In parallel, the development in the organizational systems continues as far as the level of semi-military systems. At the political level at this stage, the pragmatists of the movement will incline toward the direction of integration with the political system, struggling to overthrow it from within. Oppositely, the radical margins will continue to fight uncompromisingly to overthrow the regime. This is the point where

there is a high probability of the secession of the radical margins from the movement, and the founding of a new revolutionary movement, sometimes even more radical than the mother movement at its commencement. The decision of an Islamic movement to act inside the existing political system, and according to its rules, is, actually, the expression of a transition from revolutionism to pragmatism. The buds of this process begin as early as the end of the stage of expansion, but the process materializes in the stage of institutionalizing.

5. *Seizing the reign*: Four movements reached this stage in the life of radical movements in Iran, Sudan, Afghanistan, and in the Palestinian authority (Hamas). Most Islamic movements are in the second and third stages of their lives, and they are unsuccessful in realizing the goal of seizing rule, for a reason. To achieve this, two necessary conditions must exist. The first is the creation of broad popular support for the movement and the willingness among many levels of the population to overthrow the existing regime. The second is a substantial military and political ability of the movement, making it possible for it to seize the reign and, more importantly, to keep it. At this stage, some movements either disappear or assimilate into the existing political system.

Summary

Islamic movements are similar in their characteristics and evolutionary trends to revolutionary protest social movements in other cultures; but, notwithstanding, they bear certain uniqueness, originating from the environment in which they grow. This uniqueness stems from the existence of Islamic cultural codes of behavior and constant social, political, and religious tension within the Muslim states, between the ruling elites and wide groups in the population. This tension causes the development of social and political conflicts and the challenging of the existing governmental systems by Islamic movements. The reciprocal relationships between these movements and the systems they operate next to, and the processes occurring within them, create dynamic behavior patterns based on cost-benefit considerations. The movements develop action policies of walking the edge in their relationships with the regime; some adopt a pragmatic approach and integrate themselves into the institutionalized system, and some continue to operate with revolutionary characteristics outside this system. The pragmatists strive for the realization of the Islamic visions in stages and base themselves on a strategy of combining religious fundamentalism with political realism. These movements, which grew after the appearance of the modern state, learned in the last few decades to acknowledge not only the might of the systems around which they operate such as the state, the regional system, and the international system, but also their limitations. Accordingly, they navigate their activity from within a framework of constraints and opportunities to promote their affairs.

The Shiite Community in Lebanon and the Background for Hezbollah's Emergence

Introduction

The Hezbollah movement emerged at the height of a crisis in the Lebanese political system as an expression of political and social processes within Lebanon and in the region, from the 1960s on, that paved the way for the emergence of radical elements in the Shiite community. The Islamic revolution in Iran and Israel's invasion of Lebanon shook the Shiite community in Lebanon and sparked off a poignant internal debate. This debate raged between the followers of the pan-Islamic approach, who advocated loyalty to Khomeini's leadership and did not recognize the validity of the Lebanese state, and the Amal movement, which perceived itself as a national-secular Lebanese movement operating within the framework of the Lebanese political system. In July 1982, Amal leader Nabih Berri decided to join the Lebanese National Salvation Front.[1] A schism occurred in the movement following this step, and some of its members, including Berri's deputy, Hussein al-Musawi, retired from it. These dissidents, in full agreement with Shiite fighters and a group of young clerics who had graduated from the religious seminaries in Najaf, founded Hezbollah in the summer of 1982 with Iranian assistance.[2]

Hezbollah grew on the infrastructure of premovement groups that took shape among the members of the Shiite community and within the Amal movement in the 1970s and early 1980s. This chapter in the movement's life, explaining the reasons leading to its foundation, is lacking. As an introduction to the discussion of the processes and reciprocal connections between the movement and the community within which it grew, it is worth describing the fundamental trends in its development on the basis of the five stages model.

1. *The foundation stage (1982–1983)*: This stage was characterized by uncontrolled acts of extreme terrorism, carried out by clandestine groups and cells with an affinity to the movement's framework.
2. *The formation stage (1983–1985)*: During this stage, the ideological framework became crystallized, and the extreme violence, led by a charismatic pro-Iranian revolutionary leadership, continued.

3. *The expansion stage*: Between 1986 and 1991, an embryonic institutional system of the movement appeared as a consequence of the increase in the number of its activists and the scope of its activities. Alongside this, the extreme violence continued and reached its peak in the late 1980s with the eruption of the struggle for control of the Shiite community against the Amal movement.

4. *The institutionalization stage*: This is the stage at which the movement has been from 1992 on. During this stage, it integrated into the political system of Lebanon. Its activities are characterized by pragmatism and political realism, and it is driven by cost-benefit calculations.

5. *Seizing rule/decline*: This is the fifth stage in the model of the development of protest movements. Hezbollah has not reached this stage yet.

It should be noted that Hezbollah was created between 1970 and 1982. Understanding this period is important to comprehend the causes of the movement's foundation.

The Shiite Community in Lebanon—from Passivity to Revolutionary Activity

The importance of this community in Lebanon stems from the unique nature of the Lebanese state, which involves a diverse social mosaic of numerous communities, an authoritarian and hierarchical family structure, narrow elites, and a wide stratum of petit bourgeoisie. Its population is spread out in communal or clannish concentrations over a narrow area and faces continual political instability. The civil services system, educational and religious institutions, charitable organizations, budgets, and even employment domains usually operate within the borders of the communities' systems. Those who control the economic basis of the community and its institutions, in essence, control the community.[3]

In light of this, the struggle for power in Lebanon was conducted in two circles that fed each other. The inner circle comprised the struggle between the traditional elites and new subgroups that challenged them over domination of the community. The outer circle encompassed the struggle between the community and the rest of the communities for control of the power sources of the state. Demographic, social, economic, and political processes from the 1960s on, including the religious awakening in the Shiite community, fundamentally changed the social and political order in the community and in the Lebanese system.[4]

The Shiite awakening in Lebanon is a social-political protest movement in its essence.[5] The man who led and shaped the patterns of this social Shiite protest in the 1960s and 1970s was Imam Musa al-Sadr, a Shiite cleric with the characteristics of a religious and political leader. He was born in Iran to a family of privileged religious scholars of Lebanese descent and was educated in the Shiite seminaries of Najaf and Qom. There he absorbed the fundamentals of the Shiite activist thought that was developed in those years by the greats of the Shiite Ulema. In 1959, he started to serve as the Shiite mufti of the city of Tyre. In less than two decades, he succeeded, with strenuous activity, charisma, and high rhetorical ability, in organizing the Shiite community, characterized for hundreds of years by passivity and isolationism, and in mobilizing it into collective activity for the realization of social and political goals.[6]

The Shiite Community—Old Social Stratification
versus the Rise of New Powers

The Shiite community, which was the third largest in Lebanon, according to the results of a general census from the 1930s, lacked any degree of influence on the political system of Lebanon during the first few decades of its independence. It comprised mostly ignorant rural people and was represented in front of the authorities by a handful of feudal families.[7] The geographic concentration of the Shiite population in the mountainous periphery of southern Lebanon and in the Beqaa valley isolated it from the focus of political events in Beirut and created three Shiite communities, with different social structures, behavior patterns, and characteristics. This dissimilitude made it difficult to find a common denominator that would enable the recruitment of community members for collective action to further clan interests and even fundamentally acted as a fracture line, which split the community into moderates and extremists in the early 1980s.[8]

The social structure of the community, until the mid-1960s, can be separated into three strata. The political-economic elite, the "Zuama," included the members of the rich families in the south and in Beqaa. The religious elite, the "Ulema," included the members of the families comprising the Shiite religious establishment, some holding a distinguished familial pedigree. The third stratum included all the peasants, laborers, and small merchants. The developments that took place from the mid-1960s on changed the power relations between the elites and their reciprocal connections and paved the way for the emergence of new social groups, such as the bourgeoisie/petit bourgeoisie and the newfangled clerical group, challenging the status of the traditional elites.

The economic-political elite (Zuama) controlled all the power sources of southern Lebanon. It included a number of families and manned the power focus reserved for the community in the Lebanese parliament, the role of parliament chairman, until the mid-1980s.[9] These families led in southern Lebanon a social order in the standard of the feudal model, meant to preserve and expand their power and to prevent a threat to their status as the ruling elite. The social structure of the Shiite community in Beqaa, on the other hand, was tribal in essence. The social order in this region was largely determined according to the importance, property, and genealogy of the family within the tribal frame.[10]

The rise of new forces in the community in the 1960s, the move from the village to the city, the expansion of education, the change of employment patterns, the emergence of new competitors in the form of the Lebanese leftist parties, and the power struggles taking place within the elite posed an actual threat to this elite and gradually diminished its control over the power sources and its influence within the community.[11]

The appearance of the Palestinians in southern Lebanon in the early 1970s and the escalation in the security situation in the south further weakened the status of this elite. During the late 1970s, following Operation Litani and the disappearance of Musa al-Sadr (1978), its members succeeded in partially rehabilitating their position for a short period.

The religious elite (Ulema) consisted of the families of the old Shiite religious establishment. They were greatly dependent on the Zuama, and many of them were appointed by it. The members of the Shiite religious establishment in those years were conservatives, somewhat disconnected from the masses, and found it hard to digest the rapid changes taking place in the community during the 1950s and 1960s. [12] In the 1960s and 1970s, changes in the composition of this elite took place with the arrival of the new activist spirit, blowing from the religious seminaries in Najaf. The first generators of change in Lebanon were two senior clerics with similar cultural and religious backgrounds: al-Sadr and Muhammad Hussein Fadlallah.[13] Their arrival in Lebanon, parallel to the social and demographic transformations taking place in the community in the 1960s, paved the way for them to set in motion processes of social change. Though they did not walk the same path and though, to a large degree, a concealed rivalry existed between them, they succeeded in acquiring many disciples and students from within the Ulema and the new classes. The followers of al-Sadr united within the framework of the Amal movement, while the followers of Fadlallah were among the founders of the Hezbollah movement.

The transformations taking place in the community in those years also radiated to this social stratum. More and more students joined religious studies in the seminaries of Najaf and Qom and the new seminaries founded in Lebanon. This process strengthened from the 1970s on, following the expulsion to Lebanon of several Lebanese religious students from the Najaf seminaries by the Iraqi authorities.[14] Some of them were integrated into the seminaries and religious schools in Lebanon, where additional generations of clerics were trained in the spirit of activist ideas. Later, the Najaf expellees became the backbone of the Hezbollah movement.

If one were to examine the process of the development of the Shiite community in Lebanon over the course of time, one would find that the change in the scope of religious studies in Lebanon increased significantly in the 1970s. The number of clerics increased significantly from a few dozens to approximately 420 in the early 1970s. This increase was a result of the activities of al-Sadr and Fadlallah, who broadened and encouraged the religious training in Lebanon and supplied stipends for the funding of the studies of talented students in the seminaries of Iraq and Iran. The Iranians contributed as well to the expansion of the circle of students of religion in Lebanon, even more enthusiastically after the Islamic revolution in Iran.[15] The students' revolutionary approach, and the way the new Najaf-graduated Ulema conducted themselves, stood in total contrast to the conservatism and obedience that characterized the relationships of the traditional Ulema with the Zuama. These two groups (students and graduates) constituted the revolutionary vanguard, who laid the foundation for the formation of Hezbollah in Lebanon and provided the human resources for the leadership class of the movement.

The middle class developed in the Shiite community from the 1960s on in the cities and included members of the liberal professions, such as lawyers, clerks, merchants, doctors, and military men, alongside the nouveau riche, who made their fortunes abroad, acquired education, and returned to Lebanon. This social group worked to realize its abilities and to influence political processes, but was rejected by the governmental system due to its Shiite descent. As a result, its members sought ways to change the existing social and political order in Lebanon. For them, the leftist parties, and later the Amal and Hezbollah movements, provided an admission ticket to the political world without their ancestry being an obstacle.[16]

The lower class comprised farmers, small merchants, and peddlers residing in remote villages in the mountainous regions and townships, whose decrepit access roads made connectivity with the outside world difficult. This was practically the largest social stratum in the community. The detachment between Beqaa and southern Lebanon created two Shiite subcommunities with different temperaments, occupations, and interests. The people of southern Lebanon were engaged in agriculture, small commerce, and peddling. They were regarded as submissive and subdued, and the authorities did not find it difficult to impose their rule on this region. The people of Beqaa, on the other hand, engaged in growing and trading drugs. They were tough and assertive and opposed any representation of authority in their region.[17]

The members of this class, who resided in the periphery, were completely dependent on the graces of the Zuama, who ensured that the immense gap between them and the villagers was maintained and any attempt to promote education and improve the standard of living in the territories under their control was nipped in the bud. Oppositely, those members of this class who immigrated to the cities experienced firsthand the feelings of frustration and relative discrimination more strongly than their fathers, a fact that made them attentive to the absorption of new religious or radical social messages. They were attracted, like to a magnet, by any framework that offered them even the haziest hope for the improvement of their situation. For them al-Sadr was the first of the community who delivered the necessary goods and paved the way for their integration into a communal organizational system, with the goal of improving their condition.[18] The members of this class became, in time, the manpower pool upon which the two big movements, Amal and Hezbollah, grew. The importance of this sector of the population was great for both movements, and they fought for control over it. Each boasted itself as a popular movement, deeply rooted in the Shiite community.

Processes of Demographic and Social Change in the Shiite Community

Lebanon is one of the prominent examples for the fact that accelerated demographic and social processes are among the main causes for the rise of social protest movements, waving the flag of social injustice. The transition from the village to the city, changes in the natural increase in the various communities, immigration, the impacts of modernization, and the appearance of new players in the Lebanese arena changed the intercommunity power relations and disrupted the delicate balance characterizing the intra-Lebanese system.

The transition from the country to the city: The modernization and urbanization processes in Lebanon toward the end of the 1950s and the severe economic condition in the Shiite rural areas caused an internal immigration from the country to the city and, externally, from Lebanon to other countries. The immigrants mainly comprised youths who were unable to find their place in the traditional rural frameworks and who sought a way to improve their status. The immigration and accelerated urbanization changed the face of the Shiite community and its spread in Lebanon significantly.[19] The Shiite immigrants established a belt of slums surrounding Beirut. This belt was, since its inception, a fertile ground for the growth of social protest forces. The encounter of the Shiite youths with the big city and with the members of the other communities, whose economic condition and social status was immeasurably better than their own, caused feelings of frustration and discrimination. This target audience was fought over by two new social forces, the leftist parties and the Shiite clerics.[20]

The Shiite immigrants arriving in Beirut settled in the slums on its fringes, in communal settings with some common denominator (family, tribal, or village kinship). The communities preserved their communal framework and clannish solidarity and absorbed new immigrants from their group.[21] The strained reality of the Shiite immigrants on the fringes of cities and the sense of discrimination they experienced were exploited by the clerics for broadening their influence. They provided religious and charity services, but not only. Their activities were aimed at widening the Islamic message, stopping the process of westernization, and reducing the impact of the leftist parties.

The natural increase: The Lebanese governmental system is based on the national charter. It is, in fact, an intercommunity agreement for the division of the governmental posts among the communities on the basis of their relative weight in the population as calculated in the 1932 census. In this census, it was found that the Christian community was the largest, followed by the Sunni community and then the Shiite community. On this basis, the governmental posts were divided: the post of president was given to the Christian community, prime minister to the Sunni community, and chairman of parliament, the lowest of the three, to the Shiite community.[22]

The demographic processes in Lebanon completely changed the balance of power in the country within three decades. The Shiite community became, in the course of time, the largest in the country due to a higher birth rate than the other communities', as well as due to the scope of the high rate of emigration of the Christian population from Lebanon.[23] The demographic changes were not translated into changes in its political status or in the bases of the clan's power in the governmental system, due to the fact that a Sunni Maronite coalition stood before it, preserving the governmental pie in its hands. With the increasing social and political tension in Lebanon due to the crises of unfulfilled expectations from the 1960s on, voices rose within the Shiite community demanding a redistribution of the political cake in light of the significant changes occurring in the structure of the Lebanese population.

The impact of modernization: At the same time as the transit from the country to the city, the impact of modernization penetrated the rural areas. The Lebanese economy started to increasingly rely on commerce and services and less on agricultural production. As a consequence, the economic status of the Zuama families, who dominated most of the lands and the agricultural production, was increasingly undermined. In the townships and burghs, centers of small industry and commerce were established. The improvement in the level of infrastructure in the country and the increase in the number of vehicles connected the isolated villages to the cities and tightened the contact and influence of the city on everyday life in the villages. Radio and television broadcasts made villagers more aware of the changes occurring around them. The stories of family members who emigrated abroad and came back for summer holidays emphasized the gap between the material and physical conditions of the villagers and the opportunities open before them and increased the sense of relative discrimination and frustration with the existing situation. The prominent expression of the penetration of modernization into the rural areas was the level of immigration of the Shiite population to the cities, which burgeoned significantly in the 1960s and 1970s. This population immigrated to the cities with the aim of finding employment, welfare, and better education and cultural life, as well as escaping the cycle of poverty and ignorance that characterized its lot in the villages.[24]

The emergence of the Palestinians: The Palestinians have been part of the social fabric of Lebanon since 1948, with the settlement of Palestinians in the refugee camps around the major cities of Lebanon. In the beginning of the 1970s, members of the military Palestinian organizations, operating in Jordan, arrived in Lebanon. With their appearance, the center of gravity of the Palestinian anti-Israeli activity shifted to southern Lebanon. This situation transformed Lebanon into a battle arena between Israel and the Palestinians, with the immediate and direct casualties being the Shiite inhabitants of southern Lebanon. As the conflict between Israel and the Palestinians escalated, the situation of the residents of southern Lebanon worsened and many of them abandoned their homes and emigrated to the north. The Shiites, who were opposed to the Palestinian activities, found it difficult to prevent or reduce them in the 1970s.[25]

Musa al-Sadr—the Generator of Change in the Shiite Community

The most essential conceptual change in the Shiite community occurred in the 1960s. It symbolized, most of all, the transition of the community, as a body, from passivity and political isolationism to activism and political involvement. It developed due to the feelings of discrimination and frustration, the acceleration of the processes of modernization and urbanization, and the appearance of a charismatic Shiite leadership in the form of al-Sadr. The latter, using impressive rhetoric and organization abilities on the one hand and religious pedigree and economic independence on the other, succeeded in recruiting the support of the Shiite masses while simultaneously challenging the traditional elite and the political system. He demanded from them an end to the discrimination against the community by giving it the representation appropriate to its size in the Lebanese population.[26]

Al-Sadr embodied the qualities of a political leader and a Shiite cleric and worked toward the organization of the community at several levels simultaneously:

1. At the social level, he established educational and charitable institutions that were financed from the monies he collected in fundraising campaigns, from tax budgets, and from the contributions he received from his patrons in Iran.[27]

2. At the organizational level, al-Sadr worked to cultivate close ties between all members of the community in Lebanon. For that, he sought to bridge the divide between the various elements in the community by finding a wide-enough common denominator to exercise the community as a whole toward the outside.[28]

3. At the political level, he held negotiations with the authorities, demanding recognition for the Shiite community as separate from the Sunni community and equal rights for it in the Lebanese system. The state's acceptance of the Shiite demands was expressed in the foundation of the "Supreme Shiite Council" in May 1969.[29]

The foundation of this council was the turning point in the social power relations within the community itself. The traditional elite, the Zuama, and the Ulema became weak and lost some of their power to new social subgroups. These subgroups supported al-Sadr and his strategy of establishing the position of the council, at the intracommunity level, as standing above the internal struggles and rivalries and, at the Lebanese level, as leading the campaign for the abolition of ethnic discrimination. He never concealed his aspirations to combine political activity with religious preaching.[30]

Members of the new subgroups, starting to form on the Shiite society, educated youths, freelance professionals, and the nouveau riche. All those subgroups succeeded, to a certain degree, in securing their economic status and sought a way to translate this into a new social and political status. The activity of al-Sadr provided them the framework they were seeking for the realization of their wishes and suited them better than the framework offered by the Lebanese leftist parties, thanks to the motif of clan and communal solidarity and to the exacerbation of ethnic conflicts within Lebanon.

The activity of the Shiite community opposite the political system, outlined by al-Sadr, was characterized by walking on the threshold. On the one hand, he had an interest not to destabilize the fragile foundations on which the Lebanese state stood, and on the other hand, the discrimination of the community by the state created feelings of alienation, frustration, and rage, a fact that obliged him to organize activities that would bring about a change in the authorities' attitude toward the community. The sequence of events in the 1970s dictated the nature of activity of the community versus the political system and the other communities in Lebanon. Generally, the trend that characterized the Lebanese system in that period was the sharpening of the intercommunity struggle parallel to the weakening of the central regime. This was evident in the increasing levels of violence employed for political purposes or for the protection of clan interests. The civil war was the most prominent and extreme expression of that trend. This war represented the desire for a redistribution of the state's "public goods." It should be noted that the Shiite community underwent adjustment processes in relation to the dynamic changes that occurred in the 1970s in Lebanon, but it was, in those years, one step behind compared with the organization of the other communities.

In the development of the clan's activity frameworks in the 1970s, several primary stages and subprocesses can be observed.

1. *The foundation of the Supreme Shiite Council*: The aim toward which al-Sadr strove in his demand to establish the Shiite council was the equalization of the status of the community with the rest of the Lebanese communities and its release from the Sunni control that existed theretofore.[31]

2. *The foundation of a political movement*: Al-Sadr founded the first Shiite political movement in Lebanon—the Movement of the Deprived. Its goals were social and political, such as fighting social exploitation, discrimination, the ethnic political regime, imperialism, and attacks directed against Lebanon, all of which indicated that the movement was a national Lebanese movement. At the intracommunity level, the movement claimed to be based on the true faith in Allah and the torchbearer in the struggle against feudalism.[32] The achievement was in the very foundation of the movement. It constituted a change in the patterns of political behavior of the Shiite community that, from now on, had political institutions and organizations working within it and struggling among themselves for control of the community and its representation in the Lebanese system.

3. *The foundation of military force*: The foundation of the military force, eventually called the Amal movement, was a supplementary move made by al-Sadr. He understood that in the 1970s Lebanon it was no longer possible to maintain political power without military might and that, in a violence-saturated environment, a militia was an existential necessity for the survival of the community. On July 6, 1975, al-Sadr announced the foundation of the movement of "Lebanese resistance battalions"—Amal. He stated that it was designated to be the political-military arm of the Movement of the Deprived.[33]

The eruption of the civil war was the best possible proof for the necessity of the Amal movement. Already in 1976, a year after the war broke out, the community was forced to evacuate, without combat, the Shiite residents of the Nabaa quarter in east Beirut. This event was perceived as traumatic and humiliating in the collective Shiite consciousness and among its causes was the nonexistence of an adequate military force capable of fighting the Christian militias and protecting the neighborhood. The community absorbed this hard blow that had injured its political and social status, internally and externally. This retreat caused exchanges of internal accusation, scathing criticism, and a challenge upon the leadership of al-Sadr, whose critics went as far as perceiving him as a traitor.[34] This event is still carved in the clan's collective memory, and it also influenced Fadlallah's essay "Islam Wa Mantek Al Kouwa," written in that period.[35]

The Community during 1978–1982, "A Nut Shell upon Raging Waters"

The seeker of the explanations and the direct and logical connection to the emergence of the Hezbollah movement in the Shiite community as an alternative to the Amal movement is bound to locate them in that period. A sequence of intercommunity and regional events directly influenced the directions of the development of the community and greatly increased the use of religious fundamentalism and violence as the preferred tools for confrontation and survival in the Lebanese system. Among the events holding strategic impact in the period were Operation Litani, the disappearance of al-Sadr, and the Iranian revolution.[36]

Operation Litani (code name for the Israeli defense forces 1978 invasion of Lebanon up to the Litani river) started in March 1978 against terrorist departure bases and Palestinian infrastructure in southern Lebanon. This operation directly harmed the Shiite population in southern Lebanon and transformed thousands of the community into refugees. Following the operation, the need in the community for the foundation of a force capable of protecting its interests and living areas became much clearer.[37]

The mysterious disappearance of al-Sadr in August 1978 fitted perfectly with the tradition of the "disappearing Imam" deeply rooted in the Shiite consciousness and tradition and created a mythological aura around him, which expanded the circle of supporters of his ideas. His disappearance provided the community with the necessary motivation for the continuation of the social protest. Owing to the lack of an heir possessing the same qualities and the inability of identifying a common denominator that would enable the continuation of the management of the community as one piece, the succession of the Imam was divided between the cleric members of the Supreme Shiite Council and the pragmatic, secular leadership of the Amal movement, following the disappearance of al-Sadr.[38]

The Islamic revolution in Iran (February 1979) changed the regional power equations and, at the same time, became a source of pride and emulation for the Islamic revolutionary movements in the region, especially the Shiite movements, which regarded it as not only the victory of the Iranians against a heretical ruler, but also the victory of Islam over the West, represented in Iran by the regime of the Shah. The Shiite community in Lebanon, which was connected to the new Iranian system through Iranian exiles, opponents of the Shah's regime staying in Lebanon, family ties, and membership in the common network of the Iranian Shiite Ulema in Najaf and Qom, was deeply influenced by the success of the Islamic revolution in Iran.[39]

This influence was expressed by the changes that took place in the community in the years following the revolution. The first was the changeover that occurred in the community's self-image. It became, in the eyes of the Lebanese Shiite radicals, from a passive marginal clan in a multiethnic country to an activist community, belonging to a global Islamic entity under the leadership of Iran and standing at the forefront of the Islamic struggle against the West.[40] The second change was the expansion of the Islamic influence within the community, by way of activation of Iranians and the graduates of Najaf, in an organized and institutionalized way by Iran, in accordance with the policy of exporting the Iranian revolution outside the country's borders. The third change was the aggravation of the intracommunity struggle in relation to the activity pattern that should adopted in order to change the community's status within the Lebanese system— a struggle that ultimately led to the foundation of the Hezbollah movement as the Islamic alternative to the Amal movement.

Indecision Over Social and Political Issues among Conservatives and Extremists

These events, taking place at the threshold of the 1980s, brought to the surface extremely fundamental issues related to the activities of the Shiite community in Lebanon. First, how should the problem of southern Lebanon versus the Palestinians, Israel, and the Lebanese system be dealt with? Second, what tools and approaches should be adopted to abolish the ethnic discrimination and to improve the community's economic and political status? The third issue arose following the Iranian revolution and touched upon the community's most exposed and sensitive nerves—the question of its identity and loyalty and how it defined itself. Was it a clan with a pan-Islamic identity, acting from a commitment and loyalty toward the framework of an Islamic nation under the leadership of Iran, or did it identify with, and accept the framework of, the Lebanese state?

With the lack of a religiously and politically unifying leadership, as manifest by the figure of al-Sadr, the opinions became divided according to the attitudes of the men who headed the elements of power and the social and political trends that marked the community after the disappearance of al-Sadr. The conservative trend, headed by Kamal Assad, bound within it the traditional political elite. The religious trend was headed by Muhammad Mahdi Shams Al-Din, the head of the Supreme Shiite Council, and the secular trend was headed by Berri, the general secretary of the Amal movement.

In the background, although at a local level at this point, an unformed militant trend operated through independent groups, usually surrounding charismatic Najaf-graduate clerics such as Fadlallah. These stood for a direction of action different from the others. Some of them even operated within the Amal movement and the Supreme Shiite Council. The difference in approaches with regard to the following three issues were among the causes for the establishment of the Hezbollah movement.

1. *The issue of southern Lebanon*: The expansion of violence in southern Lebanon and Beirut toward the end of the 1970s (Operation Litani, 1978) instigated two processes that fed each other. The first was the strengthening of the militant trend in the community, calling for taking an offensive direction for the advancement of essential interests. The second was the growth of a stratum of young and dominant military leadership, which drew its power from its control over the regional fighting units of the Amal movement and worked toward the translation of its status to influence the directions of development and the movement's policy vis-à-vis its opponents at the external level and in front of its supporting public at the internal level. The prominent expression of this new spirit was the election

of a new leadership council within Amal, headed by Berri. However, in actuality, until the first Lebanon war (operation "Peace for Galilee") and the expulsion of the Palestinians from Lebanon, the declarations of its leaders, calling for resistance and sacrifice, were not translated into action. The Amal movement, which, until then, constituted a marginal force in the Lebanese power equation, focused on defending the living areas of the community versus the leftist movements and the PLO.

The militant approach, from a different angle and for different reasons, was adopted by the new clerics. They, the students of Fadlallah, followed his approach as was developed in his book "Islam Wa Mantek Al Kouwa," according to which individuals have a duty to rise up against their oppressors. This duty meant the use of violence to counter the opponent's aggression. This group worked toward the strengthening of the individual's spiritual power, the enhancement of the individual's willingness for acts of sacrifice, and the deepening of social solidarity as a tool for mobilizing for aggressive collective action. This group, as well, started its belligerent activity after the Lebanon war.[41]

In any case, the Shiite society of the 1970s absorbed belligerent activist elements—of both those who walked the secular path of Amal and the leftist parties and those who walked the Islamic path within Amal and, at a later stage, within the Hezbollah movement.

2. *The issue of ethnic discrimination*: In the late 1970s, the three leading trends in the community were unanimous concerning its unbearable state, stemming from its continued discrimination. The leaders of the three trends attempted to change the clan's status within the framework of the rules of the game in the existing Lebanese political system and, to a large degree, from within the system itself. In parallel, new Islamic forces that regarded the existing regime as illegitimate started to appear, and they preached for its overthrow by a revolutionary act as a preceding action for the foundation of an Islamic regime based on the Iranian model.

3. *The issue of national identity*: The issue of national identity versus the identity and loyalty in terms of the community arose for the first time most acutely after the success of the Islamic revolution in Iran. The connection to Iran was perceived with pride because of the common religious foundations and the long-standing ties between the Lebanese Shiite leadership and the community of Iranian exiles in Lebanon. This community was an active partner in the Islamic revolution, and some of its members even belonged to the higher echelons of the Iranian leadership. It assisted in the founding of the Amal movement and the organization and training of its military forces.[42] Notwithstanding the strong affinity to Iran, the leaders of the three trends saw themselves primarily as Lebanese, committed to identify with and be loyal to the Lebanese state and its laws and to work for the promotion of their interests within its framework.

Alongside these, another branched and cross-border relationship existed, which included family ties between Lebanese clerics educated in the Shiite seminaries in Najaf and the Shiite Ulema who led the Iranian revolution.[43] In these seminaries, the revolutionary Shiite outlook, in its new version, was molded and bequeathed to the Lebanese students, who later became the bearers of the Shiite revolutionary message in Lebanon. The alternative they proposed to their supporting public was the foundation of an Islamic regime. The loyalty and identification of these was given to Iran and Khomeini, whom they regarded as a leader and figure for emulation.

The success of the Islamic revolution of 1979 in Iran, and the Lebanon war in 1982, further inflamed the Shiite revolutionary fervor and widened the gap between the extreme groups and the three trends. Owing to these events, the debate over the needed course of action versus the intra-Lebanese and the regional systems raged in full force even within the Amal movement. Berri's controversial decision to join the Lebanese National Salvation Front in 1982, regarded as crossing the red lines by the Islamists, caused a rift in the Amal movement, and some of its seniors, including Berri's deputy, retired from the movement.[44] The Shiite community was split into two: the pragmatic and moderate majority, regarding itself as part of the Lebanese state and working toward changing the regime on the basis of the accepted rules of the game, and the extremist minority, denying the legitimacy of the secular and pro-Western Lebanese regime and working toward its overthrow in a revolutionary act. For this minority, Khomeini was the sole source of authority.

The Emergence of the Hezbollah Movement—Organizational Infrastructure and Action Strategies

In the early 1970s, Lebanese clerics, graduates of the Shiite seminaries in Najaf, laid the foundations for the activist Shiite education in the religious seminaries and the Islamic educational institutions that were founded in Lebanon. In these institutions, thousands of students were trained and educated, in the course of the decade, in the spirit of the Shiite militant Islam. A Lebanese researcher claims that the Islamic revolution in Lebanon occurred in two consecutive stages: the first before the Iranian revolution and the second after it. The centers of religion and education played a vital role in fanning the revolution. This was Khomeini's action strategy, and this was also how the new ideas were disseminated in Lebanon.[45] Like Khomeini, Abu Yasser, the head of Hezbollah's political bureau, argued that the movement had existed culturally and conceptually even before the Iranian revolution, based on different groups with a common idea, seeking the way to execute it.[46]

The Islamic seminaries in Lebanon taught religion in combination with military training and instruction. Their target was to train Shiite youths to serve as agents of change, the bearers of a revolutionary social message. The life of Sheikh Ragheb Harb, a cleric who combined military and religious activity, demonstrates how the process of religious training and recruitment for violent activity with Hezbollah occurred. Harb was born in the township of Jibshit and studied religion with Fadlallah in the Islamic college Almehad Alsharaai in Beirut. On the completion of his studies, he went to Najaf where he studied for four years and was expelled to Lebanon as the rest of his friends. He continued his studies in the religious college at Burj Hamud in Beirut, and on completing them in the late 1970s, he was appointed as the Imam of Jibshit in southern Lebanon. A circle of youths, looking for an Islamic action setting, crystallized around Harb. His activities were funded by the Iranians. Following the Islamic call to resist Israel's presence in southern Lebanon, Harb started to initiate, plan, and lead violent action against the Israel Defense Forces (IDF) in 1983. In February 1984, he was killed. After his death, he became the symbol of sacrifice and resistance to the Israeli occupation of Lebanon and a model worthy of emulation by Shiite youths and the new clerics, who integrated into military activities across various locations in Lebanon and outside it.[47]

The prominent members of the group of activist clerics included Sheik Subhi al-Tufayli from Beqaa, a graduate of the seminaries of Najaf and Qom; Sheik Abbas al-Musawi from Jibhsit, a graduate of the seminaries of Najaf; and Sheik Ibrahim Al-Amin from the region of Zahle, who studied in the seminaries of Qom. These clerics joined the Amal movement with the aim of influencing it from within and retired from it in the summer of 1982.[48]

The departure of the radical margins from the Amal movement, the existence of additional premovement social networks with a similar affinity, and an Iranian effort to create an Islamic-Shiite replacement for the Amal movement in Lebanon created the necessary conditions for the emergence of a new movement framework. The new movement was founded and organized in the Beqaa region, not unintentionally. Three important conditions existed in this region, making the organization of Hezbollah easier:

1. *The existence of an environment conducive to organization*: The Beqaa valley was ideal for this purpose. It was far from the centers of control and influence of the Amal movement, the Lebanese government, and Israel. Moreover, at least in the first year, Syria enabled Hezbollah to get organized almost unhindered.[49]

2. The arrival, in July 1982, of a few hundred members of the Iranian Revolutionary Guards Corp (Pasdaran), a particularly extreme Islamic element that was crystallized during the Islamic revolution in Iran: The activists of the Revolutionary Guards Corp were sent to Lebanon, with Syrian consent, to assist in the fight against Israel. They settled in the area of the city of Baalbek in the Beqaa, began to disseminate the ideas of the revolution among the Shiite population, and assisted in the foundation of Hezbollah and in its organization from its first steps.[50]

3. The existence of a critical mass of components from all the subgroups, organizations, and premovement structures in geographical proximity in the Beqaa region: This proximity made it possible to create, in a relatively short period of time, an organizational system with a common denominator and common goals.

Hezbollah, an Umbrella Framework for Pro-Iranian Islamic Groups

Hezbollah encompassed within it various Islamic organizations and elements from the Shiite community, all having the common denominator of recognizing

Khomeini as their religious and political leader and a desire to combine their efforts in activities for the establishment of an Islamic republic in Lebanon, based on the Iranian model. The movement served as an organizational framework for the following pro-Iranian groups.[51]

1. *The Ulema*: This group comprised the leadership backbone of the movement in the 1980s and 1990s. It included the graduates of the seminaries in Najaf and Qom, who headed institutions and religious seminaries in Lebanon. Some belonged to the Lebanese Dawah movement and operated as an opposition group within the Amal movement. Among the notable members of this group were Subhi al-Tufayli , Abbas al-Musawi, and Sheik Mohammed Yazbek. [52]

2. *The Amal Al-Islami movement*: The Amal Al-Islami movement was an important and essential component of Hezbollah. It was founded in the summer of 1982 by Hussein al-Musawi, the deputy of Berri, who left with his followers and took control of some of the Amal handholds in the Beqaa region. The movement adopted the pro-Iranian line and received Iranian support and funding for its military and militia activity. It was only natural that, with the founding of the framework of Hezbollah, Amal Al-Islami would constitute a central component of it.

3. *The members of the "Kabadiat" arm*: The Lebanese system, including the Shiite community, was teeming with thugs—veterans of the battles between the rival militias in Beirut and other places in Lebanon. With the crushing of the Sunni-Palestinian militia, the Shiite groups, and the individuals working within it, were expelled into the Lebanese "job market." Those who were unsuccessful, for various reasons, in joining the Amal movement, lent their services to the new movement, which was lacking in material and military knowledge needed for the actualization of its goals into military action on the ground and which, at that point, absorbed any one who could assist it in furthering its interests.[53]

4. *Dawlat Hezbollah Libnan*: It constituted one of the central pillars of the Hezbollah movement. The spiritual leader of this group was Fadlallah.[54] Among the seniors of this group who should be mentioned was Ibrahim Al-Amin, who served as the Amal representative in Iran and later on became the official spokesman of Hezbollah.[55]

5. *Al Iitihad Al Libnani Lltulaba Al Muslimin*: The Lebanese Muslim Student Organization, which had an intimate affinity to the Lebanese Dawah party and, similarly, regarded Fadlallah as its spiritual leader, joined the movement with the consent of Fadlallah.[56]

6. *Tajamu Al Ulama Al Muslimin Fee Lubnan*: The creation of this organization was inspired by the Iranian revolution, constituting both Shiite and Sunni Ulema, working toward the advancement of the Islamic revolution in Lebanon, from the vision of combining the two trends. This organization was supported by the Iranians and later merged with the Hezbollah movement.[57]

7. *Tajamu Al Ulama Fee Jabel Amel*: This group included clerics who operated in Jabl Amel, and some of its members belonged to the Amal movement.

Their common denominator was their clear affinity to Iran. This group controlled and influenced a network of community and educational institutions in southern Lebanon, including mosques, schools, religious seminaries, and charitable organizations. At the same time as Hezbollah's organizing, the members of this group started to act against the IDF in southern Lebanon.[58] The person who symbolized most of all the stratum of these clerics was Harb, whose story of life and death epitomized the new Shiite activism in Lebanon. Hezbollah based its organization of "Islamic resistance" in southern Lebanon on the framework of this group.[59]

A few months after the organization of the nucleus of the movement in Beqaa, activities with similar characteristics began in additional Shiite-dominated areas in Beirut and southern Lebanon. Here, as well as in Beqaa, the clerics, religious institutions, and Iranian representatives served as the focal point around which the activists gathered.[60]

The Struggle Over the Control of the Community as an Expression of the Expansion of Hezbollah's Influence

Hezbollah was founded in the summer of 1982 as the successor of the premovement groups in Beqaa. From the day of its establishment, it waged a struggle against Amal, its rival for control over the community. A comparison of Hezbollah and Amal—their statuses as movements, their attitudes, and their funding sources—reveals the existence of fundamental ideological, political, and religious differences, which affected the paths and methods of their activities, goals, rivals, and conduct:[61]

1. *The status of the movement*: At the time of the founding and crystallizing of Hezbollah, Amal was already a secular social protest movement in the stage of institutionalization. Its power and influence on the community peaked in early 1984. Hezbollah was a new movement in the stage of foundation with a rising trend, which invested in the widening of its popular base.
2. *The ideological aspect*: The ideological framework of Hezbollah was religious and pan-Islamic, regarding Khomeini and his successors as the source of authority. It aimed at the establishment of an Islamic regime in Lebanon. As such, it considered the Lebanese government as illegitimate and worked toward its overthrow in a revolutionary act. In contrast, Amal defined itself as a secular, national Lebanese movement, striving to reform the existing political system with the aim of abolishing ethnic discrimination and advancing the community's interests.
3. *The sources of support*: Iran was Hezbollah's patron. It provided inspiration, funding, training, weapons, from a generous close accompaniment in the initial years of the movement. In return, Hezbollah took a clear pro-Iranian stance, compatible with the positions of its benefactor. In contrast, Amal leaned on Syria, from which it won reserved support according to the Syrian interests in the Lebanese system. This support was expressed by guarding the movement's status within the Lebanese system.[62]

4. *The goals*: Hezbollah defined three main goals, which were derived from its political and ideological platform: first, the expulsion of all foreigners from Lebanon; second, the liberation of Jerusalem; and third, the establishment of an Islamic regime in Lebanon. These goals committed the movement to confront three very powerful elements in significantly inferior conditions, even if in front of each one separately: the foreign forces in Lebanon, the Lebanese government, and Israel. The achievement of its goals necessitated actions outside the borders of Lebanon. Amal, in contrast, was opposed to the overthrow of the Lebanese government and worked from inside the borders of the political system. It supported the goal of removing foreigners from Lebanon, but not in a sweeping manner and not with Hezbollah's methods. In addition, it was not interested in the ideological goal of liberating Jerusalem and in actions outside the borders of Lebanon.

5. *The target audience*: The two movements competed for the same target audience, the Shiite community. Hezbollah was engaged in seeking the path to all strata in the Shiite society. The fact that it was outside the establishment assisted it in offering numerous groups in the community an alternative to the path of Amal and provided them the springboard they were seeking for the improvement of their condition. The existence of Hezbollah as a movement in the first few years was conditional on its abilities to develop as a popular movement. This task was not easy at all. Hezbollah was forced to compete with Amal, which experienced in that period (1982–1985) a significant surge in its power within the community and, at the same time, in the intra-Lebanese system.

Hezbollah's Efforts to Establish Its Social-Popular Infrastructure

One of the main issues facing the leaders of Hezbollah during 1982–1985 was how it should act to broaden its base and establish itself as a popular movement with firm roots in the community versus the rising power of the Amal movement. The strategy it eventually employed was the initiation of activities at three levels: the *ideological-religious*, with the aim of mobilizing society and incorporating into it motifs such as religious activism, resolve, and willingness for personal sacrifice for the sake of the whole; the *social*, with the aim of abolishing ethnic discrimination and social injustice and improving the living conditions of the Shiite population; and the *military*, with the aim of bringing about the expulsion of all foreigners from Lebanon.

The weakness of the government throughout the 1980s, the effects of the first Lebanon war, and Israel's lasting presence in Lebanon assisted the movement in operating on all the three axes simultaneously. The movement's successes acted as a lever for it to expand its base and influence within the Shiite population, while gnawing at the support base of its main adversary, the Amal movement.

The mission presented to the crystallizing leadership nucleus of Hezbollah was not at all easy, particularly in its first year of operation. The Lebanon war changed the balance of power within the Lebanese system and indirectly caused the transformation of Amal into the strongest Muslim militia. Amal reached the peak of its power with the completion of the conquest of west Beirut and the enlistment of thousands of Shiite soldiers who deserted the Lebanese Armed Forces in February 1984.[63] However, despite the fact that Hezbollah still did not constitute a concrete threat for Amal, its radical slogans, gaining the sympathy of the Shiite community, caused a radicalization in the positions of the Amal movement and the conservative religious trend.

From February 1984 on, a process of disintegration started in the Amal movement, and it lost its assets to its adversaries. Its leader, Berri, joined the Lebanese national unity government as a minister in 1984, a factor that made it difficult for him to advance community goals. Amal became, in the opinions of many, part of the very Lebanese establishment it acted to change. It also failed to fulfill the socioeconomic expectations of its supporters.[64]

With the withdrawal of the IDF to southern Lebanon in 1985, the struggle between Amal and Hezbollah intensified, overflowing into violent activity on the ground. The tension created within the community had erupted from time to time in the form of shooting incidents and clashes between the two sides along the borderlines of the southern neighborhoods of Beirut, gradually expanding to the south as well. These incidents carried a local character, and with the lack of interest of both movements to move the struggle between them at this stage (mid-1980s) into violent lines, they were located, isolated, and dealt with. In fact, the more power and sense of security in Beirut and the south that Hezbollah accumulated, the more did the centers of friction between Hezbollah and Amal expand and, respectively, so did the number of incidents between them.[65]

Hezbollah, with the aid of the Iranians, conducted a propaganda and information campaign, with the aim of causing key men from the Amal movement to defect to its ranks.[66] An especially prominent defector was Mustafa Dirani, who functioned as the head of Amal's security apparatus and the commander of its terrorist acts wing, the "faithful resistance." He defected from Amal and joined Hezbollah with his loyal followers. [67] The internal struggles within Amal played into the hands of Hezbollah. It absorbed into it ranks activists who were either disappointed with Amal or expelled from it and expanded its control over the neighborhoods of Beirut's southern suburb until, in 1986, they became a Hezbollah stronghold.[68]

The expansion of the Islamic trend in Lebanon was reflected in the questions posed by journalists to their militant Shiite interviewees. The questions that were repeatedly asked dealt with the ideology of the movement, its political goals, its policies, and its leaders. From an analysis of the questions of reporters in 1986–1987, it seems that, as estimated above, Hezbollah was at the climax of a process of growth and influence within the Shiite community, at the expense of the Amal movement.[69]

Amal's weakness made it easy for Hezbollah to penetrate additional areas and strata within the community. In Beirut, for instance, Hezbollah exploited the network of Islamic community institutions that operated in the southern neighborhoods of the city as a lever for the deepening of the Islamic consciousness among its residents, an activity that paved the way for the enlistment of many into the movement.[70]

In 1987, Hezbollah's presence in southern Lebanon was a fait accompli. Nevertheless, it was defined as a presence with the aim of resisting Israel's stay in the south. The Amal movement accepted this presence as long as Hezbollah operated within the policy lines dictated by Amal in southern Lebanon, meaning as long as it accepted the fact that Amal had sole responsibility for security in the area, avoided carrying out rocket attacks on Israeli territory, and refrained from harming the UN forces. It looked like, for a while, there existed cooperation between the military arm of Hezbollah, the "Islamic Resistance," and that of Amal, the "Faithful Resistance."[71] This cooperation and harmony in the relationship between the two movements was brief, however. In late August 1987, Daud Daud, Amal's political head in the south, poignantly expressed that he was against Hezbollah. He forbade the distribution of its publications and threatened action against anyone who would undermine Amal's control in the south.[72]

The challenge posed by Hezbollah to Amal was complex, multifaceted, and lasting. Hezbollah took advantage of every opportunity it came across to expand its influence within the community. One of these opportunities was Amal's entanglement in the "War of the Camps" (1984–1987). It acted as a lever for Hezbollah to ram its opponent and to erode away its public support by portraying this war as inefficient and lacking in an intra-Lebanese solution, military or political. Hezbollah's message to the Shiite community was clear and easy to remember. It claimed that Amal's involvement in the War of the Camps harmed the advancement of the most important interests of the community in the Lebanese system, such as the management of the abolition of ethnic discrimination and of the resistance against Israel.[73] This war affected its prospects. It caused a schism in the movement's leadership, a phenomenon of internal rebellions, and activists' desertion of Amal for Hezbollah.[74]

The Crystallization of Hezbollah and Its Expansion in Lebanon

The Hezbollah movement followed, from the day of its founding, an action strategy aimed at expanding its influence to all layers of the Shiite population. This strategy combined social and religious propaganda activity and initiating and leading violent action for the achievement of goals common to the entire community as a means of expanding the potential for recruitment and support of the movement. The means and circumstances to realize this strategy were found in abundance in Lebanon from the 1980s onward. Primarily, the existence of a human infrastructure (groups of organized or semiorganized activists and individuals with a political awareness) showing perviousness to receive the revolutionary Islamic message and maturity for violent action for the advancement of Islamic goals, together with Iranian funding and guidance, the presence of foreigners in Lebanon, revolutionary Islamic ideology, and a violent environment, created the common denominator that facilitated the emergence of the movement. Its successes served as a lever for the expansion of its influence in additional regions of Lebanon. This expansion, propelled by the military actions, came at the expense of Hezbollah's moderate and secular adversary, the Amal movement.

The Struggle during 1983–85, the Formation Stage, and the Mutual Influences

Hezbollah joined the struggle against the IDF within the framework of the National Lebanese Opposition Front in 1983. Its targets were the multinational forces in

Lebanon and Israel. The movement was surprising in its innovativeness and the level of determination and sacrifice that characterized its attacks. In 1983, its activists caused numerous casualties among the multinational forces in Lebanon through a series of suicide and bombing attacks against the American Embassy (April 1983) and the bases of the multinational forces in Beirut (October 1983). The attacks were attributed to Hezbollah, even though an unknown organization, called the "Islamic Jihad," claimed responsibility for them. The leader of the Amal al-Islami movement, al-Musawi, was charged with the responsibility for the series of attacks, including the one on the IDF headquarters in Tyre in November 1983.[75]

The operations produced immediate results. Since their stay in Lebanon exacted from these forces a price higher than they were willing to pay, they left Beirut in the beginning of 1984. From the point of view of Hezbollah, this was a significant success. It was credited to Hezbollah in the Lebanese public opinion and gave further validity to its arguments that Jihad, resolve, and willingness to sacrifice are the necessary means for the expulsion of foreigners from Lebanon.[76]

The suicide attacks in Lebanon gave a new meaning to the concept of sacrifice from the pro-Iranian revolutionary cradle. They even bore far-reaching strategic results from the standpoint of Hezbollah and abolished the power gap between the movement and its adversaries. The international resonance and exposure created by the suicide attacks focused the attention of the international system on the Lebanese issue in general and the Shiite community in particular. The success spurred other terrorist organizations from here on to adopt the action pattern of suicide attacks.

The escalation of violencein the Lebanese arena in 1983 caused the radicalization of the positions and actions of all players in the Shiite community (Hezbollah, Amal, and the Shiite public opinion) and the development of waves of violence and protest that fed themselves from one outburst of violence to the next.[77] In October 1983, following an incident in Nabatieh between the IDF and the locals, the head of the Supreme Shiite Islamic Council, Muhammad Mahdi Shams al-Din, promulgated a religious edict (fatwa) calling for civil disobedience and forbidding contacts with Israel. A month later, on November 4, 1983, a Shiite activist carried out a suicide attack on the residency of the Israeli military government in Tyre, in which sixty people were killed. The attack, and Israel's response to it, completely shattered the fragile set of relationships between the pragmatic Shiite leadership and Israel.[78]

The successes of the extreme Shiite groups, displaying a political and organizational affinity to the umbrella framework that just came to being (Hezbollah), on the one hand, and the lack of an appropriate response from the Amal movement, which chose to sit on the fence, on the other hand, combined with the feelings of frustration and rage of the Shiites toward Israel, influenced the Shiite community. Radical clerics organized and led groups of Shiite youths, who began carrying out attacks against the IDF forces. One of the prominent figures in these lineups was Ragheb Harb, who combined religious preaching and military activities.[79]

The Amal movement, which suddenly realized that Hezbollah was breathing down its neck and that it was in danger of losing control in the south in favor of its adversary, radicalized its positions over the Israeli presence in Lebanon and began initiating and organizing activities against the IDF in southern Lebanon, with the aim of maintaining its control in the region. In March 1985, Muhammad Mahdi Shams al-Din promulgated another fatwa, calling for "defensive Jihad" against Israel as long as it stayed on Lebanese soil. This fatwa was a command to the faithful believers to join Jihad activity. This type of Jihad in Islam is perceived as the duty of the individual and not only the duty of the community, as in the case of offensive Jihad.[80]

The withdrawal of the IDF from Lebanon in 1984–85 and its consolidation along the border of the safety zone resulted from, inter alia, the profusion of attacks against it. This success was claimed by the two movements. However, the fruits of this success were reaped by the Hezbollah movement, which improved its position and scored points in the struggle for control over the community.[81] On the first anniversary to the memory of Harb, Ibrahim al-Amin, the official spokesman of the movement, assembled a press conference where he publicly uncovered for the first time, and in an official manner, the movement, its ideological doctrine, and its goals.[82]

The Struggle in the South during 1985–87, the Expansion Stage, and the Mutual Influences

The withdrawal of the IDF from southern Lebanon created a new situation. The two movements began a race to establish their foothold in the areas from which the IDF had retreated and in the Shiite public opinion. The changes in the public opinion within the community radiated onto the movements' activities and functions on the one hand, and on the other, their activities faithfully reflected their assessment of the level of support they had in the south and the level of support the actions of their adversary movement had. Hezbollah was quick to institutionalize its activity in the south, with the aim of leaving facts on the ground, before Amal managed to make arrangements for blocking its activity.[83]

Abbas al-Musawi, from the founders and leaders of Hezbollah, was chosen for the task of organizing infrastructure in the south. During 1985–1988, he established the organizational entity called the "Islamic Resistance" and led its terror attacks during these years.[84] In an interview in December 1987, al-Musawi outlined the nature of the Islamic Resistance, its goals, and its areas of activity in the south. The content of the interview indicates that the resistance operated on three parallel planes. First, it used its successes as a tool to recruit its ranks, to enhance the fighting spirit of its activists, and to strengthen the aspect of sacrifice and determination. Second, it neutralized Israeli deterrence by portraying the Israeli soldier as an oppressor on the one hand and as very vulnerable on the other hand. Third, it strengthened the affinity of the residents of the south to Islam and Hezbollah. In the interview, al-Musawi mentioned that impressive progress had been made in the achievement of the goals of the resistance in those years. He emphasized that the population's fear reactions against Israel's responses had diminished and the popular support basis of the resistance had expanded; it now encompassed a wide strata of the population, and the phenomenon of the objection of family members to the recruitment of their sons to Hezbollah had disappeared. According to him, the goal of creating a mobilized and fighting revolutionary society has not been achieved yet due to erroneous education of the Muslims in Lebanon. For the budding of this goal, in the form of disillusionment of the population and its realization that Israel is the main enemy, he gave credit to the activity of the new clerics, the leaders of the activist approach.[85].

Hezbollah put great emphasis on operational innovation and focused on carrying out quality operations that gained widespread resonance and were exploited as propaganda, for the expansion of the movement's foothold in the south. It outlined an action plan that included three stages:

1. *First stage*: The operations of the first stage featured fire ambushes, the placement of roadside bombs, and demolition charges. The most common operation characteristic of this stage was that it was carried out from the very first days of the Islamic Resistance's appearance against the IDF in Lebanon.

2. *Second stage*: This stage included attacking SLA (South Lebanon Army) posts with the aim of causing its collapse and began in late 1986. The movement reached its goal, and Israel was required to invest further forces in the safety zone in order to prevent its collapse. The victory parades, showing captured weapons and armored personnel carriers (APCs) plundered from conquered SLA posts, alongside the footage of the operations themselves, which were shown in the channels of Lebanese television, added many points of favor to the balance of the movement in the Shiite and Lebanese public opinion and embarrassed its opponents. The movement took full advantage of its successes as a lever for recruiting activists into its ranks.

3. *Third stage*: This was the most pretentious stage and included using the same formula that proved to be effective against SLA posts to attack IDF posts and thus force the IDF to withdraw from Lebanon. The movement failed in reaching the goals of this stage. After a series of humiliating defeats in attacking IDF posts in 1987, during which dozens of the movement's activists became casualties, it began seeking new ways of action against the IDF. In September 1987, it was announced that the Islamic Resistance was operating to cut off the security zone in the area between Marjayoun and Jezzine and create territorial continuity between Beqaa and southern Lebanon. In December 1987, al-Musawi declared that a new type of sophisticated activity against Israel is to be expected.[86]

The issue of resistance against Israel created a dilemma for the Amal movement. It was obvious that the support in the continuation of the resistance in the Shiite public opinion was very broad. Oppositely, the theater of operations against Israel was under the security control of Amal, who found it difficult to oppose the activity of Hezbollah for fear of being portrayed negatively among its own crowd. The issue was exacerbated sevenfold following the escalation in incidents in southern Lebanon and the damage to the feeling of safety of its residents.

The policy applied by the movement on this issue was, in a sense, the lesser of two evils. It enabled the continuation of the resistance in southern Lebanon, as long as the conflict was conducted against IDF forces, not with artillery bombardment or Katyusha fire. Despite the different nature of activities of the two movements in the south—Amal keeping civil order and security and Hezbollah acting within the framework of the resistance—they had numerous frictions and conflicts of interests, sometimes sliding from the level of public discourse to violent clashes. This state of affairs reached such an extent that the man in charge of Amal in the south, Daud, ordered his men, in a ceremony held in September 1987 in one of the villages of southern Lebanon, to forbid the distribution of Hezbollah publications in the south.[87]

The conclusions reached between the Amal movement and Hezbollah in southern Lebanon in 1987 on the issues of joint terrorist attacks policy, activity in the framework of the lines of Amal's security policy, forbearance from ostentatious operations, forbiddance of firing rockets and harming UN personnel were all broken by Hezbollah. The reason for that was probably Hezbollah's sense of security, stemming from its understanding of the levels of the expansion in its influence over the Shiite public opinion.[88] In May 1987, Subhi al-Tufayli, from the leaders of Hezbollah, declared that the "*Islamic Resistance is a growing phenomenon,*" and is stronger than ever and that the movement will not make it possible to sign a peace agreement with Israel.[89] In October 1987, Abbas al-Musawi reinforced Tufayli's statement by saying that, following the developments taking place in the Islamic Resistance and in its public support, it can withstand any difficulty. He further argued that Israel's policy of "driving a wedge," successful in the Palestinian-Lebanese case, is not applicable in the case of Hezbollah, due to the deep rooting of the movement. According to him, the Islamic Resistance was waging a campaign to convince the "Islamic nation" that it was capable of confronting Israel successfully.[90]

The rise in Hezbollah's sense of security in the south was expressed in the spreading of strife between it and Amal and in the deterioration of their relationship. This tension reached a new peak following two kidnappings carried out by Hezbollah activists in territories in southern Lebanon, which were under Amal's security control. Amal had no choice but to react. In February 1987, two employees of United Nations Relief and Works Agency for Palestine Refugees in the Near East (UNRWA) in Tyre were kidnapped and released after a few days. On February 17, 1987, the chief of the UN's Observer Group, Colonel Higgins, was kidnapped as he was returning from a meeting with Amal's man in charge in Tyre. From here, the distance between the total deterioration and the widening of the battles between the two movements was short.[91]

The Kidnappings and Their Impact on the Relationships between the Community and the Movement

The effects of Hezbollah's activity exceeded the borders of both the Lebanese and the regional systems. Its activities included executing suicide attacks against the foreigners in Lebanon, operations with various characteristics against the

IDF and the SLA, as well as hijacking airplanes and western hostages in Lebanon for the advancement of the movement, pan-Islamic, and Iranian interests. Kidnapping hostages, an action pattern that characterized the activity of the movement all along the 1980s, projected on its status in the intra-Lebanese as well as the international arena. This action pattern was not always perceived as beneficial for the interests of the Shiite community in general and Hezbollah in particular, and it stirred much debate between the extremists and the pragmatists.[92]

The main objector to this activity was Fadlallah. He argued that it harms the image of the movement. Opposite him stood the leadership of the movement, which supported this activity and viewed it as a tool to advance pan-Islamic objectives. Notwithstanding this fact, the movement avoided from taking direct responsibilities for the kidnappings and denied any connection with the Islamic Jihad organization.[93] The internal debate on the issue of the continuation of kidnappings, raging in the 1980s within the community and between the followers of the two movements, was influenced by the successes and failures of this modus operandi and from lack of Syrian satisfaction.[94]

One of the peaks of this modus operandi came in June 1985. An American passenger jet belonging to the Trans World Airlines (TWA) company, flying from Cairo to Rome, was hijacked by Hezbollah and forced to land in Beirut's airport, which was under Amal's control. This event, lasting for sixteen days, was covered by the television networks in the world and played into the hands of Hezbollah. It served Hezbollah as a means to enhance its exposure in the international system and turned it, for a while, into a meaningful player in the international system. This event had all the components that characterized the struggle between the two movements for control over the community. On the one hand, it showed violent action of Hezbollah to realize common community interest, such as the release of Shiite prisoners jailed in Israel in exchange of the release of the hijacked airplane, while challenging the passivity of the Amal movement and its leadership. On the other hand, it reflected the desire of the Amal movement to not only be portrayed as one that does take care of the release of its prisoners, but also be portrayed as a Shiite movement that is not radical in nature. The success of Amal's leader, in this case, to navigate well between these two constraints added points to his impoverished balance and also gave points to Hezbollah, which, due to its operation, achieved the Israeli release of Shiite prisoners.[95]

This way or the other, the phenomenon of the kidnappings instructs on the innovativeness that characterized the operations of the movement. The innovation was in the use of a simple and relatively easy action tactic, such as "kidnapping," as a mean of achieving strategic goals versus the Western states. The kidnapping of over a hundred foreign hostages, staying in Lebanon between 1982 and 1990, advanced Hezbollah interests and mostly those of its patron—Iran. The Western states, in exchange for the release of their citizens, were forced to make political payments in the form of releasing terrorists jailed in their countries, advertising political statements, releasing Hezbollah activists, and, in the French case, stopping the shipping of French arms to Iraq. Moreover, this activity made a laughingstock of the superpowers, which exhibited impotence in maintaining peace and security for their citizens and found it difficult to act against Hezbollah for the fear of harm coming to the hostages.[96]

In the early 1990s, Hezbollah stopped the kidnapping operations. During this period, the last of the Western hostages, held by radical Shiite groups with an affinity to the movement and to Iran, were released.[97] The main reasons for this release were, so it seems, the change in Iran's policy, the increased Syrian pressure on Hezbollah to stop the kidnappings, and a change in the public opinion of the Shiite community.[98] The modus operandi of kidnapping foreigners in Lebanon did not improve the status of the movement in the community. On the contrary, from a certain stage onward, it even hurt the movement's efforts to expand its influence in the community. Despite its denials and attempts to cut off any affiliation between itself and the kidnappings, most of the kidnappings were attributed to groups operating under the inspiration of the movement, and they were perceived in the public opinion as a means of advancing Iranian interests.[99]

The Social-Islamic Activity—the Struggle on the Shiite Family Unit

The economic situation and the difficult living conditions of the Shiite community in general and the Shiite immigrants in the margins of the cities from the 1970s onward in particular, alongside the government's inability to provide the necessary services, created a vacuum into which the Islamic agents entered. These agents funded by Iran and by donators from abroad, established and managed a branched network of religious, charitable, and educational institutions, through which they expanded their circle of influence in the Shiite society. This process, starting before the founding of Hezbollah, gained momentum from the mid-1980s onward. During this period, institutions grew and additional intramovement organizations or organizations with affinity to the movement and to Iran emerged, dealing with extensive social activity within the community as a means to recruit activists to the movement. The social activity of Hezbollah was carried out simultaneously with its Islamic activity. Wherever Hezbollah felt secure in its control over the region, it introduced and enforced strict Islamic rules, such as changing the manner of dress and lifestyle, closing houses of entertainment, and forbidding the sale of alcoholic beverages.[100]

One of the most fundamental struggles between Amal and Hezbollah was waged in the social field. The real struggle in this field was, in fact, carried out in southern Lebanon. For every sector in the Shiite population in southern Lebanon in which Hezbollah invested, so did Amal. In the 1980s, Amal had a relative advantage over Hezbollah. This advantage stemmed from its control over government budgets transferred to the development of the south, by virtue of it being the militia responsible for security in the south and by virtue of the areas of civic activities it took care of.[101] The social activity of Hezbollah was based on a number of tiers and action strategies, all aimed at reaching the family circle, directly or indirectly:

1. *Economic assistance to families in distress or the families of the movement's casualties*: It was carried out through Iranian institutions, institutions of the movement, and independent institutions with an affinity to the movement. Among these institutions and bodies were the "assistance council of

the Imam Khomeini," a network of charitable institutions under the management of Fadlallah,[102] and "Mu'asasat Al-Shahid" ("institution of the martyr"). The activity of the institution of the martyr was aimed to increase the affinity between the community, Iran, and Hezbollah and to encourage recruitment of activists to the movement. It was established in Lebanon after the first Lebanon war as a branch of the "Mu'asasat Al-Shahid" of Iran. In 1987, it already included seven branches in Beirut, Beqaa, southern Lebanon, and Tripoli, a wide deployment indicating the status of the movement as well as the extent of the Iranian investment to advance it. The institution took care of all the needs of the families of the movement's casualties and provided employment and vocational training for them. Its activities were taken advantage of as propaganda and as a tool for recruitment and first-class influence.[103]

2. *Medical assistance*: This included the foundation of medical infrastructure and assistance to the individual. Within this framework, the movement established between 1985 and 1987, with Iranian assistance and funding, two hospitals in Beqaa and Beirut, seventeen medical centers, centers for civilian defense, and dental clinics.[104] The members of the movement, casualties, and needy Shiite families received large discounts, and some even received free medical treatment in those centers and in the Islamic health network established by Iran.[105]

3. *The area of education and culture*: The movement attributed great importance to Islamic education. The Islamic seminaries under the leadership of the new clerics first bore fruit in the beginning of the 1980s. Their graduates were among the first activist nuclei in Hezbollah. The investment in education as a basis for recruitment and dissemination of the Islamic message, parallel to the resistance activities, characterized the activity of this system from its first days.

   With the foundation of the movement, the educational activities expanded into further circles, which were identified as holding recruitment potential and marked as important to its development. The "culture and recruitment committees" of the movement operated among the student organizations in the colleges and universities, organized assemblies and teaching days, distributed scholarships for students, and supported their continued studies in Iran and abroad.[106] In the southern suburb of Beirut, the movement also determined the nature of the settings of study, according to the Islamic line. Thus, for example, the student-recruitment center of Hezbollah notified, in September 1987, the headmasters of the public and private high schools in the southern suburb to segregate the studies of boys and girls.[107]

The educational activity included the youth as well as infants. In this framework, elementary schools and kindergartens were founded or renovated, and education programs and educational settings for infants were operated according to the spirit of the movement. Those who attended these programs were provided all necessary requirements from Iranian funding sources. The best of these pupils were given scholarships for their continual education in the Islamic seminaries.[108]

The movement also worked toward the expanding of its influence beyond the operation hours of formal schooling by organizing the youth in the setting of "youth brigades" and the "Islamic Scouts." These held various types of competitive sports activities, combined with activities that deepened the affinity to Islam and the movement. The members of these groups participated in the ceremonies and marches of the movement, alongside the fighters of the military units. Some of them underwent basic military training in summer camps, held annually in the Beqaa area.

The second facet of the Islamic education was the media. It was meant to reach various target audiences, mainly the family unit. For that purpose, the movement made use of two main channels of communication: the traditional channel, based on the network of mosques and religious centers, where its representatives performed recruitment activities[109] and the modern channel that included the movement's journal "Al-Ahd" starting from the summer of 1984, the radio stations "Voice of the Deprived" and "Voice of the Islam," and the station "Radio al-Nour," from 1991. An important element in the dissemination of the Islamic message was the television station "Al-Manar," starting its broadcasts in 1989. These media broadcast a variety of programs, including news, Islamic programs, political topics, current events, and the resistance to Israel. They served as a means for advertising and marketing the principals and goals of the movement. Using them, it expanded and perfected the propagation of its messages, shaped Islamic cultural patterns for its audiences, and constructed new symbols and myths related to its activity.[110]

Summary

There is no doubt that Hezbollah transformed from a nascent movement that just arose (summer 1982) to a weighty element in the internal, regional, and international systems. The stage in which the movement was in 1988 was the third in its career, the expansion stage. The short duration from its founding to the appearance of indicators pointing to a process of expansion is not an insignificant matter. The rapid growth rate of the movement stemmed from processes and circumstances that took place simultaneously, thus creating the opportunity for growth.

The rapid growth in the number of its activists and areas of operation caused the appearance of embryonic organizational systems, which controlled, to a certain degree, the activities of the movement. However, under the organizational umbrella, extremist groups with affinity to Islam operated independently or in direct activation of radical elements in the Iranian leadership. The activities of the above did not take into consideration either the reactions or changes in the Shiite public opinion or the damage such activity causes to the expansion of the movement's influence.

On February 17, 1988, Colonel Higgins was kidnapped in southern Lebanon by Hezbollah activists. The kidnapping raised the struggle between Amal and Hezbollah to a new height. It was an expression of Hezbollah's confidence in its ability to defeat the Amal movement in the battle for Shiite public support, even in Amal's stronghold in southern Lebanon. This point in time marked the beginning of a savage fight between the two movements, at whose termination the boundaries of influence and action of both movements were shaped by their patrons.[111]

The violent struggle taking place between the two movements in the years 1988–1991, and the changes in the systems surrounding the movement, also generated a change in the activity patterns of Hezbollah and the areas of action to which it turned. The explanations for this directional change, from radical to pragmatic and from pan-Islamic to Lebanese, are in fact found in one of the most violent and difficult periods that the Shiite community in Lebanon faced, during which a war between brothers (*Fitna*) erupted over positions of power and influence in the community.

4

Expansion and Institutionalization of the Movement—Constraints and Adaptation

Introduction

August 1992 was a very successful month for Kulta Al-Wafa Lal-mukuma (Arabic for Loyalty to the Resistance Bloc, generally referred to as Al-Wafa), the party that represented Hezbollah in the first parliamentary elections held in Lebanon in some twenty years. Eight Al-Wafa representatives were elected to the parliament in these turbulent elections. Hezbollah's decision to field candidates in the elections signified, first and foremost, that it recognized the legitimacy of the Lebanese political system. For a movement that had spent the previous decade waging a violent battle to bring down the government from outside the system, such a decision constituted a drastic change in strategy—conflicted sharply with the movement's policy and ideology.[1]

The dramatic changes in the movement did not occur in a single day. They embodied insights that had crystallized following internal and community power struggles over whether to take the reformist, secular approach, or the revolutionary, religious approach as well because of the sensitivity of the movement's leaders to changing public opinion within the Shiite community. This was accompanied by organizational pressure both from within the movement and from outside the community. Sayyed Hassan Nasrallah's decision to participate in the elections increased the internal tension as to whether the movement should adopt a radical approach based on an uncritical belief in the values of Shiite Islam, revolution, pan-Islamism, and the uncompromising heritage of Iran's Ayatollah Khomeini or follow a pragmatic approach based on the belief that reality had left the movement with no choice but to join the renewed Lebanese political system and that doing so was necessary to advance the movement's goals, even at the price of temporarily accepting the rules of this system.

There are no objections to the fact that this decision is a demonstration that pragmatism and rationality could be found even in the most fundamentalist and radical stronghold in Lebanon. However, it is important to note that Hezbollah's integration into the Lebanese political system is not necessarily an indication that it had abandoned its goals of overthrowing the existing regime and establishing an Islamic republic. This decision was considered another step on the path toward realizing the movement's long-term goal of ruling Lebanon. Unlike advocates of the radical approach, who aimed to achieve this goal by violent revolutionary means, the advocates of the pragmatic approach wanted to do so gradually, both from the top (through Lebanese institutions) and from the bottom (through wide-ranging social activities).

Ironically, the change in policy occurred during one of the most difficult periods that the Shiite community in Lebanon had faced, in 1988–1990, when Hezbollah transitioned from "the expansion stage" to "the institution stage." During this period, Hezbollah and Amal fought for dominance within the community. The change embodied the movement's sensitivity to the processes and influences of the domestic and regional systems, which were amplified as the movement expanded and established itself.

The 1988–1990 Amal-Hezbollah Struggles—A Sign of the End of the Movement's Expansion Period

In December 1990, on the eve of the establishment of the reconciliation government led by Rashid Karami, it was clear that the Shiite community had become an actor that had to be considered. Indeed, there were even those who thought that the Ta'if Accord did not provide a satisfactory formula for integrating the community into the "new order." It is important to emphasize here that, in these years, Lebanon suffered a severe legislative crisis—two governments (the Aoun and the Al-Hoss) operated simultaneously without a president. This period was characterized both by violent incidents between the Aoun government and the Syrians and by great tension that led to violent incidents involving players in the regional system and Hezbollah. Some of the problems that characterized the Lebanese system during this period were solved by reaching and implementing the Ta'if Accord.

The struggle between Amal and Hezbollah (1988–1990) determined to a great degree the borders and regions of influence of the two movements as well as the balance of power between them in the Lebanese system. Hezbollah defeated the Amal movement in Beirut and won recognition as an organization with military and political power that must be taken into account. However, its failures in the south distanced it from the circle of anti-Israel activity, a situation that the movement found difficult to accept. For the Amal movement, which had already lost more than a little of its power and prestige because of its entanglement in the Camps War, the war against Hezbollah further lowered its status in the eyes of both the community and the powers active in Lebanon and led to the further erosion of its power and internal unity. Only the fact that it was a popular movement with deep roots (mainly in southern Lebanon) allowed Amal to maintain its status as an important player in the community and in Lebanon. As a result, both movements worked constantly to improve their relative status and their image in the Shiite community.[2]

The struggle between Amal and Hezbollah escalated into a real war at the beginning of 1988. It continued, with ups and downs, until late 1990. The war, which was characterized by great violence and cruelty, took a heavy toll on the

Shiite community. Throughout the war, all of the operative methods that characterized militia battles in Lebanon were utilized, including heavy weapons (tanks and artillery), terrorist acts that targeted the commanders of both movements, kidnappings, various bombs and explosive devices, and psychological warfare.[3] The war included three periods of fighting: April 1988–May 1988, concluding with a cease-fire agreement between the parties; January 1989, concluding with the signing of the first Damascus Agreement; and March 1990–September 1990, concluding with the signing of the second Damascus Agreement. The second agreement was brokered by and signed under pressure from Syria and Iran, with the support of the Shiite community, which had had more than enough of the bloodshed. It was implemented at the same time as the Ta'if Accord and the disarming of the militias.[4]

The pretext for the war between the movements was the kidnapping of U.N. staff Col. William R. Higgins, of the United States, by Hezbollah activists from territory that had been under the control of Amal. However, the actual reasons were more complex; they involved the growth of Hezbollah's influence and infrastructure in the south to the extent that they endangered Amal's status. A glimpse of Hezbollah's viewpoint was revealed in an interview with the first Hezbollah secretary general, Subhi Al Tufeili, in October 1989. He claimed that the war between the movements broke out because of differences in their outlook on three major points. (1) The dilemma of liberating Palestine: Hezbollah was actively striving to liberate Palestine via the dissemination of propaganda and the creation of an atmosphere conducive to launching a process of revival among the Islamic nations. At the same time, it was initiating and executing operations against the (Israel Defense Forces) IDF in Lebanon. In contrast, Amal, he said, had adopted a passive policy and did not consider the liberation of Palestine to be a priority. (2) Stance on Israel: Hezbollah did not believe in agreements or conciliation with Israel and took action to expel it from Lebanon via resistance. Amal, on the other hand, supported coexistence with Israel and thought that it was possible to bring about its withdrawal from Lebanon via diplomatic negotiations. (3) Advancing the Shiite community's interests: While Hezbollah wanted to end the ethnic leadership approach and hold free elections, the Amal movement was behaving inconsistently. It supported "cancelling the ethnic leadership approach" in theory, but at the same time, cooperated with the government to formulate agreements that clashed with the logic of doing so,[5] such as the Trilateral Agreement and the Ta'if Accord.[6]

The two kidnappings that occurred in February 1988 stemmed from Hezbollah's confidence that residents of the south would support its actions. The kidnappings were a challenge to Amal's status and a severe blow to its reputation, mainly due to the fact that Amal considered itself responsible for security in southern Lebanon.[7] Amal's response, which included searches and the arrest of Hezbollah activists, sparked off a chain of violent incidents in southern Lebanon.[8] At the beginning of April 1988, it appeared that Hezbollah had succeeded in defeating Amal: it attacked Amal roadblocks in the south, conquered Amal positions and offices in Jazia and Nabatia, and kidnapped a number of Amal activists. However, in a counterattack Amal regained control of Nabatia and the entire south, including villages such as Jibshit, Duweir, and Zawtar that had been considered Hezbollah strongholds. It arrested and evicted most of the Hezbollah activists from villages in the south; those that remained went underground. By September 1988, dozens of additional Hezbollah activists and their families had been forced to leave the south.[9]

The fighting in the south signified the beginning of the difficult battle between the movements for the upper hand in the community's public opinion. The movements' leaders and spokespeople exploited the successes and failures in the battlefield to wage psychological warfare through the media and any other platform or means possible. Evidence of the importance of this campaign in shaping and influencing public opinion in the Shiite community can be found in the conclusions of the Quadripartite Committee that was formed in May 1988 to resolve disputes; the committee decided that in addition to a cease-fire, the sides should also halt the propaganda war.[10]

The psychological warfare began at the same time as the outbreak of violence. Amal leader Nabih Berri was the first to adopt the technique of exploiting the events on the battlefield to wage a psychological war. He emphasized that Amal had overcome Hezbollah because of the Amal movement's broad public support. He pointed an accusing finger at Hezbollah and claimed that it was severely violating the agreements between the movements intentionally, causing their relations to deteriorate, and neglecting the resistance. At the same time, he turned to the Islamic sector in the Shiite population and told them that Amal operated according to Islamic principles and opposed the actions of irresponsible religious figures who published fatwas to serve the interests of parties in the community. Encouraged by the victory, he called on Hezbollah to sign an agreement, under the auspices of the Supreme Shiite Council, that would regulate relations between the two movements, under the auspices of the Supreme Shiite Council.[11]

The Amal movement's actions, which were characterized by the application of direct and indirect pressure upon Hezbollah, continued during the month-long marathon fighting in Beirut in May 1988. Amal organized mass protests and rallies in the south, where denunciations of Hezbollah and praise for Amal and its role as the leader of the resistance to Israel could be heard. Its leaders pressured Syria to enter the southern suburbs and, at the same time, pressured the *mukhtars* (leaders) of the villages in the south to declare their support for Berri and his policies.[12]

Hezbollah's expulsion from southern Lebanon harmed its ability to manage the resistance against Israel. Therefore, from this point onward, returning to the south became vital for Hezbollah and a major bone of contention between it and Amal. At the same time, Hezbollah searched for ways to minimize the harm this caused by continuing its resistance activities from the western Beqaa region and Iqlim al Tufah and by reinstituting an operational policy involving suicide attacks.[13] Abbas Al Mosawi, who led the Islamic Resistance at that point, continued to organize activities, to expand infrastructure, and to establish Hezbollah's beliefs among the Shiite population.[14]

In May 1988, the struggle expanded from southern Lebanon toward Beirut. The expansion served the interest of both movements. Amal hoped to exploit the momentum of its victory in the south to expand into Hezbollah territory.

Hezbollah, on the other hand, wanted to salvage its reputation in the community's eyes, to avenge its humiliation in the south, and to create conditions that would allow it to return to the south. The results of the fighting in Beirut reflected the balance of power between the movements in the city and ended with Hezbollah's victory and Amal's expulsion from western Beirut.[15] The fighting in Beirut was characterized by greater violence than the fighting in the south and severely lowered the quality of life of members of the Shiite community who lived in the city. Heavy damage was inflicted upon property, hundreds of citizens were injured, and tens of thousands abandoned their homes and became refugees.[16] The fighting also extended into the Beqaa and threatened Hezbollah control of it. In May 1988, the tension in the region rose to the point where there was a danger of an outbreak of hostilities between the two leading families in the Beqaa: the Jaffar family, which supported Hezbollah, and the Nasr Ad-Din family, which supported Amal. By July 1988, skirmishes between the two movements were occurring in this area as well.[17]

The Syrians and the Iranians were summoned to mediate between the sides in order to bring the struggle to an end. In mid-May 1988, at the height of the battles, Syria and Iran initiated the establishment of the Quadripartite Committee, which included representatives of Syria, Iran, Hezbollah, and Amal. The committee was formed to resolve disputes, to enforce the cease-fire agreements, to monitor the implementation of agreements, and to identify those responsible for violating agreements. The committee received Syrian and Iranian support for its activities, though this did not deter the parties from violating new agreements.[18]

The first wave of battles ended in late May 1988 following domestic and international (Syrian and Iranian) pressure on the two movements. Upon its conclusion, a balance of power was reached between the movements in which Amal won control of southern Lebanon and Hezbollah of Beirut. Each movement strove to exploit its military victories to improve its standing in the eyes of the Shiite community and used the media to wage psychological warfare and to strengthen its positions against the other party. For example, on May 29, 1988, Amal publicized claims that Hezbollah received assistance from Christians in its battle against Amal. It claimed this information came from its interrogation of Hezbollah prisoners. The Hezbollah movement responded quickly by confirming that some of its activists had been captured and denying that it had any ties whatsoever with Christian militias.[19]

The reinforcement of positions by both movements made it difficult for the Quadripartite Committee to find a mediation formula that would make it possible to end the crisis.[20] Hezbollah demanded political and military freedom of action in southern Lebanon. Amal vigorously opposed this. In contrast, Amal demanded that the Supreme Shiite Council be recognized as a supramovement body in the community and be accepted as a higher authority that would mediate between the positions of the parties and help end the conflict. Hezbollah rejected this demand.[21]

The failure of the mediation efforts increased the tension between the movements and consequently the number of incidents and their severity. Thus, for example, from September 1988 onward, the incidents in Beirut grew increasingly severe. They included heavy exchanges of fire, kidnappings, and executions. One of the most notorious events that influenced the rest of the reconciliation efforts was the Hezbollah execution of three senior Amal figures. Amal accused Hezbollah of trying to destroy it and responded by expelling Hezbollah activists, those who were identified with the movement, along with their families, from the areas under its control. Hezbollah objected and accused Amal of attacking and torturing its activists in the south and pressured the Iranian leadership to take steps to minimize and prevent this phenomenon.[22] The increase in incidents between the movements and the difficulty the Quadripartite Committee had in enforcing its authority led Syria to intervene with force in order to halt the escalating hostilities between the parties.[23]

At the same time, the psychological warfare between the movements also escalated and came to resemble a conversation of sorts. At a mass protest Amal organized in the south, Berri called Hezbollah a group of blood-sucking vampires and called on Hezbollah activists to rebel against their leaders.[24] In December 1988, he launched an especially harsh verbal attack on Hezbollah. He accused it of using Nazi and radical operating patterns and of creating a distorted image of the Shiite community and Iran as terrorists and radicals in the international public opinion. He emphasized Hezbollah's use of "excessive violence" against Amal and claimed that this violated Islamic principles. He taunted Hezbollah about its defeat in the south, claiming that its activists had fled and that his movement now organized resistance activities in the south. However, Berri left the door open for dialogue and reconciliation, though he made it contingent upon the surrender of the murderers of the three Amal leaders and the fulfillment of Amal's basic demands.[25] Hezbollah did not sit by idly. It condemned Amal's activities in southern Lebanon and gave Berri the questionable nickname "Slaughterer of the Shiites."[26]

In January 1989, a new round of violence broke out. This time, the center of violence was Iqlim al Tufah, a hilly region east of Sidon that extends toward the security zone. Hezbollah took steps to establish its control in this area. The area enabled Hezbollah to continue its resistance activities and served as a convenient starting point for regaining control of the south in general and of the Nabatia region in particular. Amal was sensitive to the developing threat and initiated actions to eliminate Hezbollah presence in the region.[27]

The Syrians, who were concerned about the extensive flare-ups in the Beirut suburbs and other parts of Lebanon, took severe and unprecedented steps to restore security. They stationed troops along the entire line of conflict in Beirut, increased patrols and roadblocks in the areas under their control, and launched a joint campaign with the Iranians to exert pressure on the parties to accept a cease-fire agreement and normalize their relations in all areas.[28] On January 30, the parties signed the first Damascus Agreement, which included agreeing to a comprehensive cease-fire, effective immediately; ceasing of the verbal attacks on one another in the media; and immediately opening negotiations to achieve a peace agreement and establish a framework for relations between the parties. The agreement also declared that Hezbollah activists would be permitted to return to a number of areas in southern Lebanon, provided the Quadripartite Committee approved, and that Amal would be able to function in Beirut.[29]

In the months that followed, both sides took steps to implement the agreement. However, the implementation of the agreement faltered under constantly increasing difficulties, starting with a protest organized in villages in the south against the decision to allow Hezbollah activists to return and continuing with mutual recriminations and local skirmishes. These ultimately led to the outbreak of the third wave of fighting, which lasted from February to September 1990.[30] It began at the most sensitive point of friction between the movements—the Iqlim al Tufah region. Hezbollah accused Amal of intentionally escalating the situation and preventing the transfer of supplies to Hezbollah activists in the region, as well as of collaborating with Israel to destroy Hezbollah. These circumstances, the movement explained, forced it to launch an attack. Amal's demand to restore the previous status quo in the area was summarily rejected. Al Tufeili rejected the approach of solving individual problems as they cropped up in Iqlim al Tufah and emphasized the need to find a comprehensive solution to all the problems that had developed between the movements and, on top of that, to return Hezbollah to southern Lebanon.[31] Hussein Mosawi, the leader of Amal Al-Islami and a senior Hezbollah figure, also made this demand, saying that the movement would be prepared to withdraw from the positions it had conquered in the Iqlim al Tufah region if the following conditions were met: prohibiting Amal from returning to these areas, allowing Hezbollah's supply channels to remain open, and beginning talks to fully implement the Damascus Agreement.[32]

The Amal movement, which had not succeeded in defending its positions in Iqlim al Tufah, tried to minimize the damage and pressured the Lebanese government to intervene. In September 1990, it released a statement expressing concern over the domestic security and economic situation and warning about the danger this posed. The statement emphasized the need to take action quickly to neutralize this danger. Therefore, the movement called on the Lebanese government to do its duty and to implement the decision to deploy the army in Iqlim al Tufah. Immediate intervention was needed, the statement said, due to the increase in the number of displaced persons and refugees from the battle zones and the fact that Hezbollah had escalated its activities in Iqlim al Tufah and Baalbek and its leader, Al Tufeili, was foiling every attempt to end the conflict.[33] In October 1990, the chairman of Amal's political bureau accused Hezbollah of befriending Maronite Christian leader Michel Aoun with the aim of forging a coalition to oppose the Ta'if Accord and establishing a new Lebanon. He also claimed that the intentional escalation in Hezbollah activities was the result of power struggles between moderates and extremists in Iran.[34]

In November 1990, the second Damascus Agreement was signed. Hezbollah and Amal pledged to implement it with the support, involvement, and close supervision of Syria and Iran. A joint follow-up committee, consisting of representatives of all the parties, was formed to monitor its implementation.[35] The agreement was based on the following principles: involvement of all parties, including representatives of the Lebanese government, at the highest level; immediate implementation of the cease-fire; cessation of propaganda; release of captives and prisoners; handing over of responsibility for security in Iqlim al Tufah to the Lebanese Army; and the return of all displaced persons, from both sides, to their homes.[36]

The signing of the agreement was accompanied by a commitment from the two movements' leaders to act to implement it. For them, the agreement was the ladder that would allow them to descend the tall tree they had climbed. Each of them had an interest in ending the war. Hezbollah was watching, with growing concern, the regional and domestic changes, such as the crisis in the Persian Gulf, the end of the Aoun government, and the beginning of the implementation of the Ta'if Accord, which were liable to leave the movement in a position in which it would not have any justification for continuing its existence as an armed Lebanese movement unless it succeeded in gaining a foothold in southern Lebanon. All this influenced Hezbollah's desire to hasten its return to southern Lebanon to further the resistance. Indeed, the resistance was the main mechanism it used to gain legitimacy in the coming years. It was especially important due to the timing—the beginning of the process of rehabilitating the Lebanese system in accordance with the Ta'if Accords. The resistance activities were the main justification for its claim that Hezbollah was not just another Lebanese militia, since its weapons were intended only for use against Israel. Therefore, it claimed, the agreement to disarm militias, which was anchored in the Ta'if Accords, did not apply to Hezbollah. This claim was the main ammunition against the demand to disarm and was emphasized repeatedly in statements by the movement's leaders. Hezbollah also declared that its obligation to implement the agreement was contingent upon receiving guarantees of freedom of activity, political expression, and managing the resistance against Israel.[37]

Berri declared that Amal was prepared to fulfill its part of the second Damascus Agreement and called for the agreement to be implemented quickly due to the situation developing in the Gulf. However, unlike Hezbollah, he ordered his movement's commanders to begin to collect light and heavy weapons. He saw the Ta'if Accord as an opportunity to restore Amal's status, which had suffered a severe blow, by integrating into the new political system and the framework of the Lebanese Army.[38]

Fighting Words alongside Mediation and Dialogue—the Leading Strategies in the War for Public Opinion

The war between the movements was obviously influenced by their struggle to win the public-opinion war in the Shiite community during the period when both movements were conducting internal ideological debates and formulating their stances regarding the Ta'if Accord. Hezbollah, which remained faithful to the pan-Islamic vision, presented the struggle in pan-Islamic terms. It rejected the legitimacy of the existing Lebanese political system and saw itself as the elite Shiite opposition that was in the process of expanding and gaining influence outside of the political system.[39] Hezbollah acted to advance the issues that it considered critical, with an emphasis on maintaining its military capability and guaranteeing its access to southern Lebanon. Amal, in contrast, dedicated itself to implementing the Ta'if Accord and disarming the militias as part of its aim to become part of the Lebanese political system.

The Shiite community's dissatisfaction with the bloodbath raging within it was expressed in the accusations being voiced by all the streams within the community. Some focused on hurling accusations, while others tried to find formulas to mediate between the two sides. Religious figures from both camps and others tried to bridge the differences, but were rejected repeatedly by both sides. The most prominent religious leaders who took a stand and worked toward ending the conflict were Muhammud Husayn Fadlallah, Mahdi Shams Ad-Din, and Abd Al-Emir Kabalan. Their initiatives, which directly reflected their personal opinions and indirectly reflected the changing opinions in the Shiite community, changed in accordance with the circumstances and developments in the field.[40] Indeed, the movements' decision to end the war was ultimately influenced by their understanding that its continuation was causing both of them real harm.

Fadlallah was sure that the kidnapping of Higgins would not cause an outbreak of violence, despite the constant tension that characterized Hezbollah–Amal relations at that time. Therefore, he supported it indirectly and claimed that Higgins was a spy who collected information about Hezbollah.[41] As the fighting expanded, he made veiled accusations that elements in the community were acting out of their own narrow, personal considerations and harming efforts to advance the resistance. Fadlallah predicted that the war would create a new balance of power and that Shiite public opinion would be a restraining factor if there were an escalation in fighting. He called for the parties to refrain from harming civilians and to quickly end the war and for the Quadripartite Committee to intervene to end it.[42]   Fadlallah believed in the existence of "balanced relations" between Amal and Hezbollah. Such relations, he said, are not anchored in the agreements that guarantee political coexistence of the movements. Restoring the Amal movement's status in Beirut depended upon its willingness to enable Hezbollah to return to southern Lebanon.[43] In his opinion, the main reason for the continuation of the struggle between the movements was the imbalance between them in southern Lebanon, which stemmed from Amal's unwillingness to allow Hezbollah to have an equal degree of freedom of action in the area.[44] Fadlallah's inability to bring the war to an end led him to cooperate with the Iranians and Syrians. In January 1989, at the height of the fighting in Lebanon, he met with the Iranian foreign minister and called again for an end to the war and the creation of conditions to enable conciliation between the movements.[45] In January 1990, in light of the escalation in Iqlim al Tufah, he called on the Syrian president to intervene to bring about a cease-fire.[46] In November 1990, he supported the second Damascus Agreement and warned against attempts by interested parties or Israel to thwart it. Therefore, he urged its signatories to hasten to implement it and to renew the resistance activities against Israel as soon as possible.[47]

At the end of 1989, the Hezbollah secretary general, Al Tufeili, presented a series of allegations that justified Hezbollah's stances and cast the blame on its opponent. He admitted that both movements had failed in their efforts to win the war, which he labeled as destructive. However, he placed most of the blame on Amal, which he claimed was trying to destroy Hezbollah. He emphasized that, despite this, even at the most difficult points in the war, his movement had refrained from taking steps that were liable to destroy Amal and was dedicated to coexistence with it. Therefore, he called on the Amal movement to act wisely and to end the fighting in accordance with the agreements they had signed.[48] Naim

Qassem, the Hezbollah deputy secretary general, expressed a similar opinion in January 1990 and claimed that Hezbollah had laid down its weapons for the first time out of a desire to reach peace and not out of fear or inability. He said that Hezbollah's tolerance stemmed from its lack of desire to continue the war between brothers and from the hope that they could reach an understanding, adding that Amal had interpreted this as a sign of weakness.[49] In February 1990, in light of the events in Iqlim al Tufah, Al Tufeili berated Amal for not honoring the agreements, for wanting to continue the state of war, and for attempting to create a rift between Hezbollah and the community with its recent claims that Hezbollah was responsible for torpedoing the agreement in Iqlim al Tufah. He threatened that Hezbollah would react harshly to any violent action and that it had the means and the ability to do so. He said that the movement had won wide support in the Shiite community and among elements in the Sunni community as well.[50] In January 1990, after the agreement was signed, he declared that the movement would act with determination and seriousness to implement it and that, from that moment onward, its weapons would be aimed only at Israel.[51]

The Supreme Shiite Council and its leader, Mahdi Shams Ad-Din, sided with Amal. However, concerned about the possible results of a war between the movements, it too called on the movements to refrain from engaging in a confrontation that could endanger the future of the Shiite community.[52] In August 1988, Ad-Din hinted that Hezbollah was to blame for the failure to make peace and again urged both movements to agree to a cease-fire and a halt in the mutual recriminations as an initial step toward future reconciliation.[53]

The Shiite mufti of Lebanon, Abd Al-Emir Kabalan, who was identified with Amal, had reservations about Hezbollah's activities and put forward his own proposal to end the fighting. In July 1988, he estimated that another wave of violence was likely in Beirut or the south and warned Hezbollah, which he held responsible for the violence that had occurred until that point, not to try to launch another round of violence in the south. He said that Amal's fall in Beirut was the result of the poor organizational and operational level of its forces in the city.[54] At the end of 1988, the growing violence in Beirut led him to call on the sides again to halt the bloodshed.[55] In January 1989, at the height of the fighting, he presented a plan to establish a framework that would make it possible to end the conflict. Hezbollah responded by calling for an immediate, unconditional cease-fire, but completely rejected the demand to withdraw from Iqlim al Tufah, claiming that would not help end the conflict.[56] In March 1989, after his initiative failed, Kabalan published a fatwa forbidding members of the community to join Hezbollah. He accused it of taking actions that would turn Lebanon's Shiite community into a pawn of Iran.[57]

Hezbollah and the Shiite Community—from Expansion to Institutionalization and from the Old Order to the New Order in Lebanon

A series of developments in the domestic, regional, and international arenas at the end of the 1980s and the beginning of the 1990s affected the system in Lebanon.

They had a significant impact on both the movements, which prepared to fight for their standing in the Shiite community and the Lebanese system. The Ta'if Accord symbolized the end of Lebanon's "old order," in which the militias set the tone and agenda, and the beginning of the new order, in which the Lebanese government, operating under Syria, gradually assumed the responsibilities of state. The developments in the domestic Lebanese arena played into the hands of Amal; they provided Amal with the ultimate political opportunity to climb out of the mud in which it had been stuck through the second half of the 1980s. Amal defined itself as a secular, national Lebanese movement that supported strengthening the government and its authority. It was prepared to enjoy the fruits of joining the new order—even if that meant it had to disarm. Furthermore, the new order pulled the carpet out from under the feet of Amal's opponent, Hezbollah, and weakened its standing in the community because of the obvious incompatibility between Hezbollah's platform, which called for overthrowing the Lebanese government, and the new order, which required acting within the framework of the existing political system and obeying its laws. Therefore, the Amal leadership aimed its attacks at Hezbollah's soft spot—its stance on the Lebanese government. Amal claimed that Hezbollah was trying to overthrow Lebanon's legitimate government and intentionally thwarting efforts to end the civil war and achieve national reconciliation. In contrast, Amal emphasized its own responsible, patriotic approach that involved advancing the community's concerns through the Lebanese system, strengthening Lebanon's status as an independent state, and continuing to lead the battle against Israel until it withdrew.[58] Amal, and particularly its leader Berri, acted behind the scenes and openly to gain power in the government institutions being formed, in the army, and in other central institutions in order to use this as a base to increase its power and influence within the community.[59]

There is no dispute that Hezbollah saw these developments as significant threats to its status and used all the means at its disposal—both direct and indirect—to frustrate them. It took steps to minimize the impact these processes had on the community and to present them as being more harmful than beneficial to the community. At the same time, Hezbollah worked to achieve two intertwined goals: first, it wanted to make the movement the standard bearer of the resistance against Israel by increasing its attacks on Israel, and second, it wanted to end the war with Amal and to restore its standing in the Shiite community. In October 1990, the movement announced that it was prepared to end the war and that it was taking steps to transfer control of Beirut's southern suburbs to the Lebanese Army. Both steps served the goals stated above.[60]

The struggle to win the public-opinion war in the Shiite community led the movement's leaders to change the tone of their dialogue. In a series of interviews with the media, and in the conversations that Al Tufeili had with journalists, from December 1990 to the middle of 1991, the movement presented various target audiences with its positions and policies on the following topics on the Lebanese, community, and movement agendas:[61]

A. *Ta'if Accord and the disarming of militias*: The movement opposed implementing the Ta'if Accord in its current state and would continue to advance the idea of establishing an Islamic republic in Lebanon. He noted that in such a republic, the movement's religious ideas would not be forced on the public, but would only be promoted via persuasion, and the public would have free choice. He also demanded that Hezbollah be removed from the list of militias to be disarmed, declaring that, from that point onward, its weapons would be aimed only at Israel. He responded to critics that Hezbollah activists had been forced to bear arms in the cities due to the fighting with Amal.

B. *Integrating military power into state institutions*: This issue was placed before all of the militias in general and Hezbollah in particular. The movement refrained from participating in this process claiming that it was too early to consider this.

C. *Political freedom of action*: Al Tufeili emphasized that the movement made its decisions independently and was not the emissary or agent of another source. According to Al Tufeili, one does not need to be a member of the government or parliament to conduct political activities, and the activities are legitimate if they are in the public and national interest. He added that he was taking steps to establish a broad opposition front to the government with national and Islamic elements.

D. *Representation in the government*: Al Tufeili clarified that Hezbollah's decision on whether or not to join the government depended upon the character of the government to be established, its policies, and the extent to which joining the government would benefit the movement and the community. He announced that a decision on the issue would be made soon and that the movement was waiting to see what the government's policy would be. In any event, he refused to join a government that included the movement's great adversary, Amal. In actuality, the movement announced that it would not join the reconciliation government since it did not recognize the existing political-community regime as legitimate.

E. *Representation in the parliament*: Aware of the new rules of the game that were developing, and changes in public opinion in the community, Al Tufeili did not completely rule out the idea of joining the parliament. However, he opposed the government's proposal to appoint representatives to the parliament with the claim that it was an unfair step and that parliament members must be elected only by the people.

F. *Relations with the Supreme Shiite Council*: Al Tufeili claimed that the movement's troubled relations with the council were the result of the council's policies. In his opinion, a policy change toward joint activities would bode well for their future relations.

G. *Second Damascus Agreement*: He declared it a good agreement for the movement and emphasized his commitment to working toward its successful implementation, despite the possible difficulties posed by parties interested in torpedoing it. He assumed that all the problems related to the Lebanese Army's deployment in Iqlim al Tufah and Hezbollah's deployment in southern Lebanon would be solved in the spirit of the agreement.

H. *Hostages*: In accordance with the movement's policy on this issue since the mid-1980s, Al Tufeili denied having any connection to, or involvement with, anything related to hostages.

The demand that Al Tufeili should respond to his critics in the media and present the movement's positions on many issues was not a pointless exercise. It was the inevitable result of the dynamic reality that characterized the Lebanese system in the early 1990s and the first steps of implementing the Ta'if Accord. The identification of processes and changes in a shifting and complex situation, such as that in Lebanon, is an especially difficult task. However, formulating a new policy of action and having it absorbed by the target audience is no less complicated and, in some cases, it is more so. It demands conceptual changes that, at times, are so significant that the movement's fundamental principles must be annulled. Wide-ranging action must be taken to soften opposition so that the new policy is absorbed. All this is significantly more difficult for a movement such as Hezbollah, which is composed of various groups and operates in a competitive environment in both the community and in Lebanon. The need to formulate a policy of action for the movement on the many weighty dilemmas listed above, while maneuvering between centers of power within the movement, required virtuoso leadership, a high degree of unity in its senior levels, and extensive control over internal sources of opposition.

Toward the end of 1990s, differences of opinion and discrepancies in approach within the movement regarding the central dilemmas and the methods and policies that should be adopted in the ever-changing reality began to appear in Lebanese media reports on the movement. This can be seen in the questions that journalists asked the Hezbollah activists and, even more so, in the answers that they gave, trying to dispel these rumors as much as possible. The media coverage paints a picture of the situation by pointing out the qualitative differences in the approaches favored by the senior levels of the movement, from the extremists to the pragmatists, and the unrest within the movement. In December 1990, Al Tufeili was asked by a Lebanese reporter to confirm or deny the rumors of unrest within the Hezbollah movement. He denied the accuracy of the rumors. In June 1991, Qassem gave a similar, more thorough answer to that question. He claimed that the movement was operating in accordance with the same values that guided it in the past and completely rejected the rumors about the existence of ideological camps within the movement. He emphasized its tradition of hierarchical organizational discipline, noting that the movement had a single, unanimous platform and that the discipline in the movement is the basis for solidarity among its members. Therefore, in his opinion, the different versions of the platform expressed by various Hezbollah members are simply the result of their different styles of expressing themselves and should not be interpreted as discrepancies.[62] The sensitivity of the issue and the importance the leadership placed on it is evident in the extraordinary clarification Abbas al-Musawi made regarding certain statements of an imam from Jibshit. He emphasized that the imam's words had not expressed the official opinion of Hezbollah.[63]

The most concrete and significant step the movement took was to elect a new leadership. This step was a combination of the movement's own initiative and a response to external pressures. At the movement's second organizational confer-ence in May 1991, al-Musawi was elected to head the movement. To the outside world, the movement presented the election of the new leadership as a routine, democratic event; it made it clear that the election should not be interpreted as a change either in policy or in the movement and that the new leadership would continue to advance the same decisions and policies as the outgoing leadership. However, despite the reiteration of the familiar, old Hezbollah platform, small indications that the platform was in the process of changing began to appear.[64] The claim was already being made that al-Musawi's election as secretary general was part of a new trend that would include joining the Lebanese political system as an opposition party with a Lebanese character.[65]

The rumor mill, which continued grinding out tales of unrest and different camps within Hezbollah during the conference, posed a challenge that the new leadership had to tackle immediately. This was particularly true for al-Musawi, who had previously minimized his contact with the Lebanese media. In the initial months after his election, he appeared frequently in the media to clarify his positions and policies on many issues in the movement's agenda. The main issues that the new secretary general addressed on a routine basis were as follows:

A. *The Hezbollah elections*: Only days after being elected, al-Musawi declared that the elections were a routine operation conducted in accordance with the movement's bylaws, that the senior levels of the movement had not changed, and that all its members would remain in leadership positions after the elections.[66] This declaration filled his need to create a sense of continuity between the present, past, and the future. He also defined the topics he intended to address in the near future:

> At this stage, we are interested in the Palestine problem and liberating Jerusalem, as well as in maintaining the intifada and the Islamic resistance in Lebanon, in addition to activities within the Lebanese domestic arena. . . . Since the Ta'if Accord, we have said that this regime is rotten and does not serve the interests of the residents and the downtrodden of Lebanon. As it is a community-based regime, it must be destroyed down to its very founda-tions in order to be rehabilitated with a new base.[67]

On another occasion, al-Musawi clarified the movement's positions and principles in a few succinct sentences:

> We are one leadership that decides upon a path that is not open for discus-sion. We are walking in the path of Imam Khomeini and we see the problem of Israel and the conflict with the Israeli enemy as a topic on which all of our leaders and youth have an unequivocal opinion. That is to say, between us and the Israeli enemy there is only the riffle. Therefore, we reject any type of ceasefire, conciliation, or cooperation with the Israeli enemy. This has been the stance of the Hezbollah leadership from the beginning until this moment. The same is true of the developments in Lebanon. We have a clear policy and anyone who enters the ranks of our leadership only does so in order to realize that policy. This is a set policy that is not open to debate.

We are not a party or a community movement or anything like that. We hold fast to political principles that cannot be appealed and unchangeable ideological and philosophical principles. When the leadership changes or some person or other changes, that does not mean we have changed our foundations or ideas. We all believe in a single way and a single platform.[68]

B. *Ta'if Accord*: Al-Musawi, like his predecessor, summarily rejected the Ta'if Accord with the claim that it was based on the community approach and would not advance national reconciliation. However, he added, the movement would support any issue that would enhance the welfare of the citizens.[69] He accused the government of leading the residents astray and of adopting investment policies that discriminate against the population of the suburbs.[70] He proposed establishing a government based on the principles of resistance to Israel, social justice, and mutual respect instead of implementing the Ta'if Accord, which was based on exploiting the communities.[71]

C. *Disarming the militias*: Al-Musawi opposed this with the claim that the Hezbollah's weapons were used in the war of resistance against Israel and that the movement is not a militia.[72] This dilemma was still on the movement's agenda in 1992. Its spokespeople presented an uncompromising stand on it, as expressed by Qassem: "Whoever wants to take away our weapons must first liquidate us since the weapons are holy to us and we will not give them up and will continue to fight until all of our land is liberated."[73]

D. *Representation in the parliament*: The movement's participation in the Lebanese parliamentary elections, in his opinion, depended on the principles on which the Lebanese government would be based. Hezbollah would participate in the elections, he said, only if they were free and based on justice and mutual respect. He rejected the notion of entering the parliament through an appointee system, even if it were only temporary, with the argument that such a situation would make the appointee dependent upon the body that appointed it. In July 1991, he declared that if parliamentary elections were held in accordance with the will of the people, then the movement would find it necessary for its activists to contest the elections.[74]

E. *Serving in the Lebanese Army*: Al-Musawi rejected the idea of recruiting Hezbollah activists to serve in the Lebanese Army. In a July 1991 interview, however, he said that the movement would submit a list of Hezbollah candidates to serve in the army for two reasons: doing so furthers its overall approach of disseminating the message of Islam throughout the entire society, and [75] if the army remains in the Christians' control, they are liable to use the army to attack citizens.[76] In actuality, there were no signs of Hezbollah activists serving in the Lebanese Army.

F. *Hostages*: The secretary general addressed the issue of hostages right from his first days in office. He was willing only to discuss the release of the two Israelis, for the kidnapping of whom the movement had claimed responsibility. He denied having any connection to, or involvement with, hostages from Western countries. He fully exploited the Israeli release of dozens of Lebanese prisoners and the return of the bodies of the fallen Hezbollah activists to attract members to the movement and to improve the it's reputation in the community by presenting Hezbollah as working nonstop for the release of prisoners and return of bodies.[77] There are those who believe that al-Musawi became involved in the hostage issue out of a desire to improve the movement's reputation and to prepare it to join the new order.[78]

G. *The Islamic resistance*: The resistance to Israel was one of the major issues on the secretary general's agenda throughout his entire term. He frequently repeated the message that they must stand fast in their resistance to Israel until it disappeared. He even pushed his forces to increase the pace of their resistance activities and called on the state to participate in them.[79] At the same time, he was careful not to deviate from the limits of the framework established in the Damascus Agreements and took steps to open a joint operations room with Amal in southern Lebanon, in accordance with the agreement.[80] He sharply attacked the government, some of whose members saw the movement's existence as a barrier to reaching a solution via diplomatic channels, and claimed that removing the weapons of resistance from the south would actually encourage Israeli aggression. He believed that the way to defeat Israel was to forge a "society of resistance" based on the concept of self-sacrifice. He said that the Islamic resistance draws its legitimacy from the existence of a broad popular Islamic network in Lebanon that sees Jihad as a religious obligation.[81]

H. *Relations with the government*: Despite his disagreement with the government's policies, al-Musawi adopted a policy of openness and dialogue with the political system, owing to the movement's interests. As a result, the movement received an official authorization of sorts to conduct political activities and handle various aspects related to the daily life of the residents of Beirut's southern suburb.[82] This relationship opened Hezbollah up to pressure to curb its activities and had a direct impact on its status within the community. This pressure was partially successful—al-Musawi was forced to explain activities that deviated from the consensus. For example, in October 1991, he had to respond to accusations that the movement caused residents to flee from their homes due to its unsuccessful attempt to fire artillery into the security zone. He told his critics that the movement refrained from initiating exchanges of fire with the exception of cases that involved rescuing forces and rejected the charge against the movement, claiming that it was part of the campaign to besmirch and weaken the Islamic resistance.[83] Thus, during al-Musawi's term, the first signs of a policy of openness toward the Lebanese government appeared, which stemmed from an understanding of the process of change occurring in the community system and the domestic Lebanese system and from a desire to preserve and even expand the movement's sphere of influence within the community.[84]

The atmosphere of change and the need to integrate into the new order was supported as expected by Fadlallah. In January 1992, he declared that there had been a change in the Hezbollah movement's stance and that it was prepared to play the Lebanese political game and present a list of Hezbollah candidates to run in the upcoming elections, provided that the nation's right to express its opinion was guaranteed. He said that the change was due to "political considerations," but that the ideological line that characterized the movement had not changed. He also claimed that this was not a new phenomenon and that there has been a trend of Islamic movements participating in the political systems in their countries as a means of expanding their influence over public opinion and advancing their goal of seizing power.[85]

In conclusion, during the term of al-Musawi, which ended when he was killed by Israel in February 1992, some nine months after his election, Hezbollah was in the initial stages of preparing for the new order in Lebanon. Al-Musawi succeeded in internalizing and comprehending the rapid changes in Lebanese reality in general and within the Shiite community in particular. He took action to improve the movement's image and standing within the community by formulating new approaches to integrating the movement into the new Lebanese order, on one hand, and by stubbornly advocating the continuation of the resistance and the exclusion of the movement from the agreement to demilitarize militias on the other hand. His actions not only took the sting out of Amal's claims that Hezbollah was working against the national interest of Lebanon, but also improved the movement's image in the community and broadened the circle of its supporters. The best evidence of this is the movement's impressive success in the Lebanese parliamentary elections in August 1992.[86]

Hassan Nasrallah—a New Pattern of Leadership

Hassan Nasrallah succeeded al-Musawi as the secretary general of Hezbollah.[87] Like his predecessor, he spent his first few months in office establishing his leadership by emphasizing the direct connection between his approach and activities and al-Musawi's legacy, the movement's unchanging principles, and the leadership of Khomeini and his heirs. During Nasrallah's term, Hezbollah continued the process of transition from radicalism to pragmatism that resulted in the movement's entrance into the Lebanese political framework. This was one of the most influential topics on Nasrallah's agenda during his first year in office. He needed to address it in order to operate simultaneously on several levels (movement, community, and Lebanon) to promote the election of the movement's representatives to parliament. On the internal-movement level, he needed to dissolve opposition, clarify the change, and lead the movement to absorb it. On the community level, he fought to gain the community's support. Finally, on the Lebanese level, he needed to stand watch in order to guarantee the realization of the movement's interests and to prevent legislation that would harm the community and the movement.

Unlike his predecessors, Nasrallah appeared in the media frequently. He made optimal use of his strong rhetorical abilities and exploited the platform that the media provided to disseminate the movement's messages to various target audiences. The Hezbollah of 1992—and Nasrallah in particular—was more aware of the media's influence. Of himself, Nasrallah said that, before he was elected to his position, he dealt with organizational matters behind the scenes and rarely appeared in the media.[88] This did not prevent him from using the media wisely from his very first days as secretary general. At the same time, he took advantage of the movement's and Lebanese channels of communication to spread his message to the broadest audience possible, both supporters and opponents. In his appearances, he would voice the same stances and messages repeatedly in clear, easily comprehendible, and fluent words. His speeches and statements on topics on the movement's agenda accurately reflected how he—and apparently most of his colleagues in the leadership—viewed the movement's principles, position, and situation vis-à-vis those of its opponents and the surroundings. In his first public appearance as the movement's secretary general, he touched on all of the points that appear below, establishing himself as the movement's leader at the same time.

On the personal level, Nasrallah focused on two issues. The first issue was to establish his status as the leader. He emphasized that he had been elected "unanimously" to head the movement soon after the announcement of al-Musawi's death.[89] The second issue that of continuity, affected him directly as a leader, but he used the first-person plural when he spoke about it as a technique of emphasizing to his audience that he was continuing in the path of his predecessors. "The policies adopted by the late secretary general were not his personal policies, but were determined by the collective leadership of the movement—the Shura Council. We will continue to work for the same things as the late secretary general," he said.[90] In an interview a month later, he emphasized the same point using the first-person singular: "I will adopt the line adopted by al-Musawi and I will work in accordance with the line that the Hezbollah has always followed."[91]

On the movement and community level, Nasrallah's messages were intended to establish the movement's status and image in the future Lebanese system by presenting Hezbollah as a popular Lebanese movement with roots, a tradition, and goals:

A. With regard to the movement's roots, Nasrallah emphasized the movement's connection to Lebanon and the fact that it is not a passing phenomenon: "I would like to emphasize that the Hezbollah in Lebanon is not an atypical or ephemeral movement, but a movement with deep roots in the Lebanese people that is fighting for the land."[92] A few days later, he responded to a question by saying, "We are not a military group, but a popular and political movement and we have our own political program for how things in Lebanon should operate."[93] These statements, which are also important on the internal movement level, contain an extremely important message regarding the movement's relationship with the Lebanese system. At another point, he emphasized that "from time immemorial the Hezbollah has fought to defend the land and liberty of Lebanon . . . . The Islamic resistance will continue to make a sacrifice for Lebanon."[94] During the Lebanese parliamentary elections, Nasrallah declared, "The Hezbollah will play a part in all of the affairs of the state . . . . We have a comprehensive plan that covers all aspects of the life of the simple people . . . ." [95] He deemphasized the pan-Islamic approach and based his stance on that of

Fadlallah, who saw the Hezbollah as a Lebanese movement with ties to Iran.[96] He said:

> For the leadership of the Islamic revolution, keeping the faith does not con-
> tradict the fact that I am a Lebanese citizen since we believe in the authority
> of the religious sage and through our religious commitment we are able to
> provide important services to the Lebanese people . . . . It is not a secret that
> we see ourselves as part of the Islamic revolution and are bonded to it in
> friendship and cooperation.[97]

B. Regarding the movement's goals, Nasrallah emphasized two goals that
were not only on the leadership's agenda, but also determined their priority.
The first was continuing the resistance and the second was fighting community-based discrimination. The concessions to Israel were the reason for
the great devastation in Lebanon and only resistance would restore
Lebanon's sovereignty and honor, he said. Thus, the only answer was to liberate Lebanon from the occupation of Israel and every citizen of Lebanon
had a responsibility to do so. In his opinion, the resistance's success
depended on its ability to use its power to implement an integrated policy of action that included waging a war of attrition that would make the
price of remaining in Lebanon too high for Israel and destroy Israeli society from within and overcoming the differences in strength between Israel
and the movement by using distinctive fighting tactics and to strengthen
the steadfastness of the Lebanese population in the face of Israeli pressure.
He boasted of the resistance's most significant strategic achievements in
the region thus far, which included causing Israel to withdraw to the border of the security zone in 1985, preventing progress in the normalization
process between Israel and the Arabic-Muslim world, and even serving as a
model for the development of the Palestinian intifada.[98]

C. Like his two predecessors, Nasrallah was asked to confirm or deny rumors
of internal struggles and different camps within the movement, and like
them, he claimed, "The talk of streams within the Hezbollah is inspired by
various intelligence sources or based on the speculations of journalists in
media reports."[99] He emphasized that the movement's leadership is "a collective leadership that is engaged in a continual process of learning from
our past experiences in order to improve weak points, if there are any."[100]

On the domestic Lebanese level, Nasrallah considered continuing the movement's policy of openness to the Lebanese system as vital to advancing its status
within the community. Therefore, despite his extensive criticism of the conciliation process, which clashed with some of the movement's principles, he was careful to emphasize his commitment to the process as part of his efforts to dispel the
idea current on the Lebanese street—that Hezbollah intended to turn Lebanon
into an Islamic state through a revolutionary act. In his words:

> "There are those who wish to distort the Hezbollah's image and to present it as
> a source that wants to bring about an Islamic republic by force. We believe in the

principles of Islam, but these statements are nothing but an attempt to distort the Hezbollah's image[101]

He added that despite the fact that the movement rejected the Ta'if Accord, it supported any program that would lead to the end of the internal warfare.[102]

After his election, Nasrallah was asked about his policies regarding the possibility of the movement's integration into the new Lebanese political system. He gave an ambiguous response that could be interpreted to mean either that, unlike his predecessor, he had not yet made a decision about whether the movement would contest the parliamentary elections or that, for tactical reasons, he had decided not to reveal the internal workings of the movement and put the cart before the horse. For example, in March 1992, he responded to a question from the *Al-Hayat* newspaper by saying,

> We are seriously considering the issue of elections since in principle we support the idea of holding parliamentary elections in Lebanon as soon as possible so that representatives can be elected for the Lebanese nation after 17 years of not having elections. We support holding elections even if the Hezbollah does not participate in them and we will announce our decision on this issue in the future.[103]

Even when he was asked to clarify his stance on this question in May 1992, very shortly before the elections, he responded, "The Hezbollah has not yet made a final decision about participating in the parliamentary elections."[104]

Integration into the Lebanese Political System—the Reasons, the Explanations, and the Justifications

Lebanon had been preparing for the parliamentary elections since 1991 owing to the fact that the elections were an important ingredient in the new social order that was beginning to take shape. Hezbollah, like the other powers operating in Lebanon, needed to reevaluate the situation and formulate policies and operational plans in response to the processes occurring in both the Lebanese arena and the community. On various occasions in 1991, al-Musawi had declared that Hezbollah would participate in the national conciliation process in Lebanon, including the parliamentary elections, provided that the elections were fair and just and did not conflict with the movement's principles. At the same time, he began to implement a policy of dialogue and openness toward the government and other powers in Lebanon.[105] The atmosphere of change also began to occur from the bottom and found expression even in the movement's strongholds. In January 1992, Fadlallah claimed that Hezbollah's stance had changed and that it was ready to participate in the Lebanese political game.[106] In November 1997, Nasrallah revealed to his audience that the policy of openness had begun in 1990–1991 and added:

> No one can claim that the policy of openness is skipping a step since in general things happen gradually. The Hezbollah's participation in the 1992 elections was a very important element in the policy of openness.[107]

Qassem's book (*Hezbollah—Al-Manhag Al-Tajriba Al-Mustakbal*, the Arabic edition) reveals some of the processes, questions, and dilemmas surrounding the movement's decision to participate in the elections. He wrote that topics such as stabilizing the security situation in Lebanon, restoring national institutions so they could function normally, and the Lebanese system's handling of the Ta'if Accord's continued implementation and the parliamentary election also aroused discussion in various forums in the community and the movement. As a result, the Shura Council formed a twelve-member internal committee to formulate recommendations on the following dilemmas. What is the significance of joining the parliament for the movement, considering the parliament is built on the Ta'if Accord, and what are the benefits of doing so? What responsibilities would the movement face in the event that its representatives are elected to the parliament? What are the costs and benefits of joining the parliament and to what extent would this step effect the resistance?[108]

The committee found advantages and disadvantages and decided—following a vote of 10:2—to recommend participating in the elections. In the committee's opinion, the movement's resistance activities were likely to benefit if the movement were to serve in the Lebanese parliament since the movement could then use the parliament as a platform for promoting its policies. In addition, a presence in parliament would give the resistance legal standing and help it in its struggles with elements in the political system. The committee also claimed that a presence in parliament would enable the movement to advance the interests of the nation in a variety of areas, such health and welfare, since the movement would be able to influence the allocation of the national budget and new legislation. In addition, the parliament would provide the movement with a platform for cooperating with, and advancing openness to, other communities and religions. The negatives, according to the committee, included participating in a parliament that did not have an Islamic character and the fact that they expected to encounter deceitful opposition from the parliament members. In the end, the committee decided to recommend participating in the elections; this decision reflected the opinion prevalent among the movement's leadership.[109]

The elections were scheduled for August 1992, which meant that Hezbollah needed to make an operative decision about whether or not to participate in the political system and take the appropriate steps. At the beginning of that month, the secretary general revealed the names of the movement's candidates for parliament at a press conference. Ibrahim Al-Amin, a senior member of Hezbollah, headed the list that was composed of well-known, influential figures. Nasrallah also announced that Hezbollah would cooperate with other movements whose political platforms were similar to its own, irrespective of the community they represented.[110] This announcement to the press launched the campaign of the last movement to enter the parliamentary race. After it was made, the movement expanded its activities to promote its candidates. In the governmental sphere, it strove for a change in the election laws. In the contest for Lebanese public opinion, it decided to present itself as a social movement that fought for the fair representation of the underprivileged, irrespective of the community they hailed from, and as the director of the legitimate battle to force Israel out of Lebanon. Internally, that is, before its own activists and the Shiite community, the movement emphasized its devotion to its ideological path and to Islam and justified its decision to run for parliament on moral, religious, and social grounds. These messages were disseminated to the appropriate target audiences through the media and all other possible channels, including the Lebanese and movement's media networks, mass election rallies, sermons at Friday prayers in mosques, candidates' campaign appearances, parlor meetings, and even a dialogue with the government and leaders of other communities.[111]

To a large extent, the movement's decision to contest the elections was a decision to take a risk at one of its most critical periods. A failure in the elections was liable to have a boomerang effect and endanger the movement's existence.[112] Why then did it decide to take this path? Did it have other options? It is difficult to provide definitive answers to these questions owing to the unavailability, for obvious reasons, of inside information on all the considerations that affected the movement's decision to participate in the election. That said, the activities and statements of the movement's leadership, as well as the propaganda that accompanied the election campaign and continued throughout the 1990s, show that the community's public opinion played a significant role in the leadership's decision to participate in the elections, despite the danger of creating a rift within the movement. It should be emphasized that the difference between a movement that generates change in the opinions of its supporters and a movement that is influenced by the opinions of its community is very small. Comments by Mohammad Fneich, one of the Hezbollah candidates for parliament, show that Hezbollah tried to grasp the stick from both ends to satisfy its different audiences. He made it clear that the movement tried to adapt itself to the new reality without compromising its ideological goals.[113]

The research that a faculty member of the American University of Beirut (AUB) conducted in June 1993, revealed a surprising picture of the divergent positions and opinions in Lebanon's Shiite community. A survey of students that a researcher named Hilal Khashan conducted in Beirut a year earlier supports some of the data found in the AUB study. The AUB study surveyed a representative sample of the Shiite community and found that Hezbollah was the most popular party: 41 percent of those surveyed supported Hezbollah as compared with 31 percent who supported Amal. A small percentage, some 12 percent, of those surveyed defined themselves first as Shiites, as compared with the 43 percent that defined themselves as Lebanese. Furthermore, 24 percent supported the establishment of an Islamic state in Lebanon, while 41 percent preferred the existing political system, and 33 percent supported adopting a Western system of government. The findings of the study demonstrated that Hezbollah and Amal depended upon similar social strata and that their supporters consisted of groups and individuals from all levels of society.[114] Even if the findings of this study were not placed on the table of the movement's decision-makers during their discussions on changing policy, it appears that they were sensitive to public opinion in the community and had drawn similar conclusions.[115] Beyond that, statements by senior Hezbollah figures from the mid-1990s onward show that the movement was not only merely aware of the direction the wind was blowing in the community with which it was in daily contact through its various institutions and organs, but also actually relied on surveys and analyses of the situation, which it conducted both routinely and before making major decisions. In a January 1997 interview, Nasrallah said, "Before the 1992 elections, we conducted a data survey in all the areas in which we would have an electoral presence."[116] Similar surveys were conducted before the 1996 elections and the 1998 municipal elections. Therefore, it is not surprising that the movement's propaganda system and its messages were fashioned based on the movement's understanding of public opinion in the community in order to provide a response that would satisfy all its members, from the radicals to the relative moderates.

At times, the movement's leadership and candidates provided clear, unequivocal answers to the questions raised above and other questions, while at other times they disseminated ambiguous hints through all the channels at their disposal. Their arguments appeared gradually throughout 1992, with increasing frequency from May onward. In general, it can be said that Hezbollah appears to have decided to participate in the elections in response to a rational analysis and prudent, shrewd evaluation of the changing factors in general and particularly in the in the movement's arena of operation. These factors included the new reality taking shape in Lebanon, changing sentiments in the Shiite community, the movement's standing vis-à-vis that of its opponent and the new Lebanese political system, and concern that regional and internal pressure would succeed in isolating and weakening the movement.[117] In August 1992, Qassem said:

> In Lebanon, we must work within the framework of the political situation . . . . When the Hezbollah isn't in this framework, it loses all influence . . . . We are a movement that wants change. We want to change the situation and one way to do that, no matter how many limitations it involves, is entering the parliament.[118]

Fadlallah was even sharper and clearer than Qassem on this. In an interview with a reporter from the *Al-'Ahd* on the eve of the elections, he claimed that the only way to break the tightening stranglehold on the Islamic opposition and Jihad was to participate fully in the Lebanese political system.[119]

Until May 1992, Nasrallah adopted a hazy line that could be interpreted in two ways—he supported holding free parliamentary elections in principle, but refrained from responding to questions as to whether the movement would participate in the elections.[120] The fatwa that Ayatollah Ali Khamenahi, the Supreme Leader of Iran, issued in May 1992 regarding participating in the elections paved the way for Hezbollah to do so. The fatwa provided the movement's leaders with a religious stamp of approval and moral justification in the community and made it possible for them to claim, on one hand, that the movement was remaining faithful to its ideological path and vision and, on the other hand, to emphasize that entering the parliament would help further resistance activities. Qassem, the deputy secretary general, one of the leaders who shaped the propaganda campaign and the head of the central committee formed for the elections, clarified this in the speech he gave at the height of the campaign in Nabatia. He said:

> There were those that said, "We are disturbed that the Hezbollah will enter the parliament, but we are also satisfied since the parliamentary activities will in fact prevent the resistance activities." Well, we say to them, "Don't worry since you are

not facing a mere political party and a group that changes with the circumstances and international platforms or those in office. You are facing a nation whose leaders are Mohammed and El-Hussein."[121]

There is no dispute that the movement's decision to participate in the elections had significant implications on its future steps and required a change in the thinking of its activists and supporters. The real meaning of this decision was the revocation, or at least downplaying, of the pan-Islamic and revolutionary policies that had characterized the movement in the 1980s and their replacement with a new pragmatic policy that took into consideration the rules of the game in the Lebanese political system. The fashioners of this policy adopted new operational patterns to "seize control" in a gradual process and integrate from above via institutions and from below via welfare and movement activities in the Shiite community and in other communities in Lebanon. It was clear to the movement's leaders that serving in the parliament contradicted the revolutionary, antiestablishment approach, but it provided the movement with status and legitimacy within and beyond the community, a public platform for disseminating the Islamic message, a means of preserving and advancing the status of the resistance, as well as a base for establishing frameworks for cooperation with other powers in Lebanon.[122] The movement's secretary general summed up the decision with the following words: "I don't see any contradiction between participating in the elections and serving in the parliament and between continuing the battle for your true rights."[123]

An analysis of the speeches and interviews published in the second half of 1992 reveals the existence of a propaganda line in which the messages are intended to justify participating in the elections, to gain the support of the community, and to bridge the gap between the movement's ideological values and the decision to participate in the election. This line was formulated in response to three significant issues that occupied the movement's activists and its inner circle of supporters: first, the fear of a change in the ideological platform; second, the clear deviation from the moral commandment to reject the legitimacy of the Lebanese political system; and third, the extent of the expected benefit of changing the platform. This line was formulated to conquer public opinion in the movement by utilizing the phrase "cost-benefit" since the benefit expected from the movement was greater than the payment it had to make. In addition, this line was designed to convince the community and the Lebanese arena that the movement was changing its face and preferred an open, pragmatic policy to radicalism.

The response to the first dilemma included messages to relax the audience and promises that the movement would continue to be devoted to its ideological path and to Islam in all events. In January 1992, Fadlallah said that the change occurring in the movement was in policy only and that the ideological framework would not be changed by participating in the elections.[124] Statements such as this, which emphasized the movement's commitment to its ideological line, were also made by the movement's candidates for parliament. For example, one of them said, "I will continue the struggle out of devotion to the principles of Islam within the walls of the Lebanese parliament and anywhere else I find myself."[125]

The secretary general also was called on to address this issue. He did so clearly, emphasizing the movement's devotion to its principles and way. In an interview published in August 1992, he said:

> From time immemorial the Hezbollah has fought to defend the land and liberty of Lebanon. However, we do not intend to waiver in our resistance or to adopt a defeatist attitude. The Hezbollah also does not intend to sink into the swamp of petty haggling that is the Lebanese political system or to abandon shaping awareness of the Arab-Israeli conflict. The Islamic resistance will continue to make a sacrifice for Lebanon.

At another point, he added, "The Hezbollah will continue to man its positions in the battlefield and in the political field."[126] This issue also dominated the statements made by Qassem. On the eve of the elections, he declared,

> Participating in the parliament will not bring about a change in the principles that we exalt and we will continue to fight for . . . our struggle in the parliament will be conducted at the same time as the struggle outside it. I want to emphasize that our participation in the elections will not cause us to give up our principles and there is no reason for fear on that front.[127]

In October 1992, he rejected the claim that the entry into the parliament was an attempt to "tame" the Hezbollah.[128]

Fneich, who was elected to represent Hezbollah in parliament, presented an original and interesting formula to ease the fears of the movement's supporters. He claimed that, on the one hand, armed resistance to the Israeli occupation is the highlight of all types of resistance (such as cultural, political, economic, and so on). On the other hand, the other types of resistance should not be overlooked since they support the armed resistance and draw their strength from it. He explained,

> Our entrance to parliament is one of the types of resistance on the political level. That is because it is natural that the resistance fighters have a political base to back them up. And that is because the armed resistance needs assistance in the political arena . . . . Our entrance to parliament will be a source of assistance to the armed resistance to the occupation.[129]

The response to the second dilemma, which stemmed from the fear that the movement was deviating from the religious-moral commandments that had guided it until that point, was making the movement's decision valid according to religious law by harnessing it to sources of religious authority in the movement and Iran. The most important religious stamp of approval that the movement's leadership attained to justify participating in the elections was the fatwa that Khamenahi issued in May 1992, supporting the decision.[130] This provided the movement's leadership with a formula to bridge the apparent contradiction between the religious commandments and the political process. Thus, Qassem could declare, during one of the demonstrations the movement organized, "The Hezbollah is participating in the elections in accordance with a political decision that is at one with Islam and the will of the people."[131] This statement is especially important as it contains an additional explanation for participating in the elections—the will of the people. Fadlallah, who was a senior religious authority in the Shiite community, supported the movement's decision and claimed that penetrating the institutions of authority is liable to serve the movement's interest and frustrate attempts to constrict the movement's footsteps.[132]

The response to the third dilemma, regarding the expected benefits of entering the political system, was integrated into the movement's platform and made prominent in its leaders' statements. They promised that participating in the political system would not only advance the realization of the movement's vision in the long term, but also would advance its short-term goals. Qassem emphasized that Hezbollah had not abandoned its strategy, but changed tactics since "entering the parliament is not our ultimate goal . . . . It doesn't erase the Hezbollah strategy, but gains us political capabilities which will help us achieve our goals."[133] At another point, he pledged that the movement would fulfill its promises to its activists and continue its activities against Israel and the United States.[134] Nasrallah connected the decision to participate in the elections to the will of the people. He said:

> The Hezbollah's obstinacy on the issue of parliamentary elections stems from its desire for an opportunity to establish a parliament of all the communities of Lebanon in accordance with the will of the people and desire not to sign an agreement similar to the May 17 agreement with the Israeli enemy . . . . The movement's goal is not to allow administrative corruption to run rampant in Lebanon.[135]

A weighty claim was added to this in the interview that Qassem gave to *Al-'Ahd*:

> The Hezbollah has decided it has a responsibility to take steps to provide representation for the stream that fights against the Israeli enemy, which will be the vanguard of the resistance movement to Israeli occupation and bring together around it all of the elements fighting the Zionist enemy. We came to the conclusion that, unlike in the past, participating in the elections will enable us to send representatives to parliament who will voice our positions without having to relinquish our principles.[136]

At another point, Nasrallah said that Hezbollah had decided to participate in the elections in order to advance the interests of the downtrodden by legislative action in parliament, on one hand, and, on the other hand, to clarify to the movement's opponents, and particularly to the West, that Hezbollah was not "a small group or some local organization."[137]

The propaganda system's messages in preparation for and after the elections were intended to bring about the necessary change in mentality in the movement's nucleus of activists and supporters, convey the importance of the decision to the movement and the community, and convey the expected benefits of the decision, that is, to continue to achieve the movement's goals. These messages were the base of the platform designed to appeal to the Shiite community and the downtrodden of other communities. Along with the call to continue the resistance, end political corruption, and bring about social justice for the Shiite community, the platform included slogans to appeal to Lebanese society such as the

return of displaced persons to their homes and a readiness for dialogue and cooperation between communities. The platform was based on a broad common
denominator that enabled various groups and individuals inside and outside
the community to support the movement's representatives in the parliamentary
elections. The platform itself is evidence of the extent of influence public opinion
in the community had on the movement. Its messages were formulated to be
inclusive and easily absorbed by the ears of the community and other segments of
the Lebanese population. One example of this is the mollifying messages woven
into the speech of a member of Hezbollah's political bureau at an election rally in
Al-Sharkiya in August 1992. He said,

> The Hezbollah did not decide to participate in the election in order to compete
> against other candidates or to win additional seats to use to gain political power, but
> out of a desire to defend the honor and rights of the residents and to defend the
> land, which some want to present to the Zionist enemy on a silver platter.[138]

Another claim, which was extremely interesting, was made by the Hezbollah
parliamentary candidate in Beirut. He appealed to the city's entire Muslim population, particularly the young, by promising to cooperate with them and do the
groundwork to enable them to attain a position of influence. He said,

> If I am elected as the Hezbollah representative for the Beirut electoral region, I will
> work to revoke the community policy. We will cooperate with the young generation
> of Muslims so that they can attain influence in the state without suffering from dis-
> crimination and community hegemony.[139]

The platform that the movement presented at numerous rallies and conferences
across Lebanon and in the movement's and Lebanese media included the following
points:[140]

A. *Supporting the resistance*: This was not the first issue on the movement's
   platform for nothing. The movement discerned that there was a broad
   consensus in Lebanon regarding the resistance and used this to expand the
   circle of its supporters in the elections and to justify participating in them.
   It called on all Lebanese citizens from all the communities to support the
   continuation of the resistance through its activities and to support the
   steadfast, brave residents of the south. The platform called for establishing
   a fighting society, based on the principle of sacrifice, and for working
   together to force Israel out of Lebanon.[141]
B. *Eliminating community-based politics*: The second most important point
   on the platform was eliminating community-based politics that was responsible for the continuing discrimination against the Shiite community. This
   point was formulated and presented in a broad, inclusive manner so that
   it would appeal to other target audiences.[142]
C. *Release of hostages*: The platform also included a demand that the government take immediate action to free the Lebanese hostages. This was
   included due to the understanding that it was likely to increase support for

the movement in the Shiite community in general and particularly among residents of the south since the hostage issue was closer to their hearts.[143]

D.   *Return of displaced persons*: This was another social issue that the movement championed to establish itself as the leader of the struggle to improve the social status of the underprivileged of all communities. It was part of the clear, political platform whose principles Qassem presented in his speech at the election rally in Nabatia. It included returning all displaced persons to their homes, including those from the security zone.[144]

E.   *Cooperation*: This clause became an important component of the movement's political platform and lessened the impact of all those who wanted to isolate and weaken the movement. It included a call for an agreement of cooperation between the movement and Lebanese parties that opposed the government. This step was intended to improve the movement's standing and enable it to advance its resistance activities. In addition, the movement fielded a joint list with other parties in places where it calculated it could gain a significant political advantage from doing so. The most remarkable and significant cooperation was that with the movement's opponent, Amal. Qassem claimed that this cooperation was intended to foil the activities of troublemakers and to prove that the south was united by the resistance. It is reasonable to conclude that the Hezbollah leaders calculated that cooperating with Amal in southern Lebanon would be more beneficial than competing with it owing to Amal's status in that region, and so they fielded a joint parliamentary list there.[145] In addition, Syrian pressure to move in that direction was an influence; indeed, at the end of the day, Amal and Hezbollah would not have been able to join forces in the south if it were not for Syrian pressure.

The success of the Hezbollah candidates in the parliamentary elections strengthened the stand of the leaders who spearheaded the change, established the movement's status, and improved its image in the community and the Lebanese political system.[146] This provided the movement with tools and additional means, such as the platform of the parliament, to advance its goals in the short- and medium-term. At the same time, the process of change widened the gap between the extremists and the pragmatists. The internal debate in the movement continued to intensify until July 1997, when former Secretary General Al Tufeili, the most senior member of the leadership to oppose the changes within the movement, led a group of radicals to leave Hezbollah.

Summary

The Hezbollah leadership's decision to join the Lebanese political system was born of an understanding that the movement reached during its two-year, blood-drenched war of survival against Amal and following a meticulous examination of the expected advantages and disadvantages of this process. Control of the street, that is, the public opinion of the community was, and remains, the real reason for the battles the movement waged both through violence and through competition that swung from dialogue to restrained struggle. The April 1988 commitment toward rectifying its relations with Amal reflected Hezbollah's confidence (which proved wrong) in the extent and stability of support for it in Lebanon's Shiite community. The end of the war allowed it to invest its resources in improving its standing in the community and expanding its infrastructure in preparation for the expected competition for sources of power and influence in the community and the right of representing the community in the Lebanese political system.

The community's weight in Hezbollah's considerations became even greater when the Lebanese political system began to take the first steps to implement the Ta'if Accord and decided to hold parliamentary elections. The movement's leadership had good reason to express the need to participate in the Lebanese political system—concern that the movement would find itself excluded from the circle of real influence and on the margins of society and the community. Therefore, the real battle for the community's public opinion was the one that was decided in the voting booth. To that end, the movement used all the tools at its disposal, from conducting public opinion polls of the community and using the rousing rhetoric formulated by Nasrallah to playing down the radical Islamic approach in the movement's original platform and adopting an inclusive, political tone that was easily absorbed by Lebanese ears.

The impressive success in the parliamentary elections contributed to the movement's efforts of establishing its reputation as a renewed movement, but at the same time placed a complex challenge before it: proving to its supporters that the price it had paid on the way to the parliament was semantic only and that the movement had not abandoned or changed its ideology or the path of resistance. The Shiite community demanded that the movement prove and clarify the extent of the veracity of the pragmatic image that it was trying to project to the public as well as the nature of its relations with the Lebanese state, considering its special ties with Iran.

Political Institutionalization and Public Discourse—Adaptation and Legitimization

Introduction

The importance of the Shiite community's public opinion was very evident in the conduct of the Hezbollah movement in the 1990s. It worked, not without errors, toward the shaping of a policy that would support the resistance on the one hand and establish the legitimacy and the Lebanese character of the movement on the other hand while it blurred its image as a radical pan-Islamic movement. The voices of the electors in the ballot boxes determined, to a large degree, the legitimacy of the movement, its power versus the Amal movement, and its ability to influence the distribution of the public goods.

The Political Purview—the Campaign for the Shiite Community's Public Opinion between the 1992 and the 1996 Elections

The results of the 1996 elections to the Lebanese parliament astonished Hezbollah. Its power declined from eight representatives in the parliament to only six. Oppositely, Amal, headed by Nabih Berri, succeeded in actually increasing the number of its members in parliament significantly. A demand for a thorough examination and mutual accusations were only a few of the actions taken by the movement.[1] However, there were those who had noted the first signs of a disconnection between the movement and its audiences already in late 1994. Lebanese journalists and commentators argued that the fighting against Israel's security zone came at the expense of the treatment of social problems.[2] Between the two election campaigns, a feeling was growing in the high echelons of the movement that the support it enjoyed from the members of the Shiite community and other communities across Lebanon originated mostly from its role as the standard bearer for the resistance against the Israeli occupation of Lebanon. This is how Hassan Nasrallah expressed himself at the launch of the second campaign for the parliamentary election: "We hold the opinion that the people who voted for us in 1992 did not do so due to the services we gave . . . but due to support of the resistance."[3]

The issue of the resistance stood first in the list of priorities in the 1992 elections and was, since then, consistently maintained as such—both declaratively and operationally. Therefore, there is no wonder that in Hezbollah's fourth organizational conference (July 1995), it was decided to allot half of the movement's resources to promote the resistance.[4] The movement's assessment, based, inter alia, on the results of polls it conducted on the eve of both election campaigns, held that the popular support of the movement is on a trend of constant increase since the 1992 elections.[5]

Lebanese government elements, opponents, and commentators referred to the expansion of the popular support base of the movement. In February 1995, the Lebanese minister of defense commented that the movement represents a large popular political trend, which has roots and shoots in the public, and should be expressed in the government. Even Rafik Al-Hariri, on the eve of the 1996 elections, held the opinion that the movement had attained wide popular support as a result of Israel's activities in operation "Grapes of Wrath."[6]

In the beginning of 1997, Nasrallah revealed details about his conduct in the 1996 election campaign. He argued that the failure in the first election cycle in the mountainous regions and in Beirut led to his decision to cooperate with Amal. He emphasized that the popularity of the movement among the Shiite and Islamic public, as well as other publics, is on a rising trend, even though this was not reflected in the ballots.[7] Abdallah Kassir, one of Hezbollah's delegates in parliament, did well in expressing the sentiments of the high echelons of the movement in light of the disappointing results:

> With regard to the popularity of Hezbollah after the last elections, we admit here that there was embarrassment and shock following the election campaign with regard to our base of popular support. . . . Hezbollah is currently trying to overcome this crisis . . . . We will work toward the renewal of mutual trust and restore the relations between Hezbollah and its supporters.[8]

Kassir emphasized, for a reason, the movement's intention to work toward renewing mutual trust and restoring the movement's relationship with its audiences. The Shiite community was the main, and the foremost, environment of activity for the movement. It influenced its activity and was influenced by it. It constituted the base and the soil on which the movement grew and expanded during all the years of its activity. Evidence of the importance of the Shiite community's public opinion, and the degree of its influence over the movement, is found in abundance in the statements of its seniors and in the manner of its conduct between the two election campaigns, and after them.[9]

Emphasis of Achievements from Parliamentary Activity as a Means of Establishing the Conceptual Change among Its Audiences

The first task facing the decision makers of the movement, following its success in the 1992 elections, was to prove to its voters that its entry into the political system was not harmful, but actually helpful in promoting its aims. Nasrallah emphasized to his electorate that parliament served the goals of the movement and provided it with a stage for the propagation of its messages.[10] He praised the members of the Al-Wafa in the parliament and declared that the movement would continue operating in this arena, despite it being a new one for it.[11] His deputy, Naim Qassem, explained that the movement's entry into parliament stemmed from its desire to express its power in the Lebanese and regional systems.[12] The necessity of Hezbollah's presence in parliament received backing from Fadlallah, who argued that this presence served an Islamic interest and that it should be exploited as much as possible until the reign was seized. As far as he was concerned, even sitting in the government was possible in principle, but subject to certain provisions.[13] The achievements of the movement in parliament were emphasized in a speech by Nasrallah on the eve of the 1996 elections. He emphasized that the movement had kept the promises made to its constituents in the last elections and that it had attained the social and organizational goals it had set for itself.[14]

The assimilation of change among the movement's activists and in the Shiite community was based on two complementing directions of activity. At the practical level, "purges" were made in the high echelons of the movement and at the intermediate levels. When they ended, the objectors to the change were removed, including the former secretary general, Subhi Al-Tufayli.[15] At the propaganda level, Nasrallah strove to present a unified and convincing front in the movement to emphasize its achievements and work to promote the needs of its constituents.[16] Among the topics that stood out in this propaganda discourse between the movement and its audiences, between the two election campaigns, the following fundamental issues should be emphasized:

1. *Promoting the resistance*: The propaganda line taken by Nasrallah on this issue all along the 1990s was based on three main messages: that the preparations for elections and the movement's parliamentary work did not harm the resistance activities, that the resistance was the movement's top priority, and that there was a trend of increase in the quantity and quality of its military actions.[17] In February 1995, he said, "Today the enemy admits that in 1994 the resistance's operations were more important, fierce, numerous, and valuable from the standpoint of quantity and quality, than those of 1993. Every year, between 1991 and 1994, surpassed its predecessor."[18] In December 1995, Nasrallah emphasized that the apprehensions prevalent in the public opinion were proved false, and that, in a perspective of three years, a qualitative and quantitative rise was seen in the resistance operations and in its popular and political base of support.[19] He argued that "Al-Wafa has become the mouthpiece of the resistance in parliament, and outside it" and made it clear to his listeners that the movement's parliamentary activity actually benefited the resistance and gave it the necessary popular backing.[20] The activities of the faction in parliament contributed, in the opinion of the movement's leadership, to the promotion of the official recognition in the resistance, to the unique status of southern Lebanon, and to the allotment of assistance budgets to its inhabitants. The statements of Prime Minister Al-Hariri, one of the main opponents of the resistance, that the resistance would not

be disarmed as long as Israel stayed on Lebanese soil, comprised an irrefutable proof of this argument.[21] The movement recruited on its side the Lebanese political system, which, either willingly or out of a lack of choice, stood, at least outwardly, behind the resistance and presented a unified front that emphasized the commitment of the government of Lebanon to the resistance as long as the occupation lasted.[22]

2. *Establishing an Islamic regime*: The leaders of the movement were aware of the existence of two positions in the public opinion of the Shiite community: one that did not recognize the legitimacy of the existing government and wished to establish an Islamic regime through a revolutionary act, and second that worked toward changing the regime through an evolutionary process within the framework of its institutions. The messages of the movement were shaped to provide a formula that would bridge the different opinions. For example, in May 1993, Qassem declared, "Our participation in parliament does not necessarily mean recognition in the Lebanese government, but the waging of a struggle for change."[23] Notwithstanding, a trend of change in the messages of the movement was evident as a consequence of its integration into the Lebanese political system and from the desire to portray the image of a Lebanese national movement. In parallel to the parliamentary activity, the movement continued the propaganda line with which it started before the elections. Its gist was that Islam is the best solution for Lebanon and that the movement does not intend to impose it by force. Hezbollah of 1994 marketed itself as a tolerant movement that stopped all expression of religious coercion, even in the southern suburb of Beirut.[24] Qassem emphasized the rationality and tolerance embodied in the movement's attitude. He said that the Lebanese rejected the movement's suggestion to adopt Islam owing to the complex situation with the various communities in the state, but still the movement would be willing to participate with all the powers in Lebanon in establishing a regime based on dialogue, which would reflect justice and equality for all and fit the principles of the movement.[25] Nasrallah, who was very aware of the population's fear of Hezbollah's intentions to establish an Islamic regime through a revolutionary act on the one hand and the fear of the movement's hard core abandoning the Islamic ideology on the other hand, combined in his messages a response to both sides simultaneously. He denied coerced religious conversion and supported the dissemination of the Islamic message in pleasant ways. In 1993, he still toyed with the idea that "the circumstances might change, and what is unrealistic now might become realistic in the future . . . it is possible to convince the non-Muslims to accept the political concept of the Islamic state."[26] In late 1994, he declared that the movement would strive to promote individuals' freedom, national reconciliation, and the prevention of oppression. The movement would temporarily accept a government that would appease a wide strata of the population, and might even participate in it.[27] Nasrallah perfected and softened the aforementioned message and strove to create among his listeners a separation between the movement's conceptual and practical layers.

On the conceptual-ideological layer, he argued that the movement regards Islam, as does the Iranian model, as the solution for every political society as long as it desires it by choice alone. On the other hand, on the practical layer, the issue of the establishment of the Islamic state did not occupy the movement, and it was more troubled with the functioning of the political regime in Lebanon.[28] The realization for the need to act in "a reality in which it is impossible to realize radical ideas" is evident from the words of Mohammad Fneich, one of the movement's delegates in parliament, who commented that despite the movement's objection to the formula of a clan-based regime, it still operated in parliament.[29] The continuing occupation of the Lebanese press with the issue of establishing Islamic rule in Lebanon, between and after the two election campaigns, helped the movement to portray a new image of itself as a Lebanese national party and to score points in its favor in the Shiite community's public opinion.[30]

3. *Maintaining a dialogue with Lebanese parties and elements of power*: The "openness policy" of Hezbollah toward the Lebanese parties and its backing of this policy with propaganda messages contributed to the improvement of its image in the public opinion of the Lebanese in general and of the Shiite community in particular. The movement emphasized the fact that parliament constitutes for Hezbollah a stage for rapprochement with Lebanese parties and other elements of power.[31] The movement's first year of activity in parliament was assigned to establish pacts and agreements with parties and various figures in the Lebanese system and to hold discussions on the issue of the resistance, on politics, and on the social and security situation. This policy of openness was perceived as "serving the resistance."[32]

4. *Operating versus the government*: The movement carried on two types of activity in this area. The first involved the waging of a struggle versus the government for an official recognition of the resistance and its necessity, and the second, promoting the establishment of an opposition front for the foiling of those activities of the government that were contrary to the movement's principles. The contribution of the movement's attendance in parliament for the attainment of success at both these levels of action was widely emphasized in various media. At the opposition level, the activities of the national reconciliation government, and those who followed after it between the two election campaigns, for the implementation of the Ta'if Agreement placed Hezbollah, which was opposed to the implementation of the agreement, in opposition to the serving governments in a clear and visible manner. This position made it possible for Hezbollah to present to its audiences, in a more convincing manner, that its presence in parliament helped it to defend the interests of the Shiite community and the movement and provided it with the right to use all the means that this stage offered for its oppositional activity. Therefore, in any opportunity that presented itself, its delegates attacked the decisions and actions of the government and worked toward the establishing of pacts with elements in parliament to foil the same. Now and again, they called on the government to step down due to the "peace talks," "failure of the economic

policy," and "the perpetuation of the political clan-ness" and even initiated, led, and participated in demonstrations and protest strikes against the policies of the government.[33] Awareness of the sensitivity of the Shiite community's public opinion to the status of the government as an institution was evident in the messages of the movement. It made a clear distinction between the government as a legitimate institution of authority and the policies of the government that it criticized.[34] In July 1995, Qassem defined the situation of the movement's relationship with the government as one in which a dialog is maintained alongside an oppositional stand. According to him, Hezbollah maintained "a constructive and logical opposition."[35]

5. *Handling the release of Lebanese prisoners*: Hezbollah recognized the potential embodied in dealing with this issue and the degree of influence it had over the Shiite community and Lebanese public opinion. Therefore, the issue did not leave the movement's agenda, which appropriated to itself the handling of the issue of the Lebanese prisoners. Whenever the negotiations with Israel faded a bit, it repeatedly energized it in the various media, using different tactics.[36] The movement even chose the timing for "closing deals" so that it served the movement's policy and promoted its interests in the Lebanese system in general and the Shiite community system in particular.[37]

The Military Purview—Security of the Inhabitants of the South as a Determining Factor in the Decisions of the Movement

The need to provide a sense of security for the inhabitants of southern Lebanon and of the Beqaa valley and to appear as the one who protects them became central to the movement's policy and its conduct in Lebanon. The movement strove to achieve two opposing goals simultaneously: the first was to create social solidarity around the resistance and to shape a sympathetic public opinion toward its actions, and the second was to avoid being portrayed as harming the life habits and the subsistence needs of the inhabitants of the south.[38] In front of the temptation to act against Israel, always stood the question of the price that the "southerners" would have to pay. An escalation in the movement's activity caused an escalation in IDF activity, damage to the quality of life of the inhabitants of the south, and direct and indirect pressure on the movement from both its supporters and opponents. The movement was required to provide explanations and answers to scathing questions, to soften objections, and to prevent the desertion of the south.

The lasting conflict between the IDF and the movement, reaching its peak in operations "Accountability" (July 1993) and "Grapes of Wrath" (April 1996), took a heavy toll on the lives and property of the inhabitants of southern Lebanon.[39] The economic infrastructure of Lebanon was damaged. The Lebanese economy found it difficult to function, and the economic problems pressed on the members of the Shiite community, particularly the inhabitants of the villages on the frontline. Their life routine was disrupted, farmers found it difficult to cultivate their fields, crops were damaged, and the southerners who emigrated abroad avoided going to the south for their summer vacations. The lasting damage to the feeling of security and to the livelihood of the members of the Shiite community had an influence on the positions of the Shiite community's public opinion, and it expressed discontent and apprehensions regarding the situation.[40] Hezbollah saw in the actions of Israel an attempt to drive a wedge between it and the population and the Lebanese government, to disarm it, and to force it to act within a framework of rules and stiff constraints.[41] The accusations of the public opinion were not only pointed at Israel, but also against Hezbollah when its response policy, especially rocket fire, brought about escalation in combat.

In an interview given in September 1995 to the Lebanese TV channel LBC, Nasrallah was asked not only to explain the advantage that his movement saw in the use of rocket fire precisely when the peace talks were at their height, but also to answer the allegations leveled against Hezbollah that it supplied Israel with justifications to shell Lebanese villages.[42] Two months earlier, he had been asked to remark on the state of mind of the community, defined by the reporter in the following words: "Every so often there is a wave of restlessness among the residents towards the war of attrition that is waged on their land between the resistance and the enemy."[43] Berri, the Lebanese government, and Israel, who identified this phenomenon, acted, each according to its calculations, to attack Hezbollah and undermine its status within the population.[44]

In light of this, and owing to the importance of the Shiite community's public opinion in its considerations, Hezbollah prepared to explain its actions. It emphasized its avoidance from initiating activities that might disrupt the life routine of the inhabitants of the south and, in parallel, presented itself as the one responsible for their safety. Its messages were meant to explain its military activity both to its audiences and to its rivals and to establish its status in the pubic opinion of the Shiite community and beyond. The movement even made efforts in shaping and "maintaining" public opinion that was supportive of the resistance by emphasizing activity against the occupation and the duty of Jihad, the need for protection of Lebanese honor, and praising the steadfast standing of the population of the south.[45]

The main difficulty facing the movement was the explanation of the rocket fire policy, which was perceived as the main cause for the escalation of the security situation in the south. Nasrallah was aware of this, but assumed that this was an appropriate response to the Israeli aggression. In August 1994, he dedicated an extensive explanation to the development of the phenomenon. According to him, this policy was initially implemented during his tenure as secretary general, and its effect on Israel had made it a proven and effective means of response. Therefore, even though this modus operandi was controversial, it was used whenever firing toward Lebanese villages occurred. According to him, the current situation (at the time of this speech) was different because, in the Understanding of July 1993, it was agreed that Israel and Hezbollah would avoid firing toward villages on both sides of the border.[46]

The July 1993 Understanding did not endure for long. In 1994, the movement renewed its response policy, arguing that Israel repeatedly violated the July Understanding. Because of the awareness of the apprehension of the residents of the south from an escalation of incidents and a desire to explain the motives for firing and calm the residents, the incidents of rocket fire were accompanied by the movement's announcements in the media and by calming messages. Thus, for example, in October 1994, Hezbollah announced that it fired rockets toward Israel in response to the death of Lebanese citizens in an IDF operation. Nasrallah himself sent a calming message to the residents of the south, saying that he did not anticipate an escalation of the situation.[47] In February 1995, he declared that Hezbollah foiled the intentions of Israel to drive a wedge between it and the population and forced upon it the cessation of aggression against the citizens of Lebanon. He emphasized that the deterrence against Israel was maintained owing to Hezbollah's response policy.[48] During that same month, while appearing before students, he said that the relations between the resistance and the civilians was never better and praised the moral strength of the inhabitants of the south. He reiterated and emphasized the success of the response policy in deterring Israel and added that this policy was applied cautiously, responsibly, and judiciously for fear of being dragged into an Israeli trap.[49] In April 1995, the movement's policy gained encouragement from Fadlallah as well. He argued that the resistance should protect its people from Israel's madness and barbarity and that it " . . . acts from political maturity, and does not carry out shelling in an unplanned manner, but every firing of a missile and every laying of an explosive are done judiciously."[50]

If one were to follow the statements of the Hezbollah movement in this matter, he would learn that it made educated use in the response policy it developed, with two goals in mind. The first was to deter Israel, and the second was to improve public relations in the internal Lebanese system. Against Israel, the movement threatened to respond in the same fashion, and in front of the internal Lebanese system, it emphasized that it was attentive to the population and its needs and that this was why it avoided actions that might harm the activities of the farmers or the security of the residents. In addition, it reiterated in countless opportunities the formula "every offense against our civilian residents will be answered with a multifold response and with additional operations, with the means we will see fit."[51]

The movement made it clear that it was not "trigger happy" and that rocket fire was used only as a response and only after a situation assessment and a warning to Israel. It declared, more than once, that it would choose the method, time, place, and severity appropriate for response. In statements advertised on its behalf after the firing of rockets, it linked its reaction and the Israeli violations, specified the reasons for its reaction, and blamed Israel for the escalation in the security situation and held it solely responsible.[52]

In spite of that, the movement was repeatedly required to explain its policy and to respond to the allegations presented against it. In July 1995, Nasrallah rejected outright the argument that the resistance operated from within the villages, calling it a lie. According to him, the movement distanced its activities from the villages as much as possible, and only rarely was it forced to open fire from within buildings.[53] During the same month, he was again asked to explain the policy of rocket fire, emphasizing the affinity between the movement's commitment to protect the civilians and the firings it opened. Nasrallah boasted of the success of this policy of rocket fire, during the two years that passed since the establishment of the July 1993 Understanding, in providing protection to the inhabitants of southern Lebanon and exhausting Israel.[54] The proof for that, according to one of the seniors of the movement, was the large number of summer vacationers arriving that year (1995) in southern Lebanon.[55]

The escalation in southern Lebanon, on the eve of operation "Grapes of Wrath" (January–March 1996), worried the movement's seniors, but more so the inhabitants of the south. In light of the delicate situation, the movement adopted increased caution in its conduct in front of the public opinion. Its actions were accompanied by the statements and clarifications of the movement's seniors, and Israel was blamed for the deterioration in the situation. On March 21, 1996, owing to the continuing escalation, Nasrallah assembled a press conference dedicated to explaining the actions of the movement. According to him, these actions were "well planned, so that they do not cause damage to civilians on our side." He emphasized the responsible policy of restraint taken by his movement, despite the continuing Israeli aggression. He said that he was aware of the possibility of widespread Israeli operation and made an effort to prevent further escalation. He added that if Israel violated the Understanding again and harmed Lebanese civilians, the movement would be forced to react.[56] Nine days later, after he learned of the deaths of two Lebanese civilians from IDF fire, he expressed that he had no choice but to react with rocket fire toward Israel and that "the period ended where we alone died and our homes were wrecked."[57] On April 9, after an episode of rocket fire toward Israel, Nasrallah assembled another press conference and announced that the firing was carried out as a response to the death of the civilians of the village of Barashit. He blamed Israel for the continuance of the aggressive policy and emphasized its contrast with the responsible policy of restraint that the movement had enforced upon itself.[58]

Nasrallah was sometimes required to answer especially difficult questions. One such question dealt with the price in property and lives that the inhabitants of the south had to pay owing to the movement's activities. In his reply, he indicated that every resistance has a price and that fighting is required in order to free the land from the occupation. He argued that, alongside the price paid in lives by the movement's activists, who arrive from all parts of Lebanon and fight and die in the south, there is also the price that the southerners are required to pay. In his words, "Our people living in the villages of the front line are a fighting people in the full sense of the word, and this is the tax that must be paid."[59]

The main culprit responsible for the suffering of the inhabitants of the south, from the point of view of the movement, was Israel, which took an aggressive policy toward civilians. During a meeting in October 1995 between the chairman of the political council and the farmers of south Lebanon, the former argued, among other things, that "aggression is one of the idiosyncrasies of the Zionist entity, which strives for expansion."[60] To justify their argument, the leaders of the movement presented numerical data that expressed the aggression of Israel versus the policy of restraint that characterized the movement during that period. Nasrallah argued that Israel violated the July 1993 Understanding 231 times, for which Hezbollah responded only ten times by opening rocket fire toward Israel, owing to the harming of civilians.[61] The movement also argued that operation "Grapes of Wrath" was one of the products of the Sharm el-Sheikh summit, where

Israel received American authorization for its aggression in Lebanon, regardless of rocket fire [62]

Actually, Hezbollah met the opportunity to prove its striving toward achieving safety for the inhabitants of the south on one of the most difficult moments in its conflict with Israel, toward the end of operation "Grapes of Wrath". The allegations made against it, and the community's blaming of it for the suffering caused to the residents of Lebanon, were quickly replaced by the issue of the village of Qanaa and the blaming of Israel for the massacre of civilians.[63] Factually, the movement was successful in marketing its messages to the public opinion and in concealing its part in the current escalation. The direct proof for that was in the increase that occurred in the Lebanese public's sympathy to the activities of the resistance. Nasrallah reminded his critics, who regarded the rocket fire policy as the cause for "Grapes of Wrath," of the large number of Lebanese civilians who died in the preceding month, which forced the movement to respond with fire. This fire, according to him, was exploited by Israel as a pretext for its attack, which was, in any case, planned and aimed at destroying the movement.[64] From then on, the matter of ensuring the security of the civilians and of removing them from the cycle of violence became the central topic in the cease-fire agreement.

The "Grapes of Wrath" agreements (April 1996) were exploited for propaganda to emphasize the movement's part in their shaping and its insistence that international guarantees be given to the ensuring of the security of the inhabitants of the south. Nasrallah extolled the movement's part in reaching the April Understanding as an expression of its efforts in caring for, in every way, the safety of the inhabitants.[65] He viewed the Understanding as a new mechanism that would make it possible for the movement to protect the civilians and, therefore, he committed himself to be strict in fulfilling them. These Understanding, as far as he understood, limited not only Israel's space of operation, but also that of Hezbollah for the benefit of the civilians. The movement even conditioned (and extensively publicized this) its agreement for the cease-fire in the presenting of reliable guarantees so that Lebanese civilians would not be attacked again.[66]

During the first months after the cease-fire became effective, the movement demonstrated sensitivity to the situation of the population, which had just experienced a particularly difficult period, and adopted a cautious policy. In early May 1996, Nasrallah declared that the new Understanding were entering a trial period and that the movement would stop rocket fire until further notice, but it would follow events and reassess the situation following Israeli violations. During the same month, Hezbollah argued that Israel violated the Understanding, but that the movement refrained, at that stage, from renewing the policy of response fire out of a desire to give a chance to the follow-up committee to prove its effectiveness.[67] The movement, either willingly or owing to the necessity of the circumstances, rolled, at least at that stage, the responsibility for the lives of the residents of the south to the doorstep of the Lebanese government, urging it to realize its responsibility for the safety of the civilians, to conduct serious tracking of the Israeli violations, to submit grievances, and to act at the diplomatic level for the denouncement of Israel.[68]

The Understanding of April 1996 made it possible for Hezbollah to prove that its activities were motivated primarily by concern for the safety and welfare of the inhabitants of Lebanon, and not by extremism for its own sake. It took care to keep the issue of Israeli violations and the way to deal with them at the top of the Lebanese media's agenda for a long time. Alongside expressions of losing patience and of the need to respond with rocket fire, the movement, in fact, emphasized its self-imposed national policy of restraint, taking into consideration the safety of the civilians and not providing Israel pretext for the rocket fire policy.[69] This policy of restraint apparently stemmed from the understanding of Hezbollah's leaders that public opinion did not support the rocket fire policy and that it would harm it at the present timing. Therefore, it refrained from conducting fire in response to what it perceived as Israeli violation and harming of civilians and left the dealings to the oversight committee.[70]

The movement's policy of restraint was exploited for political gain. In an election speech in 1996 in Nabatieh, Nasrallah exalted the movement's responsible policy that took into account the public's state of mind and made it possible for the Lebanese government to realize its responsibility.[71] Muhammed Raed, the head of the political council of Hezbollah, explained this as a desire to regard the interest of the civilians and to assist the state in dealing with the violations within the framework of the oversight council.[72] The fact that, in the year after the April 1996 Understanding, three Lebanese civilians were killed as opposed to the twenty-four killed in the preceding year was emphasized by the movement's leadership as another means to gain sympathy and political support.[73]

It took Hezbollah more than a year of mobilizing rhetoric until the propaganda message permeated, portraying it as a responsible movement that was concerned with the safety of the residents of the south, "does not use power in an arbitrary way," did not provide pretexts for Israel, and curbed its activities according to the circumstances.[74] In September 1997, one of the senior of the movement said that the change in the position of the public's opinion was expressed in articles, commentaries, and letters that the movement received as well as in the number of people who visited Nasrallah on the occasion of the death of his son, Haadi.[75]

The movement's return to the policy of response fire was carried out in a controlled, tiptoe manner while wishing to demonstrate to the population its sensitivity to its needs and its contribution to its safety versus the continuing ineffectiveness of the resolutions of the oversight committee. In the first stage, the movement clarified that it could not restrain itself after the harming of civilians. When it became clear to the movement that the warning message was not received, it reacted on July 1997, for the first time since the Understandings of April 1996 became effective, by rocket fire toward IDF posts located along the border of Lebanon accompanied by the threat that it might respond to the harming of Lebanese civilians by fire toward Israeli settlements.[76] The first rocket fire toward Israel was carried out in August 1997 in response to South Lebanon Army (SLA) fire towards Saida. Following it, the movement publicized a clarification, stating that use of the response fire policy would be made only in cases where it felt that the lives of civilians are dependent on it. The fire itself was reasoned as the desire of the movement to remind everyone of the basis of the April Understanding and to revive them. This goal, in Nasrallah's opinion, was crowned with success.[77] The renewed implementation of the policy of response fire originated, inter alia, by the movement's assessment that the political conditions for it had matured and that its activities would probably gain support in the public opinion.[78]

A testimony for the relatively successful conduct of the response policy during the 1990s was, in fact, heard from the representative of the Amal movement in parliament. According to him, the policy of response fire was disapproved by the Lebanese public opinion in the 1980s due to its low effectiveness. However, this policy proved itself as an effective defensive measure in the 1990s owing to the July 1993 and the April 1996 Understanding. Use of this defensive measure strengthened the status of Hezbollah and promoted it to the center of the political stage.[79]

In parallel to the media campaign to shape a sympathetic public opinion, Hezbollah worked in the social-economic area as well for the advancement of the welfare of the members of the Shiite community, using the economic, medical, educational, and cultural institutions that it founded and operated as well as giving social services in the centers of the Shiite population. Hezbollah's leaders estimated that its social activity was one of the factors responsible for its success in the 1992 parliamentary elections and, therefore, continued it.[80]

Reconstruction of the war's damages: The activity to repair the damages from the fighting in southern Lebanon and the Beqaa valley was evident after operations "Accountability" (July 1993) and "Grapes of Wrath" (April 1996). The damage caused to the civilian infrastructure and the need to compensate the casualties and make it possible for the residents to return to their life routine obligated a quick mobilization and significant resources. In August 1993, Nasrallah revealed some of the reasons for the movement's decision to mobilize for the task of reconstruction, saying "we decided to help the people to rebuild their homes, and this will help in strengthening the connection between the people and Hezbollah."[81] On another occasion, he referred to the importance of the movement's rapid mobilization to carry out the task of reconstruction as a means of establishing social peace and preventing the fleeing of residents from their home.[82] It was said that, among other actions, the movement removed its offices and bases from population concentrations and established social institutions in their stead.[83] In August 1994, the Lebanese newspaper *Al-Sharaa* pointed out the changes in Hezbollah's policy in southern Lebanon and revealed to its readers that the movement worked to prevent the fleeing of the residents of the south during periods of tension by exhibiting their presence in the villages, conducting calming talks with the residents, and promising assistance to residents who suffered damages. According to one of the newspaper's sources in southern Lebanon, this activity, symbolizing the movement's considerations of the civilians' interests, gained the sympathy of the residents.[84]

Assistance to farmers: Most residents of rural southern Lebanon earned their living mainly from farming and small industry. The agricultural life cycle dictated the inhabitants' agenda, while the escalating violence disrupted it. Hezbollah presented an appearance of consideration for the needs of the agricultural sector in southern Lebanon and the Beqaa valley. It conducted meetings with the farmers and their representatives, provided them with consulting and professional guidance, compensated them for their damages, established factories, managed agricultural projects, and in the high seasons, such as the olive picking season, it even searched for solutions that would assist the farmers whose plantations were in the range of IDF fire.[85]

Islamic training: The movement put special emphasis on the Islamic training and education of all age groups in the population. The movement applied great attention in training teachers, organizing widespread activities among students in the religious seminars and the universities, and publishing articles and reports on issues of Islamic culture in the media that was available to it.[86]

Nabil Qauq, one of the seniors of the movement in southern Lebanon, said in January 1995 that the movement offered its services to all residents. He defined the movement's role in the region as "greater than a party and lesser than an executive authority" and presented data on the extent of its educational institutions and its activity in southern Lebanon. He announced that it had four schools, six colleges for women's technical training, four seminaries for religious studies, fifteen public institutions, and sponsorship of about 130 sports teams in the villages of the south.[87]

At the national level, the movement operated, according to Qassem, about fifty Islamic schools. This activity created a potential for manpower available for recruitment, thus constantly feeding the ranks of the movement and its supporters. The activity even made it possible for its leaders to reject applications of non-Lebanese volunteers to join its ranks and to boast about being a "pure" Lebanese movement. Nizar Hamzeh, a researcher in the American University of Beirut, estimated Hezbollah's strength in early 1998 at about 6000 trained fighters and about 10,000 active supporters.[88]

To conclude this discussion, it should be emphasized that the media campaign and the practical work done by the movement complemented each other. They provided its representatives at the local and national levels tools to better deal with accusations pointed at them and with the resentment in the Shiite public opinion. In any case, and even though these things were not said wholeheartedly, it can be seen from what was aforementioned that public opinion significantly influenced the use of the policy of response fire, its nature, quantity, and timing. Vice versa, the mobilizing rhetoric and the continuing propaganda campaign of the movement in this area created the atmosphere that made it possible to continue using this policy.

Extraorganizational Political Struggles

The Struggle against Amal for the Shiite Public Opinion—New Action Strategies and Mutual Influences

The rivalry between Amal and Hezbollah for the Shiite public opinion did not stop for a moment, even when they decided on running a joint roster in the 1992 and 1996 elections. Both regarded themselves as popular movements with a wide and stable base of support, but each strove to increase its hold on the Shiite community and on additional publics at the expense of the other. Berri, holding the role of chairman of parliament in addition to being Amal's leader, acted to control Hezbollah's steps and to maintain decision making authority in relation to the affairs of the Shiite community in his hands. On the other side, Hezbollah combined struggle and dialogue, striving to gain positions of power in the Shiite community and in the administrative systems.[89] As far as the leaders of the movements could influence things, they prevented the struggle for the public opinion from sliding into violence and maintained a mutual framework of restraints.[90]

The Hezbollah movement worked to change its image from an extreme Islamic movement, as it was portrayed in the public opinion of the Shiite community and of the other communities, to a legitimate and institutionalized political movement with a wide base of support. For this purpose, it employed various action strategies with the aim of influencing Shiite public opinion directly and indirectly. It put its most talented spokesmen, led by Nasrallah, at the forefront of its propaganda and repeated its messages countless times while meticulously presenting a trustworthy, responsible, and moderate image.[91] Nevertheless, the movement found it difficult to translate the popular support that its activity against Israel gained into significant political power and identification with its platform. Its failure in the 1996 elections only strengthened this statement. This failure, and even the departure of the radical faction from the movement, did not stop the campaign it conducted for public opinion. The movement learnt its lessons, formalized action plans, and with hard work, as Nasrallah testified more than once, it succeeded, once again, in establishing its status in the public opinion.

The struggle for the Shiite public opinion, as mentioned above, did not occur at one point of time and at one level; it was based on the conduct of a continuing propaganda campaign, accompanied by social and public activity within the Shiite community and the Lebanese system. The movement did so by emphasizing its unique contribution to the Shiite community and to Lebanese society, while dealing with the difficulties and the challenges posed to it by it rivals: Amal movement on the one hand and the Lebanese regime on the other.

In the first area, the security arena, Hezbollah emphasized three central messages that, as far as it was concerned, expressed its contribution to the Shiite community and to Lebanese society in this area and its superiority over its rivals. The first message emphasized its role as the leader of the resistance, the liberator of the land, and the restorer of the Lebanese national honor.[92] The second message aimed at sinking in the concept of it being legitimate.[93] The third message emphasized its role in protecting the well-being and safety of the residents of southern Lebanon and the Beqaa valley.[94]

Its incontrovertible domination in the arena of security activity gave it an advantage in the struggle for public opinion over its rivals, which it used well to promote its messages and to produce political gains. The movement even used the fact that support of the resistance crossed the borders of the Shiite community's public opinion and acted to promote initiatives in this area with Lebanese society.

The Amal movement, from its side, claimed primacy in the establishing of the resistance and its leadership. It supported the need for resistance, but reduced Hezbollah's role in this area and urged the government to implement its comprehensive responsibility in Lebanon, including the issue of the resistance.[95] In parallel, it actually emphasized the movement's activities from within the

Lebanese villages, claiming that these activities harm the south and its residents more than they gain militarily and politically. Berri denounced these activities and called for a reorganization of the resistance in such a way that it would help maintain its popular support.[96] Similar criticism was voiced from the direction of the chairman of the Supreme Shiite Council, Mahdi Shams al-Din, who argued that the activities of the resistance should match the current political reality, reflecting the positions of the Lebanese public opinion.[97]

The importance of the resistance in the Shiite public opinion, the understanding that it can be translated into political support, and the resistance being a Hezbollah monopoly motivated the Amal movement to renew, for a brief period, its activities against Israel. Indeed, on the eve of the 1996 elections and during operation "Grapes of Wrath," Amal carried out a few operations that gained wide media resonance.[98]

The second area, the public-social arena, constituted one of the main penetration paths of the movement into the heart of the Shiite population and was based on its public and social institutions. The competition for control in the public-social field in the Shiite centers of population in the 1990s was more difficult and complex than before and required significant resources, which the movement found difficult to mobilize. In this area, it competed against the governmental apparatus and the chairman of parliament, Berri, who controlled the sources of public funding, budgets, and the system of administrative nominations and could adjust them according to political considerations. Nasrallah complained more than once about this, arguing that "there is an attempt to restrict the movements of the Hezbollah organization in every field, except for the area of the resistance, and this is expressed in the areas of nominations for executive positions and in providing services."[99] Notwithstanding, the movement was perceived by itself and by the civilians as promoting the welfare of the residents of the south and the Beqaa valley through its institutions spread out in the Shiite population centers in Lebanon.[100]

With the lack of real executive capability in the public-governmental system, Hezbollah representatives in parliament worked to promote the affairs of the Shiite population either through bill initiatives or objection to government bills presented for parliament's approval.[101] The faction members in parliament made sure that the issue of the resistance and the government's obligation to assist the residents' steadfast stand were not removed from the parliament's agenda. They criticized the government on its failing conduct with regard to the issues of assistance to the south and treatment of poverty and demanded it to invest budgets in protecting the south and improving its preparations versus the Israeli threat in parallel to compensating the casualties of Israeli aggression.[102]

The movement met with difficulties in dealing with its rivals in this arena. Testimonies of that were found in journalists' reviews of the erosion occurring in its treatment of the socio-economic problems of its constituents, the criticism from within of Al-Tufayli, and even the statements of its seniors. Thus, for example, Fneich, the faction's delegate in parliament, admitted in November 1995 that the difficult economic situation in Lebanon deepened the social gaps and caused discontentment, resentment, and criticism against the movement. According to him, these originated from, among other causes, the gap that was created between the anticipations of change and reality.[103]

The "Revolution of the Hungry" that erupted in July 1997 brought the socio-economic problems of the Shiite community in the Beqaa valley to the surface and exposed, to a large degree, the movement's difficulty in solving the economic hardships and social discrimination. Al-Tufayli, the leader of the "revolution of the hungry," argued that Hezbollah of 1997 simply abandoned the treatment of the economic problems of the population owing to political considerations, arguing for giving the resistance priority.[104]

This powder keg, threatening to explode and annihilate the achievements of the movement so far, obligated it to take immediate action to neutralize feelings of frustration and alienation, some of which were pointed toward it, and to find a solution to the problem. Nasrallah took a combined approach including explanations and actions. He explained the social policy of the movement as aimed at achieving two goals. The first was protecting the freedom of the entire society, and the second was achieving social justice and realizing the demands of the poor regions. He admitted that the movement, using legitimate means of sometimes criticizing the government and sometimes holding dialogue with it, found it difficult to foil the government's economic plan. In the area of actions, he emphasized the efforts of the faction in parliament to cancel the budget cuts in the area of healthcare, to expedite budget allocations for the inhabitants of the Beqaa valley, and to promote assistance for agriculture. He argued that the purpose of the action strategy in the social area was to achieve the aforementioned goals not by overthrowing the regime, but through dialogue and cooperation.[105] In the beginning of 1998, Nasrallah revealed that the budget allocated to public-social activity had increased and that the movement was operating the construction department in full swing to repair property damages, assisting and guiding farmers, and, in parallel, providing health services through mobile and permanent clinics in the villages and continuing to operate its network of institutions. He added that the public's expectations had changed since the civil war and that the movement's struggles to integrate itself into the executive system stemmed from its desire to promote more effectively the interests of the underprivileged.[106]

In the late first-half of the 1990s, a strategy was formalized, whose purpose was to portray Hezbollah as a moderate and trustworthy movement in the Shiite community arena and as one that is open for cooperation and dialog with Amal and the Lebanese system. It coordinated its positions on Shiite community and internal Lebanese issues with Berri, organized joint meetings, avoided repeating the mistakes of the past in regard to its relationship with the population in the south, and curbed phenomena of internal violence among its activists.[107] At the practical level, it worked to encourage tourism in the Beqaa valley and exhibited a civilized and moderate image to replace the radical image that had characterized it in the past. For that purpose, it cooperated with the Lebanese Ministry of Tourism and assisted it in preparing archeological sites for tourist visits, renewing the appearance of the township of Baalbek and erecting billboards in English.[108]

In 1994, in a message aimed at a Shiite community audience, Nasrallah emphasized Hezbollah's part in promoting cooperation with the Amal movement, "I can say that the reciprocal killings between us and Amal became a thing of the past, and progress has been achieved with all Shiite factors and institutions."[109] In May 1996, because of incidents between the movements stemming from disagreements concerning "ownership" of the "Qanaa incident," he reemphasized his commitment to keep a restrained framework in the relationship with Amal and to prevent irregular phenomena.[110]

The preparations and attitudes of Hezbollah toward the Ashura events of 1995 constitute an informative example of its desire to present a new face. Traditionally, these rituals constituted, since Hezbollah's foundation, an explosive focus for the development of clashes between the two movements and between Shiites and Sunnis and a matter of criticism of the primitiveness of the self-flagellation rituals that characterized the Hezbollah processions. On the eve of the 1995 Ashura events, coordination meetings between the two movements were conducted regarding the nature of the processions and their locations, and lines of cooperation were set to prevent violent incidents.[111] The Ashura rituals, carried out between June 2 and June 8 of 1995, were conducted "in a natural atmosphere and no difficult problems arose," according to Qassem. The eruption of violent incidents in several locations stemmed, in his opinion, from the violent nature of solitary individuals and the existence of a phenomenon of hooliganism in both movements. He denounced provocative behavior of any kind in the rituals and supported the punishment of lawbreakers by the authorities.[112]

Mobilizing the public opinion of the Shiite community was a task that obligated "field work" and large presence everywhere and for a long time. Hezbollah, on its part, invested significant resources to be in the center of the Shiite community and public stage, using control over the Shiite community public discourse and all possible means and types of meetings possible. It made extensive use of the media and the parliament podium together with initiating and organizing assemblies, conventions, ceremonies, and parades in Shiite centers of population. Its leaders, who saw great importance in disseminating the Islamic message, appeared often in funerals and memorial services, schools and education institutions, and public events. They met with delegations of residents from all parts of the population while tightening their contact with and hold over the Shiite community and other populations and rounding support for their activities.[113]

The leaders of Hezbollah exploited their clear advantage over the Amal movement by the fact of their ownership of a variety of media, such as Al-Manar television, Radio Nur, and *Al-Ahd* newspaper, in addition to their influence over additional Islamic media that served them as a stage for the passing of messages related to their movement and to Islam. Therefore, there is no surprise that Berri urged the Hariri government to promptly order the stopping of the activity of Hezbollah media in the framework of the implementation of the Media Act, and in parallel, he sought opportunities for cooperation with other media for the dissemination of the message of the Amal movement.[114]

Ahmad El Assad, one of the seniors of the declining old Shiite community elite, argued in one of his interviews that "there is a whole political sector of the population that is not convinced of a certain political line. I am convinced that the people's belief is not stable, and that it will change and develop." This insight was probably not exclusively his, but rather expressed the assessments of the two major players in the field, Hezbollah and Amal, who were carrying out between them a struggle for the recruitment of those segments in the Shiite community through persuasion and mobilizing rhetoric.[115]

One of the examples characterizing this struggle is the dispute that broke out between Hezbollah and Berri owing to the arrangement of ceremonies of a "day of rapport" with the south on March 14, 1995. Hezbollah argued that Berri intentionally worked behind its back for the "nationalization" of the ceremonies to make them popular with the aim of overshadowing its achievements and, at the same time, to enjoy the fruits of the initiative and expand his circle of supporters in the Shiite community. Despite the hard and fundamental argument, the movement refrained, probably in light of its desire to present a responsible appearance, from deteriorating the relationship and taking aggressive steps. Local violent incidents, erupting between the movements' activists in the field owing to the crisis, were treated and, despite the casualties, their spreading was halted.[116] Examining the events of the "day of rapport" of 1997, two years later, instructs on the development of the relationship between the two movements. This time, Hezbollah representatives were integrated into the organizing committee in parliament, and even though the disagreements between the movements' activists in the field slid into confrontations in a few villages, it was evident that there was satisfaction in the movement from the way the ceremonies were conducted.[117]

Another arena where the two movements fought for recruiting the support of public opinion was surrounding the question of Hezbollah's status and future, assuming that the peace process would indeed reach the finish line. The opinion prevalent in the Lebanese system held that, in an era where military resistance was no longer required, the need for Hezbollah's existence as an independent movement was doubtful.[118] Questions regarding the path of the movement, if and when a peace agreement was established, were directed to its leaders now and again. Their answers included two messages: the first and most important message held that the movement would continue to operate independently even if a peace agreement were signed between Lebanon and Israel. According to Nasrallah, despite the existence of mutual influence relations between the military activity and the other activities, the existence of Hezbollah did not depend on the future of military activity. Even if this avenue of action were closed, the movement would continue and expand in other areas. This was because of the fact that Hezbollah was a mass movement, "Islamic Jihadist political social cultural and popular," and that it had social and cultural institutions, as well as presence across all levels of Lebanese public action, in the municipal system, and in parliament.[119] Nasrallah's deputy, Qassem, declared in 1995 that Hezbollah was a mass movement with institutions and supporters that represented a wide stratum in Lebanese society and, therefore, it would continue to exist even if there were pressures in the future. In 1998, he emphasized that the question of Hezbollah's continuity was totally not on the agenda and that the media should stop dealing with this subject as if there were a state of emergency.[120]

The second message regarded the future and the nature of the movement's activities against Israel. This message was deliberately dimmed, and the movement avoided specifying what action policy it would employ after Israel's withdrawal. It excused this with its lack of desire to provide Israel with free information and made it clear that its policy would be revealed in due course. It was read between the lines that it would continue to oppose the phenomenon of normalizing relations with Israel by using other means. The radical faction in the movement, led by Al-Tufayli, took a clear stand and announced that the military resistance would continue even after the establishing of peace between Lebanon and Israel.[121] In July 1995, Nasrallah attacked the Amal movement and Berri, arguing that "some of the Lebanese power elements hurry to reach an agreement in order to get rid of Hezbollah and its power because it is their political rival." He pointed his criticism toward Berri, arguing that he exploited the pressure under which the population of the border villages was and worked manipulatively to incite it against Hezbollah with the aim of damaging the image of the movement.[122]

Hezbollah's failure in the parliamentary election campaign of 1996 versus Amal's impressive success constituted a hard blow to its prestige in the Shiite community arena and obligated it to rethink and draw conclusions. It decided to continue the policy of openness, to rehabilitate its relations with the rest of the Lebanese parties, and to deepen its connection with the Shiite community. Renewal, sensitivity to public opinion, a series of military successes against Israel, and its habit of taking advantage of political opportunities already caused changes in Hezbollah's status in the Shiite community public opinion and in the Lebanese system in the course of 1997.[123]

The 1996 Election Campaign—Marking False Expectations

The activity of the movement in the political arena provided Hezbollah with additional tools for competing for the Shiite community and the Lebanese public opinion versus the Amal movement. This activity transformed it into a legitimate movement and helped it improve its image and reach new target audiences among the members of the Shiite community. The movement based its legitimacy on its military activity, the price it paid for the liberation of Lebanese land, and its presence as the people's representative in the Lebanese parliament.[124] The movement did not rest on its laurels after its success in the 1992 elections, but strove to use it for promoting the resistance, expanding cooperation relations with additional elements in the political arena, and influencing the distribution of the state budget and the executive positions.[125]

The second parliamentary election campaign found Hezbollah more ready and more experienced, as far as demonstrating too much self-confidence in relation to the anticipated results. Its victory in the 1992 elections, and the data it had in its hands regarding the levels of support it had in the Shiite and the Lebanese public opinion, raised its leaders' levels of expectation. As election date neared, the expressions indicating the expansion of popular support of the movement multiplied. On the practical side, Hezbollah worked to promote its preferred bills toward the elections.[126] The preparations for the elections gained momentum in late 1995. During this period, the various meanings of the Election Act bills as well as the level of influence each bill had on the chances of the movement were studied. Also studied was the significance of a joint running with Amal and other power elements in the Shiite community. Hezbollah did not conceal its ambition to increase its power in parliament and expected its constituents to staff most of the seats assigned to the Shiite community.[127]

As the election date arrived, the movement's contacts in the Shiite community and the Lebanese arenas, for coordination of positions and the examining of frameworks for possible alliances, expanded. The main struggle for the Shiite community's public opinion positions was waged between Amal and Hezbollah. Both movements discussed the possibility of running a joint roster, but found it hard to reach an agreement on the number of representatives from each movement. Hezbollah demanded an equal division in southern Lebanon, arguing that, in 1992, it was not aware of its electoral strength, while Amal demanded more presence in the Beqaa valley roster. Both threatened that they would run competing rosters in the south and in the Beqaa valley if their demands were not met.[128]

The Understanding of April 1996 gained, as far as the Hezbollah leaders were concerned, sympathy and wide support in the Lebanese public opinion and strengthened their assessment that the movement would succeed in increasing its strength in the 1996 elections. In May 1996, Ibrahim al-Amin, one of Hezbollah's senior leaders and founding members, said, "We are close to the Lebanese parliamentary elections, and we assume that Hezbollah, who gave and contributed much to Lebanon in the present period, particularly in the area of the resistance, will increase the number of its delegates in parliament."[129] Captured by the concept of an "easy victory," as Abed El Hamid Beydoun, a member of parliament from Amal, put it, the seniors of Hezbollah made a mistake in their assessment of their electoral strength; therefore, their demand to increase the quota of their members in parliament was not realistic.[130]

In July 1996, the movement announced its position regarding the election areas and urged the government to avoid unnecessary delays and to accelerate the phrasing of the Election Act. It opposed the Election Act that the government passed for the approval of parliament, but did not cancel its participation in the elections themselves.[131] In parallel, it reduced its activity against Israel to the essential minimum. Its seniors were mobilized for the promotion of the faction's nominees; they appeared in election rallies and met with potential allies and dignitaries in the election areas. The movement's media were mobilized for the propaganda effort as well, to broadcast election propaganda.[132]

Its failure in the elections in Beirut and in the mountainous area shocked Hezbollah. The seniors of the movements complained of fraud and irregularities in the elections, of being "victims of fierce community incitement," and of intentional conspiracy by the heads of government.[133] In this state of affairs, as Nasrallah explained in his speech at an election rally in Nabatieh, the only choice available was to establish a coalition with the Amal movement for running a joint roster in the south and the Beqaa valley. Implementing this decision from theory to practice was not an easy task. The negotiations between the movements reached an impasse a few days before voting and were stopped. Only three days before the vote was the crisis finished, with the arbitration of Syria. Nasrallah also admitted to the existence of strong opposition within the movement for joint running with Amal, but justified his decision as his desire to preserve the future of the south and the resistance and to avoid explosion and conflicts within the Shiite community.[134]

At the end of the elections campaign, it became clear that the big winner was Berri. He succeeded in increasing the attendance of Amal ("Al Tahrir" faction in the new parliament from six to ten delegates and his supporting parliamentary bloc to twenty delegates, while the number of Hezbollah delegates to parliament

(Al-Wafa) was decreased to six, and its supporters in parliament shrank to only three delegates. Hezbollah indeed succeeded in increasing its strength in southern Lebanon and in preserving its support in the mountains and in Beirut, but between that and the goal it set to itself, the distance was great.[135]

The Municipal System as a Means of Strengthening the Connection between the Movement and the Shiite Community

Islamic movements hold great importance in integrating into municipal systems. These systems have sources of authority, the ability to act, and means and budgets that directly influence the daily life of the Shiite community, but these do not have the political–public responsibility existing in the public-executive-national system (government). This makes it possible for Islamic movements to gain power and influence without being reliant on the government's favor.[136]

Entry into the municipal system constituted a very important political opportunity for Hezbollah, all the more so after its failure in the elections for parliament. Involvement in the municipal system provided the movement with control and direct influence over public goods and their use on the one hand and made it possible for them to maintain continuous and direct contact with the residents on the other. Hezbollah saw the advantages latent in this system and were prepared to run in the Shiite villages. Therefore, whenever the possibility of postponing the municipal elections or replacing them with a system of appointments was talked about, the movement cried aloud and expressed objection to the principle of appointments.[137] The Lebanese government did not hurry to decide on the system for the municipal elections, while Hezbollah urged it repeatedly to accelerate the legislation in this matter and made sure that the issue would not be removed from the Lebanese agenda. The occupation with the municipal elections legislation was expanded at the end of the 1996 election campaign.[138] Hezbollah, for which it was the first time, as a party, to run representatives on its behalf to the municipal authorities, examined ways to cooperate with Amal and other elements while taking into consideration the unique nature and family structure of every authority.[139]

The municipal election campaign became particularly interesting in the Shiite community because its results expressed the power ratio between the two movements in it, in light of the changes occurring in public opinion since the 1996 elections. Both movements were required to undertake a complicated task, taking into account certain considerations, such as the power ratios between families and local power elements as well as local sensitivities. Both were required to consider the fact that their activists lived and worked side by side in all Shiite population centers in the rural periphery and in the towns. In light of this, the two movements concluded operational principles that took into account the social-political composition in the various areas and defined the way they were involved in the election campaign. Still, as the election date neared, the competition between them intensified as far as the throwing of mutual accusations and the eruption of violent incidents in several locations.[140]

Hezbollah attached great importance to the election results and got prepared for them. It established an election headquarters that carried out opinion polls and studied possibilities for local cooperation and announced that, contrary to Amal, it would not prevent its people from running for election. The movement operated with extra caution in the Beqaa valley because of the delicate situation after the schism within itself and the removal of Al-Tufayli from its ranks.[141] Generally speaking, it can be said that Hezbollah was successful in basing its status within the Shiite community in the municipal elections. It won half of the councils in the Shiite settlements, including the southern suburb of Beirut. In southern Lebanon, it succeeded in introducing about 150 of its representatives and supporters into the local authorities. Notwithstanding, it failed in the Beqaa valley.[142]

The Movement in Processes of Internal Change

Pan-Islamism and revolutionism, the central pillars of Khomeini's teaching and the export strategy of the Iranian revolution, were assimilated by the Hezbollah movement from the day of its founding by the members of the Iranian revolutionary guard who stood behind its organization and operation in the first years. The assimilation of this ideology was made possible due to the common background of the Ulema, graduates of the Shiite seminaries in Iraq and Iran, who founded the movement. The Ulema expressed their limitless loyalty to Khomeini and his leadership and regarded themselves as his envoys for the realization of the pan-Islamic goals, as part of a worldwide Islamic revolution, whose boundaries were inferred by the geography of Islam. This perception disregarded the limits of the Lebanese system and worked to overthrow it by a revolutionary act.

The official position of the movement, formed in 1985 with Fadlallah's pressure, indeed determined that the movement would strive to apply Islam in Lebanon by way of persuasion, but the influence of its violent acts on the public opinion was stronger than its statements. Therefore, the Lebanese were not particularly impressed with Al-Tufayli's suggestion in April 1991 to carry out a referendum regarding the nature of government desirable in Lebanon.[143]

The decision of the movement to participate in the 1992 parliamentary elections marked a reference point in the time between the revolutionary pan-Islamic period of the movement and the period where it marketed itself as a pragmatic Lebanese national movement. The changes occurring in its policy stemmed from the implementation of its organizational decisions and were reflected by its entry into the Lebanese parliament, the organizational changes it made, its conduct in the Lebanese arena, the nature of the political Islamic discourse that developed then, and the sensitivity it developed for the Shiite and Lebanese public opinion. These changes occurred in parallel and affected one another.[144]

Notwithstanding the realization of the new policy, the movement found it difficult to convince its audiences and rivals that the changes it announced were indeed genuine and that it had abandoned in earnest the revolutionary pan-Islamic path in favor of the pragmatic national-Lebanese path. Here and there, expressions that characterized the previous policy were still being heard, such as the one made by al-Amin, the faction chairman in parliament, who explained that "Hezbollah's entry to parliament does not symbolize a change in the organization's plan, working towards the establishment of an Islamic republic in Lebanon."

According to him, "Hezbollah will work inside the organization [meaning parliament—author's comment] for a radical change in the current clannish and unjust regime, which carried out crimes against the people."[145]

The Islamic rhetoric, based on concepts of Jihad and sacrifice; the managing of a policy of independent resistance, sometimes in total opposition to the interests of the Lebanese state; and the lack of dramatic changes in the leadership of the movement and in its intermediate ranks, as necessitated from far-reaching policy changes planted doubts regarding the depth of the change and the degree of its assimilation in the movement. Moreover, the ambiguous and opaque formulas provided by its leaders in the first half of the 1990s did not help in promoting its new image and prevented the blurring of the revolutionary pan-Islamic one.[146] One way or the other, the political rivals of the movement made sure that its revolutionary image was not forgotten. Hariri's roster, competing for the constituents' votes in Beirut and the mountains, defined the contest with Hezbollah as a struggle between moderation and extremism. Its slogan, "A conflict between moderation and extremism and the ending of Islamic fundamentalism," placed Hezbollah at the extreme margins of Lebanese society and emphasized the need to annihilate Islamic fundamentalism.[147]

Therefore, there is no surprise why the Lebanese and foreign press often dealt with the question of Hezbollah's Lebanese pragmatism, despite the expressions of discontentment and unease from the side of the movement's leadership, which strove to instill its new image in the public opinion. In August 1992, Nasrallah emphasized that Hezbollah was "a Lebanese party, whose leadership is Lebanese and its men are Lebanese, and its public is Lebanese and it has a connection with a specific country ... Hezbollah did not rise to serve an Iranian plan. Hezbollah rose to fight the occupation, and therefore it is more Lebanese than all the others."[148]

However, despite the efforts to conceal the revolutionary image and to present a Lebanese appearance, the Hezbollah leaders were repeatedly required to ward off their opponents' arguments that emphasized the movement's acceptance of Iran as the source of authority, a fact that, in their eyes, cast a doubt regarding how Lebanese was the movement. Qassem tried to settle the contradiction between obeying the leadership of Khomeini and his successor, Khamenei, and the fact of Hezbollah being Lebanese. According to him, Hezbollah believed and obeyed the rulings of the world scriptural Muslim leadership in Iran and, as such, was no different from other groups obeying a world leader. The movement's affinity to the Iranian religious source of authority did not stand in contradiction to it being a Lebanese movement. There was a clear boundary, reflected by the movement's exclusivity in decisions on internal Lebanese issues. To strengthen his argument, Qassem added that the members of the movement were Lebanese patriots with Lebanese identities, who sacrificed their lives for Lebanon.[149]

Nasrallah strove to position his movement in the same status as other Lebanese parties and argued that, excluding the issue of the resistance, Hezbollah is "a movement that operates like other movements in Lebanon in the social, cultural, and political areas."[150] Another argument from Nasrallah's school of thought that strengthened the Lebanese message was based on the fact that Hezbollah was a homogenous movement whose members were Lebanese only. He emphasized that his movement avoided receiving foreign volunteers, despite this being an acceptable phenomenon in other Islamic movements.[151] In March 1999, Nasrallah rejected outright arguments regarding Hezbollah being an Iranian movement that was imported into Lebanon. According to him, the Islamic idea on which the movement was founded was not based on a specific country. He provided an original explanation to the nature of the Lebanese–Iranian connection and argued that its source was, in fact, the Islamic point of view that was shaped by Lebanese religious scholars who operated in Iran.[152]

Another fear that the movement strove to relieve in the public opinion of the Shiite community and in Lebanon concerned the degree of Iranian influence on the movement's attitude toward an Islamic state. The propaganda message was based on the differences between Iran and Lebanon and the lack of basic conditions in Lebanon to the founding of an Islamic state. Nasrallah made it clear that an Islamic state necessitates popular support with a special majority and that it cannot be founded with a military coup or with party activity. The Iranian experience, as far as he was concerned, constituted an example for the foundation of an Islamic state through a nonviolent revolution. Its success stemmed from the wide popular support that the country's Islamic regime had. According to him, the situation was fundamentally different in Lebanon; the conditions were not ripe for the foundation of an Islamic state and preparing the ground for the foundation of such a regime might last hundreds of years. Therefore, the realistic solution, from his point of view, was the continued existence of the current regime while conducting a dialog concerning the nature of the desired regime.[153]

In an effort to convince the target audience on this matter, Fadlallah took part as well. He regarded the Lebanese nature of Hezbollah as a matter of course and even presented it as such. In a series of statements made in the first half of 1995, Fadlallah argued that the Islamic phenomenon in Lebanon is not an Iranian phenomenon.[154] In 1998, faithful to his rational approach, Fadlallah said, in the most lucid way, that the foundation of an Islamic state in Lebanon was not even on the agenda "and that a realistic approach should be taken." He added that "we dream that the whole world will be Muslim . . . the Islamic wishes to continue to maintain freedoms in Lebanon because this serves its purposes more than a striving to realize an unrealistic goal of establishing an Islamic state in Lebanon."[155]

National Lebanese expressions and symbols had started to appear bit by bit in the movement's discourse since 1995. In June 1995, Raed, a member of the Al-Wafa, referred to the nature of the relationship between the movement and its audiences and the state in the following words: "The Islamic resistance leans on national tendencies and makes an effort to take into account reservations and weaknesses that arise in secrecy, far away from the battlefield. This is because the resistance wishes to liberate the territory in an atmosphere of internal agreement."[156] In another place, in the same month, he said "there is an identity of interests between the state and the resistance movement, and there is no justification to say that there is an abyss gaping between them."[157]

Islamic expressions that were not compatible with the national line were refined, dimmed, and made vague. The message of liberating Jerusalem, one of the goals of the movement, took another form. The responsibility of liberating Jerusalem was turned over to the Palestinians, and the movement positioned itself in the status of assisting the Palestinians to achieve this goal.[158] Nasrallah was even willing to "risk" the cooperation ties with the Islamic movements in Lebanon and outside it by publicly criticizing them, as long as this served the movement. He called upon the Islamic movements to strive for reconciliation with their governments in order to make it possible for resources to be directed for the struggle against Israel, and even offered his help.[159]

The movement's emphasis on affinity to the country also found expression in its celebrating the Lebanese Independence Day and national memorial days, playing the national anthem, and waving Lebanese flags in the movement's rallies. In December 1995, Nasrallah emphasized that the occupation prevents the movement from celebrating the Lebanese Independence Day, but that it would celebrate it when the occupation was over. In April 1996, during the events of the national day of rapport in memory of the Qanaa dead, Radio Nur declared a moment of silence, after which it played the national anthem.[160] The first indication of the waving of Lebanese flags in the movement's rallies appeared in 1997 during the memorial service on the occasion of the death of Nasrallah's son. Following it, the movement declared that, from then on, the Lebanese flags would be raised in its rallies, explaining this in the implementation of a new policy.[161] An additional national symbol, which an "invisible hand" took care to announce, appeared in Nasrallah's letter to the president of Syria, in which he used expressions of national Islamic resistance.[162]

The continuing propaganda campaign for the changing of its image among the Lebanese public opinion reaped gains as well. The movement was successful in blurring its old image, in projecting credibility in its intentions to change, and in creating a basis of legitimacy in the Lebanese system. A testimony to that would be the words of the Amal delegate to parliament on the eve of the 1996 elections, who, while attacking Hezbollah as representing foreign interests in the eyes of the public, said that "the Hezbollah organization recently succeeded in changing its image, but is yet to succeed in removing all barriers" and that "the people of Hezbollah are trying to argue that there is no contradiction between the Islamic program and the national-Lebanese program. In late 1997, the Amal delegate remarked that Hezbollah began a process of Lebanonization at the very stage where it separated ideology and politics.[163]

One of the high points of the campaign to change the movement's image in the public opinion was the initiation and leading of a widely covered media move to establish a supraclan party framework for the promotion of national and internal Lebanese issues. This initiative, starting in April 1997, provided the movement with the necessary means, stage, and setting to prove to the Shiite community and Lebanese public opinion that it was indeed a renewing, legitimate, and moderate movement, operating within the limits of the national Lebanese system. A persuasive proof for that was provided by the movement in the shape of the document of principles that it distributed to the Lebanese parties as a basis for defining a common denominator. The document presented a moderate image that accepted Lebanon's cultural, religious, and political diversity and called for the strengthening of the national unity and the formation of a national identity with an Arab shade, while maintaining political freedom of action, public freedom, and freedom of expression and action of the social elements. The style of Hezbollah's document of principles of April 1997 was fundamentally different from the style of its "open letter" of February 1985. It suggested pragmatism and a national-Lebanese approach, as opposed to its predecessor that exhibited pan-Islamism and extremism and revealed Iranian connections.[164] In August 1997, the movement initiated a second conference for the approval of the revised document of principles as another means to emphasize its new image and the seriousness of its positions as well as its attitude toward concepts such as nationality and Lebanese nature.[165]

In September 1997, after the death of Nasrallah's son, the movement registered another achievement in the story of its relationship with the Shiite and Lebanese public opinion, and its support increased, according to many opinions. This was evident from the number of delegations who arrived to console Nasrallah, from the presence of representatives from the entire Lebanese political spectrum, and from the masses attending the rally organized in memory of his son. Nasrallah took advantage of the political opportunity presented to him and announced an additional step in the "policy of openness" of his movement, whose purpose was to increase openness toward the Lebanese system. The Lebanese flags raised in the memorial rally were, in fact, proof of the expression of this policy, and they were meant to establish its image as a national-Lebanese movement that holds real importance in the symbols of the state.[166] In his statement, Nasrallah laid the foundations for the establishing of a new Lebanese apolitical resistance framework that would operate with affinity to Hezbollah. This initiative was recycled from the idea of the "society of resistance" (previous attempts to implement this were unsuccessful) and the giving of a national dimension to the activities of the movement. This step, which was added to a series of steps and initiatives of the movement in front of the Shiite community and the Lebanese systems, was aimed at convincing public opinion that the movement had indeed changed its way and that it was now acting out of pragmatic national-Lebanese considerations.

Nasrallah's announcement bore immediate fruit in public opinion. A month later, as he was aware of the increase in public support for the resistance activities, Nasrallah said "we are aware that a heavy responsibility is placed upon us to transform this sympathy into political action, cultural action, and military action, to which all Lebanese will be partners."[167] An *Al-Ahd* reporter boasted that "the Hezbollah organization was wise in merging into its strategic goals a pragmatic rational which is characterized by realism." He further argued that the policy of openness toward the Lebanese system and the understanding of the existing reality and its constraints, alongside intellectual flexibility and pragmatism, caused increase in the popular support of the movement and its activities. These generated the necessary changes in the Lebanese system and made it possible to execute the new initiative for the foundation of the Lebanese resistance squadrons.[168]

The initiative to establish an additional pan-Lebanese framework of resistance that would operate in affinity to the Hezbollah movement provided an excellent opportunity for the movement to establish its status and its reliability as a legitimate national-Lebanese movement.[169] It derived from this framework all possible benefits by revealing it to the public opinion, emphasizing its tasks and its affinity to the movement, the progress of recruitment and training processes, and the level of readiness of the framework to carry out its tasks. This propaganda activity continued also in the first half of 1998, and it was cautiously managed with the aim of not harming the movement's relations with the other parties and the desire to maximize the profits from this initiative. The name that was chosen, not unintentionally, for the new framework was "Lebanese Squadrons for the Resistance of the Occupation." It was meant to create a link between the movement and additional target audiences in the Lebanese system and to provide additional and very meaningful legitimacy to the Lebanese character of the movement.[170]

The Revolution of the Hungry as an Expression of Processes of Change and Internal Struggles

In the beginning of July 1997, Al-Tufayli, who was the first secretary general of Hezbollah, declared a "revolution of the hungry" in the Beqaa valley and called on its residents to start a civil disobedience against the Lebanese regime. He challenged the leadership of Hezbollah and Nasrallah as its chief and blamed them for neglecting the treatment of the issues of the Beqaa valley and its residents. Al-Tufayli's departure, along with his followers, constituted the climax of the crisis within the movement between the radical trend, clinging to the continuance of the revolutionary pan-Islamic way, and the pragmatic majority. The roots of this crisis are found in the movement's conference of 1991, with the selection of Abbas Al-Musawi as the replacement of Al-Tufayli and with the preferment of Nasrallah over him after the assassination of al-Musawi in 1992. The departure of the radical stream, led by Al-Tufayli, is a typical phenomenon in the life cycle of social protest movements and usually occurs in the institutionalizing stage. Similarly, the Hezbollah movement was founded in the beginning of 1980s on the basis of the radical margins of the Amal movement.[171]

The internal dispute on the shaping of the movement's path and policy was decided in the early 1990s, with the making of the decision to participate in the parliamentary elections. This decision exacerbated the crisis in the high echelon of the movement, between the supporters of the move and its objectors. The more integrated into the renewing Lebanese system the movement became, the more disputes and gaps between the pragmatic majority and the radical margins that opposed it appeared. The dominating group in the leadership of the movement, headed by Nasrallah, neutralized the power of the radicals by removing them from centers of influence and expanded the basis of support for the new policy within the movement and among the members of the Shiite community. As long as the leadership of the movement felt that there was a chance to solve the crisis through internal dialog within the movement and away from the eyes of the media, it denied the existence of "camps" as well as assessments heard of a possible schism.[172]

The interesting thing is that, despite the removal of Al-Tufayli from the leadership of the movement, his authority was preserved by the force of his religious status, and the movement's media continued to interview him and quote his weekly sermons.[173] The attitude toward him as the head of the radical trend in the movement was not comfortable for Al-Tufayli as well. He preferred to lead Hezbollah and keep it on the revolutionary path of the 1980s. Therefore, he used ambiguous language when referring to Hezbollah and avoided initiating a disconnection from it.[174]

Despite all that, Al-Tufayli did not conceal his criticism. He objected to the movement's decision to participate in the parliamentary elections and to its conduct during the elections. He offered an alternative in the shape of an Islamic program to handle the executive corruption, the economic hardships, and the distress of the farmers. He held a different opinion also with regard to Hezbollah's role if and when the peace process materialized. While the movement preferred to deliberately cast a fog over the issue, he emphasized that the military resistance against Israel should continue and that any Lebanese attempt to hold direct and indirect commercial ties with Israel should be prevented. At the end of 1995 and during 1996, Al-Tufayli worked to prepare the ground for the foundation of a new movement in the shape of the 1980s revolutionary Hezbollah. He ordered his listeners and readers to join the new movement, to acquire arms, and to be ready to act in the way of the military resistance.[175]

Hezbollah's failure in the 1996 election campaign deepened the gap between the radicals of the movement and the leadership. Al-Tufayli, who estimated that his position acquired more supporters after the election campaign, blamed Hezbollah for giving Berri the leadership in the south and almost in the Beqaa valley as well and for turning the movement's parliamentary delegates into prisoners. He emphasized that the reason for that was the flawed functioning of the movement's leadership.[176]

Al-Tufayli's declaration of the launch of "the revolution of the hungry" in July 1997 in Baalbek and his call for its expansion to additional Shiite population centers in Beirut and in the southern Lebanon marked the "point of no return" in the relations of both sides. Al-Tufayli began a combined move, whose purpose was to create delegitimization of the current government, to energize the Shiites in the Beqaa valley and Beirut through the use of the media and proclamations, and to act against the government. He instructed people in these regions to stop paying taxes, water bills, and construction fees to the state; to stop obeying its laws; and to physically harm government goals and symbols. He was not content with appealing to his listeners through the media, so he worked with the organized action plan he had conceived on the eve of the revolution. According to the plan, in the first stage, the movement would establish itself in the Beqaa valley and erect its institutions. From there, it would expand toward Beirut, the south, and the north. In July 1997, he instructed his supporters to open fire on the representatives of the Lebanese government. This decision on violence as the preferred path of action was, according to him, a result of methodical thinking and the exhaustion of all other options.[177]

Al-Tufayli properly identified and used the feelings of alienation, rage, and frustration of the Shiite residents of the Beqaa valley and Beirut for the purpose of launching the initial wave of protest, which he chose to base on a common denominator of social discrimination. He hoped that this would make it possible for him to create the momentum that would bring about the overthrowing of the regime and the foundation of an Islamic state. His words influenced the residents of the Beqaa valley, particularly those who had lost their source of income as a result of the government's control over the prices of agricultural products and the ban it placed on growing narcotics. The government's tardiness in providing budgets for the development of the area and the creation of alternative sources of income only made it, in the eyes of the residents of the area, the main culprit in their situation. The fact that the Beqaa valley's was second in Hezbollah's list of priorities (after the resistance and the south) did not help to change the gloomy condition of its inhabitants and actually contributed to the Shiites joining Al-Tufayli's movement.[178]

The launching conditions of his movement appeared to be better compared to those of Hezbollah in the early 1980s. According to a few sources, thousands of people in the Beqaa valley (around 3,000 were present in the opening ceremony) answered Al-Tufayli's call, and the movement gained the support of a number of Shiite clerics and parliament members. This troubled Hezbollah and Amal. It threatened to disrupt the balance that formed in the power odds within the Shiite community and to drag the community, once again, into a campaign of violent conflicts. Al-Tufayli's radical doctrine, his religious status, and his call for the delegitimization of the government only strengthened these fears. Each movement used its means to fence in the phenomenon, prevent the expansion of Al-Tufayli's movement beyond the Beqaa valley, and to minimize the damages that were already caused.[179]

The government, which was no less worried by this phenomenon and its potential for damage, responded to the challenge posed by Al-Tufayli by a combined strategy of simultaneous repression and containment (enabling). This included directing forces to the Beqaa valley, arresting activists, and suppressing demonstrations, alongside expediting the approvals for budget allocations for the region. The government line of combining dialogue and repression was not sufficiently solidified. It created confusion and disputes within the government and invited external criticism. Al-Tufayli's attitude toward the government was much clearer; his strategic decision to act violently was immediately translated into operational instructions to his supporters. He conducted a short dialogue with the government, but he dedicated the rest of his time to organize the civil disobedience, instructing his supporters to go out and demonstrate, open protest strikes, and shoot government representatives.[180]

As time went by, it became apparent that Al-Tufayli had difficulties lifting off. The security activities of the Lebanese army in the field made it difficult for his activists to move around and greatly reduced the scope of the economic activity in the Beqaa valley. The Hezbollah movement did not undergo any far-reaching organizational tremor due to his activities, and it did not seem like economic assistance was about to arrive as a result of the violent action. Due to this trouble, voices started to be heard calling Al-Tufayli to take a more sensible approach and to promote the matters of the Beqaa valley through Hezbollah's members of parliament.[181] In parallel, Al-Tufayli suffered another blow from the direction of Hezbollah, which, after a long period of restraint and unsuccessful attempts to bridge the gaps, officially declared, in an unusual step, the expulsion of Al-Tufayli from its ranks while blaming him with attempting to cause its splitting and sparking a war between brothers.[182]

The crisis in the new movement reached its climax with the eruption of a shooting incident between Al-Tufayli's faithful followers and the Lebanese army during negotiations with regard to the evacuation of the religious seminary in Baalbek. Following the incident, the government decided to pass the handling of the Al-Tufayli matter to the judicial instances, contrary to the position of Hezbollah and Amal. Al-Tufayli was forced to flee from the Lebanese army outside Baalbek and go underground.[183]

Al-Tufayli did not disappear entirely. He continued to operate at a low profile in the Beqaa valley region under a Syrian umbrella. In April 1999, the activists of his movement broke into a Hezbollah weapons depot in the Beqaa valley. During the last months of that year, Al-Tufayli started appearing in public again and continued in the recruitment efforts for his movement. He was also seen in the memorial ceremonies in Syria after Assad's death. On September 2003, in an interview conducted with him for the first time after a long period, Al-Tufayli said that he founded his movement with the aim of forcing the state "to examine the problems of the Beqaa valley inhabitants," and that he was surprised by the fact that Hezbollah supported the government's position against him. He made it clear that the last word was not yet said with regard to this issue and that he was ready to continue acting.[184]

Al-Tufayli's initiative caused a stir in the Shiite community's public opinion and in Hezbollah's base of support in the Beqaa valley. Hezbollah, the main casualty of the initiative, adopted emergency measures and worked to minimize the effects of the damage caused by Al-Tufayli's departure by conducting an internal overhaul. It located, isolated, and expelled his faithful followers from its ranks. In contrast to its harshness in its internal purge activities, it exhibited, as long as it could, a moderate appearance in its activities for the public opinion. In this framework, it clung to its position that no schism occurred in the movement and displayed a position supportive of Al-Tufayli's demands, but renounced his operational methods and the nature of the messages he disseminated. It tried to improve its image by increasing its activities among the members of the Shiite community in the Beqaa valley, in parliament, and in front of the government representatives for discovering solutions to reduce the hardships of the Beqaa valley residents. In parallel, it emphasized its oppositional activity while accusing the government, arguing that it employed destructive economic activity.[185] Amal, for its part, tried to take advantage of the situation and, as Hezbollah argued on the eve of the municipal elections in the Beqaa valley, Berri assisted Al-Tufayli with the purpose of promoting the movement's affairs in the elections.[186]

Conclusion

The Hezbollah leadership, at least outwardly, was wise in internalizing the processes occurring within the Shiite community and within Lebanon at the end of the civil war and in shaping a political path that suited the renewing Lebanese system. The change, backed by widespread propaganda and explanatory activities, was aimed at establishing the movement's status within the Shiite community and inside the Lebanese system, making use of the existing tools and means available to the establishment for the advancement of the goals of the movement, and increasing the exposure of the Islamic message. However, this change involved an overly high price as far as the radical margins were concerned. It obligated abandoning the revolutionary pan-Islamic approach and working within the boundaries of the Lebanese political system.

Hezbollah, in my humble opinion, assumed, in the last third of the 1990s, that it had succeeded in convincing the Shiite community's public opinion, as well as others, of the sincerity of its moves and its new image, and it worked to translate this into political power and to prepare the ground for activity in the era after Israel's withdrawal from Lebanon.[187] Lebanese journalists and commentators, and researchers specializing in the Lebanese arena, referred to the change that took place in its image during the 1990s in comparison to the previous decade.[188]

It is hard to decide whether Hezbollah was successful in convincing its various audiences that it had indeed undergone a process of change in earnest and how far and whether the sophisticated propaganda and the endless reiteration of its messages in the various media had indeed achieved its goals, but there is no doubt about how important the Shiite community's public opinion was to the leadership of the movement. The majority of the movement's messages were aimed at changing the Shiite public opinion. For the sympathy of the public opinion, it waged a continuous, sometimes violent, struggle with the Amal movement, and as a result of its understanding of the community's state of mind, it studied its actions and policies.

A sympathetic Shiite public opinion was essential for the existence of the movement, more so since the 1990s, from the stage in which it put itself to the judgment of the elector. Therefore, its moves in the Lebanese political arena were, in many cases, meant to serve its goals in the internal Shiite arena and to establish its status as a patriotic popular movement that worked for the advancement and improvement of the conditions of the underprivileged among the members of the Shiite community, in parallel to its war against Israel.

Hezbollah as a Player in the Lebanese Political Arena—Mutual Influences

Hezbollah and the Lebanese System—Mutual Influences since the Foundation of the Movement (1982) to the Ta'if Agreement (1990)

The Lebanese System—Main Characteristics

Lebanon is a unique example of a multisectarian country with a complex social and political structure. This fact has influenced the stability of the political system of the country and was one of the main factors leading to the split of Lebanon, the outbreak of waves of violence, and the eruption of power struggles.

At the national level, Lebanon split into two ethnic groups: Christians and Muslims, who struggled against one another to determine the character of the Lebanese state (Arab or Western) and the desired type of regime. Within the camps, the heads of the groups were fighting over the leadership of their own group. Even within the communities, power struggles were going on for domination of the community. It is worthwhile to emphasize that the 1980s were characterized by the use of violence by all the sectarian players as a means of achieving their goals.[1]

During this period (the 1980s), the Lebanese system comprised six players who exhibited between them reciprocal power relations, which reflected upon the process of occurrences in Lebanon and, as an exception, also upon Hezbollah and the Shiite community:

A. *The Lebanese government*: The Lebanese government was a weak player of marginal influence throughout the 1980s. It was established on the traditional elites, who had lost their power during the civil war. The Lebanese president Amin Gemayel, two prime ministers (one of whom was murdered), and a paralyzed parliament found it difficult to control Lebanon during the 1980s.[2] The anarchy reached its peak toward the end of Amin Gemayel's regime. In the absence of an agreed-upon presidential candidate, two governments reigned in Lebanon (a Christian government headed by Aoun and a Muslim one headed by al-Huss) alongside each other, without an acting president and with no real influence upon the occurrences in the country. In 1989, under the pressure of regional and international factors, the framework of the relations between the Muslim and the Christian camps was regulated and validated under the Ta'if Accord (October 1989). The elimination of Aoun's power bases in October 1990 and the election of Elias Hrawi as president in November 1990 paved the road to Lebanon's political and institutional recovery as well as that for the termination of the regime of the militias in the country.[3]

B. *The Christian group*: This group was a major player in the Lebanese arena.[4] Its influence on Hezbollah's expansion was indirect, yet of great importance. It largely contributed to the ongoing violence and chaos in Lebanon and systematically obstructed the Syrian efforts to stabilize the condition in Lebanon, as it also did concerning internal sectarian initiatives and Lebanese internal initiatives to terminate the civil war. Its weakening toward the end of the period, as a consequence of continuous power struggles, had prepared the groundwork for redrafting the national treaty and finding the formulas to permit the restoration of the political system.

C. *The Muslim group*: This group included players from all three sects: Shiites, Sunnis, and Druze. Violent struggles for control of the community had been taking place within these sects, and all of them wanted to be the backbone of the Islamic community. In the Shiite sect, there were struggles between Amal and Hezbollah. The Druze sect was ruled by Walid Junblat's militia, one of the three strongest militias in Lebanon during these years. The struggle within the Sunni sect concerned the control of powerful positions within the Lebanese political system.

Actually, we can say that four major players were operating within the Islamic community: Amal, Hezbollah, the Druze militia, and the Sunni sect, whose major power derived from its status in the political system. The interactions between players within the Muslim group, the aspirations of each one of them to intensify their own political strength, alongside the dysfunctional government, as well as the fact that the Lebanese system provided a loose framework for aggressive players with conflicting interests were some of the main factors for the ongoing violence along the contact lines between the different militias.

Hezbollah and the Lebanese System—Mutual Influences during the Movement's Establishment

The interactions between the Shiite community, the government, and other power factors in Lebanon, as well as the violent activity typical to the Lebanese system ever since the mid 1970s, formulated the activity patterns of the Shiite community in general and of Hezbollah in particular. Its members' feelings of frustration and discrimination were translated into acts of collective protest, challenging the regimes and the longstanding elites. As the intersectarian struggle worsened, the political system weakened. The outbreak of the civil war in 1975 was the expression of this struggle. This war brought armed groups to the front of the stage, bringing about the development of new elites, who based their power on the militias they had established.

Until the outbreak of the civil war, the community's struggle with the administration included two components that complemented one another: dialogue and organized and controlled protest. This strategy of struggle had gained partial success, such as the government's decision to establish the "Southern Council" and to allot resources for its restoration, but the decision became ineffective from 1975 on.[5]

The civil war emphasized the necessity of the Shiite militia's existence. This had been demonstrated after the banishment of about 100,000 Shiites from their homes in the Naba'a quarter (in Beirut) in 1976. During this period, Sheikh Fadlallah, himself an expellee from Naba'a, wrote his famous treatise, "Al-Islam wa-mantiq al-quwwa" (Islam and the logic of force), in which he rejected the passive Shiite approach and laid the foundations for the use of force against oppression, invigorating faith in God, and crushing the infidels. The Naba'a expulsion was engraved into the collective sectarian memory and, from hereon, the use of force was increased as a means of survival in the chaotic Lebanese environment and as an instrument to attain political goals.[6]

The first significant challenge of the Shiite community, in regard to the Lebanese government as well as the use of force to achieve political goals, occurred after the Islamic revolution in Iran. From 1980 to 1982, violence broke out between the Amal movement and pro-Iranian groups on the one hand and between the Palestinian organizations and left wing organizations in Beirut and in Southern Lebanon on the other. The Shiites, who had suffered from the Israeli-Palestinian conflict, fought to expel the Palestinians from the Shiite population centers.[7]

This activity environment, governed by the sectarian militias, in which violence was the main way to survive, provided suitable conditions for the emergence of protest movements. From time to time, essential disagreements concerning the goals, the manner of activating the forces, and the conduct within the Lebanese political system took place within the militias themselves. In the case of the Shiite community, this created a serious split—seclusion of the radical margins and the establishment of the Hezbollah movement. The deep split in the Shiite community took place during the summer of 1982, when Amal joined the "National Salvation Front."[8]

To conclude, an ongoing discrimination on behalf of the Lebanese government and the development of an environment of chaotic activity in which the idea of "might is right" forced the Shiite community to adjust its activity patterns with the condition created. With somewhat of a delay, it managed to internalize the fact that the Lebanese government was incapable of providing the community with security and basic services and started enlisting from its internal resources in order to form a sectarian militia force. The weakness of the political system has influenced the internal sectarian procedures, causing disputes that grew wider and wider as the war went on. All these, in turn, inflicted changes in the inner-sectarian balance of power, causing the emergence of new elites and radicalization in the sectarian public opinion. As a consequence, and more increasingly following the success of the Iranian revolution, a new militant Islamic wing developed in the community, which adopted revolutionary pan-Islamic concepts, striving for the founding of an Islamic state in Lebanon. This wing became a movement during the summer of 1982 under the encouragement of Iran and while exploiting the weakness of the Lebanese political system.

Hezbollah and the Lebanese System—Mutual Influences during the Movement's Consolidation

This period, which lasted for three years, was characterized by the Israeli control over Lebanon. It corresponds with two phases in the lifespan of Hezbollah: the establishment of the movement in 1982 and its consolidation between 1982 and 1985. During this period, changes occurred in the internal balance of forces of the Lebanese system. Since 1982, the Palestinians ceased to be a military and political force in Lebanon, and the Lebanese left wing, which was greatly dependant upon the PLO, weakened severely.

On the other hand, the Amal movement and the Progressive Socialist Party under Waleed Junblatt became very powerful and expanded their areas of influence in Beirut.

In September 1982, Amin Gemayel was elected to the presidency under the patronage of a multinational task force that had arrived in Lebanon. After his election, he commenced an act to regulate a new governmental order in Beirut as a preliminary move to implementing the regime over all of Lebanon. A short-sighted political standpoint and an anti-Shiite policy, ignoring the rising power of the Shiite sect, had already failed his initiative in its primary stages. His decision to sign the May 17, 1983 agreement with Israel only worsened a condition that was anyway complicated. The opportunity to set the Lebanese political system back on the track of stability and rehabilitation was missed out on, and it got carried away by another wave of violence, which ended only during the 1990s with the implementation of the Ta'if Accord, under Syria's leadership.

The president's refusal to conduct a dialogue with the Shiite community and his policy of oppression against it and, simultaneously, the renewal of the Sunni-Christian alliance pushed the Shiites into taking an oppositional position toward the government. In August 1983, Nabih Berri instructed the Shiite militia to take actions to secure the control over the city's neighborhoods, and in February 1984, he called on the Shiite soldiers in the Lebanese Army to defect and join the Amal movement. By the end of February 1984 and after a series of clashes with the army forces, the Amal movement expanded its control over the Beirut centers of power and economy.[9]

From there on, the sect became a significant factor in the Lebanese political system and was integrated into every negotiation toward a plausible arrangement in Lebanon. So, for example, Berri was invited to the reconciliation conference in Lausanne in March 1984 as the community representative, and in May 1984, he joined a national unity government headed by Rashid Karami and consistently served in the Lebanese governments until the 1992 parliament elections. Berri's tenure in the governments of Lebanon and the financial resources at his disposal facilitated him to establish his influence within the sect. These resources provided, as far as he was concerned, a counterbalance to the generous Iranian funding that the Hezbollah movement was enjoying during those years. [10]

The reciprocations between the Shiite community and the political system were directly influencing Hezbollah as well. The weakness of the political system allowed the establishment, training, and operation of the Hezbollah movement without any interruptions. Creativity and extreme violence allowed it to break into the center of Lebanese and international attention and to simultaneously become well structured and consolidated as an organizational entity. From a fragile central framework with an Islamic common denominator, unifying unorganized radical groups during the second half of 1982, Hezbollah became a movement with an ideological framework and an organizational outline during the first half of 1985. Its consolidation, during a very brief span , was facilitated, inter alia, due to the existence of chaotic environmental conditions and the intensification of violence in the country. The more "successes" it celebrated, the wider its circle of supporters became from among the members of the Shiite community.[11]

In the purview of Lebanese internal affairs, the movement had placed the goal of overthrowing the regime on a high priority and acted to fulfill it. The government's weakness had turned the goal of changing the regime by using force into a seemingly applicable one and even allowed militias to operate in order to achieve this, almost without any actual threat from the regime itself. The signing of the Israel-Lebanon Draft Peace Agreement on May17, 1983, provided a catalyst for waging a violent campaign against the Lebanese government, overthrowing it, and thwarting the agreement. This campaign included the following:

1. Attacks against the Lebanese armed forces in Beirut and in the Beqaa valley, calling the Shiite soldiers to defect, and the Hezbollah overtaking of the "Sheikh Abdullah" camp, which served as the main base of the Lebanese Army in the Beqaa valley, in September 1983.[12]
2. The execution of a series of violent activities against the MNFs in an attempt to force them to withdraw from Lebanon and thus weaken the regime's strength resources.
3. The escalation of the activities against Israel in an attempt to accelerate its withdrawal from Lebanon.[13]

In February 1985, Hezbollah publicly declared its goals, including establishing an Islamic republic in Lebanon. As long as the Lebanese regime was weak, the movement operated to fulfill them by using violent means.[14] Naim Qassem wrote in his book that, during its first years, Hezbollah operated confidentially while avoiding political activity because of the need to organize its ranks, to consolidate the movement and to protect it from the infiltration of Israeli intelligence. Qassem stated that the movement avoided dealing with the political issue during this time, out of fear that it might divert the movement from promoting the resistance activities. According to his claim, this fear evaporated during the late 1980s.[15] Simultaneously with the violent activity, the movement expanded its propaganda campaign for purposes of modeling an Islamic society in Lebanon through the Daawa and preparing the groundwork for the reign of the religious sage (Velayat-e faqih). This was supported by deepening the social community activity and by providing a variety of services for the sect members, with an emphasis on welfare and education.[16]

The Lebanese government, which identified the potential threat placed by the movement to its stability, was dissatisfied, to say the very least, by Hezbollah's style of activity and acted to limit and minimize it as much as possible. It has been claimed, for instance, that Karami, who agreed to head the national reconciliation government in 1984, did so on the condition that the Syrians would restrain Hezbollah's activity in the Beqaa valley.[17]

To conclude, the weakness of the Lebanese political system provided political opportunities for the emergence of the Hezbollah movement and permitted its rapid consolidation and propagation among the Shiite populace in the country. Furthermore, it allowed the movement to threaten the regime's very existence and to bring down the force bases that it depended upon. The chaotic conditions that prevailed in the country on the one hand and political creativity in all that concerned the initiation of violent activity on the other hand allowed the Hezbollah movement to become organized, get equipped, as well as recruit and train new activists.

Proof of the importance of the impact of the chaotic environment on the consolidation of the movement was provided by the Lebanese system in 1997–1998. During these years, the attempt made by Subhi al-Tufayli to repeat Hezbollah's model and to establish a new movement in the Beqaa valley, named "Revolution of the Hungry"(also known as Revolt of the Hungry), was oppressed. The failure of al-Tufayli derived, among other things, from the essential differentiability that had taken place concerning the movement's activity environment and, as a consequence, of the Lebanese government's ability to enforce its reign in Lebanon.

The Hezbollah and the Lebanese System—Mutual Influences during the Movement's Expansion

In general, there was no essential change in the relations between the movement and the Lebanese government during the second half of the 1980s, and it went on in the same pattern as before. The movement, which underwent a process of accelerated expansion during these years, completely avoided dialogue with the government under the claim that the regime was cooperating with Israel and the United States, and strove to establish an Islamic republic.[18]

Altogether, an internal discussion took place within the movement concerning the question of whether an Islamic republic, according to the model set by Iran, would be viable in Lebanon. The first approach set by Fadlallah claimed that the conditions of the Lebanese system differ from those in Iran; therefore, activity guidelines must be presented to befit this system. On the other hand, part of the movement's leadership upheld a militant approach, striving to establish an Islamic republic through a violent act, as part of a pan-Islamic world system, under Iran's leadership. The discussion concerning this issue was principally decided in 1985, with the publication of the movement's ideological framework, drafted according to Fadlallah's guidelines. Yet, the operative activity executed under the leadership of the young Ulema actually emphasized the violent standpoint of Islamic fundamentalism and was one that created among the Lebanese people in general, including amid members of the Shiite community, the all-encompassing objection to and fear from the establishing of an Islamic republic.[19]

Fadlallah had often expressed his positions concerning the need to change the existing regime. He was waiting for the proper political opportunity to do so.

In early 1988, during one of the most significant low points of the Lebanese government, he identified such an opportunity, claiming that the governmental framework in Lebanon was devoid of any content and, therefore, the desirable condition for the Hezbollah movement was to drag Lebanon, at the end of Amin Gemayel's regime, to a condition of "constitutional vacuum." This condition, as far as he was concerned, "would make the Lebanese people change their way of thinking in an extreme manner," forcing them to adopt an inclusive solution, clear of narrow sectarian interests and considerations.[20]

In May 1988, Fadlallah said that the Iranian model was not viable in Lebanon because of the essential differentiability between the two countries and that the Lebanese Islamic movement was operating according to the conditions, the status in the Lebanese arena, and the restraints of the regional and international systems. Therefore, he offered the Lebanese people the solution of an Islamic republic. In his opinion, if the Lebanese would adopt the Islamic solution, it could pave the road to its implementation. If it were rejected, the Islamic movement would remain, just like the other political movements, a solution not applied in Lebanon. Fadlallah added, "The question of whether we wish to coerce this opinion through terror, as they say, or whether we wish to coerce it in the framework of radical-ization, as they say, meaning either we'll have everything or we'll have nothing, we denounce and condemn this kind of talk."[21]

He emphasized that the primary hurdle that the Islamists were facing was that of convincing the Lebanese public of the purity of their intentions while clarifying that their offer derived from faith and that the Islamic solution was the right one for Lebanon.[22] He also called for the integration of the Hezbollah movement into the Lebanese political arena.[23]

In contrast with Fadlallah's approach, part of the movement's leadership upheld a radical militant approach, based on loyalty to Khomeini's leadership and the commitment to impose Islam all over the world, as a part of the Islamic Iranian republic, while using all available means—political as well as violent.

Hussein al-Musawi, one of the prominent representatives of the radical militant approach, said in August 1986: "We don't believe that the regime has a legitimate right to survive . . . since we assume that it is possible to overthrow this regime, we're using all the means at our disposal in order to make this regime illegal and powerless . . . we may not be able to overthrow it in the near future, yet we are not dissatisfied with our methods of overthrowing the regime."[24] In late 1987, he said, "As Muslims, we don't believe in the existence of a separate country called Lebanon, we relate to the entire Islamic world as our homeland."[25] The problem with the Lebanese regime, as far as he was concerned, was not the presi-dential image, but its being a depriving regime, and therefore, according to him, "We are ready to overthrow the regime in Lebanon in order to establish a just regime. Whoever rules over Lebanon must adhere to the laws of Islam. It doesn't matter to us whom the next President of Lebanon shall be, because we are not in the Lebanese regime." [26]

In late 1989, al-Tufayli expressed a slightly softened position, in accord with the principles set by Fadlallah, and said, "We wish to persuade the world to become Muslim through dialogue, yet we do not wish to compel Islam by force. As to Lebanon, we do want to allow the Lebanese people to elect the regime which most people would want to have. When they choose Islam, we will accept this and if they will choose another form of regime, we shall accept that as well".[27]

One way or another, most players in the Lebanese system were following, with concern, the movement's efforts to change the existing regime, and most of them denounced the idea of an Islamic republic. The establishment of enclaves, according to the model of the Islamic Iranian republic, in Baalbek and in the southern suburb of Beirut, with all of the accompanying characteristics (external physical appearance, public administration, education, and services) signified, as far as the Lebanese people were concerned, the movement's serious intentions and the commencement of the plan to enforce Islam over the state.

No wonder, therefore, that they doubted the sincerity of the movement's declarations, which stated that it did not intend to forcefully apply Islam in the country.[28] The nearly complete paralysis of the Lebanese system, with the founding of Aoun's government and the outbreak of the war between Amal and Hezbollah, had intensified the anxiety of the fundamentalist Islamic plan and of Hezbollah's rising power. The Hezbollah movement, on the other hand, claimed that the Lebanese media was hostile toward its movements and activities, was taking a negative stand, regarding it as "a foreign entity on Lebanese soil."[29]

The environment of violence and chaos that prevailed in Lebanon during the 1980s allowed for the rapid emergence of the Hezbollah movement, from a network of secret cells and prepolitical groups to an organized, semiconfidential movement, operating through two wings (military and civilian) that complemented one another. The movement was taking advantage of the anarchy in the Lebanese system in order to expand its bases of supporters amongst the members of the Shiite community, by translating the feelings of discrimination and alienation into acts of violence against the political system and its institutes as well as against foreigners in Lebanon. It refrained from getting involved in internal Lebanese power struggles. Yet, it did not hesitate to act violently against the Amal movement, in a battle for domination over the Shiite public opinion, just as long as the violence served its purposes.

The longstanding deprivation of the Shiite community played into the hands of the Hezbollah movement. It founded and operated many institutions and organizations, which satisfied the populace's needs, from health and welfare services to acquiring education and Islamic culture. Lebanon's split into sectarian-based living zones and the location of most of the Shiite communities in the rural margins and the poverty-stricken slums in the outskirts of Beirut facilitated the movement's penetration, permitting the establishment of Islamic enclaves, in which life was administrated according to the model of the Iranian Islamic republic.

While other militias were knee-deep in exhausting struggles over power and control, Hezbollah was striving to translate its successes (in the activities against foreigners in Lebanon and Israel) to an expansion of its circle of supporters, to the recruitment and training of new activists, and to the creation of a military and civilian organizational infrastructure in the Shiite population centers. The war against Amal, "War between Brothers," was initiated only after it felt secure in its ability to defeat its rival and even identified an opportunity to execute this task. The increasing anarchy in Lebanon from late 1988, the absence of an acting president, and the simultaneous existence of two governments (Aoun and al-Huss) had nearly dragged the Lebanese political system to the threshold of an abyss, yet afforded significant grounds of activity for the ongoing struggle between Amal and Hezbollah.

Hezbollah and the Lebanese Militias

The anarchy in Lebanon served well the goals of the Hezbollah movement. It operated to expand its infrastructure, to model a combatant Islamic society, and to overthrow Amin Gemayel's government.[30] Hezbollah even refrained from getting involved in the militias' wars and objected to agreements that could have essentially changed the condition.

1. In December 1985, it objected to the "Tripartite Agreement," signed under Syria's arbitration between the heads of the three strongest militias: Berri, Junblatt, and Elie Hobeika.[31]
2. In 1987, it objected the Syrians' entry into the southern suburb, fearing that this activity might restrict its steps. Only in 1988, following ongoing Syrian pressure, did it agree to this move.[32]
3. In November 1989, the movement objected to the contents of the Ta'if Agreement. This objection was accompanied by a call to formulate an alternative plan of action that should coerce a change, without violence.[33]

The rivalry between the Lebanese militias, and mainly the two most eminent conflicts during this period, "the War of the Camps" and the "War between Brothers," played into Hezbollah's hands, influencing its continued expansion. The War of the Camps took place from 1985 to 1987 between Amal and the Palestinians in Beirut and in southern Lebanon. It wore off Amal's power and caused its branching and the depletion of its ranks. Hezbollah's success against Israel, on the other hand, had turned it into a center of attraction for young Shiites who couldn't find their place with the Amal movement.[34] Hezbollah was very careful not to get dragged into the War of the Camps and chose to take advantage of this "window of opportunities" to expand it's organizational and community-based infrastructure, to include activities against Israel, and to over-throw the regime.[35] The War between Brothers, on the other hand, was between Amal and Hezbollah during the years 1988–1990, concerning the control of the community. Hezbollah's achievements in this war had established its status as a weighty movement in the Lebanese system.

Despite its rising status in the Lebanese arena, the Hezbollah movement had difficulties creating frameworks of cooperation with other force factors.[36] Being well aware of this and attempting to change the situation, the movement adopted a policy of activity based upon two components: the first was to sustain the preservation and to establish connections with the Islamic movements, and the second was to strive to create a common denominator, which would allow them to commence a dialogue with the prominent players in the Muslim camp (and even with the Christians, under certain circumstances).[37] However, a majority of the players refused to cooperate with it, because of its extremist Islamic image.[38]

An in-depth study of the relations between Hezbollah and the Druze militia in 1987 tells not only of the movement's difficulties in establishing correlation connections with the militias, but also of its determination in striving to do so. This relationship pattern moved from mutual accusations and hostility to cooperation.[39] All through the 1980s and the early 1990s, a pattern of relations of ups, downs, and suspicion alongside connections of cooperation characterized the movement's relations with other militias as well. .

The Hezbollah and the Lebanese System—Mutual Influences from the Ta'if Agreement (1990) On

In August 2000, the third election campaign for the Lebanese parliament (since the application of the Ta'if Agreement) took place. This election campaign pointed out the entry of the Lebanese system into a course of stability and continuity. The armed militias, Lebanon's dominant players during the 1980s, had turned into parliamentary parties during the 1990s. From then on, they struggled and cooperated with each other, within the limits set by the rules of the game for the renewing political system. Violence, as a means of achieving political goals, was replaced by oppositional activity in the parliament and in the public arena. The feasibility of renewing the Lebanese political system occurred as a result of the Ta'if Agreement, which was signed on September 30, 1989. This agreement determined the principles and set the activity guidelines for the future Lebanese political system. Several days later, on November 5, 1989, the parliament convened to elect a president. The elected candidate was René Moawad. Seventeen days later, he was murdered. William B. Harris, a researcher proficient in the Lebanese political arena, claimed that the murder was carried out by Hezbollah in an attempt to thwart the implementation of the Ta'if Agreement.[40] On November 24, 1989, the parliament convened once more to elect Elias Hrawi as Lebanon's next president.

The signing of the Ta'if Agreement was the turning point in the administration of the Lebanese system. From hereon, a process of gradual restoration of the political system, under close Syrian leadership and supervision, was set in motion. It influenced the relative status and position of the players in the system and mainly the government's position. In the course of the 1990s, the regime had turned from a weak and powerless player into the major player in the Lebanese system. Because of the lack of real power and independence, the government was forced to maneuver between internal pressures and Syrian restraints and dictations. Despite this, the government succeeded in leading a long and complex process of restoration. The essential milestones in this process are as follows:[41]

1. *The government of national consent*: The Ta'if Agreement determined that the government should be established by national consent, which should delineate a security plan and act to materialize it. It further determined that the militias should be disarmed and steps should be taken for the restoration of the army and the security forces. Accordingly, on September 24, 1990, Omar Karame's government was established, in which most of the

militias' leaders served . The leaders of the Lebanese Communist Party and the leaders of the Islamic movements, including Hezbollah, were not incorporated into Karame's government of consent.[42] Syria operated, on its side, to facilitate the success of the security plan. It overthrew Aoun's government in Beirut in October 1990 and paved the road for the establishment of the government of consent. The next stage in the security plan concerned disarming the militias as a preliminary step toward dispersing the army all over Lebanon's territory. On March 28, 1991, the government decided that by April 30 all militias would be disarmed and the amalgamation of their members into the state institutes would be confirmed. Most of the militias, except the Palestinian terror organizations and Hezbollah, implemented the decision and handed over their weapons and the lists of their members on the predetermined date. The disarmament of the militias established the regime's status versus the other players, allowing it to reconstruct the state institutions and reestablish the boundaries of "right and wrong," which were practically -nonexistent during the 1980s.[43]

2. *The parliament election*: The Ta'if Agreement redefined the composition of parliament representatives on the basis of the demographic changes that had taken place in Lebanon. The agreement determined that the number of Christian and Muslim representatives in the parliament should be equalized; a redivision of the representatives within the camps should be carried out in accordance with the relative size of the sects and that the elections should be held on the basis of territorial division. An election date was set for the summer of 1992. From here on, the competition over power and political strength had shifted from the military arena to the parliamentary one. The oppositional parties were compelled to choose between struggling from within the system or outside of it. The campaigns for parliament from 1992 on saw the participation of most of the force factors, which had been operating in the chaotic system of the 1980s; only this time, they were operating within the game limits of the restoring political system.

3. *The reforms in the public administration system*: It was determined that the government should act to carry out a modification in the public administration system and should restore the administrative mechanism. The first Hariri government started performing inclusive reforms in order to reinforce the power bases of Lebanon's heads of regime. The administrative reform infuriated Hezbollah, which claimed that Berri and the Lebanese government had joined forces to prevent the movement's activists from entering the public administration system.

4. *The reforms in the media*: Within the framework of implementing the Ta'if Agreement, the government acted to regulate the media's activity in the country by legislating a communication law. The process of legislation was laden with struggles. The law, which became valid in 1996, permitted only a few stations to continue broadcasting, including two Hezbollah stations. Dozens of other channels that had been operating in Lebanon during the 1980s were outlawed and forced to cease broadcasting.

5. *The municipal elections*: In May and June 1998, municipal elections were held in Lebanon. This was yet another milestone in Lebanon's road to

establishing a stable political system and securing regular order of regime in the country.

6. *The presidential elections*: As Hrawi's tenure ended, Emile Lahoud was unanimously elected as the next president of Lebanon by 118 members of the parliament on October 15, 1998, after a deliberation that lasted only thirty minutes. That this wall-to-wall consensus, in a country that, ten years before, had no chance of convening the parliament representatives at all, testifies for the progress that had been made in the restoration of the political system and of Syria's degree of control over the Lebanese parliament.

The Players in the Renewed Political System

The Ta'if Agreement changed the odds between the players in the Lebanese system, and new patterns of activity and relations of power were gradually being molded. Oppositional players were shifting to the coalition and vice versa and ex-opponents were cooperating in order to achieve mutual goals. In general, we can say that, in the Lebanese system of the 1990s, a regimental equilibrium was achieved, at least "on paper," between the Christian and the Muslim camps in Lebanon, and a delicate balance had been created within it, between two principal world perspectives—a Western perspective and an Oriental perspective. But in practice, the power relations between the players, which had operated during those years, were much more complex.

The leading player during this period was the Lebanese government. Its moves were greatly dictated not only by Syria, but also by the relations between its three components: the president, the prime minister, and the chairman of the parliament or the "Troika," as they were called. The Ta'if Agreement redefined the power relations between these three entities. In its framework, the Christian president's authorities were reduced in accordance with the expansion of those of the government and the parliament chairman. The government's domination over the country's power resources, through its institutions, had turned it into the mightiest and most dominant player in the Lebanese system. The decisive use of force in the enforcement of the state laws and the regime's decisions gradually formed the activity expanse of the other players.

The Ta'if Agreement was perceived by most Christians and mainly by the Maronites as a move to eliminate the power of the Christian camp, and thus, they opposed it and the regime, conceiving it as a Syrian dummy. In the absence of charismatic secular leadership, especially after the eloignment of Bashir and Aoun from office and, as a result of ongoing internal and external struggles, the Christian camp had become greatly weakened and worn down. The religious leadership, which took the place of the secular-military leadership in the Christian camp, was finding it hard to promote the sect's interests and its status in the Lebanese system.[44]

The Ta'if Agreement, on the other hand, was bettering the Muslim camp in Lebanon, especially the Sunni sect. The authorities of the prime minister, a member of the Sunna sect, was expanded, thus making him a significant power center in the Troika. Within the Sunna sect, power struggles were going on between the longstanding and conservative elites and the new forces that had emerged during the 1990s, whose obvious representative was the Lebanese prime minister, Hariri.

The status of the Druze community within the Muslim camp, which was derived from its relative size, not from its military strength, was greatly weakened. Junblatt was forced to switch from a pattern of a "state" in the Druze canton to the status of a regular political party. Out of the desire to preserve the sect's position versus the other players in the new national system, Junblatt exercised complex political moves, which included getting closer to the Christians, his ex-rivals; moderating his objection to the activities of the government he was serving in; and avoiding harsh confrontations with Hariri.

In the Shiite community, the activity of the two players, Amal and Hezbollah, went on, and they upheld a complex and dynamic system of relations of cooperation and struggle. The Amal movement nearly completely gave up its military and militia components and was assimilated into the regime's institutions. Hezbollah, on the other hand, adopted a combined strategy: it continued operating as an armed militia movement (although it totally objected to being defined as a militia) in order to achieve the goal of Israel's expulsion from Lebanon; simultaneously, it integrated within the Lebanese political system as a party, and competed in the election campaigns for parliament from 1992 on. Its ability to continue in this pattern derived from the existence of mutual interests, Syrian and Iranian, for maintaining the movement's activities against Israel. The movement's success in the resistance activities; its potential threat to the stability of the Lebanese system, alongside its investments in the social field; and its conduct in the political arena, reinforced its status. Although it stayed in the opposition, its influence went far beyond the limits of the Shiite and the Lebanese systems.

As a rule, the relations in the Muslim camp were characterized by a multitude of power struggles concerning the position of seniority in each sect, between old and new elites and between the secular and the fundamentalists. The main sectarian struggle in the Muslim camp was between the Shiites and the Sunnis and mainly between Hezbollah and the Lebanese prime minister, Hariri.

Hezbollah and the Lebanese Government—between Rivalry and Reciprocity

The relations between Hezbollah and the Lebanese government during the 1990s were mainly those of rivalry, entwined with very little cooperation. It is no secret that the governments of Lebanon found it hard to accept Hezbollah's independence and its activities, which did not always fit the regime's interests, and therefore, they tried to minimize the movement's freedom of activity. Despite the fact that the governmental efforts were not always deemed as completely successful, they did impose changes in the movement's policy and in its manner of conduct in Lebanese politics. The first and most essential change was the transition from activity outside of the political system to oppositional activity from within it. This was expressed by the participation in the elections for parliament in August 1992 and in the acceptance of the rules of the game of the Lebanese system.[45] The second change was a transition from a comprehensive oppositional policy to a "constructive" opposition, according to a definition by one of the members in the movement's high echelons. The third change was manifested by a transition from nonrestrained and unconstrained military activity to a policy of restraint, partially influenced by governmental pressures. Hezbollah's decision to compete in the election campaign for parliament vested within it the practical consent to operate within the limits of the renewing Lebanese system and according to its rules. The gradual, yet decisive and systematic, application of the Ta'if Agreement by the governments of Lebanon and Syria often stimulated struggles and confrontations between the movement and the regime, to the extent of using military force against the movement on several occasions. Altogether, the movement refrained from allowing the relations to deteriorate to a condition of violence and defined red lines with regard to its activity against the government. Despite the mutual hostility between the sides, rules of the game and activity frameworks were drafted during that period, allowing them to operate alongside each other. This restrained activity concerning the government derived from the movement's assessment that, in the new reality, which was taking place in the Lebanese arena, violence might end up turning against it like a boomerang.[46]

The Ta'if Agreement placed new challenges before Hezbollah and required it to determine its policy of activity. As far as the regime was concerned, it was obvious that the application of the agreement was a necessary stipulation for the rehabilitation of Lebanon, as early as possible as its first stages had already brought upon some essential changes in the Lebanese system as well as upon the power relations between its components. As far as the movement was concerned, the agreement posed a real threat to its future; it decisively objected to it and even strove to thwart it or to change it completely. However, this did not prevent it from simultaneously holding a dialogue with the regime and integrating within the political system that has been established in its premises.[47]

The struggle for the cancellation of the clauses of the Ta'if Agreement was simple compared to the necessity of finding an appropriate answer to the issue of disarming the militias. From the movement's point of view, giving up means of warfare and resistance was equal to political suicide, and thus, it could not give up on this matter.[48] On the other hand, the government's leadership and its ability to enforce its decisions were put to test. Giving up on such an essential matter could have been interpreted by the other players as weakness and could have borne implications upon the continuation of the rehabilitation process. Thus, Hezbollah's request not to be included in the list was rejected out of hand by Hrawi, the Lebanese president and by Karami, the prime minster, who were both of the opinion that the role of the resistance was over and demanded that Hezbollah agree to disarm itself. Hezbollah refused to accede to this demand, claiming that it could not accept an equal decree to that of the rest of the militias in Lebanon, because it was not a militia but a resistance, whose weapons were primarily intended for fighting against Israel. It explained that its use of weapons was forced upon it due to the circumstances in Lebanon, yet as this period ended, it still needed weapons in order to maintain its resistance to Israel. In the above-described confrontation, Hezbollah emerged victorious.[49] Its victory was only the first round in the ongoing battle to disarm the movement. From then on, on every opportunity, whether due to the movement's temporary weakening or following domestic and international procedures, the subject of disarming the movement was placed on the Lebanese and the international daily agenda.[50]

In 1992, corresponding to the disarmament of the militias, the government launched military forces in southern Lebanon and announced its readiness for full dispersion in the south—if and when decision 425 (U.N. Security Council Resolution 425 March 14, 1978 included Israeli withdrawal from Lebanon, formation of the United Nations Interim Force in Lebanon [UNIFIL], and help to the Lebanese Government restore its effective authority in the area) was to be carried out. The existence of the Lebanese Army in south Lebanon served two governmental goals: it demonstrated the continuing activities to implement the Ta'if Agreement and also had a restraining influence on Hezbollah's activities in south Lebanon. The possibility of a confrontation between Hezbollah and the government was, seemingly, just a matter of time. It was obvious that both sides wished to avoid confrontation—Hezbollah, out of fear of loosing the capability to continue with the resistance and the Lebanese government, due to its weakness. In March 1993, the Lebanese minister of labor, Abdullah Amin, suggested that Hezbollah would concentrate on controlled and specific activities against Israel as not to provide it with an excuse to harm Lebanese citizens. He warned that continuing with Hezbollah's current pattern of activity would bring calamity upon the resistance and upon other factors afterwards. The minister criticized Hezbollah's use of the resistance for the promotion of political purposes and claimed that the government would protect the resistance as long as it acted within his suggested framework.[51]

From Inclusive Oppositional Activity to Constructive Oppositional Activity

Hezbollah's unique status, both within and outside the institutional system, allowed it to make use of the advantages of both worlds altogether. On the one hand, it established and applied an independent activity policy, outside of the establishment, against Israel, based on using violence as a means of expelling Israel from Lebanese soil, and on the other hand, it operated within the institutional system by using political tools to achieve its objectives. Al-Tufayli defined this by using the following words: "We are waging a military campaign against the Zionist enemy alone, while maintaining a public and political system in regards to the Lebanese regime, without using force."[52]

Hezbollah's activity at the inner level was characterized by a constant strife to promote support for the resistance through the Lebanese public opinion and by constructing frameworks for cooperation with political figures and parties, while willing to pay a price by moderating its positions, in an attempt to overthrow the government. Altogether, the movement had exhibited caution and political wisdom and did not cross the line in its relations with the government although it was regularly pretty close to that. Declaratively speaking, the movement was emphasizing its commitment to act within the permitted legal framework and had placed clear borders and red lines, as Nasrallah said, "We . . . shall act to establish the internal security and the internal peace and quiet and we shall make every effort to cast away the threatening shadow of a civil war."[53]

The movement's entry into the political arena and the establishment of the first Hariri government did not essentially change the movement's approach toward the government. In June 1993, al-Tufayli called the government of Lebanon "an American extension of the first degree in Lebanon," and Husayn al-Musawi emphasized that the movement would resist the government until it placed the resistance and support of its citizens on the top of its list of priorities.[54]

The expressions of Hezbollah's higher echelons and the adopting of the "walking on the brink" strategy concerning its relations with the government increased the tension in the relations between the sides as well as the chances for the outbreak of a crisis between them. In such a charged atmosphere, there is no wonder why Hezbollah's activity, which blatantly ignored the government's decisions, were culminated by a violent incident between the Lebanese soldiers and Hezbollah's activists. On September 13, 1993, Hezbollah initiated a demonstration, on the background of the Oslo Accords (officially called the Declaration of Principles on Interim Self-Government Arrangements or Declaration of Principles—DOP), opposing the governmental decision, forbidding conducting of unauthorized demonstrations. The Lebanese Army, sent to break up the demonstration, opened fire at the demonstrators, killing nine Hezbollah activists and wounding dozens more. The incident spurred upheaval among Hezbollah and the Lebanese political system. The government was forced to embark upon an investigation, but did not retrace its principal decision to prevent such demonstrations in the future.[55] The crisis was used by Nasrallah to intensify his attack on the government. He tied the event with the peace process, claiming that the government did it in order to "reconcile" with the United States and out of a desire to exhibit influence and control in Lebanon. He demanded that the perpetrators of crime and their senders be put on trail, called for the Lebanese Army to disobey the orders of their commanders, and demanded that the parliament denunciate the murder. Nasrallah accused the government of administrating a dictatorship policy and of suppressing the freedom of speech and expression in Lebanon. He notified his intention of taking steps to overthrow the government through non-violent, popular political struggle and informative propaganda. Others in the movement's leadership regarded the event as an attempt to limit the steps of the resistance. They attacked Hariri verbally, presenting him as a political rookie lacking expertise and experience in Lebanese politics. They also called for continuing with the struggle according to the political rules of the game.[56]

In light of all this, in order to coordinate positions and establish activity patterns, the movement initiated meetings with national parties, Islamic parties, and other Lebanese power factors, including the Lebanese Communist Party, the National-Social Syrian Party, the Fatah-Revolutionary Council, and the Islamic Unity Movement. At the same time, the movement's leadership met with the Syrian vice president and expressed before him its concern about the Lebanese government's manner of conduct and its anxiety about the deterioration in the country's condition to the extent of its destruction.[57]

The crisis influenced the decisions and considerations of both sides from then on. As for Hezbollah, it determined the rules of the game within the

Lebanese system and the government; it influenced the decision-making with regard to Hezbollah matters. For both sides, there was no point in overthrowing the exiting order by means of a violent act.[58]

From 1994 on, the government has expanded its law enforcement activities by exercising the security forces in Beirut, south Lebanon, and in the Beqaa valley. Factors in the Lebanese government have clarified that these steps are not intended directly against Hezbollah, but aimed to prevent breaches of law and order, which might harm the country's stability and sabotage its moves in the international arena. In March 1994, another confrontation broke out between the Lebanese security forces and Hezbollah activists during a parade in the Beqaa valley, displaying various means of warfare, to celebrate Jerusalem day. The Lebanese security forces arrested fifteen Hezbollah activists on the charge of participating in an armed demonstration. In July 1995, Lebanese and Syrian security factors conducted extensive arrests in the Beqaa valley, following shooting incidents between two Shiite clans. In February 1996, the Lebanese security forces imposed a curfew on the southern suburb of Beirut, on the basis of information concerning Hezbollah's intention to send many of its activists to participate in the professional unions' demonstrations. In September 1996, the Lebanese government sent thousands of soldiers and security personnel to south Lebanon in order to maintain law and order on parliament election day.[59]

The government law-enforcement activities also expanded to the media. It prohibited the broadcasting of news and propaganda on private radio and television stations, including those owned by Hezbollah and took measures to minimize the number of broadcasting and communication channels operating in the country. The governmental initiative encountered harsh criticism on Hezbollah's part, as also from the rest of those who were negatively affected by the proposed law. Naim Qassem claimed that the government was striving to establish a military regime that would harm the freedom of speech and expression, although he emphasized that the movement would obey the law, but fight to change it.[60] One way or another, the government's conduct in the internal arena of Lebanon was more aggressive and decisive than that which characterized its struggle to restrain Hezbollah in south Lebanon, and it definitely set clear limits of right and wrong in the internal arena, even at the cost of a frontal confrontation with Hezbollah and other oppositional factors.[61]

The downfall of the first Hariri government and the establishment of a second government headed by him cleared the way to improving the murky relations between the government and the movement. An examination of the contacts concerning the establishment of the Lebanese governments during the 1990s teaches of a change that occurred in the movement's oppositional position toward the government, from complete rejection and unwillingness to enter the government during the early 1990s, to conditioned rejection and willingness to enter the government under certain conditions toward the end of the decade.[62]

In July 1994, Nasrallah declared that "Hezbollah is willing to participate in a government that will not negotiate with the Zionist enemy and will not sign a peace treaty with it."[63] In October 1994, it was claimed in the Lebanese press that meetings were being held between Hariri's government and Hezbollah in order to promote issues on the movement's and the government's agendas.[64] Eventually, the movement rejected outright any possibility of participating in the government, claiming that "Hariri's government has a plan, which we regard as dangerous for the future of Lebanon, and therefore we think that we naturally belong in the opposition."[65]

With the disassembling of Hariri's government in May 1995 and the commencement of negotiations for the establishment of his second government, the discussions on the issue of the movement's integration in the government were renewed. One of its seniors even said that the movement was examining the benefit of participating in the government and that it would give notice of its decision when the time was right.[66] Fadlallah even provided the authorization for such a move by claiming that there was no legal religious prohibition that concerned entering the government, but one must examine the benefit of the move and place conditions on joining. He said that a decision on this matter should be accepted by people with political and Islamic consciousness.[67]

In practice, despite the extensive publication of the matter in the media, there was no official or practical offer on the part of Hariri for Hezbollah to include movement representatives in his government. Qassem claimed that the discussions between the faction representatives and the Lebanese prime minister concerned the policy guidelines of the new government and the mishaps of the previous one. He accused the United States of intervening in the Lebanese internal affairs and imposing a veto on the movement joining the government. The movement voted "no-confidence" in the government, yet called it to cooperate "for the benefit of the homeland and the civilians."[68] Fadlallah clarified that "the Islamic movement is not taking an oppositional stand just to object to the government at any cost, yet this concerns a matter-of-fact examination of the government's positions."[69] The prevailing feeling among Hezbollah's high echelons and among Lebanese journalists, during the first months of tenure of Hariri's government, was that a compromise was taking place in the relations between the government and the movement concerning the issue of the resistance. In light of this, the movement decided to encourage this relationship, without abandoning the ongoing struggle against the government's social and economical policy.[70]

After the establishment of the government, new ways of tightening the connection between the movement and the government were examined. The Lebanese president even called on Hezbollah to invest efforts in integrating the movement into the political life in Lebanon.[71] A parliament faction member expressed himself in November 1995, stating that there was no principle obstruction or religious problem preventing Hezbollah's entry into the government, even if the government was negotiating with Israel. In his words, the entry depended upon the existence of political circumstances.[72] In practice, the movement did not join the government, and there were those who thought that the reason was the fear that the move might limit the resistance activities.[73]

A similar progression also characterized the contacts previous to the introduction of Hariri's third government to the parliament in November 1996. During this period, the relations between Hariri and Nasrallah had worsened, following Operation Grapes of Wrath and Hezbollah's failure in the election campaign for parliament. The chairman of the faction in the parliament, Ibrahim El-Amin, said that the possible entry of a Hezbollah representative into the government was discussed at a meeting with Hariri, but was rejected out of hand. On October 14, 1999, Nasrallah announced that "Hezbollah's way is opposed to that of the regime and the entry of one or two ministers in the government would not change a thing."[74] In this case as well, the movement had made it clear that its oppositional stand was matter-of-fact and conditioned by the government's policy.[75] Altogether, it should be emphasized that although Nasrallah objected to the government's policy in many aspects, he refrained from activities containing a potential for a violent clash with the security forces. He feared that this would divert the movement from its main goal—the resistance to the occupation—and that it might play into the hands of Israel. As far as he was concerned, this was not the time for other solutions as well—less violent solutions, such as a civil rebellion to overthrow the government.[76]

In December 1998, Salim al-Huss presented his new government to the parliament. Hezbollah supported the candidacy of al-Huss and made it public. It expressed hope that he would succeed in initiating a change in the nature of the government and its activities and promote national reconciliation. Altogether, the movement did not change its principal position, which opposed joining the government, claiming that the basic conditions by which it had decided against joining the government had not changed and it did not wish to be a partner in realizing a policy it had no influence over.[77]

Despite everything, the movement did not support the government on the elections for parliament, and this was explained by its ideological position, by its unfamiliarity with the new ministers, by the government's ambiguous economic message, and by the American ambassador's involvement in the consolidation of its platform. At the same time, Nasrallah praised the new government's position concerning the resistance and declared an essential alteration in the movement's approach toward the government in terms of "a transition from decisive objection to serious cooperation," which in his words "was made possible due to the government's composition, whose stands . . . match those of Hezbollah." He gave his blessing to the new government's declared policy on internal affairs, its support of the resistance and the relations with Syria, and suggested that it acts quickly to apply it.[78] In August 1999, Hezbollah circles were quoted clarifying that they were indeed satisfied with the Lebanese government's positions toward the resistance and that the foundations were placed for "a full understanding and non-artificial relations, yet spontaneous and natural relations." These sources stated that what makes the current regime unique is its positive approach toward the movement and its stands and that the movement supported the government's positions in all that concerns the political process and the economic reform.[79]

To conclude, the movement's relations with the Lebanese governments during the 1990s faced ups and downs and often severe crises, especially while dealing with Hariri. The movement traditionally avoided a vote of confidence with respect to the various governments.

Altogether, it is worthwhile to note that the question of its joining the government became from an "experimental media scoop" during the early 1990s to a heavy weighted issue from 1996 on. The contacts for the establishment of four different governments during the 1990s and the question of joining the government provided the movement an opportunity to influence the basic guidelines of the established governments in the field of the resistance and concerning social issues. This and more, it seems that the total oppositional approach that had characterized the movement during the early 1990s in its relations with the government switched to a conditioned opposition and partial cooperation at the end of the decade. This was made possible, among other reasons, due to the election of Lahoud as the president of Lebanon and of al-Huss as prime minister.[80]

The Revolt of the Hungry—As an Example of the Connection between Social Environmental Conditions and Possibilities for the Development of Social Movements

In late 1997, al-Tufayli announced the commencement of the "Revolt of the Hungry" by an act of civil rebellion against the Lebanese government in an attempt to overthrow it. By doing this, al-Tufayli laid the foundations for the establishment of a new fundamentalist movement that would compete with Hezbollah. The chain of events from there on proved the assessment that the chaos, which characterized the Lebanese system during the 1970s and the 1980s, was one of the main factors that allowed Hezbollah's rapid development. Al-Tufayli's attempt to establish a new movement using the same tools and principles that had been applied in the foundation of the Hezbollah movement ended up being a miserable fiasco. Al-Tufayli ignored the changes that had taken place in the Lebanese system and was surprised by the government's intense response to the early stages of his movement's organization. The Lebanese government's determination to eliminate the new movement was expressed through the combined use of all the means at its disposal.

It held a dialogue with al-Tufayli and, at the same time, instructed the army and the police to prevent the convergence of his supporters at the rally in which they announced the movement's establishment and their activity at the Beqaa valley in the days that followed. Military and security forces were dispersed in advance throughout the Baalbek area and along the routes leading to it. These forces confronted the movement's supporters and carried out searches and arrests in the Beqaa valley settlements. During the confrontations, al-Tufayli's deputy, Khader Tlays, was killed in a firing incident. This fact did not influence the continuance of military activity. The government did not refrain, despite Hezbollah's resentment, from ordering the transfer of the treatment of the al-Tufayli affair to the judicial instances.[81] Eventually, al-Tufayli was forced to go underground out of fear of being arrested or assassinated; his movement did not gain the sufficient momentum it required in order to consolidate, and its remnants, in the form of preorganized groups, operated in town and villages in the Beqaa valley without bearing real influence or actually threatening the stability either of the Lebanese regime or that of Hezbollah.[82]

Hezbollah and the Lebanese Parties—Dynamic Relations

The movement's entry into the Lebanese parliament had set the conditions, as far as it was concerned, for the expansion of its activity in the political arena, as a means of increasing the pressure on the Lebanese government and promoting the movement's goals. The statutable stature that the movement had received upon its integration into the Lebanese system allowed it to operate more effectively, facing the other parties and upholding alliances and cooperation. Its electoral success provided it with the proof of the widespread support of its concepts amid the Lebanese public, and it strove to increase the size of its adherents. The target public it addressed for this purpose was the Lebanese parties. Cooperating with them, in its view, contributed to the promotion of its objectives in the internal and sectarian Lebanese arenas. The only stipulation set by Hezbollah was the outright disqualification of the Christian Maronite movements that had been cooperating with Israel.[83]

The efforts to form alliances with the Lebanese parties were carried out in two arenas, in accordance, which complemented each other. In the political-parliamentary arena, Hezbollah acted to expand the opposition to the government's moves through reciprocal agreements with various figures and groups in the parliament that objected to the governmental policy. The basis for these alliances was the temporary or regular existence of mutual interests.[84] In the "outer-institutional" arena, the movement strived to establish a multipartisan mutual front, which would operate to promote the resistance and to create external pressure on the government. Its desire for cooperation in both arenas was, in a way, making the best of both worlds. It had to preserve its Islamic ideological framework and, at the same time, be more flexible and operate on the basis of a wide common denominator that was not always in accord with its ideological doctrine.

The need to expand contacts with the Lebanese parties, including the Christians, and the need to make concessions, even if only seemingly, was clear to the movement's leaders. They continued the propagandist line, designed to change its negative image among the Lebanese public opinion.[85] In late 1994, Nasrallah expressed his satisfaction with his movement's successes in establishing cooperation and alliances concerning various matters. He was disappointed that his movement did not succeed in harnessing the political system into an active participation in the resistance activities. In his opinion, this failure stemmed from the unwillingness to make a sacrifice on the side of this system.[86] The movement's conduct in the internal Lebanese system also gained the support and encouragement of Fadlallah.[87]

Until 1997, the entire apparatus of contacts and relations of cooperation between the movement and the Lebanese parties moved along sluggishly and had no apparent breakthroughs. The Lebanese parties treated the Hezbollah's intentions with suspicion, avoiding any deepening of reciprocal relations. The escalation of the Israeli-Lebanese conflict between 1996 and 1997, in which Hezbollah played a major role, promoted it from the fringes of the Lebanese political agenda to its center. The movement's growing influence on the Lebanese public opinion, despite its failure in the parliamentary elections of 1996, prepared the groundwork for Hezbollah's new initiatives and made it difficult for the rest of the parties to ignore

The first initiative reached the stage of maturity in April 1997, in the establishing of an all-encompassing multipartisan, multisectarian cooperative framework, in which the movement was a central delegate. The principles of this framework, which was mutually formulated, acquired the movement a moderate and responsible image and reinforced its position in the opinion of the Lebanese public.[88] The second initiative was in September 1997, a week after the death of Nasrallah's son, as, in the midst of a wave of support and sympathy for him and his movement, Nasrallah declared the commencement of a new organizational policy, whose purpose was to increase the movement's openness toward the Lebanese society and the political system. This initiative, which led to the founding of the "Lebanese Resistance Squadrons," increased the correlation between the movement and the Lebanese society and expanded its influences far beyond the limits of the Shiite community. These moves reinforced the movement's status in the Lebanese political system and provided an additional influential factor in the system of reciprocal relations and influence between the movement and the government.[89]

Hezbollah as a Political Body—from Activity Devoid of Restraints, to a Partially Restrained and Controlled Activity Policy

From 1992, Hezbollah was eminent as the only movement that operated simultaneously as a political body within the Lebanese system and as an armed militia outside the limits of the political structure. This fact created a problem for the Lebanese regime, which had difficulties enforcing its reign upon the Hezbollah, as long as it received Syrian-Iranian backup for its unique status. From 1992 on, Hezbollah was actually a nonstate player operating as a state within a state. The movement's independent policy created conflicts and tensions in its relations with the Lebanese regime. One of the essential points of conflict between the movement and the Lebanese government was its policy of exercising the resistance, which, in many cases, completely opposed the government's interests and thus damaged the procedures that it was trying to promote. This web of relations was defined in the two expressions of Naim Qassem. In June 1991, he said, "So far, neither a positive nor a negative position have been taken concerning the resistance . . . the declarations of the Lebanese government officials are contradictory. Some of them stated that the resistance must be stopped, while others expressed support of the resistance." In February 1993 he added and said that "we are aware of the fact that some of the heads of the regime are operating against us and wish to limit our steps, while they know that the people are unifying around us."[90]

The movement conducted a campaign to change the government's approach toward the resistance. It demanded that the government acknowledge the right to resist and allocate resources for this purpose. In June 1991, it tried to market the idea of "combatant society" to the government and to the public opinion and even suggested that the movement provide the base for establishing such a society. This initiative was rejected out of hand.[91] In October 1991, the first stage of the movement's struggle with the government was deemed successful. On the eve of the Madrid Conference, the Lebanese government published an announcement acknowledging the resistance's right of existence, as long as the occupation continued. In 1992, the government declared the granting of priority to the steadfast withstanding of south Lebanon's inhabitants. In practice, the government's declarations were not translated into actual in-field actions. Yet its actual acknowledgement of the right of resistance and of the movement's activity to realize it created a commitment on its behalf that it found hard to ignore every time an escalation took place in southern Lebanon.[92]

Hezbollah stood against the government's policy, which was strove to get Israel out of Lebanon in diplomatic ways, and upheld an unequivocal position that objected to any kind of negotiations or acknowledgement of Israel and regarded violent resistance as the only way of clearing Israel out of Lebanon. Altogether, the government, in a paradoxical manner and probably because of an ensemble of internal and external restraints, refrained from using aggressive means against Hezbollah on this matter. Some of its members even supported Hezbollah's continuance of activity. The official position adopted by the government, rejected out of hand the demands to disarm the movement, as long as Israeli forces remained on Lebanese soil.[93]

The difference in approaches between Hezbollah and the government reflected upon their activities during the 1990s. Hezbollah continued its violent activity even while the regional peace talks were taking place, and the government continued to limit the resistance's steps and to convince it or force it to consider the national interests and considerations. In practice, the achievements of both sides were partial. Every time the security condition escalated, or each time the conditions for the promotion of political initiatives were created, the resistance activity was somewhat restrained, either by the government directly or indirectly exerting pressure on the movement. Four significant occurrences in the regional and the internal Lebanese arena gave the Lebanese regime the opportunity to formulate a restraining (though only partially) framework of relations concerning the movement's military activities:

A. *The movement's entry into the political arena*: The government hoped that the movement's parliamentary presence would help restrain its activity. This assessment was also shared by the movement's supporters.[94] The movement made it clear to its supporters, as well as the Lebanese regime, that it did not intend to give up its principles and that its entry into the parliament should serve to promote the resistance.[95] Its position was reinforced in its fourth conference, held in July 1995. At its closure, Qassem emphasized that, although the movement was a part of the political system, in all that concerned the resistance, it neither accepted orders nor became influenced by any factor or country.[96]

B. *The regional peace talks (1991–1996)*: The involvement of Lebanon and Syria in the regional peace talks was of great concern to the Hezbollah movement. The diplomatic activity concerning Israel was totally opposed to its policy and it completely rejected this. In an attempt to stop the process, Nasrallah organized demonstrations and protest rallies all over Lebanon.[97] He presented the movement's position on the matter and stressed that "Islam cannot live in coexistence with the Jews." Qassem added that the peace conference was "a great danger to the Islamic nation and its problems" and that "only a rifle can liberate the lands and eradicate the enemy." Accordingly, the movement was intensifying its activities against Israel in an attempt to thwart the continuance of the talks.[98] The more things moved along in the diplomatic purview, the more the movement became exposed to governmental and Lebanese public opinion pressures and the less the military solution seemed attractive. On February 1992, the government instructed the Lebanese Army to prevent Hezbollah's activity from the areas under its control with a special emphasis on preventing the launching of Katyusha rockets and declared its intention to disarm the movement with the establishment of a peace agreement. Yet, the gap between the declarations of the regime, which was just beginning to establish its authority, and its influence on the consequences in the field, was too great. The Lebanese government found it hard to control matters in the south, leaving Hezbollah with a broad operational leeway for activities against Israel. Each time there was an escalation in the southern Lebanon, Hezbollah called on the government to support the resistance and not to surrender to external pressures.[99]

The activities and the declarations of the government and of Hezbollah during November and December 1992, with the peace process and the escalating situation in south Lebanon in the background, teaches us a lot about the balance of power and the reciprocal relations between the sides during this era. The government was in a complicated situation, being torn between bad choices and even worse ones. The partners of its peace talks expected it to restrain Hezbollah, which went on with its independent policy, ignoring the existence of the talks as well as the government's immediate interests.[100] The government's attempts to maneuver between the various restraints and to relax the situation were rejected by Hezbollah. So, for instance, the announcement of the Lebanese minister of defense, Muhsin Dalul, at the end of a meeting with a Hezbollah delegation, that "self-control has been agreed upon, so that Israel will not have excuses to carry out acts of aggression" and that "Hezbollah's response was complete," was denied by the movement.[101] Furthermore, Nasrallah fiercely attacked the governmental policy and rejected out of hand the demands to stop the resistance activities.[102] In the absence of any real ability to subject authority upon the movement, the government approached Syria for support. Defense Minister Dalul, who was conducting the contacts on the government's behalf, asked the Syrians to act against Iran and Hezbollah in order to restrain the resistance activity.[103]

In an interview held on November 13, 1992, the Lebanese foreign minister well expressed the government's anger and frustration in regard to the existing condition and the movement's manner of conduct. He attacked Hezbollah's policy and activity and claimed that, despite the just principle guiding its activity, the resistance was causing more damage than benefit. According to him, in order to produce desirable results, the movement must act according to the policy, guidelines, and abilities of the government.[104]

Several days later, he expressed deep frustration with the situation, saying that "no such cutoff or tactical opposition exists in any country in the world like that which currently prevails in South Lebanon . . . I do not think anyone can say resistance to occupation can be carried out with disconnection from the policy and from the economic, diplomatic and security considerations."[105]

Nasrallah, of course, held a completely opposite position and claimed that "the Lebanese diplomacy must serve the resistance activities, instead of vice versa, the way Boueiz wants it."[106] Despite this, the government avoided a frontal confrontation with Hezbollah and sought a way of communicating with it. The Lebanese information minister, Michel Samaha, said that "the government does not wish to enter a confrontation with Hezbollah and does not want to oppress it." He further added that "the government disagrees with Hezbollah," yet was willing to hold discussions with it, as required in a democratic country.[107] The movement announced that it did not regard itself as responsible for the consequences of the negotiation and that it would continue objecting to the normalization of relations with Israel in any way it might see fit.[108]

Throughout 1993, the peace process made progress and there was a breakthrough in the negotiations with the Palestinians (the first Gaza-Jericho Agreement), yet the feeling of pressure in the Hezbollah movement also increased, with it feeling that its maneuvering expanse had become more and more minimized. The increasing hostility between Hezbollah and the government reached new heights because of Operation Accountability (July 1993) and the incident in the southern suburb (September 1993). As a consequence, the movement increased its efforts to overthrow the government. In October 1993, al-Tufayli called the Lebanese government "a treacherous regime, eager to reach an agreement with the Zionist enemy," but stressed that the movement would continue operating in the framework of the acceptable political rules of the game.[109] The continuance of the peace process and the signing of the agreements between Israel and Jordan and between Israel and Palestine only increased the disquiet in the Lebanese internal system. Aware of the possible developments, the government prepared for the possibility of an escalation in the movement's activity in the Lebanese arena and even declared its intention to act decisively against breaches of order after the establishment of a peace agreement.[110]

As the signs of the arrival of the peace agreement became stronger, so did the fear in the movement from the possible implications upon the continuance of its activities. The official position of the Lebanese government, which testified of its intention to disarm the movement with the establishment of an agreement, caused an inner strife in the movement. Among the movement's leadership was a consensus in regard to the movement's approach toward Israel and the continuance of struggle against it until its annihilation. The argument concerned the nature of the struggle, its means, and the ability to apply it under the conditions prevailing in the Lebanese arena and in the political system. The pragmatic wing of the movement's leadership identified a difficulty in continuing the existent policy of activity when Israel retreated from Lebanon and began preparing for the day after, formulating and consolidating a policy of activity, which the movement consistently refused to share with the media. Whatever did manage to leak out, pinpointed the movement's intentions to object to a normalization of the relations with Israel and to conduct the resistance against Israel at the economic, social, and cultural levels. The radical wing, headed by al-Tufayli, held a different position and claimed that resistance in nonviolent ways, while refraining from confrontation with the Lebanese government, was nonapplicable and called on the movement to continue its resistance with military means even after the agreement, even if meant a confrontation with the Lebanese regime.[111]

The thawing of the relations between Hariri and Hezbollah during the second half of 1995 did not essentially change the situation. On the one hand, Hariri's second government declared the resistance's right for protection, but on the other hand, it continued to operate in order to achieve an agreement through diplomatic means while avoiding direct involvement in the resistance activities.

Both sides assessed that there was the likelihood of establishing a peace agreement, and each side operated to promote its own goals. The government, on its side, tried to "embrace" the movement and get closer to it in order to restrain its activities and prevent an uncontrolled deterioration by doing so, while the movement increased the resistance, in an attempt to stop the "peace wagon" before it would be too late. As far as statements were concerned, its leaders said that the resistance had nothing to do with the negotiations—it had started before the Madrid Conference and continued to exist afterwards—and that upon the withdrawal of Israel from Lebanon, the movement would reconsider its steps. Its activities, except for the firing of rockets and missiles, were within the Lebanese consensus and retrospectively gained the government's support. The movement rejected out of hand the claims that it was worsening its activities in an attempt to inflict the failure of the process and that it was guilty of the crises that had occurred in regard to the talks.[112]

The movement also withstood the pressures exercised upon it with the establishment of the April 1996 Understanding, reluctant to alter its positions, or its approach, concerning the peace process, even when it seemed to be a finalized fact. It exposed only a small portion of the policy it was establishing and was planning to implement, if and when a peace agreement were to be signed between Israel and Lebanon, and continued fighting against Israel, within the limits of the "April Understanding," while trying to recruit the Lebanese public opinion to its side. The failure of the peace talks and the influx of voices in Israel calling for a unilateral withdrawal from Lebanon in 1997 provided, according to the movement's standpoint, unequivocal proof of its policy and placed it in a position of advantage versus the Lebanese government. The launching of two new initiatives in the same year by the movement—first, the establishment of a national Lebanese multipartisan central framework and the second, the increasing of the policy of openness—only facilitated to increase this advantage.[113]

To conclude, the efforts of the Lebanese government to frame the movement's policy and to subject it to the government's policy all along the peace process were deemed just partially successful. Concerning this, the Lebanese foreign minister, Fares Boueiz, said : "Every government wants the resistance to be correlated with it and should fully uphold its policy, but not every wish is fulfilled." In May 1998, he admitted that there were difficulties in influencing the movement's policy and decisions and stressed that he did not think that the movement could be pressured into stopping the resistance, as long as the occupation existed.[114] In practice, the movement did not change its basic position, which rejects the conducting of negotiations with Israel, and continued its activities. The absence of real governmental ability on the one hand and meager consideration of its interests by Hezbollah on the other hand tainted the relations between both sides and reflected upon their ability to act mutually in regard to other issues.

C. *Operation Accountability and its consequences (July 1993)*: Operation Accountability provided a "window of opportunity" for the Lebanese government to establish a framework of new rules of activity in southern Lebanon and to somewhat restrain Hezbollah's actions. The operation had tainted the relations between the Lebanese regime and the movement. Israel was accused by the government of killing civilians and destroying the Lebanese civil and economic infrastructures, yet more than one finger had been pointing in Hezbollah's direction. Altogether, the Lebanese prime minister, Hariri, refrained from publicly accusing Hezbollah of causing the deterioration in the situation and claimed that neutralizing Hezbollah of its military force, as long as there were Israeli forces on Lebanese soil, was impossible and bordered on suicide.[115]

In July 1993, in the midst of the crisis, a meeting was held between Hezbollah's leadership and the Lebanese prime minister, during which the movement expressed willingness to cease launching rockets and missiles, on condition that the airplane attacks be stopped.[116] At the same time, it announced that the Israeli operation intended to create a split between it and the Lebanese government and to pressure it to disarm Hezbollah.[117]

The Lebanese government wished to use the situation created following the operation to formulate a new reciprocal framework with Hezbollah, to minimize its expanse of activity against Israel, and to force upon it an activity framework that would be coordinated with the interests of the Lebanese government. At the end of the operation, the prime minister clarified that he expected that the movement's outer territorial activities be carried out in coordination with the government. At the same time, he sent the army to southern Lebanon and instructed it to keep the internal security and to disperse along the lines of contact, alongside the UNIFIL (United Nations Interim Force in Lebanon) force. This decision, which was taken after a series of discussions with UNIFIL and with the Americans, without acknowledging Syria, enraged and embarrassed the Syrians. In February 1994, when Hariri learned that the move he had plotted would not suffice to restrain the movement, he addressed Syria and tried to recruit it into making a move to try and restrain Hezbollah as well. The Lebanese foreign minister Boueiz claimed that an arrangement had been reached for the prevention of the Katyusha missiles' firing, and that Lebanon's right to resist the occupation had been reserved. He emphasized that Hezbollah's activities for the realization of this right should be carried out within the framework of an inclusive and reasonable plan.[118]

The government's steps caused the movement concern and it asked for elucidations regarding the role of the army and how this would influence the resistance activities in the future. The answers it was provided with by the government officials, according to whom the army did not intend to limit the resistance, appeased Hezbollah, and as Nasrallah stated, after studying the subject and resolving problems that came up during the first days of the army's dispersion, the movement learned to live with this decision. Altogether, he added that his movement would disagree with any move that might limit or harm the resistance.[119] Loyal to this stand, Nasrallah rejected out of hand the prime minister's demand relating to the duty of coordinating the movement's activity policy with the government and claimed that the government was doing its best to stop the resistance activities and to "domesticate" it and subordinate it to the Lebanese government and that his movement would not stand for it.[120]

Lebanese commentators and journalists reported that the combined efforts of the government and of Syria had somewhat influenced the characteristics of Hezbollah's activity and that during the first months after Operation Accountability, it refrained from using rocket launchers and from deliberately causing the escalation of the situation and concentrated on specific activities via explosive devices and firing. Nasrallah denied the claim that the resistance's freedom of operation had been limited, yet he could not hide his concern regarding the erosion that was taking place concerning the stands and statements of government officials.[121]Actually, most of the movement's efforts during this time were addressed to the restoration of the military mechanisms and the civil infrastructures that had been severely damaged during Operation Accountability and to the organization of the movement's relations with the Shiite population and the Lebanese internal system, which regarded its activity as one of the main reasons for the escalation. Within less than a year of the establishment of the July 1993 Understanding and after a series of "painful" activities by Israel against the movement's activists, including the kidnapping of Mustafa Dirani, the movement went back to operating in a similar pattern to that which had characterized it in the past. It took advantage of the opportunity that it came across in order to justify and establish its renewed policy, to demand that the government suspends its participation in the peace talks, and to remotivate the initiative for building a combatant Lebanese society.[122]

The propagandist campaign that accompanied the movement's activities from June 1994 on was intended to clarify to the public opinion and to the Lebanese government that Hezbollah was neither temporary nor marginal, but a movement with a wide popular base, upholding an independent political line and an Islamic ideology and that it would continue taking an important part in modeling the present and the future of the country and operating against the occupation, albeit the efforts to limit its steps and disarm it.[123] The escalation in the regional and the internal arena, during the second half of 1994, increased the Lebanese public's sympathy toward its activity, according to the movement, and minimized the government's influential expanse concerning its policy.[124]

During the second half of 1995, there was another escalation of the security situation in south Lebanon, which wore off the anyway-limited abilities of government to delimit Hezbollah's activities and match them with the government's interests and policy framework. In the field, the July 1993 Understanding seemed to be losing significance. The waves of violence were feeding themselves, each reaction leading to a counter reaction. The consequence was an increase of the frequency of using rocket launchers against Israel, and, accordingly, of Israel's intensity of retaliation. All that was left for the Lebanese prime minister, Hariri, to do was to conform to the Syrian line, which was claiming that "the Lebanese resistance is operating according to its legal right to protect its land and that military activities against Israel shall continue until peace is achieved with Syria and Lebanon." A more sympathetic statement with operative significance was voiced by the Lebanese defense minister Dalul in December 1995. He announced that he had instructed the Lebanese army to cooperate with the resistance "as though they were one" and called on the people to unite in regard to the resistance.[125] Hezbollah, on its side, continued to present a decisive front and conditioned its approach toward the government by its degree of support of the resistance. It exposed its decision to increase the resistance's budgets and to exercise it in the same pattern, without making any compromises.[126]

In practice, the government failed in its efforts to create a mechanism of cooperation between it and Hezbollah and to restrain the waves of violence. Its ministers blamed Israel's provocations, but they also admitted their inability to influence Hezbollah's independent policy. At the end of March 1996, Lebanese government sources claimed that, in a final effort to prevent the situation from deteriorating, contacts had been held between the Lebanese government, the Syrians, and Hezbollah concerning the matter of freezing Hezbollah's activities in southern Lebanon. They even pointed out the positive change that was taking place during the recently, regarding the security situation in the south.[127]

On March 20, 1996, at the end of a government meeting that was dedicated to the developments concerning the security situation in southern Lebanon, Hariri declared that the activities in the south "were being carried out by the resistance and the government of Lebanon has no control over them." He stressed that the Lebanese government was enforcing its authority on all that concerned the internal security and that it prohibited the performance of illegal activities or activities opposed to its policy, except for the activities of the resistance. He clarified that the government was doing everything in its power to prepare for the possibility of an Israeli attack and even instructed the security forces to resort to alertness steps and to follow the developments in the internal arena. Thus, as far as he was concerned, the solution to stopping the cycle of violence was not in the hands of his government, but on the side of Israel, which was required to withdraw from Lebanon.[128]

In April 1996, in the midst of the Operation Grapes of Wrath, the Lebanese foreign minister accused Hezbollah of being responsible for the crisis created and pinned this on the movement's overindependent policy. He added that, despite the resistance's accusations and denunciations, the Lebanese government supported the principle of resistance, as had been agreed upon in July 1993.[129]

D. *Operation Grapes of Wrath and its consequences (April 1996)*: The failure of the 1993 Understanding and the escalation in southern Lebanon caused the outbreak of Operation "Grapes of Wrath." This operation, like the previous one, provided the government with the chance to redefine its framework of relations with the Hezbollah. The existence of a sympathizing public opinion that supported the movement's continuance of activities alongside external restraints made it difficult for the government either to "bend" the movement's policy or to disarm it. The Lebanese prime minister Hariri, one of the movement's harshest opponents, testified to this, in the midst of Operation Grapes of Wrath: "We cannot disarm Hezbollah from their weapons, whether we agree with their political platform or not," because "if we start disarming Hezbollah from weapons while the occupation persists, we would be perceived by the public opinion as aiding the conquerors."[130] The government's powerlessness was not missed out by the Lebanese people, or by Hezbollah, to the extent that a delegate of the Lebanese parliament said: "You cannot pressure the Hezbollah . . . I don't think the Prime Minister has the instruments to pressure or to put an end to Hezbollah's activities."[131]

Needless to say, the prime minister was dissatisfied, to say the very least, with the existing condition that Lebanon was dragged into (as far as he was concerned, mainly because of the Hezbollah) and with the fact that the continuance of the violence jeopardized his plans to rehabilitate Lebanon. Therefore, he did all he could do to minimize the movement's influences and activities. He rejected the movement's monopoly concerning the resistance and accused it of administrating a careless and ostentatious policy undermining the country's foundations and of using the resistance as an instrument for the attainment of political goals.[132]

The struggle between the sides took place exclusively in the field of the media. Hezbollah refrained from creating belligerent provocations against the government and continued the strategy of "walking on the verge," while the government, whether due to Syrian-Iranian pressure or due to fear of the possible implications of actions against the resistance, also refrained from taking operative means to change the situation in the field. Both sides were entrenched in their positions and the prime minister's relations with the movement went back to a track of crises, mutual accusations, and suspicion. All mediation attempts carried out during the second half of 1996 between the prime minister and the leader of Hezbollah were unsuccessful. The relations between the sides had reached a new low point during the election campaign for parliament. In September 1996, Nasrallah accused the heads of the regime, and mainly Hariri, of declaring war upon the movement and of attempting to wipe it out, while using the governmental institutions and the mechanisms at their disposal.[133]

Nasrallah's declarations at the end of Operation Grapes of Wrath and in the midst of diplomatic activity for the establishment of a supervisory committee removed any doubt that the changes in the movement's policy and principles were merely cosmetic changes. On the one hand, he declared that there was a need for cooperation between the movement and the government and that it was willing to coordinate its activities with the government, but on the other hand, he stressed that the resistance activity should not be limited by political considerations and announced that it would not accept any impositions.

According to him, the resistance anyhow imposed upon itself the same limitations that the government wished to impose upon it. Therefore, he suggested that the government should continue with its current policy of disowning the resistance and the movement and protecting itself from exposure to international pressure. He added that the government should establish an unofficial people's combatant force, which would become integrated with the resistance activities, as countries under occupation had done in the past, and invest in improving southern Lebanon's strong withstanding.[134]

The new Agreement of Understanding provided the government with far more efficient means of pressure and influence than those it had until then for restraining Hezbollah's actions. The government played a major role in the cease-fire communications, in the formulation of a new framework of understanding, and in the construction of system of control and supervision to ensure the implementation of the Understanding. Hezbollah's acceptance of the Agreement of Understanding minimized the movement's expanse of activity, leaving the stage open for communications and diplomatic means of restraining those breaching the Understanding. In this purview, the government was an exclusive player, a fact that improved its capabilities of preventing the uncontrolled escalation of the situation in the field.[135]

In April 30, 1996, Prime Minister Hariri presented the main principles of the Agreement of Understanding that his government had signed. He stressed that the Lebanese government was solely responsible for its implementation, and thus it would operate via its mechanisms and institutions for the stabilization of the agreement. He added that the resistance was not a purpose, but a means of liberating the land, and therefore, it was not above the supreme national interest determined by the government. In his words, the principle guiding the government's activities   resolved the breaches in southern Lebanon by using a mechanism that would prevent unnecessary escalation.[136]

The creation of a new Lebanese system of internal forces, following the operation, obliged the movement to reexamine its policy and fit it with the dynamic reality. During May 1996, Hezbollah decided to resort to a "policy of restrained retaliation"—granting it flexibility and maneuvering space, facing the government and the public opinion. Hezbollah announced that though granting the Lebanese government precedence in finding the appropriate response to Israeli breaches, it was reserving its right to retaliate if Lebanese citizens got hurt. From then until a renewed escalation in southern Lebanon, the movement ran a media campaign intended to pressurize the government into realizing its responsibility, stressing the government's inability to successfully cope with the Israeli breaches and to prepare the groundwork for the continuance of fighting, in accordance with the movement's policy guidelines.[137]

The government did not stop with the definition of an activity framework in the military and political purviews, but strived to minimize the movement's influence on the Lebanese public opinion by shutting off the flow of direct Iranian funding, from which it had been benefiting and which comprised one of its major growth resources. On May 22, 1996, the government decided to ban the direct support of Lebanese citizens and determined that this kind of support should only be provided by the state institutions. The government and its spokespersons claimed that the inhabitants of southern Lebanon were complaining about the favored treatment that the movement's supporters were receiving.[138] The movement's chief of international relations, Ammar al-Mussawi, commented on the government's decision by saying that the movement could not monopolize any support it might receive from Iran or from any other country. According to him, most of the Iranian support passed through the states institutions, and the little that the movement directly received was transferred to its legal and official support institutions, which regularly aided the residents of the south.[139]

One way or another, it seemed that an escalation of tension in southern Lebanon was prevented during the first months after the establishment of the April Agreement of Understanding. The movement permitted the supervisory committee to perform its work and kept the framework of the agreement while launching accusations toward Israel and criticism concerning the Lebanese government's policy toward the Lebanese government. The more ineffective the supervisory committee turned out to be, the more the degree of tension in the south rose and, accordingly, between the government and the movement.[140] The latter increased its attacks and criticism concerning the government and the committee's manner of conduct while emphasizing their failure in the prevention of repeated breaches by Israel. It demanded from the government more decisive activity in the international arena, translating the committee's reports into effective measures against Israel, and called for the redefinition of the committee's roles and means of enforcement, in a manner that would grant it deterrence ability facing Israel.[141]

The movement regarded the prime minister as primarily responsible for the situation and accused him of neglecting the safety of the inhabitants of south Lebanon in benefit of personal considerations and his government of deliberately obstructing the efforts of the resistance to the occupation.[142] At the same time, the movement's leaders stressed the fact that the existing solution did not provide security for the residents of southern Lebanon and that, facing the situation, the movement might renew its retaliatory policy.[143]

The government's steps disrupted the movement's activity, and it strove to find ways of minimizing the restraints and limitations that had characterized the balance of powers created following the Agreement of Understanding. An analysis of its conduct during the months after the Agreement of Understanding shows that it resorted to a combined policy of activity that included a propagandist declarative component, which was intended to form a supportive public opinion and create pressure upon the government, and an operative component, which was intended to change the framework through field activities. In both purviews, its policy was characterized by "walking a thin line," and as the days passed after the Agreement of Understanding, its characteristics became more radicalized.[144]

In the declarative-propagandist purview: In this purview, the movement ran a media campaign while depending on an infrastructure of public opinion that supported the continuance of the resistance activities. On the one hand, the manipulative-communicative dialogue, out of the movement's doctrine, presented it as responsible and cooperative, consistently adhering to the "April Ceasefire Understanding." On the other hand, the government's malfunctioning was emphasized, along with its inability to keep its promises to provide security for its citizens. It was accused of playing into Israeli hands by imposing a policy of limitations on the resistance activities. Altogether, the high echelons of the movement made sure they did not stop "playing by the rules" and stated that a certain degree of cooperation existed between the government and the resistance and that the circumstances were not right for launching rockets against Israel.[145]

In February 1997, Nasrallah requested the Lebanese government to admit its inability to ensure the security of the citizens via the mechanism of the supervisory committee and to allow the movement, which had so far fulfilled its part of the Understanding, to return to the policy of effective retaliation. He added that the movement would not agree to change the rules of activity concluded by the April Understanding or to any kind of limitation concerning its activities.[146]

In July 1997, the movement intensified its expressions against the government and the committee and placed a big question mark around their ability to prevent the continuance of Israeli aggression. A delegate of the Al-Wafa faction in the parliament stated that the movement did not have great faith in the committee, which was "distorting the facts." He called on the Lebanese government to fully utilize all the means at its disposal to create effective international pressure on Israel. He reminded everyone that the movement had maintained its retaliation ability and would be prepared to respond to the Israeli breaches, at the proper time.[147]

In the operative purview: In this purview, the movement applied the tactics of progressing in small steps while operating to create controlled tension by lowering the threshold of response and intensifying the nature of its activities. This line of activity was characterized by the performance of rocket and missile launching (from April 1997 on) toward Israeli posts in the heart of the security zone, close to Israel's international border. This activity did not deviate from the framework of the Understanding, but was definitely considered "walking on a thin line" and had a high potential of volatility.[148] The move yielded the desired result, as far as Hezbollah was concerned, and caused a rise of tension during July and August 1997. The government, as predicted, had difficulties restraining the movement because it actually did not deviate from the limitations of the Agreement of Understanding. The latter, went on feeding the Lebanese public opinion with numbers and figures, in an effort to tailor public opinion that would be supportive of the response the movement was offering to apply.[149]

The escalation of the tension in southern Lebanon and in the Jezzine area, during July and August 1997, and the shelling of Sidon by the South Lebanon Army (SLA) provided the opportunity the movement was expecting, and it dropped the grounds for the limitations imposed by the government upon its activity. Hezbollah regarded itself, once again, as free from political restraints and reclaimed the responsibility for the security of the inhabitants of southern Lebanon. This was immediately translated into launching rockets toward Israel and a temporary thawing of the retaliation policy, or, as Nasrallah said, "We wanted to remind everyone the base according to which the April Understanding was achieved . . . we succeeded to instill a new spirit in the April Understanding."[150]

The tension in southern Lebanon was of great concern to the Lebanese government, which was also busy, during that time, attempting to thwart al-Tufayli's efforts of establishing a new revolutionary movement. In an effort to stop the deterioration in southern Lebanon, the government decided to instruct the army to reinforce its troops in the southern suburb and in the western part of the Beqaa valley, as a means of creating pressure upon the movement's leadership and its activists in the field. At the same time, it declared that it would forcefully prevent any attempt of civil rebellion in the Beqaa valley and would use force in order to enforce the state laws there. Nasrallah, who did not like either of the two components of this decision, accused the heads of the regime of incitement against the Shiite sect and criticized the decision, which he regarded as hard to understand, to reinforce the dispersion of the Lebanese Army. On the background of the decision and the movement's fears, a clarification meeting was held between a delegation on its behalf and Prime Minister Hariri.[151]

This trend of slowly gnawing away at the Understanding and the limitations imposed by the government upon the activities of the resistance was typical of the relations between Hezbollah and the government during 1998–1999 as well, until Hezbollah's return to the basic equation of the "retaliation policy," without either considering the consequences of the supervisory committee's discussions or the policy of the Lebanese government.

The Lebanese government's preoccupation with the implementation of decision 425 and the influx of voices in Israel demanding withdrawal from Lebanon on the background of the activities of Hezbollah on the one hand and changes in the government with the election of Lahoud as the new president and the establishment of a government headed by al-Huss on the other hand created a convenient climate for Hezbollah and allowed it a wider freedom of activity against Israel. In February 1999, Abdallah Kassir, one of the movement's seniors said, in the midst of an escalation in the south that "the coordination between Hezbollah and the Islamic resistance, and the government and the army of Lebanon, is the best, and no pressure is being exercised upon the resistance in this field."[152] Furthermore, the Lebanese information minister supported this close relationship at the closure of a cabinet meeting concerning the escalation in the southern Lebanon.[153]

In March 1999, Nasrallah once again clarified that the resistance was not influenced by political decisions or by any Lebanese internal procedures; security situation developments in the field influenced the movement's activities and that a fighting routine was being carried out in the field. In regard to the launching of rockets, he said that the movement had the right to retaliate. In his words, it was doing so in a limited manner, precisely and efficiently, and following an assessment of the situation at the leadership level. Thus, he strove to keep the exclusiveness of retaliation in the hands of Hezbollah and called on the other movements to "leave us the matter of using the Katyusha missiles."[154]

These four significant procedures that took place in Lebanon during the 1990s, from the movement's entry into the political system to the implementation of the Grapes of Wrath Understanding, gave the Lebanese regime the opportunity to limit the resistance's policy and activities and to subject it to the national policy. In reality, the government's achievements in this field were minor; it had difficulties restraining the movement's activities and stopping the escalation in southern Lebanon and was actually being dragged by the events more than influencing them. The explanation for this phenomenon was the existence of a system of Syrian-Iranian pressures and influences on the government on one side and wide support of the resistance on the other. These reasons, in addition to the failure of the peace process and the discovery of signs of weakness among the Israeli public opinion on the one hand and a change of personnel in the Lebanese government in 1998 on the other hand, provided the movement with pretty convenient activity grounds that it made well use of, even during the times in which Hariri's government managed to limit its freedom of operation.

It should be noted that even the Lebanese government's fifth chance to restrain the movement after the withdrawal of the IDF from Lebanon (in May 2000) was not very successful. Instead of disarming, as the Lebanese government had declared prior to the IDF's withdrawal, Hezbollah succeeded in establishing the claim that Israel was still controlling Lebanese territory and therefore the resistance's continuance of activity was required. The movement took good advantage of the Syrian and Iranian backing during this move in order to construct an array of artillery that included thousands of rockets and missiles, including missiles for ranges of hundred kilometers and above, through which the movement maintained, as far as it was concerned, a balance of deterrence against

Israel. The movement used this infrastructure in order to perform limited attacks along the Israeli border and to establish its hold in southern Lebanon.

Summary

In August 1999 movement circles had been quoted, claiming that "the Hezbollah organization hasn't changed its positions towards the Lebanese government, but the Lebanese government had become closer to it."[155]

Even if this claim by the movement was far from reality, it pointed out the movement's perception of itself and of its place as a major factor in the Lebanese system. From hereon, the question that should have been asked was this: What was really the Lebanese system's degree of influence on the movement's development? And had changes taken place in its manner of conduct?

During the 1980s and the 1990s, the Lebanese regime operated in the shadow of powerful regional players, which, in one way or another, "ran" the Lebanese system or the players influencing this system. The presence of the regional players on Lebanese soil, along the two decades, allowed them to directly influence procedures in this system or indirectly influence them by controlling the Lebanese regime. From the early 1990s, Syria was eminent as the player most influencing the Lebanese government, and it established its position as Lebanon's de facto landlord. The government's actions concerning Hezbollah were executed in accordance with the Syrian interest, which did not always fit the Lebanese government's policy. The Lebanese government operated within this system of restraints and dynamic changes to limit the movement's steps, to "domesticate" it, and to "subject" its policy to that of the government.

In fact, a strategic change took place in the policy and the nature of activity of both these entities from the Ta'if Agreement on. Hezbollah changed its policy and adjusted itself to the renewing system, but did not did not "straighten its line" like the rest of the power factors and continued developing its military abilities and administrating a war of attrition against Israel. This "independence" provided an abundant source of conflicts and struggles between the movement and the Lebanese government and waves of escalation and of violence that disrupted the routine of life in Lebanon and, mainly, the regime's plans of promoting its own moves.

The Lebanese internal system, therefore, did bear influence on Hezbollah's development as a movement. The chaos that characterized the political system from the mid-1970s to the early 1990s created an optimal environment for the emergence of the movement and provided it with plenty of political opportunities to expand and to promote its interests. The marginality of the Lebanese regime, which was one of the weakest players in the system until the Ta'if Agreement (1989), created a condition in which the sectarian system provided the most essential circle of influence upon the movement's manner of conduct. Thus, there is no wonder that the movement attributed such great importance to the Shiite public opinion in its system of considerations. Reinforcement for the claim that the anarchy of the 1980s permitted the establishment, consolidation, and expansion of Hezbollah can be found in the story of al-Tufayli's failure to reproduce, during the late 1990s (in post-Ta'if Agreement Lebanon), his success of the 1980s by establishing a new movement in the image of the original Hezbollah.

During the 1990s, the chaos that had characterized the pre-Ta'if Agreement era had disappeared, a fact that obliged the movement to suit its policy with that of the renewed Lebanese system. The policy of "walking a thin line" that the movement had adopted, promoted it in the field of the resistance albeit it created conflicts between it and the government in the Lebanese internal department. The government's decisiveness in regard to internal issues formed the limits of "right and wrong" in this arena, and the movement was forced to operate in its framework.[156]

On the other hand, the Lebanese government could not "bend" the movement's policy and force it to consider the national interests. In the absence of the ability to achieve this on the background of internal and external restraints, the government was exercising a flexible policy, supporting the activities of the resistance on the one hand, at least declaratively and operating to limit its steps, as much as possible, on the other hand. It prevented its entry into the administrative system and removed it from involvement and influence concerning the regional system of relations. In the critical locations, as far as it was concerned, such as Beirut, it acted decisively to enforce its reign, while in southern Lebanon and in the Beqaa valley, it refrained from fully implementing its sovereignty and from a direct confrontation with the movement and allowed it to operate against Israel. A reshuffle of personnel in the Lebanese government during the late 1990s improved the movement's position in the political system, and its activities gained further backing in the government as well. In fact, it refrained from disarming the movement even after the IDF left Lebanon.

In May 2003, a full three years after the IDF's withdrawal from Lebanon, Gebran Tueni, the chief editor of a well known Lebanese newspaper, wondered why Hezbollah hadn't been disarmed and asked, "What does Hezbollah want? Does it want to drag Lebanon and the entire region to a total suicidal war? Does it wish to make Lebanon commit suicide or lead to its slaughter?" He reminded the Lebanese regime of the clauses of the Ta'if Agreement, and accordingly demanded that "all armed militias in Lebanon be disarmed from their weapons, and Hezbollah be disarmed from its weapons, which are illegal weapons."[157]

Surprisingly, or maybe not, his questions were not neither extensively echoed nor did they arouse a profound public debate or political dialogue, and the Lebanese daily political agenda just went on as usual, a fact that reinforced the assessment that the government was choosing, owing to various considerations, not to confront the Hezbollah.

The inability to "domesticate" Hezbollah probably derived from a combination of the government's inability to efficiently influence the movement due to its political, economic, and military weakness and also due to its unwillingness to confront the movement (following the pressures of public opinion and fear of the situation's deterioration in Lebanon); Syria's dominance; and the profound involvement of the players of the regional system in what was going on in Lebanon, particularly Syria's and Iran's backing of the Hezbollah movement.

Hezbollah as a Regional Player

Introduction

The Middle Eastern regional system has developed around two central lines of confrontation: an internal competition over the hegemony of the Arab world and the Arab-Israeli conflict. The establishment of the state of Israel at the very heart of the Muslim world played an important role in designing the pan-Arab and the pan-Islamic identity. It provided a common denominator for the players of the regional system—the animosity toward Israel and regarding it as a foreign entity that must be rooted out so as to ensure the Arab identity of the entire area.[1] Within the regional front there are two subsystems that are important for our discussion in this chapter. The first is the "Arab regional front," which includes Syria, Lebanon, and Hezbollah (a nonstate player). Iran, though it is not an Arab player, shall be analyzed along with this system. The common denominator for all of the above players is the struggle against Israel. The second is the state of Israel. The current discussion shall examine the level of the regional system's influence on the movement's development and on the characteristics of its activity.

The Shiite Community and the Arab Regional Front—Mutual Influences on the Eve of Hezbollah's Establishment

During the first half of the 1970s, Musa al-Sadr founded the Shiite militia Amal and began establishing client-patron relations with Syria. He used Syria as his trump card to survive in the violent Lebanese arena and as a counterbalance to his relations with the Shah's regime in Iran. This system of relations between the Amal movement and Syria was kept even during the days of his successors in the Amal movement.[2]

The community's relations with Iran during those years were complex. On one side, Iranian exiles, opposing the Shah's regime, operated among the Shiite community in Lebanon and, on the other side, the congregation's leadership maintained relations with the Shah's regime. The relations between the Shiite community and the Shah's regime became undermined toward the mid-1970s, and at the same time, the Iranian revolutionaries increased their influence upon the members of the community in Lebanon.[3]

The year 1976 was a turning point as far as the Syrian involvement in Lebanon was concerned. Syria entered Lebanon under the invitation of the Christian

Lebanese government, which was about to collapse, and started acting to fulfill its policy and to maintain a new Syrian order in Lebanon. As more time went by, it became more apparent that the application of this policy was encountering difficulties stemming from the complex nature of the Lebanese society and the more the Syrian leadership tended to adopt an integrated policy that relied, on one hand, on a high absorption ability and, on the other hand, on the use of considerate diplomacy that made use of violence.[4] The Amal movement, which depended on Syria, became an instrument in its hands in carrying out its policy in Lebanon. This fact did not bother Syria in "allowing" the establishment of the Hezbollah movement, during the summer of 1982, despite the potential threat its establishment posed to Amal's hegemony among the Shiite community.[5]

Along with the increasing Syrian influence upon the community, changes occurred in the influence of the Khomeini supporters on groups among the Shiite community, mainly among the graduates of the Shiite colleges in Najaf and their followers. This process was further accelerated after the outbreak of the revolution in Iran. The sympathy and the identification of the Lebanese Shiites with the new regime in Iran permitted the laying of the first foundation for the adoption of the Iranian model in Lebanon as well. Connections between the Lebanese Ulema and their Iranian colleagues and teachers, along with work contacts and proximity to the Iranian exiles who operated in Lebanon facilitated the distribution of the Islamic message and increased the affinity between the Shiites in Lebanon and the Iranian revolution.[6] The new Iranian regime, under the pressure of the religious clerics, refused to acknowledge Lebanon's sovereignty and even regarded secular Amal as a factor delaying the exportation of the revolution.[7] Revolutionary bodies established in Iran started organizing and supporting Islamic fundamentalist Shiite groups in the region's countries, including Lebanon. In December 1979, Mohammad Montazeri, one of the leaders of radicalism in Iran, initiated the sending of 400 Islamic activists to Lebanon. The initiative was blocked by internal-Iranian, Lebanese, and Syrian opposition, and the first wave of volunteers that landed on Lebanon's soil was sent right back to Iran.[8]

In 1982, after the outbreak of the *Shlom Hagalil* (also known as the first Lebanon War), Iran sent, in coordination with Syria, hundreds of Revolutionary Guard Corps activists to Lebanon, not only for the stated purpose of supporting the ongoing struggle against Israel, but also for the purpose of fulfilling the policy of exporting the revolution. These activists settled down in Baalbek and began operating among the Shiite population in the area.[9] In June 1982, the Revolutionary Guard Corps activists helped the Islamic groups that operated in the Amal movement's margins and outside of them establish an all-encompassing framework under the joint leadership of the Lebanese Ulema and the Iranian Revolutionary Guard Corps.[10] This loose organizational framework, founded in the summer of 1982, provided the organizational foundation upon which the Hezbollah movement was based.

The Shiite Community and Israel on the Eve of Hezbollah's Establishment

The Shiite community, mainly the part that resided in southern Lebanon, was significantly influenced by the war of attrition that was going on between the Israelis and the Palestinians, despite the fact that it wasn't directly involved in it.

This war had been taking place from within the Shiite villages and from "bases in the nature" in their vicinity. The results of the crossfire between the sides were apparent throughout southern Lebanon and influenced the quality of life of its residents. Against this background, feelings of frustration developed among the members of the community toward the Palestinians as well as toward Israel. The Israeli occupation of dozens of Lebanese villages during Operation Litani in 1978 and the reinforcement of Saad Haddad's Christian militia only made things worse.[11]

In 1976, Syria entered Lebanon. Its entrance created a new reality that necessitated the design of new rules of game, "agreeable" to the main players of the regional system. These rules were achieved between Israel and Syria through the brokerage of the United States. In the summer of 1981, they were breached by Syria, which intervened in the fighting in Zahlé, very close to the international border of Israel. This fact accelerated the process of escalation in the regional arena.[12]

In May 1982, the *Shlom Hagalil* broke out. Israel took action in order to destroy the infrastructure of the Palestinian terrorists in Lebanon and to establish a pro-Israeli Christian government while refraining from a total war with Syria.[13] Israel was received with a blessing by southern Lebanon's Shiite inhabitants, who had long grown weary of the Palestinians and their behavior and wanted them expelled from southern Lebanon, and yet found this hard to actually apply.[14] The identity of interests between Israel and the Shiite community was short and temporary. Israel's support of the Christian community and the marginality of the Shiite community in the Lebanese political system did not allow relations of cooperation to be formed between Israel and the Shiite community, despite its demographic dominance in southern Lebanon. When the Shiite community realized that Israel was in no hurry to leave Lebanon, it joined the resistance front and acted for the banishment of Israel from Lebanon with violence.

To conclude, the collapse of the Lebanese order, the government's weakness, and the outbreak of the civil war in Lebanon led to the intervention of the regional system in the internal Lebanese conflict. The simultaneous existence of Syrian and Israeli forces on Lebanese soil divided the country into different areas of control and influence and reflected upon the relations between the militias and the government and the regional players. As long as, in the relations of the Arab and the Israeli systems, one didn't deviate from the defined and agreed-upon borders, the regional system's stability was maintained and frontal confrontation was avoided. The "breaking" of these rules of game by the Zahlé events and the missile crisis in the summer of 1981 was one of the main reasons that caused the outbreak of the first Lebanon (*Shlom Hagalil*) War.[15] The first Lebanon War and the Syrian-Iranian alliance provided the Iranians with the opportunity to get their foot in the door of the Middle Eastern conflict.

Hezbollah and the Arab Regional System—Mutual Influences from the Establishment of the Movement (1982) until the Ta'if Accord (1990)

The *Shlom Hagalil* (summer of 1982) changed the balance of forces in Lebanon and the internal and regional players' areas of control and influence. Syria, whose status in Lebanon reached a new low point, followed the moves of the

United States and Israel for the establishment of a pro-Israel regime in Lebanon. The election of the Maronite Bashir Gemayel to the post of president threatened to cancel even the little that remained of Damascus's achievements in Lebanon until then. The elimination of Bashir Gemayel and the election of his weak brother, Amin Gemayel, for the post of president of Lebanon blocked the Israeli-American move and wrecked Israel's achievements in the internal Lebanese arena. This fact did not satisfy Syria; as far as it was concerned, the Israeli threat upon its interests in Lebanon was still intolerable, and it was getting ready to continue minimizing and thwarting it.[16]

The Syrians faced three major challenges during this period. The first challenge was the cancelling of the Agreement of May 17 , signed between Israel and President Amin Gemayel. The second was the banishing of the multinational forces (MNFs) from Beirut, and the third was the expelling of Israel from Lebanese soil.

The Syrian response to these challenges began with signing the cooperation agreement with Iran in the summer of 1982. From then on, Iran became a regional player bearing direct influence upon the Lebanese system in general and upon the Shiite community in particular and thus also upon the procedures in the regional system.[17] Following the agreement, a Revolutionary Guard Corps force arrived in Lebanon, which included military experts and religious clerics. Its objective, according to its commanders, was the establishment of an Islamic movement in Lebanon and the training of the Shiites to fight against Israel, covering the ideological and the military aspects.[18] The building project saw the participation of the Revolutionary Guard Corps along with the Iranian Foreign Ministry's representatives in Syria and Beirut. They provided the movement with the ideological framework and the organizational and financial infrastructure it required.[19]

In October 1987, Abbas al-Mousawi "let the cat out of the bag" concerning the Revolutionary Guard Corps activists' contribution to the establishment of the movement and the formulation of its patterns of activity. Al-Mousawi said that he had participated in the very first military course given by the Revolutionary Guard Corps in Lebanon and claimed that its share in the movement's establishment was significant. He said that the course included military studies as well as ideological training. According to him, the first suicide activity, executed a short time after the arrival of the Revolutionary Guard Corps to Lebanon, provided the proof of the quick and positive results of the Iranian training.[20] In October 1993, in an attempt to minimize or conceal the real involvement of the Revolutionary Guard Corps with Hezbollah, Hassan Nasrallah said that this was not a military force but "a group of experts and scholars, dealing with granting information, in the cultural and conceptual field, to several movements operating in Lebanon."[21]

In practice, a short while after Hezbollah was established, its activists started carrying out terror attacks. In July 1982, the president of the American University of Beirut was kidnapped; in April 1983, two suicide terrorist attacks were carried out against the American Embassy and against an IDF convoy in Lebanon; in August 1983, an Air-France aircraft was hijacked on route to Paris; in October 1983, two car bomb explosions rocked the French and the American headquarters in Beirut; and in November 1983, another car bomb went off at the IDF headquarters in Tyre. The responsibility was assumed by the Islamic Jihad Organization, but Hezbollah and Iran, with Syria's support, were behind the planning and the execution of these terrorist attacks.[22]

As long as the movement's activities served the Syrian interest, Damascus refrained from limiting its moves although it was concerned of the possible influences of Shiite fundamentalism over the Muslim extremists in Syria itself and of the implications of the approach toward Syria on the inter-Arab and the international fields.[23] In March 1996, Nasrallah revealed that "when the Hezbollah organization was established during 1982 . . . Syria gave its party [the Hezbollah movement] political coverage, moral support and facilities." According to him, Syria was not behind the establishment of the movement and did not even finance it; yet, it supported the movement and allowed the provision of means of warfare.[24]

Syria's return to Lebanon's center of influence after removing most of the obstacles that had been eroding its status since 1982 raised establishing a hold of the Lebanese government and modeling it according to Syrian interests and policy guidelines to the top of its list of priorities. The direct result was the establishment of a government of national consent headed by Rashid Karami in March 1984.[25] During the first half of 1984, Syria achieved the goals it had set for itself. First, the Lebanese regime under Amin went along with the Syrian policy line. Second, the foreign forces withdrew from Lebanon, except Israel, which had commenced a gradual process of withdrawal. Third, the agreement of May 17 was cancelled.

During this time, Iran continued its work of organizing the organizational, operational, and cultural infrastructure of the Hezbollah movement and expanding it beyond the borders of the Beqaa valley to all the Shiite population centers in Lebanon. Iran operated through the Revolutionary Guard Corps and the embassies in Damascus and Lebanon, facing the Shiite population in Lebanon, in order to promote the concept of the Islamic revolution and to expand the circle of Hezbollah recruits. The organization of the movement was carried out in accordance with the Iranian model while being established on the principle of the authority of the religious sage. The movement's leadership council was composed of Shiite religious clerics and Iranian delegates.[26] The presence of the Iranians in the movement's supreme council directly influenced its activities. The council's decisions on various issues were influenced by Iranian interests in the regional and international arena. So, for instance, in early 1984, three Americans and a French citizen were kidnapped in Lebanon. The purpose of the kidnapping was to inflict American and French pressure upon Kuwait during the trial of Lebanese Shiite detainees suspected of involvement in terrorist attacks against the American and the French embassies in Kuwait. The kidnapping of the hostages in Lebanon and other terrorist attacks against Kuwait were carried out throughout the 1980s with Iranian support and encouragement.[27]

Hezbollah's activities according to the Iranian policy guidelines and its striving to establish an Islamic republic in Lebanon endangered Syria's interests, and it began increasing its control over Hezbollah and its patrons, the Revolutionary Guard Corps, and the Iranian Embassy in Damascus.[28] Following a series of terror attacks by Hezbollah in 1984, which damaged Syria's status in the international arena, Syria resorted to a restraining policy toward the movement. This included, among other things, arresting the activists of the Revolutionary Guard Corps and Hezbollah, sending some of the activists of the Revolutionary Guard Corps back to Iran, and cutting off the line of supply between Iran and Lebanon.[29]

Consents alongside essential disagreements were the motifs that characterized the relations of influence and reciprocity between Syria and Hezbollah during the second half of the 1980s. Syria supported activities against Israel, yet strongly objected to Hezbollah's kidnapping policy. Its attempts to restrain or to completely thwart this phenomenon failed completely. It faced difficulties in preventing the kidnappings or even effecting the quick release of the hostages. Hezbollah, on its side, completely denounced any responsibility or connection with either the kidnappers or the kidnappings.[30]

The chaos that characterized the Lebanese political system during the second half of the 1980s enforced Iran's position in the Lebanese arena. Iran administrated an independent policy in Lebanon, ignoring the existence of the Lebanese regime and often also the Syrian interests, mainly in all that concerned the kidnapping of foreigners through Hezbollah. Syria, on the other hand, operated to minimize the Iranian involvement not only via diplomatic means, but also by exercising force against Hezbollah and the Revolutionary Guard Corps in Lebanon.[31]

The Syrian activity for restraining Hezbollah and the radical Sunni militias and for the stabilization of the Lebanese system expanded during the second half of 1986.[32] The Syrian forces dispersed again through West Beirut in an attempt (as far as Syria was concerned) to prevent the activities of terror factors endangering the interests of Syria and Lebanon.[33] The Syrian presence and activity in West Beirut did not prevent the continued kidnapping of foreigners in the city, but it increased the potential of conflict between Syria and Hezbollah, and it was just a short way from there to the outbreak of violent incidents.[34]

In July 1986, at a meeting held by the Syrian foreign minister, Farouk al-Sharaa, in Tehran with colleagues in the Iranian leadership, after a series of incidents between Hezbollah and Syrian forces, he notified the Iranian partners of the dialogue that Syria would not hold back much longer in the face of Hezbollah's deviations from upholding the agreements achieved between Syria and Iran, and which had determined the limits of the movement's military activity in Lebanon. He said that Syria regarded these deviations as a threat to its security and that it would act to obliterate them.[35]

Hezbollah chose to underestimate the value of the incidents between the movement and the Syrian forces. It addressed most of its claims toward the media, which it accused of deliberately "blowing" things out of proportion in order to encourage Syria to damage the movement.[36] An incident at Hezbollah's Fathallah barracks in West Beirut in February 1987, which was nicknamed the "al-Basta Massacre," in which the Syrians killed twenty-three Hezbollah activists, provided an important landmark in the relations between Syria and Hezbollah. The Syrian activity made it clear to Hezbollah that Syria would not hesitate to confront any factor in Lebanon when it feels that the Syrian interest was being damaged.[37]

The Syrian activity, alongside the ongoing kidnappings of hostages and the Iranian fears of Syria getting closer to the United States, worsened the tension in the Syria-Iran relations. Hezbollah was forced to navigate its way between the Iranian patron and the Syrian policeman. At the beginning of April 1987, the Iranian foreign minister said that Syria must be very cautious in regard to its activities in Lebanon if it did not want to sink and drown in it. He added that no other country had as much influence in Lebanon as Iran did.[38] At the same time, Iran continued investing inputs into establishing Hezbollah's social and organizational infrastructure in Lebanon, training and qualifying new recruits, and consolidating and internalizing new activity strategies, which were successfully applied through the movement's activities in southern Lebanon.[39]

In June 1987, another severe crisis broke out in the relations between Syria and Hezbollah after the kidnapping of American journalist Charles Glass along with the Lebanese defense minister's son, who happened to be with him in West Beirut, an area that was under Syrian security control. The kidnapping was a harsh blow to Syria's prestige, and it responded by exercising heavy pressure upon Hezbollah and the Iranians. The crisis ended within a short time. The son of the defense minister was released immediately, and the journalist was released after about two months. With the termination of the affair, Syria made it clear that it would not tolerate any activity that would damage the order and security in the areas in which its forces were dispersed.[40]

At the peak of the crisis, Hezbollah continued generating a "business as usual" attitude toward the outside. A movement delegation met with Hafez al-Assad in order to discuss the relations between the sides and the ongoing resistance to Israel. Sheikh Subhi al-Tufayli claimed that the strategic system of relations between the movement and Syria should prevent any confrontation between them and that Hezbollah strived to uphold good relations with Syria because the movement's purpose was to fight Israel. He accused the media of inciting and pushing Syria into a confrontation with the movement and warned that, if Syria would be tempted to do so, it would lose the support of the "Lebanese people."[41]

The discussion concerning Syria's entry into the southern suburb was administrated alternatively from its entry into West Beirut during the second half of 1986 to its entry into the suburb in May 1988. Syria explained this as part of a plan to retrieve security and order in Beirut. In the absence of consent between Syria, Hezbollah, and Iran concerning the need for Syrian presence in the southern suburb and the fear of the outbreak of violent confrontations between the Syrian forces and Hezbollah, the entry was postponed until the right chance was created, as far as Syria was concerned, in the midst of the war between Hezbollah and Amal in May 1988.[42]

Hezbollah implicitly declared that it would continue its activity despite the steps taken by the Syrians to restrain it and that it would object to any attempt to introduce forces into the southern suburb.[43] In January 1988, the Syrian foreign minister visited Iran and expressed Syria's disapproval of Hezbollah's conduct and warned his hosts that Syria would act decisively to prevent any attempt to damage its activity in Lebanon.[44]

The outbreak of the Amal-Hezbollah war in April 1988 worsened the situation and threatened to cancel Syria's achievements so far and to thwart its attempts to maintain a new order in Lebanon. The war provided the peak of a tense relationship between Iran and Syria on the backdrop of essential disagreements concerning Hezbollah's manner of operation in Lebanon.[45] In May 1988, Iran and Syria realized that the war was damaging the interests of both countries in Lebanon, following which they decided to establish a mutual committee that would act to achieve an agreement and stop the war.[46] The mutual committee provided an instrument in the hands of the Syrians and the Iranians to enforce their desire upon their allies, yet its efficiency was merely partial. In fact, the cease-fire agreements obtained by the committee discussions were breached right and left; it had difficulties enforcing an encompassing agreement upon the sides.[47]

The changes in the relations of forces of the Iranian leadership after Khomeini's death in the spring of 1989 and the policy of openness toward the West taken by Prime Minister Rafsanjani influenced the movement and its activity. In a series of discussions in Iran and Lebanon during the second half of the year, the movement decided to formulate changes in its leadership structure and to appoint a Lebanese secretary general who would head the movement. Al-Tufayli, the elder of the movement's religious clerics, was elected for this position.[48]

To conclude, the Arab regional front made possible the establishment of Hezbollah. Syria agreed for the activity and presence of the Revolutionary Guard Corps in the Beqaa valley. It gave operational and intelligence support to Hezbollah activities against the MNFs and permitted the existence of a supply channel for means of warfare and connection between Iran and Lebanon via Damascus. The Iran-Hezbollah relations were much tighter. They were based on the desire not only to act against the foreigners in Lebanon, but also to act on the Shiite Islamic common denominator. The movement's dependence on Iran during the first half of the eighties was great (Iran provided the funding, guidance, and means of warfare). The movement became an operative arm for the fulfillment of Iran's interests inside and outside Lebanon. Identity of interests between the young Ulema, whose personality was cultivated in the spirit of the Iranian revolution and their Iranian patrons, generous funding, and a chaotic environment facilitated the establishing of Hezbollah and allowed Iran to model a fundamentalist Islamic movement that was almost indisputably under its command during the first years.

During the second half of the 1980s, Syria invested significant inputs in the attempt to restrain Hezbollah, including exercising force, but its success was merely partial. The Syrian pressure did not prevent the ongoing kidnappings by Hezbollah, yet it caused the release of some of those kidnapped. It is worthwhile to stress out that Syria's relations toward Hezbollah during most of that period was relatively "soft," and this stemmed from its unwillingness to jeopardize its strategic relations with Iran. Iran, on the other hand, continued, during the second half of the eighties, to influence Hezbollah's directions of development while harnessing this activity to promote its goals and interests.

Hezbollah and Israel—Mutual Influences from the Movement's Establishment (1982) to the Ta'if Accord (1990)

In August 1983, Bashir Gemayel was elected as the president of Lebanon. His election was the high point of the Israeli influence on the Lebanese system.

On September 14, 1983, he was murdered. His murder turned things around for Israel. The immediate Israeli response to the murder of Gemayel (which was attributed to the Syrians) was the occupation of West Beirut, and the Christians responded on September 18 with the Sabra and Shatila massacre. Following the massacre, thousands of people demonstrated in Israel and called on the government to withdraw from Lebanon. As the number of the IDF's casualties in Lebanon increased, so did the pressure upon the Israeli government to withdraw from Lebanon. On May 17, 1983, Israel signed a peace agreement with Lebanon's president Amin Gemayel and began to withdraw from Beirut.[49] The Agreement of May 17 and the Israeli withdrawal weakened Amin Gemayel's regime. Israel's unilateral withdrawal inflamed the tensions between the militias, and in the absence of a strong regimental force that would assume the control of the expanse evacuated by Israel, the militias started determining facts in the field.[50]

The more the Israeli attendance in Lebanon got prolonged, the more the tension increased between the IDF and the Lebanese population. In 1983, the increase in terrorist attacks against the IDF in Lebanon intensified the Israeli retaliation policy and created a tide in the Shiite public opinion, including among the Amal movement, which refrained from taking an active part in the terrorist attacks against the IDF until late 1983.[51]

A confrontation between the IDF, which was incidentally caught in the Ahura Parade in Nabatia on October 16, 1983, and the Shiites signified the end of the "neutrality" stage among the Amal movement. A fatwa published on the next day by Sheikh Mahdi Shams al-Din, chairman of the Supreme Shiite Council, called for a civil rebellion against Israel and prepared the groundwork for Amal movement's joining the struggle against the IDF in Lebanon. From then on, there was a significant increase in the number of activities performed against the IDF in Lebanon. Most of them were carried out by activists of the Amal movement.[52]

During this period of time, Hezbollah was prominent in the quality of the terrorist attacks carried out by its activists and in the great damage that these activities caused the IDF. The movement continued its strategy of planting car bombs and organizing suicide terrorist attacks that proved to be successful against the MNFs in Beirut, and in November 1983, it launched a suicide bomber against the IDF headquarters in Tyre. This type of activity provided a new and dangerous threat that the IDF was forced to face. The struggle between the sides was getting more and more intense. This escalation fed itself and caused the expansion of terrorist attacks and, at the same time, led to an increase in the scope and intensity of the Israeli retaliation.[53]

As strange as this may sound, Israel's presence in Lebanon played into Hezbollah's hands and provided for it particularly efficient means of establishing its position in the Lebanese political system and an instrument for the enlistment of young Shiites. A high professional level, nearly limitless war materials, operational and intelligence support, generous funding, and the willingness to sacrifice, which characterized the Hezbollah movement, turned it into a center of attraction for young Shiites.

In 1984, an escalation occurred in the activities against the IDF in Lebanon and, in accordance, in the IDF's punishing and thwarting activities in the villages from which the attacking terrorists came. The main reasons for the escalation were the withdrawal of the IDF from the Chouf mountains (September 1983), Shams al-Din's call for civil rebellion (October 1983), the suicide terrorist attack against the IDF barracks in Tyre (November 1983), and the killing of Sheikh Ragheb Harb, one of the organizers of the resistance against the IDF in southern Lebanon (February 1984). As the situation in Lebanon escalated, Hezbollah became prominent in relation to other Lebanese organizations.

Israel's decision of January 1985 to withdraw from Lebanon to the border of the security zone increased Hezbollah's motivation to hurt the IDF and accelerated the construction of the movement's operational, logistic, and organizational framework in southern Lebanon and Beirut. The Shiite southern inhabitants' support of its struggle to expel Israel from southern Lebanon helped expand the movement's ranks.[54]

Israel's withdrawal from most of Lebanese territory, except for a narrow border strip in southern Lebanon (the security zone), signified the beginning of a new stage in the relations between Hezbollah and Israel. The defense formation established by Israel was based on the Christian militia under General Lahad, which was dispersed in outposts and headquarters along the border of the security zone. The IDF prepared itself in a number of strategic sites along the security zone, as backup for the South Lebanon Army (SLA). On the other hand, Hezbollah, under Iranian guidance and Syrian backup, established an operational infrastructure in southern Lebanon and started attacking the IDF defense array in the security zone area while coordinating its policy of activity with the new reality. The Amal movement's involvement in the War of Camps and the Lebanese left wing's distance from southern Lebanon left Hezbollah the arena of confrontation with Israel and permitted the rapid expansion of its infrastructure in southern Lebanon.

The need to continue maintaining the resistance to the Israeli presence in Lebanon on one hand and the gap of strength between Israel and the movement and the IDF's retaliation characteristics on the other hand somewhat influenced the movement and its manner of development during those years. The movement's answer to the new challenge included a line of organizational steps to establish the movement's social and operational infrastructure in Lebanon, such as the establishing of new organizational frameworks and the matching of the strategies of activity with the changing reality. A designated organizational framework was founded in southern Lebanon under "the Islamic Resistance" to coordinate the resistance to Israel. It was headed by one of the movement's founders and Ulema seniors, al-Mousawi.[55] At the same time, the movement adopted a strategy of administrating a war of attrition against Israel while refraining from a frontal and apparent confrontation with it. For this purpose, it operated in a secret and compartmentalized pattern that leaned on an infrastructure of popular sympathy. The movement's operational effort was directed against the SLA.

During the years 1985–1986, Hezbollah launched a series of attacks against SLA outposts, which questioned the security array in the security zone area. This fact obliged Israel to set the IDF up at the security zone and to invest (until the withdrawal in May 2000) significant resources in the initiation and restoration of the SLA. Encouraged by its successes, the movement also tried to attack the IDF outposts at the security zone area in 1987.[56]

The resistance was central to the development of the movement; it helped promote its matters in the Shiite, the Lebanese, and the regional systems and made it attractive to the Shiites, who were joining its ranks at an ever-increasing pace.

The movement's expulsion from southern Lebanon by Amal during the Civil War in 1988–1990 dealt a harsh blow to its prestige and threatened to minimize the limits of its influence in the entire Shiite community. Therefore, there is no wonder why the movement, which came out of the "War between Brothers" victorious, presented its return to southern Lebanon as a necessary condition for any cease-fire agreement with Amal and rejected out of hand all of the intermediary solutions it was offered.[57]

Hezbollah and the Regional Front—Summary of Mutual Influences during the Eighties

The regional front played a role in the establishing of the Hezbollah movement (1982–1983) and primarily contributed to the continuance of the chaotic environment that characterized Lebanon ever since the outbreak of the Civil War. The simultaneous existence of regional players with different interests and of an international player on Lebanon's soil caused an escalation of the political violence in the Lebanese system and a worsening of the rivalries between the militias and within them. These conditions made it easy for the preorganizational groups that popped up in Lebanon during the 1970s around the Ulema level to become consolidated into a central organizational framework under Ian's support and with Syria's "consent."

The regional front's influence on the trends of developments in the Hezbollah movement was low in comparison to that of the communitarian and inter-Lebanese systems. The reason for that was the conflict of interest among the regional players and the independent striving of each player to realize its own goals. While Syria and Israel strove to limit the movement's steps and to block the process of its expansion, Iran, on the other hand, acted to accelerate it. In the confrontation between the players, Iran gained a small victory; it managed to exploit the chaos in the inter-Lebanese system well in order to promote the status of Hezbollah among the population through the funding, initiation, and activation of the movement in the social and operative fields. The Iranian activity, mainly that which pushed for the kidnapping of hostages, encountered Syrian objection in cases where it risked Syria's interests or damaged its position in the international arena. The relatively meager level of influence of the regional front on procedures in the movement during this period is also realized from analyzing the procedures and events that took place in the Shiite community between 1988 and 1990 (the period of the "War between Brothers"). Even when there was an identity of interests between Iran and Syria and a mutual understanding concerning the need to end the war in the Shiite community as soon as possible, it took them about two years to enforce an agreement upon Amal and Hezbollah.[58]

In September 1986, Iranian sources claimed that Hezbollah would continue operating while considering Syria's interests, and as long as identity of interests existed between Syria and Iran concerning Israel, it was unlikely for Syria to harm

Hezbollah. In the same context, it was claimed that the movement was relatively immune from damage owing to its being a popular people's movement.[59] Even if the above claim expressed the desire of a certain side, it had essential components, explaining the movement's circle of influences: first, the existence of a dynamic equilibrium between Syria and Iran, influencing the movement's trend of development and second, the movement's perception of itself as a popular movement. This approach, which characterized the movement's expressions during its stage of expansion, was increasingly expressed throughout the nineties in its considerations during its stage of institutionalization. During these years, the Lebanese public opinion in general and the communitarian public opinion in particular were greatly essential influence upon the movement's policy design and the trends of its development.

The movement, which was used, from day one, as an instrument for realizing the Iranian and the Syrian policies in Lebanon, provided some of the main factors that changed the reciprocal relations between the regional players in Lebanon. Its activities against the MNFs and against the IDF weakened Israel's status in Lebanon and reinforced that of Syria. The departure of the foreign forces from Lebanon and Israel's withdrawal to the border of the security zone provided proof of the effectively of its policy and made it attractive to young Shiites, who aspired to join its ranks.

But as the time went by, conflicts of interests between the Syrian and the Iranian policy in Lebanon were exposed.[60] They were expressed through Hezbollah's activities, which presented Syria with complex challenges. The Syrian interests, regional and international, were endangered due to influx of acts of terrorism and kidnapping executed by the movement, and the pressure upon Syria to force the order in Lebanon was on the rise. Altogether, there was intensification of the Syrian dilemma and of the need to decide between its desire to preserve its strategic relations with Iran on the one hand and the need to fulfill its policy in Lebanon on the other hand—a policy that was striving to uphold a secular regime (under its reign) in Lebanon, according to the Syrian model— while Iran, via Hezbollah, acted to establish an Islamic republic in Lebanon as part of the Islamic nation with Iran at its center.[61] The struggle between the two world perspectives, the Syrian one, which Amal supported and promoted, and the Iranian one, which Hezbollah executed, were some of the reasons causing the outbreak of the War between Brothers between Amal and Hezbollah in 1988.

From analyzing the things mentioned in the above discussion, it seems that the Iranian influence on the movement all along the eighties was greater that that of the other players. It seems like the series of acts of terrorism carried out by the movement during this decade, often in opposition with Syrian interests, intended to promote Iranian objectives in the international field and in the war against Iraq. On the other hand, both Israel and Syria (from the stage in which it established its hold of the regime) operated from their own reasons to restrain the movement, yet without significant success. It is worthwhile to emphasize that, from Syria's point of view, this was about choosing between damaging its relations with Iran and risking Hezbollah's strengthening at the expense of the Amal movement. Eventually, it seems that Syria refrained from jeopardizing its strategic alliance with Iran, even at the cost of Hezbollah becoming somewhat stronger.

Hezbollah and the Regional Front—Mutual Influences from the Ta'if Accord (1990) Onward

The Regional Front—Major Characteristics from the 1990s On

Three processes formulated the Middle Eastern regional front of the 1990s. They derived, in a great way, from the rise of the United States to the position of the leading powerful country in the world and from the increase in its involvement in the Middle East. The first process was the downfall of the Soviet Union, which pushed Syria to adopt a policy of getting closer to the United States.[62] The second was the outbreak of the First Gulf War (August 1990–March 1991), which signified the beginning of a new order in the Middle East under the leadership of the United States. The third included the regional peace talks between 1991 and 1996.[63] The regional players internalized the changes and the procedures that took place in the international arena and devised their regional policies accordingly.

The Syrian closeness toward the United States, its moves during the First Gulf War and afterwards, and mainly its joining of the peace process cast a heavy shadow on the strategic alliance between Syria and Iran during the first half of the 1990s. The relations between the two countries reached a new low point in late 1995, when it seemed as if the signing of a peace agreement between Israel and Syria was just a handbreadth away.[64] The freezing of the negotiations between Israel and Syria in 1996 and Assad's visit to Iran in 1997 marked the warming of the relations between the two countries and their return to a pattern of reciprocal relations as they used to be.[65]

Hezbollah and the Arab Regional Front—Mutual Influences from the 1990s On

The 1990s were marked by the application of the Ta'if Accord and by the overtaking of Lebanon by Syria. In October 1990, Michel Aoun's government, which was the last obstruction to its implementation, was overthrown. In May 22, 1991, the two countries signed the agreement for "brotherhood, cooperation and coordination," which gave the Syrian hegemony over the country official validity. From then on, Syria and the Lebanese government concentrated on activities for the restoration of the state and its institutions, stabilizing the security condition and the economic infrastructure. Under this framework, new rules of the game and a system of red lines were defined, and any deviation from them was "taken care of" either by Syria or by the Lebanese security factors.[66]

The Syrian-Lebanese mutual desire to stabilize the security condition in Lebanon was opposed to the movement's policy in southern Lebanon. The war of attrition it was administrating against Israel left southern Lebanon in an environment saturated with violence and security disquiet and threatened, from time to time, to pull the country back into violent struggles. This contradiction was eminent in its full severity after Operation Accountability in 1993 and Operation Grapes of Wrath in 1996. Following them, Hezbollah was "forced," at least for a certain period, to operate in the framework of serious limitations.

The political turn that Syria took toward the United States during the early nineties and its joining of the regional peace process in 1991 were a source of concern for the movement and for Iran. They feared of Syrian surrender to the demands of the United States and Israel. From their point of view this surrender, in the worst case, meant disarming the movement. But even the less severe scenario imposing limitations upon the resistance activity was regarded as a move that could weaken its position in the internal and regional system and accelerate its end. The profound low point in the relations between Syria and Iran only intensified these fears. Despite the uniform front that the movement presented during this period, praising Syria's tough stand in the face of the internal and external pressures calling to disarm the movement, one could read between the lines and notice tones of fear and protest against the Syrian approach toward the movement and its involvement in the peace process. The expressions of the movement's seniors during the nineties well reflected its fears.[67] The movement's fear from developments in the peace process did not cease to exist, even after the process failed.[68]

In May 1991, Hezbollah's second organizational committee was held, in which al-Mousawi was elected secretary general instead of al-Tufayli. The movement's preference for the pragmatic al-Mousawi over al-Tufayli, who is known for his radical views, probably derived from the changes in the echelon of the Iranian leadership and from an internalization of Lebanon's new reality.[69] Iran, according to several sources, was behind the decision to elect Nasrallah as the secretary general of the movement, after the termination of the service of al-Mousawi, whom it preferred over al-Tufayli, who was also after the part.[70]

The three secretary generals were completely connected with Iran and expressed their loyalty and commitment to the Islamic revolution and to its leadership, but the latter two were more befitting with the new spirit of the leadership in Iran and to integrate into the Syrian new order in Lebanon, which had been materializing ever since the early 1990s.[71] It is hard to precisely estimate what made the movement decide to participate in the elections: fear of being left behind in the margins of the Lebanese arena, the pressures of Shiite public opinion, or an attempt to imitate the model set by the Muslim Brothers in Egypt. But obviously, its decision was supported by Iran and its success in the elections was received with great satisfaction in Tehran.[72]

Despite the desire to demonstrate independence in the Lebanese arena and in general, the movement was greatly dependent upon Iran's support for funding and weapons as well as for backup facing Syria and Lebanon.[73] Iran provided Hezbollah with weapons, medical equipment, and generous funding for rehabilitation after the destruction caused to the infrastructures in Lebanon and compensated the population for the damages they suffered after the two operations in 1993 and 1996.[74] Besides, it was called on for support even when there was an escalation of the tension in Lebanon or when there was internal disagreement within the movement. So, for example, it operated enthusiastically to find a way out of the crisis the movement's leadership had encountered on the backdrop of al-Tufayli's moves, which were threatening to disintegrate the movement from within.[75]

Iran was not satisfied with activating Hezbollah within the limits of the Lebanese system. The progress in the regional peace process reflected upon the Syria-Iran relations and upon Iran's policy toward Hezbollah and the Palestinian organizations. Iran's failure in convincing its Syrian ally to abandon the peace talks provided an incentive for it to fund and establish a joint action front for the Palestinian organizations opposing Arafat in order to thwart the Palestinian authority's efforts to come to an agreement with Israel. Hezbollah played a central role in the establishment of this front. As the talks progressed via the Palestinian channel, so did Iran and Hezbollah's involvement in the doing, facing the Palestinian organizations. This trend characterized Hezbollah's activities throughout the 1990s and included support in the operative, financial, and propagandist fields.[76]

The changes in the Lebanese system and in the balance of the political forces in the country, from the application of the Ta'if Agreement onward, influenced the Iranian activity in Lebanon and minimized the expanse of activity that the Iranians enjoyed during the 1980s. Iran was forced to reacknowledge the existence of the formal institutions in Lebanon and to hold diplomatic relations with them as accustomed between sovereign countries. This fact limited its ability to influence the movement, as it did in the past, and provided another restraint in the system of restraints influencing Iran's policy toward Hezbollah during the 1990s.[77]

The reciprocal relations between Hezbollah and Iran were extensively covered by the Iranian and Lebanese media during the 1990s. Examining the statements of the movement's seniors during these years teaches of the changes that occurred in the movement's approach to Iran, and as an exception of that, also of Iran's level of influence on the movement's policy. In February 1990, the movement's secretary general, al-Tufayli said, "We uphold and respond to the orders of Ali Khamenei . . ."[78]

In September 1992, Nasrallah rejected the claim that the movement was an instrument in the hands of Iran for fulfilling its policy in Lebanon.[79] In November 1992 and June 1993, Nasrallah said that Hezbollah was an independent movement and that its activity in Lebanon was cut off from the influence of the political trends in Iran. In his words, "We are subjected to the spiritual leader, which used to be Khomeini and is now Ali Khamenei. We adhere to the principle of obeying the religious scholar." He added that "a decision by the government of Iran does not obligate Hezbollah in any way."[80] On a different occasion, he said that "we receive support from religious factors with materialistic abilities, and this is without connection to the Iranian political system."[81] In March 1993, Sheikh Khader Tlays, a delegate of the Al-Wafa faction in the parliament representing Baalbek, related to the system of relations between Hezbollah and Iran and said that they were essentially religious ideologist and that the movement was independent in its decisions in the political field.[82]

In August 1994, Nasrallah said that "Hezbollah was not established to serve an Iranian plan. Hezbollah was founded in order to fight the occupation and this is why it is more Lebanese than anyone." The movement persisted in establishing this message in the Lebanese public opinion as part of its efforts to market its new Lebanese patriotic image. In June 1996, Qassem repeated the aforementioned stand and said that "there is no connection between Hezbollah's political functioning and Iran. We accept decisions independently."[83]

Hezbollah's "independent decisions" did not always match the Syrian interests in Lebanon and although Syria objected to the disarmament of Hezbollah and supported the principle of the resistance, it acted to restrain the movement on a political military level. The escalation in southern Lebanon during the years 1992–1993 threatened to damage the application of the Ta'if Agreement and Syria's efforts to complete its "sweeping overtake" of the Lebanese system. Syria, whether under its own initiative or under the pressure of Lebanon's government or of the international system, intervened from time to time in an attempt to quiet the tension and prevent its spreading into other regions of Lebanon.[84]

The Syrian activity to restrain the movement was coordinated with Iran despite the tension in the relations between the two countries. In June 1992, the Iranian foreign minister came to Damascus and to Lebanon in order to discuss the situation in the Lebanese arena and the cooperation between Iran and Syria. He was requested by his Lebanese hosts to help restrain Hezbollah but declared that Iran supported the resistance and supported the movement with all of the possible means. In August 1992, the Iranian foreign minister and the vice president of Iran, Hassan Habibi, came to Damascus. Both figures consulted Assad and Nasrallah and discussed the situation in southern Lebanon and Hezbollah. In practice, the mutual effort made by Syria, Iran, and the Lebanese government to restrain the movement was only partly successful. In June 1993, (on the eve of Operation Accountability), the fighting between Hezbollah and Israel expanded way beyond the limits of southern Lebanon and threatened to overthrow the Lebanese regime and the new order obtained by Syria with great effort.[85]

Operation Accountability (July 1993) and Operation Grapes of Wrath (April 1996) posed a real threat to Syria's interests in Lebanon and presented a question mark on the level of influence and means of pressure that Syria had over the movement. The actual escalation, at a bad timing, as far as Syria was concerned, testified of the Syrian difficulty to impose authority upon Hezbollah. These confrontations were completely against the interests of the Lebanese government and of Syria, whose main ambition, during this time, was to stabilize and rehabilitate Lebanon and end the Israeli occupation in Lebanon via diplomatic means. Syria and the Lebanese government did not negate the continuation of the resistance, but they preferred it be put "on a small flame," according to clear rules of game concluded with the movement, with the intention of not giving Israel an excuse to worsen the violence and to expand it. In fact, the many discussions and conclusions that tried to limit the resistance activities in southern Lebanon failed miserably. The limited confrontation that went on in southern Lebanon had dynamics of its own. Israel's retaliations over the movement's activities and vice versa were influenced by the severity of the events that preceded them and mainly by the resulting casualties.

The members of the Hezbollah movement thought that Syria maintained Hezbollah's interests facing the Lebanese government and did not allow Lebanon to reach a separate agreement with Israel as a number of senior Lebanese figures wished to do. But this side of Syria had two faces, and in October 1993, sources in the movement were quoted claiming that, in the confrontation between

Hezbollah and the government of Lebanon, Syria stood beside the government, which was always striving to restrain the movement's activities. This fear increased on the backdrop of the progress of the peace process, Syria's refusal to allow Iran to equip Hezbollah with heavy artillery, and its activity to minimize the firing of missiles and rockets by Hezbollah. At the same time, Syria acted to convince Iran of the need to restrain the movement.[86] In any case, Syria was the main axis for any agreement or initiative that would end the violence and relax the situation in southern Lebanon facing the Lebanese, regional, and international systems altogether.[87]

Aware of Syria's position in Lebanon and in the regional front, the movement was careful to stress the fact that good relations existed between it and Syria and barely expressed itself in regard to the issues of the influence of Syria's involvement in the peace process upon the movement. In June 1993, Nasrallah said that "Syria is regarding the resistance from a perspective of pride and dignity" and that "important and basic strategic relations exist between us and Syria."[88] In August 1993, sources in Hezbollah's leadership claimed that there was no change in Syria's position and in the movement's policy of activity. Al-Tufayli, who was also questioned on this matter, emphasized that the resistance was totally independent and its decisions were not influenced by "the Iranians or the Syrians."[89]

These words didn't precisely reflect the reality in the field. In fact, all along the decade, most players in the inter-Lebanese regional and international system addressed the Arab regional front, with an emphasis on Syria restraining the movement. Researchers, security and intelligence bodies, and politicians, who operated during the 1990s facing the regional system, claimed that Syria had the key to restraining the movement and that it wasn't doing so because the movement's activity served the Syrian interests most of the time.[90]

It is hard to prove or contradict this claim because, in fact, during the 1990s, Syria refrained from forcing things upon the movement the way it had done during the 1980s, among other reasons, owing to the fact that Syria did not have efficient means of enforcement to use on the movement's activists, who were deployed in southern Lebanon. Altogether, Syria had a certain degree of influence on the movement's direction of development and activities, and it made use of this influence during times of tension or when it provided an important contribution to the promotion of Syrian interests. Therefore, despite the movement's repeated statements that their policy wasn't influenced by the regional system, there were indications, from time to time, concerning the changes carried out in the movement's activity patterns for short periods as a result of the occurrence of local procedures, important visits, or regional agreements.[91]

The second half of 1995 teaches us a lot about the nature of the reciprocal relations between Syria and Hezbollah and about the movement's conduct during one of the most critical times of the negotiations toward the signing of a peace treaty. The prevalent assumption toward the meeting of the generals (Israel and Syria) and for a short period afterward was that the peace treaty between Syria and Israel was nearly a finalized fact.[92] On the background of the expected developments, Abdul Halim Khaddam, then vice president of Syria, visited Iran and confided with the top of the Iranian leadership for coordinating and clarifying positions on issues that were mutual to both countries, including the question of the future of Hezbollah. As the discussions ended, both sides stressed their intention to continue cooperating. Upon his return to Syria, Khaddam summoned the leadership of Hezbollah and, according to Lebanese journalists, he ordered it to restrain its activity and to prepare for the period after the signing of the peace agreement, according to the activity guidelines concluded between Syria and Iran.[93]

Hezbollah's response to the developing condition was particularly interesting. In its fourth organizational conference, which took place in July 1995, it decided to increase the budget for acquiring means of warfare to half of the annual expense budget and to appoint one of the seniors of the movement in charge of promoting the relations with Syria. In the field, cut off from all the various pressures and contacts, the wave of escalation went on between Israel and Hezbollah with its peak being Operation Grapes of Wrath in April 1996.[94]

In July 1995, Nasrallah said that the activities of his movement actually enforced Syria's positioning of the negotiations and that Syria would not abandon the movement, which had proven its loyalty to Assad even during hard times. He belittled the importance of Khaddam's visit to Iran and the subjected discussed there. In October 1995, al-Tufayli said that there shouldn't be a contradiction between having good relations with Syria and continuing the resistance after a peace treaty was signed.[95]

Naturally, this approach greatly contributed to the ongoing escalation in southern Lebanon and, at the same time, to the increasing of American pressure on Syria to intervene and restrain the movement. In December 1995, in the midst of a wave of violence, the Syrian foreign minister declared that Syria had opposed the escalation in southern Lebanon and that action must be taken to relax things and stop the firing of missiles and rockets. The foreign minister's declaration troubled Hezbollah, and its seniors quickly asked the Syrians for clarifications and simultaneously met with their Iranian patrons in order to discuss the situation.[96] The movement's response was published in an editorial of the weekly newspaper *Al-Ahd*, from which it was understood that the movement supported Syria's position, calling on it to refrain from worsening the escalating tension in south, yet this didn't mean that the resistance would stop; on the contrary, it "shall continue daily and with greater intensity."[97] In reality, the Syrian pressure yielded a temporary relaxation and cut the chain of escalating activities. The movement excused this by the existence of technical reasons only. The escalation trend also went on during the first months of 1996. It peaked in April 1996 with Operation Grapes of Wrath. Even the Syrian intervention, in an attempt to relax the situation, was a failure.[98]

The strengthening of the Syrian hold of Lebanon, together with the progress of the talks in the Syrian-Israeli channel, placed further restraints at Iran's doorstep. Syria's exposure to American pressure was of concern to Iran, as was its Lebanese ally, Hezbollah. Therefore, alongside maintaining a loose framework of the strategic alliance, the two countries were engaged in a struggle over the movement's current and future images. The escalation of the violence during the second half of 1995 until Operation Grapes of Wrath in April 1996 played into the hands of Iran, which opposed the agreement and acted to thwart it. It caused the deviation of the negotiation from its main course. So, in fact, despite

Hezbollah's declarations concerning identity of interests with Syria, its activities promoted the Iranian interest. Iran not only "took its time" to help Syria in its efforts to restrain Hezbollah, but it also strove to thwart any idea or initiative on the eve of Operation Grapes of Wrath, during and after which it intended to restrain, minimize, or disarm the movement.[99] The movement, on its side, stressed that its position of principle negates any agreement with Israel and that it would object to any such agreement, even if it was signed.[100]

In April 1996, during Operation Grapes of Wrath, an American official said that the United States warned Syria many times that the firing of missiles and rockets carried out by Hezbollah would cause a harsh Israeli retaliation. He spoke against Syria, saying that although the escalation did not serve its interests, it did nothing to stop it. According to him, Syria was playing a double game that allowed it to gain from both worlds by continuing the war of attrition with Israel through Hezbollah along with conducting negotiations, disconnected from the Lebanese system.[101]

From analyzing the Syrian moves in regard to Hezbollah during the second half of 1995 until Operation Grapes of Wrath, it is hard to decisively determine if it was a deliberate Syrian policy of ignoring the escalation while rejecting pressures to restrain the movement or if it was an attempt on the part of Syria to directly and indirectly restrain the movement through Iran that had simply failed. Syria did try to gain from both worlds; altogether, one cannot ignore the fact that Syria acted in order to ease the tension as it broke out, particularly the firing of missiles and rockets. Its failure derived from the integration of two factors: first, a low level of Syrian determination to force things on Hezbollah concerning the resistance issue and second, the existence of additional factors such as the Iranian, Israeli, and internal-Lebanese factors influencing Hezbollah.

Operation Grapes of Wrath of April 1996 gave Syria another opportunity to restrain the movement's activity and to ensure that the scenario of an uncontrollable escalation would not be repeated. The April 1996 Understanding created new rules of game and provided Syria and the Lebanese regime with an opportunity to build a mechanism for the neutralization of an escalation that was already in its early stages.[102] But even the Syrian-Lebanese assumption that the mechanism for treating breaches of the Understanding would restrain Hezbollah's activities and allow the maintaining of a controlled level of violence in Lebanon were deemed wrong.

In May 1996, the movement renewed its activities against the security zone, and from there, it was just a question of time until a renewed escalation took place in southern Lebanon. The tension level was a function of the scope of casualties and not of the number of breaches of the Understanding.[103]

An example of the existence of a triangle of forces is evident from the Syrian vice president's surprise visit to Tehran in January 1997. The visit was supposed to straighten things out between the two countries on all issues concerning Hezbollah's future in Lebanon. This step and Khaddam's statement, which made it clear that the movement would not be disarmed as long as the Israeli occupation continued and that Syria would continue supporting the right of the resistance, provided, according to the commentators, a response to Rafsanjani's protest concerning the things that Rafik Al-Hariri said on his visit to the United States in December 1996 and from which it could be understood that Hezbollah would be disarmed.

Some people think that there were additional heavy-weighted reasons for the Iranian anger, including an Iranian evaluation that Syria decided to gradually limit Hezbollah's strength on the backdrop of the progress in the peace process. As an exception, according to the Iranians, Syria was behind the move to minimize the movement's strength during the parliamentary elections in August–September 1996, and it even imposed limitations upon its activities in southern Lebanon. In addition, an Iranian fear was rising that the Syrians were also considering canceling the regular flight line between Tehran and Damascus that served as a major pipeline of contact and supply between Iran and its activists in Lebanon and Hezbollah. In any case, this episode, like many before it, teaches of the complex and dynamic balance of forces between the players of the Arab regional front and of the movement's ability to navigate well between the various pressures and restraints exercised upon it.[104]

In October 1997, Nasrallah visited Tehran for consultations and meetings with the Iranian leadership. Nasrallah's visit after Khatami's election as Iran's President was intended, among other things, to ensure Iran's continued support of his movement and of its policy.[105] The fact that Iranian leadership stood alongside Nasrallah was important for him also in light of al-Tufayli's attempts to challenge his leadership and establish a new revolutionary movement similar to Hezbollah. The visit was a success as far as Nasrallah was concerned. He said that he received Iran's blessing for his "Openness Policy" initiative, and he began to actually implement it, and the Iranian president even urged him to take advantage of the increasing sympathy his movement was receiving, to expand its activity in the political and cultural fields, and to recruit intellectuals to its ranks.[106]

Altogether, despite declarations concerning the movement's independence, Iran made sure that it was involved anytime the subjects coming up on the regional daily agenda influenced its ally in Lebanon. Thus, for example, during the round of discussions, the Syrian-Lebanese policy concerning the Israeli initiative to carry out UN decision 425 was established. In March 1998, Iranian foreign minister Kamal Kharrazi visited Syria and Lebanon and confided with the top Syrian and Lebanese officials and also with Hezbollah seniors and Lebanese power factors with the purpose of establishing a united front against the suggested Israeli move. Even in this case, as was in the past, the basic conflicts of interest between Iran and Syria concerning the peace process clearly placed Iran alongside Hezbollah, causing tension to the Syrian-Iranian relations.[107] On the other hand, Hezbollah was dissatisfied with all the Iranian moves and mainly with the declaration of the Iranian minister of guidance concerning the future of Hezbollah after the withdrawal. Unlike his regular manner, Nasrallah responded explicitly on this declaration while clarifying, once again, his position concerning Hezbollah's independence.[108]

To conclude, during the 1990s, Hezbollah had to navigate its policy and activities according to the development of two major procedures: the implementation of the Ta'if Agreement and the peace process. The movement objected to both procedures altogether and required Iran's support every time it sensed a threat to its existence. This fact allowed Iran to continue influencing Hezbollah partially, even after the stabilization of the Lebanese regime. Altogether, the movement strictly kept the independence of its decisions in all that concerned its conduct in Lebanon while navigating efficiently between its two patrons.[109]

The same independence of decision that characterized the movement's relations with Iran also characterized its relations with Syria. Syria found it difficult to enforce its authority on the movement or to restrain it, even when its activities damaged the negotiations. Syria mainly used diplomatic tools in order to restrain Hezbollah—it summoned its leaders for explanations in Damascus, involved Iran by demanding it to exercise its influence on the movement, and, in certain cases, even threatened to operate or actually operated military forces against Hezbollah activists. The "special" treatment the movement received and the "forgiving" approach demonstrated by Syria toward the movement, even when its interests were damaged following the movement's activities, mainly derived from the Syrian need to maintain its strategic alliance with Iran.

Hezbollah and Israel—Mutual Influences from the 1990s On

In April 1996, in the midst of Operation Grapes of Wrath, the newspaper *Al-Shark al-Awsat* published a commentary on the topic of Hezbollah's status in the Lebanese arena, in which it was claimed that the military confrontation with Israel reinforced Hezbollah and granted it political legitimacy. According to the columnist, Hezbollah could not be simply removed from the Lebanese arena the way the Palestinians were. Fighting against Israel was the movement's main objective, and as long as this went on, there was justification to its existence. Therefore, the escalation of the violence, as far as he was concerned, played into the hands of Hezbollah, and the Israeli military activity did not yield the desired results, as far as Israel was concerned.[110] Nasrallah and Hariri, Lebanon's prime minister also held this opinion. During Operation Grapes of Wrath, Hariri's claim against Israel was that its activities did not weaken Hezbollah, but did the contrary, and he stressed that his government did not have the ability to control Hezbollah.[111]

Naturally, Israel and Hezbollah aimed to achieve goals that contradicted one another. Hezbollah placed two intermediary goals on the way to the termination of Israel as a state entity; first, expelling it from Lebanese soil by conducting a war of attrition against it and second, continuing to help and support the Palestinian Intifada.[112] Israel, on the other hand, placed the goal of "achieving security and peace for the residents of the North." It strove to achieve this by using its military strength directly against Hezbollah, alongside diplomatic activity facing Lebanon, Syria, and the international system. The commencement of the peace process in 1991 created an opportunity for Israel, and it used a combined strategy to create pressure upon Hezbollah on several channels simultaneously. But internal Lebanese problems, Lebanon's umbilical-cord connection with Syria, and the question of what came before what (Israel's withdrawal or Hezbollah's disarmament) did not provide for stopping the movement's violent activity.[113]

The end of the War between Brothers (November 1990) cleared the way for Hezbollah's return to southern Lebanon and to the center of the internal Lebanese arena. The quick return to resistance activities was critical for it for this permitted it to reject out of hand the pressures to disarm. Thus, the movement increased its organizational efforts in southern Lebanon and its activity against the security zone.[114] In the field of the media, it emphasized the magnitude of danger that Lebanon might expect due to the Israeli threat and the strategy of struggle that it was using against it, and presented as legitimate guerilla warfare against an occupying army force. The movement's activities in southern Lebanon were extensively covered by the movement's media at every possible opportunity.[115]

The escalation of the violence in southern Lebanon during the years 1992–1993 turned the question of restraining Hezbollah and disarming it into the main topic in the talks of the Israeli-Lebanese channel. The Israeli and American demand on Lebanon and Syria to disarm the movement was rejected out of hand, as was the demand to restrain it. Facing the increasing pressure upon it to restrain its policy and to refrain from granting an excuse for Israeli aggression, the movement presented a regular and tough stand, claiming that the resistance policy was not subjected to changes or to external pressures and that it was not being carried out for the sake of achieving political gains.[116]

Facing Israel's military action strategy, Hezbollah established a retaliation policy that it realized each time it thought Israel had deviated from the acceptable rules of conduct. This policy of retaliatory launching of missiles and rockets was adopted and performed by the movement with the clear knowledge that, by doing so, it might actually cause the escalation of things. Israel's efforts to force the movement to cancel its retaliatory firing policy failed. The Understandings achieved in 1993 and in 1996 lasted for limited periods of time, and the movement resorted to applying the retaliation policy again. Furthermore, it developed and expanded this ability even after the withdrawal of the IDF from Lebanon and dispersed throughout southern Lebanon an array of long-ranged rockets and missiles in order to create a "balance of terror," in its words, against Israel. In August 1993, Nasrallah related to his movement's retaliation policy against Israel's activity and said that this policy had been a complete success story.[117]

Leafing through a graph of the movement's activities all through the 1990s, one notices the existence of a trend of an increase in the quantity of activities and, according to the movement, their quality as well. Its senior leaders stressed this trend at every given opportunity while quoting Israeli leaders who reinforced the above-mentioned trends. In February 1995, Nasrallah said that Israel admitted that the number of activities carried out by the movement in 1994 was greater and that these were more qualitative than those performed in 1993.[118] In June 1995, the movement stressed that the retaliation policy caused a turnaround of the deterrence relations between the movement and Israel. In July 1995, Qassem declared that the movement had switched from a stage of response to a stage of initiation.[119] In October 1995, the chairman of Hezbollah's political council said that Israel's response possibilities had become more minimized and limited than they had been in the past, owing to the improvement that took place in the movement's retaliation ability and the restraints of the July 1993 Understanding.[120] In November 1996, Nasrallah said that "between 11 November 1995 and 10 November 1996, the Resistance has carried out, according to the enemy's statistics, 1,065 activities, among which 825 were carried out by the Islamic Resistance."[121] In December 1997, Nasrallah praised the significant development that had occurred in the quantity and the quality of the resistance activities and the direct damage that these had caused Israel, which was caught in a dead end and in a deep internal crisis, while Hezbollah enjoyed an unprecedented rise of its status in the Lebanese public opinion.[122]

Hezbollah testified that it learned from its own mistakes, produced lessons, and applied them.[123] In its struggle against Israel and against direct and indirect internal and external pressures, the movement's senior leaders have consistently claimed that they were convinced of the effectiveness of their policy and that they would not succumb to pressures. Whenever changes occurred in the scope and nature of the movement's activity in the field, its senior leaders quickly clarified that the changes were only tactical and derived from various restraints.[124]

The Israeli activity greatly dictated the movement's patterns of behavior. Being aware of the abilities of Israel's intelligence, it took a number of steps to ensure the survival of its leaders and military activists. The movement's operative wing remained secret and compartmentalized and was based on an infrastructure of operative activists who assimilated among the local population in southern Lebanon. The location of its headquarters was kept secret and the means of security control and prevention were increased within the movement itself, out of fears of having double agents infiltrate its ranks. Its leaders used extensive means of precaution, fearing for their own personal safety.[125]

The most challenging threat that Israel ever presented Hezbollah was the regional peace process. Its success could have essentially changed the entire situation and neutralized one of the movement's major strength components, the armed resistance. As long as the struggle for the movement's annihilation went on directly in the military field or indirectly by exercising pressure upon the Shiite population in southern Lebanon, the movement thought it had the tools to handle the threat and that the resistance was a necessary component in thwarting the Israeli efforts.[126]

But the great concern with the issue of disarming the resistance in the peace talks and mainly the existence of a Syrian-Lebanese consensus that, during the era after Israel's withdrawal from Lebanon, there was no justification in continuing the resistance in its current pattern greatly troubled the movement's leadership, which realized that its influence on the chain of events that concern this issue was limited.[127] The more the peace process progressed, the stronger became the assumption that the signing of a peace agreement among Syria, Lebanon, and Israel was definite and the more the movement was pressured into declaring its positions and intentions for the day after the signing of the agreement. In response to the consolidating threat, the movement used a combined policy; it increased its violent activity and established an activity policy for continuing the struggle and, simultaneously, rejected out of hand any notion of a peace treaty with Israel. For instance, in October 1995, Hezbollah rejected Israel's offer to stop the violence for a period of three months, as a preliminary condition for discussing the Israeli withdrawal, under the claim that this was an Israeli step whose purpose was to cause a rift in the Lebanese public opinion.[128] In addition, it deliberately refrained from declaring its policy during the peace era or as Qassem phrased it, "Each thing at its own time . . . we must leave ourselves some bargaining cards, concealed from the enemy's view, and not discuss our use of them."[129]

In accordance with the progress of the negotiations between Israel and Syria, an escalation took place concerning the confrontations between Hezbollah and Israel, which reached their peak on April 1996, during Operation Grapes of Wrath. The operation, from Israel's perspective, was supposed to damage Hezbollah's infrastructures and its ability to launch missiles and rockets, to create pressure on the governments of Lebanon and Syria to restrain the movement, to cause strife between it and the government and the Lebanese population, and to change the July 1993 Understanding.[130]

An operational failure, which triggered the killing of dozens of Lebanese civilians in the village of Qana, shuffled the cards as far as Israel was concerned, and the military maneuver gained only partial success. In reality, it was Hezbollah that harvested the fruit of the Israeli operation. It gained the support and sympathy of the Lebanese public opinion, its operational infrastructure was minimally damaged, and the movement resorted to carrying out activities in southern Lebanon within a very short period after the end of the operation.[131] In December 31, 1996, the head of the executive council, Hashem Safi al-Din, concluded Hezbollah's activities of the previous year and said that a line of successful and documented activities carried out by the movement during that year, such as exposing espionage networks working for Israel and putting those cooperating with Israel, headed by General Lahad, on trial, caused the IDF embarrassment and the disintegration of the SLA. He added that, at the same time, the movement managed to limit Israel's steps through the April Understanding and thus minimize "Israel's acts of aggression."[132] In January 1997, Nasrallah said that the movement did not use force arbitrarily and refrained from providing Israel with excuses to attack; he added that Hezbollah followed Israel's moves and declarations and responded accordingly.[133]

The results of the 1996 elections in Israel and the rise to power of Likud (the major right wing political party in Israel) indirectly played into the hands of Hezbollah. The talks on the Syrian-Israeli channel reached a dead end and the immediate threat of signing a peace treaty was removed. At the same time, the more Israel remained in Lebanon, the more the Israeli public opinion was turning against this in regard to the benefit of continuing to stay in Lebanon versus the price in casualties that Israel was forced to pay for this. The movement, which identified the trend, increased its activities against the IDF in Lebanon and its efforts to influence the Israeli public opinion by conducting an intensive propaganda campaign. The more the situation in Lebanon escalated, the more the Israeli media dealt with the Lebanese issue, and, in accordance, the more pressure was applied upon the decision makers to withdraw from Lebanon. A series of accidents with many causalities in 1997, including the collision of two Air Force helicopters on February 4 (73 casualties), the death of five soldiers in a fire during operational activity, and the failed Israeli naval command operation of September 4 (11 casualties) intensified the argument concerning whether to remain in Lebanon and reinforced the position of those supporting a unilateral withdrawal from Lebanon.[134]

Nabil Kaouk, one of Hezbollah's top guns in southern Lebanon, claimed that these events pinpointed the failure of Israel's strategy and tactics in its struggle against Hezbollah. He determined that, in the military field, Israel was in distress and that "the Resistance managed to transfer that distress, from the military field to the field of security and to the public and the political fields."[135]

The freezing of the talks in the Syrian-Israeli channel from 1996 on put the handling of the Lebanese issue back in the center of things in the regional and international systems, with one difference of principle. In return for the fulfillment of UN decision 425, Israel demanded securities and collaterals from Lebanon and Lebanon, on the other hand, demanded Israel's withdrawal without any preliminary conditions and without obliging to sign a peace agreement. Hezbollah strove to fulfill this goal by escalating the resistance activities and conducting psychological warfare, whose arrows were aimed at the IDF, the SLA, and the Israeli public opinion. At the same time, it exercised pressure upon the government of Lebanon so that it wouldn't surrender to Israel's demands.[136] Hezbollah's interest faced the Israeli interest to disarm it and to minimize the borders of its influence, while Hezbollah wished to cause Israel's withdrawal from Lebanon without any preliminary conditions and without any securities by continuing the resistance activities.[137]

As a matter of fact, it was Hezbollah that managed to realize its goals. In May 2000, the IDF withdrew from Lebanon without a peace agreement. Hezbollah was quick to take credit for its victory and, at the same time, declare that the work was not done and that it still needed its weapons because the IDF was still standing on Lebanese soil, in the Shebaa farms area, and the resistance was not over just yet.[138]

To conclude, Israel's efforts during the 1990s to disarm Hezbollah and to turn it into a marginal factor in the Lebanese arena failed. As a matter of fact, in the conclusion of the war of attrition that went on between the movement and Israel all along the 1990s and is still going on, though at a different dosage level and other characteristics, it was Hezbollah that emerged victorious. Israel withdrew from Lebanon unilaterally without an arrangement or an agreement with Lebanon or Syria. The movement continued operating from southern Lebanon against Israel directly and indirectly by helping, supporting, and activating Palestinian terror factors and recruiting activists from among the Israeli Arabs. Beyond all that, it maintained its retaliation ability against Israel by using an array of rocket and missile launchers dispersed throughout southern Lebanon. The movement's approach toward Israel and its policy, which does not solely depend on Israel's existence on Lebanese soil, was concluded by Nasrallah in his fluent speech, as early as in June 1993, by the following words: "We do not acknowledge the rogue Israeli entity, which robbed the lands from the Muslims . . . we uphold a strategy of erasing Israel from the map." The way to apply this strategy was continuing the "Jihadist doing" in Lebanon while simultaneously harnessing the Palestinian people and the entire Arab and Islamic nation to the struggle.[139]

Summary

The existence of a regional system with a multitude of players and conflicts, which most of the time had basic conflicts of interest with one another, in relation to the Lebanese system in general and to the Hezbollah movement in particular, caused for the total influence of the regional system upon the movement to be relatively meager in relation to the strengths and abilities of its players. Every player in the system acted in order to promote its own interests and to neutralize the influences of the other players.

During eras, or periods in which a consensus existed between two regional players, they succeeded, not without effort, in influencing the movement's directions of development and enforcing somewhat of an authority upon it. Things were so during the movement's stages of establishment and consolidation, between the years 1982 and 1985, when Syria and Iran acted mutually to expel the foreigners from Lebanon and to thwart the May 17 agreement. Syrian-Iranian cooperation during the years 1988–1991 (until Syria joined the peace process) allowed the ending of the War between Brothers and even the movement's integration in the procedures of restoring the Lebanese political system and into its institutions after the Ta'if Agreement.

If this assignment's concern was "what would happen if. . . ," it would be likely to assume that if a peace agreement were signed in 1996, as the result of Syrian-Israeli identity of interests, it might have had a significant influence upon the development of trends in the movement. In October 1994, Fadlallah negated an approach that was commonplace among certain circles, assuming that Hezbollah emerged as the result of a certain regional situation and might disappear as the result of regional changes.[140]

One way or another, the regional players' contradictory trends of influence and the existence of restraints that limited their activity facing the movement, allowed it to navigate its way through a twisting path between its patrons and its rival, in accordance with its policy and its needs, which did not always fit the whims of all players in the regional front. This tortuous navigation between the interests of its patrons was based on the assumption that, as long as the movement's activities benefited one of them, it shall do everything in its power to maintain the continuance of its expanse of activity, especially if this served the interests of both. The movement made it clear to everyone that, above all, it had its own independent policy and that it followed this policy consistently and decisively.[141]

Hezbollah as a Player in the International Arena

Introduction

In March 2005, the European Parliament declared Hezbollah as an international terrorist organization. Until then, only the United States, Canada, Australia, Holland, and Israel had declared Hezbollah as a terrorist organization. Till the decision was accepted in March 2005, the countries of the European Union regarded Hezbollah as a legitimate social movement represented in the Lebanese parliament, distinguishing it by calling it an "External Security Organization."[1]

The essential difference in the way the international system defined Hezbollah hindered any chance of creating effective direct and indirect pressure upon the movement. While the United States was acting to obliterate it, Hezbollah's leaders were meeting diplomats from all over the world, including the UN secretary general, Kofi Annan, during his visit to Lebanon. This international environment made it possible for Lebanon, Syria, and Iran to navigate between the European positions and the American pressure and made it difficult to disarm the movement. [2]

The involvement of the international system or of top players within it, in the complex Middle-Eastern arena, was influenced by regional and international restraints and limitations, making it hard to restrain or limit the power of Hezbollah. The absence of a consensus concerning an international definition of the term "terror" prevented effective international cooperation in fighting terror.

This fact, and the fear of the players of the international system that being involved in areas saturated with violence and terror could damage their interests, played right into Hezbollah's hands. Even during the 1980s, when the movement was launching many terrorist attacks against the international system's players, these players had difficulties cooperating in order to create effective pressure on the movement in an attempt to restraint or eliminate it. The conclusion from this analysis was that, in the absence of basic consent as to Hezbollah actually being a terrorist movement, the international system's influence upon the movement was very marginal. Despite the aforementioned, and due to the fact that the United States was, on the one hand, a superpower involved in the regional system influencing it and an enemy of Hezbollah, on the other, it is worthwhile and advisable to broaden the discussion concerning this issue. Furthermore, Hezbollah operated in the international arena from its earliest days and carried out terrorist attacks against the United States and the West and interests within and outside Lebanon.

The United States had and still has heavy weighted interests in the Middle-Eastern arena, including Lebanon. Therefore, establishing the legal regime in Lebanon and enforcing its sovereignty on all its parts, as a barrier that prevented the expansion of Hezbollah and other terror factors was and still is an important component in the United State's foreign policy toward Lebanon.[3]

In 1997, the United States declared Hezbollah as a terrorist organization whose activity provided a threat to American interests. The FBI's most wanted list included the head of the movement's Jihad council and a member of the Shura council, Imad Mugniyah, responsible for a series of terrorist attacks carried out by the movement during the 1980s and the 1990s against Western targets in Lebanon as well as outside it.[4] Mugniyah was assassinated in Syria in February 2008, an act for which no one claimed responsibility.[5]

From the second half of the 1980s, the United States had been aiming to wipe out Hezbollah's entity as a terrorist movement and to minimize its infrastructure in the regional and the international arena by exercising pressure on Syria and Iran and by cutting off the movement's funding and support resources. These moves have yet to show any significant results.[6]

Hezbollah—a Terrorist Movement with Presence and Activity in the International Arena

Hezbollah is a terror movement that maintains extensive infrastructural, operational, and logistic presence and activity in the international arena. This infrastructure grants it the ability to shorten the time between accepting a decision concerning an activity and its actual performance.[7] The movement recruits its activists from among the Shiite communities worldwide, but not exclusively. In October 2002, the American under secretary of defense, Douglas Feith, related to Hezbollah's international infrastructure and emphasized that it is one of the most dangerous terrorist networks controlled from Lebanon and supported by Syria and Iran. He added that the United States was aware of the movement's activity and was monitoring it.[8]

Analyzing Hezbollah's activity in the international arena, one can clearly notice two phases. During the initial phase, in the 1980s, it carried out terrorist attacks against Western targets on Lebanese soil as well as abroad. During this period, Hezbollah, with the support of the Iranians, established the foundations of its international network.

During the second phase, from the early 1990s on, the movement changed its activity patterns in the international arena. It was concerned with expanding and consolidating its operational and logistic infrastructure, minimizing the scope of its terrorist attacks in this arena, and concentrating on planning and carrying out terrorist attacks against "qualitative" targets. During this period, Hezbollah executed terrorist attacks against Israeli and Jewish targets worldwide. The two most prominent terrorist attacks took place in Argentina.

The first attack took place on March 17, 1992, against the Israeli Embassy in Buenos Aires, in which 29 people were killed and 250 were injured. The second attack was carried out on July 18, 1994, against the Argentine Jewish Mutual Association (AMIA) in Buenos Aires, leaving one hundred people dead and dozens injured. In 1996, Hezbollah cooperated with the Saudi Hezbollah terror organization in the Khobar Towers bombing in Saudi Arabia, in which nineteen American soldiers were killed.[9]

Since 1994, Hezbollah hadn't carried out large-scale terrorist attacks, such as the Argentina bombings, outside the Middle Eastern arena. Yet, its activists continued gathering intelligence information and planning and initiating terrorist attacks against Western targets all along that period. During the last decade, intelligence agencies and security factors worldwide reported the apprehension of Hezbollah cells in their countries and the thwarting of planned terrorist attacks as follows:

A. In 1995, the security agencies in Singapore foiled the activity of a Hezbollah terrorist cell that was preparing to launch a terrorist attack against Israeli and American vessels that were docked there. The investigation exposed a race boat that was supposed to carry out the suicide bombing terrorist attack.[10]

B. In 1997, Hezbollah activists were arrested while gathering intelligence information concerning the United States Embassy in Nicosia.[11]

C. According to the "9/11 Commission Report," Hezbollah used its camps to train the al-Qaeda activists that were involved in the terrorist attacks against the American embassies in Kenya and Tanzania in September 1998.[12]

D. In December 1999, it was reported that the combined police activity at the Tri-border area in South America hindered a mutual terror attack of Hezbollah and al-Qaeda that was to be executed against Jewish targets in Buenos Aires, Ottawa (Canada), and the Tri-border city of Ciudad del Este.[13]

E. In October 2001, it was reported that the Mexican authorities had arrested a Hezbollah cell on its way to carry out a terrorist attack against governmental targets in Mexico.[14]

F. In 2001, the Swedish authorities exposed a network of terrorist activists directly related to al-Qaeda and Hezbollah. The terrorists were charged with transferring information, using means of communication and funding.[15]

G. In December 2002, on the basis of a police report, a Canadian newspaper published that a Hezbollah network was operating in Canada and that its activists were assembling information concerning potential targets.[16]

Principles and the Dispersion of Hezbollah's Network of Terrorism in the International Arena

Hezbollah's global network is dispersed in over forty countries spanning five continents and is controlled directly from Lebanon by Hezbollah's Shura Council headed, until recently, by Mugniyah. The uncovering of affairs, the reports of agencies, and the media allow a glance into the nature and the composition of

Hezbollah's groups and cells, its methods of activity, and its manner of recruiting the activists. From the information revealed so far, it turns out that:

A. Hezbollah is involved with international crime, especially with drugs and money counterfeiting "industries"; trading of stolen property, smuggling, and fraudulent acts. These activities were intended to create another significant independent channel of finance recruitment, using professional criminal elements to improve the organization's operational abilities. The centers of the network activity are the Middle East, South America, Europe, and West Africa.

B. A local Hezbollah network usually includes the following components: a Dawa and recruitment entity, based on religious clerics, Islamic centers, Internet sites, and the broadcasts of Almanar Television;[17] a financing department whose capabilities based on the ability to raise money legally and illegally by using organized crime; and an operational team, dealing with smuggling activists and means of warfare and the assembling of intelligence concerning potential targets. The acquisition department deals with acquiring or stealing means of warfare for the organization's use and smuggling them into Lebanon or into designated countries. In some places the movement has a purchase group that buys and delivers special equipment. The last and important component is a liaison to the operational leadership in Lebanon.

C. Local Hezbollah networks exposed abroad during recent years upheld connections with the movement's activists and networks in the designated countries and the countries surrounding them, including Iranian delegates.

Here are only a few of the movement's activities, that have been exposed, in a regional scission:

North America: From the year 2000 on, Hezbollah-related activists, cells, and networks of Lebanese origin have been exposed in the United States. These groups were busy conducting diverse activities that concerned the movement, including crime, Dawa, recruiting activists, transferring finances to the movement in Lebanon, establishing contacts with other cells and networks of the movement in North America and with the Hezbollah headquarters in Lebanon.[18] In 2001, a Hezbollah activist was arrested in Canada and was accused of supplying the movement with means of warfare. In December 2002, Canada declared Hezbollah a terrorist organization and acted like the United States, thwarting the recruitment of finances for the movement from among Shiite communities in the country.[19]

South America: Hezbollah maintains a wide-scope infrastructural activity in Latin America, as an exception to the relative freedom of activity that prevails in uncontrolled areas such as the Tri-border area or in countries that have close relations of cooperation with Iran, such as Venezuela. The infrastructure in the Tri-border area of Argentina, Brazil, and Paraguay involves domestic and international crime, terrorism, logistic support, and funding. The local authorities have difficulties minimizing or restraining the movement's activities within their territory. Hezbollah maintains presence and activity in other countries of South America, such as Columbia, Guatemala, Panama, Costa Rica, and Mexico.[20]

Europe: The continent provided convenient grounds of activity for Hezbollah owing to the fact that it did not appear on the European list of terrorist movements until March 2005. Between the years 1996 and 2005, Hezbollah launched five activists into Europe to perform terrorist attacks in Israel.[21] The movement raised funds for its activity through charitable societies operating in Germany, Britain, and Switzerland. In 2002, two charitable societies, "Al-Shahid Social Relief Institution" and the "Al Aqsa Fund;" that had been raising funds for Hezbollah in Germany were closed down. Among other things, Hezbollah still maintains its presence and activity in Russia, the Balkan countries, Germany, Turkey, Cypress, and Spain.[22]

Asia: Hezbollah maintains an organizational infrastructure in the Muslim countries of South-East Asia, such as Malaysia, Philippines, Indonesia, Thailand, Korea, and India. From reports relating to this infrastructural activity, it turned out that the movement's activists were busy assembling intelligence concerning Jewish synagogues in Manila and the offices of the El-Al company in Bangkok. In Thailand, however, they tried but failed to carry out a suicide attack against the Israeli Embassy. Likewise, it was reported that the movement had been recruiting local activists in South-East Asia and sending them to train in Lebanon.[23]

Africa: Rich Lebanese Shiite residents in Africa contribute finances to Hezbollah. West Africa provides one of the movement's centers of activity. In this continent, it maintains presence in Ivory Coast, Nigeria, South Africa, Zaire, Zimbabwe, Uganda, Sudan, and other places. The movement activists and the Iranians conducted reciprocal relations with Osama bin-Laden in Sudan between 1991 and 1996. Hezbollah also operated a diamond smuggling network from the mines in Africa. In June 2004, the movement rejected American claims that it was profiting from diamond trade in West Africa.[24]

Hezbollah and the International System—Reciprocal Relations between the Years 1980 and 1985

The roots of the complex reciprocal relations between Hezbollah and the international system are vested in the 1970s. During the course of these years, Khomeini coined his famous slogan "America is the Great Satan" and, in doing so, for the first time, gave expression to a frame of mind of rage and frustration, commonplace among Muslim societies, on the background of the ever-increasing gap between the strength of Western societies and the weakness of Muslim societies. The United States was perceived as the symbol of Western supremacy. Hatred of the United States provided a common denominator for various publics in Muslim societies and a means for creating social mobilization and recruiting supporters and activists for direct activity against American targets in Arab countries and against the pro-American rulers who were administrating them.[25]

This ideological approach was well internalized among Hezbollah activists from the very first days of its establishment. Under the slogan, "expulsion of all the foreigners from Lebanon," its activists carried out suicide bombing and murderous terrorist attacks against American targets in Beirut during the years 1983–1984 and activities such as kidnapping Western citizens, including Americans, through the 1980s. In February 1985, in the first public presentation of the move-ment's platform and objectives, its spokesman declared that its activities had achieved their purpose. He emphasized that the foreign forces left Lebanon in early 1984 without achieving their objectives, while Israel was in the midst of a process of gradual withdrawal from most of Lebanon's territory.[26]At the same occasion the spokesman added , "We intend to act against the roots of evil, and these roots are the United States."[27]

In 2001, an American intelligence officer, Bill Cowan, revealed details con-cerning the principles of the American policy toward Hezbollah during the early 1980s and the considerations guiding the decision makers in the United States. Cowan was part of a crew appointed by the Pentagon in 1983 to investigate the terrorist attacks against the American forces in Beirut and to recommend courses of action for handling the terrorist threats in Lebanon. According to him, the team's findings and his recommendations were sent to the American secretary of defense and archived. Some of the recommendations, mainly those concerning the gathering of counterintelligence, were applied after the terrorist attacks of October 1983, and the rest were rejected out of hand. The root of the problem, in his opinion, derived from the differences of opinion between Secretary of Defense Caspar Willard Weinberger and Secretary of State George Pratt Schultz.The Pentagon, headed by Weinberger, supported a policy of refraining from using military activities in Lebanon, as long as there was no clear definition of the goals and objectives. Therefore, he rejected out of hand any suggestion for retaliatory military activity that was not part of a clear and inclusive governmental policy.

Secretary of State Schultz, on the other hand, had an opposite opinion. He stressed the need for an American retaliation to the terrorist attacks and pushed for the performance of counterintelligence activities in the case of preliminary information concerning intentions to launch terrorist attacks against American targets. Cowan claimed that refraining from accepting operative decisions derived, among other reasons, from the long-term influence of the failure of the hostage rescue operation at the American Embassy in Iran in 1979 (Desert One) and the fear of senior government officials of the predicted cost in the case of a failure in the Lebanese arena as well.[28]

A day after the terrorist attack against the marine forces in Beirut, U.S. presi-dent Reagan said, "We have vital interests in Lebanon," and in this he expressed Lebanon's importance to the United States. This importance derives from the existence of a profound and longstanding cultural bond between the Lebanese Arab-American community and the United States and from Lebanon being a liberal Arab country with a pro-Western orientation.[29]

This relationship was also expressed by the American involvement in the Lebanese and the regional arena. In 1982, the United States was behind the ini-tiative to position the multinational forces (MNFs) on Lebanon's soil in order to help apply the agreement to evacuate the Palestinians from Beirut and stabilize the Lebanese president's regime. At the same time, it significantly increased the scope of support to Lebanon in 1983 while placing special emphasis on the restoration of the Lebanese Army via warfare and training.[30]

Syria and Iran, which objected to the presence of the MNFs on Lebanese soil, were involved behind the scenes of the initiation and the planning of activities that would cause their expulsion. The activities themselves were carried out by Hezbollah, but it refrained from "assuming responsibility" for them out of fear of counter reactions. The leader of the Amal al-Islami movement, whose name was correlated with these terrorist attacks, rejected any connection between the terrorist attacks and Hezbollah and stressed that "we have no connection with the act of aggression" but, at the same time, added that "my intention is to emphasize to the French and to the multinational forces that the confrontation will be long-standing and that the war against these enemies shall bear a new and unique nature."[31]

To conclude, an examination of the reciprocal relations between the international system and Hezbollah during those years clearly shows that Hezbollah emerged victorious in the asymmetric struggle that it was conducting against this system. The pressure of the American public on the government caused the evacuation of the MNFs from Lebanon in February 1984. The results of the suicide bombing terrorist attacks were deeply engraved in the American political consciousness and influenced the U.S. level of involvement in Lebanon from then on. The American security and intelligence agencies, like the rest of the intelligence agencies dealing with the subject, were surprised by the method of activity and by the scope of casualties caused by the movement's terrorist attacks and had difficulties drawing a credible intelligence picture of it. Countries whose citizens had been kidnapped in Lebanon had difficulties finding an address for negotiating the conditions of their release, and in most cases, they had to use Syrian or Iranian mediators and were forced to "pay" a political or financial price for the release of the hostages.[32] Cowan, who also related to the influences of Hezbollah's terrorist attacks against the MNFs during this period stated that: " . . . it also produced a big change in our policy towards the Middle East. We'd been pursuing a very positive, active policy towards the Middle East as a whole, encouraging further agreements between the Arab governments and Israel. This put a stop to it. We really went into a period of paralysis so far as Middle East diplomatic policy was concerned. We were very much on the defensive."[33]

Hezbollah and the International System—Reciprocal Relations between the Years 1985 and 1990

In November 1989, the members of the Lebanese parliament and the representatives of prominent Lebanese power factors, excluding Hezbollah, convened in Ta'if, Saudi Arabia, to discuss matching the Lebanese national treaty with the existent reality. The conference took place following Syrian and inter-Arab pressure. The United States supported the inter-Arab move although it included components that were not in accord with the American interests. This support was the necessity of reality for the United States, whose failure in Lebanon damaged its image in Arab countries. In this context, it must be stated that, during the course of the 1980s, over 265 Americans were killed in Lebanon and eighteen more were kidnapped, of whom fifteen were either released or escaped custody, and three were executed.[34]

Hezbollah, on the other hand, reinforced its position among the Shiite public opinion during this period, using this to recruit new activists to its ranks. In October 1987, Abbas al-Mousawi, one of the leaders of the Islamic Resistance, said, "I see no possibility how the enemy, being it Israel or the US . . . could withstand the Islamic Resistance or its sons." According to him, the movement overcame the obstacles, expanded, and became strong.[35] Sheikh Fadlallah elaborated this point and claimed that the activities against the MNFs emphasized Hezbollah's ability to plan and perform and proved that "we can besiege and hinder the plan of the multinational forces, whose purpose was to turn Lebanon into an American army base in the region."[36]

Hezbollah's campaign against the United States continued throughout the 1980s and the 1990s. The movement responded to the challenges of the international system and to its indirect pressures. In July 1987, Subhi al-Tufayli said that "Europe and the US have decided to fight against us and they exercise pressure upon Syria to make it do this instead of them."[37] In September 1987, in a speech during the day of Ashura, Nasrallah defined the United States as the source of all the problems of Islamic nations and called on the movement to struggle "for the expulsion of imperialism by hurting the US, its agents and its spies."[38] Six months later, (in March 1988), at a rally in memory of the eighty Lebanese who had been killed in the explosion of a car bombing in Beirut, an activity that was attributed to the Americans, the movement's spokesmen called for the use of terrorism against the United States in order to protect the Muslim interests.[39]

One of the significant challenges placed by the movement at the doorstep of the international system in general and of the United States in particular during the 1980s was the kidnapping of Western hostages, including journalists, members of the academy, official delegates, and ordinary civilians, who either resided in or visited Lebanon. This method of activity was operatively simple, yet bore great impact upon the decision makers in the West, canceling out the asymmetry of strength between the movement and the players of the regional and international system. Hezbollah well understood this, and in July 1990 Hussein al-Mousawi, the leader of Amal al-Islami, said that "the acts of kidnapping are the only way we have in order to cope with the Israeli and the American aggression."[40]

Another prominent and particularly notorious kidnapping was the kidnapping of Colonel Higgins (April 1988) at the end of his official visit to the head of Amal in Tyre. After the kidnapping, circles connected to Hezbollah claimed that Higgins was a part of the American intelligence and was handling an espionage mission and that his kidnapping was carried out for political reasons.[41] In July 1988, al-Mousawi rejected the UN demand to release Higgins under the claim that his kidnapping was correlated with the American presence in the area.[42] Even the transferal of Higgins's body to the hands of the Americans, according to Reuters agency (August 1989), was conditioned by the release of Sheikh Obeid, who was held in Israel.[43]

The affair of the Western hostages in Lebanon emphasized the immense difficulty that the United States and the international system had to face in stopping the phenomenon or even coping with its results during the first half of the 1980s. The prolonged detention of the hostages by Hezbollah created public opinion pressures upon the decision makers in the West to act for their release. The United States itself was still under the influence of the terrorist attacks against the MNFs and was yet to establish an alternative policy of activity in Lebanon. As a result, the influence of the international system, including the United States, during the second half of the 1980s, upon the Hezbollah movement was marginal. In the absence of a Lebanese central body one could uphold a dialogue with, the United States was left outside of the direct circle of influence upon the procedures in Lebanon and fulfilled a marginal role in this system, mainly as a broker between the regional players during crisis situations.

Therefore, there is no wonder that when the opportunity was created, (in 1989) to stabilize the internal Lebanese system and to restore the political system, the United States supported the Syrian initiative, despite the fact that it did not approve of its actual presence on Lebanese soil. In July 1989, President Bush instructed his men to prepare an updated work document, analyzing the current situation in Lebanon and the significances deriving from it as the basis for updating the American policy toward Lebanon.[44]

Hezbollah and the International System—Reciprocal Relations during the 1990s

In May 2000, the IDF withdrew from Lebanon, thus closing the chapter of eighteen years of being on Lebanese soil and a decade that ranged between extreme escalations of activity facing Hezbollah and almost signing a peace treaty with Syria. During this decade, the American activity facing the regional system, including Lebanon, expanded. It derived, among other things, from the results of the first Gulf War (1990). This war created the conditions for the commencement of the peace talks between Israel and its neighbors under the brokerage of the United States. Syria's and Lebanon's joining the peace talks, the Iranian attempt to get closer to the West, and Hezbollah's entry into the Lebanese political system exposed the movement to a new system of pressures. It was forced to simultaneously struggle in several areas: the sectarian arena, facing its rival, Amal; the internal Lebanese arena, facing the increasing power of the Lebanese regime; the regional arena, facing Israel; and the international system, facing the American peace initiative.[45] Despite the pressures, the movement managed to successfully navigate between the internal Lebanese players and their regional patrons while maintaining its freedom of activity. Syria and Lebanon, which were exposed to the American pressure, rejected the claim to disarm the movement as long as the occupations persisted, yet were harnessed to help relax the tension in cases where the escalation threatened their interests.[46]

Yet, the violence in southern Lebanon had its own dynamics. It was influenced by the progress of the talks, but it also influenced them.[47] As time went by, the American means of pressure eroded and it was accused of one sidedness. This situation cleared the way for the entry of Europe into the regional arena as an additional international player. Syria, Iran, Lebanon, and Hezbollah regarded

Europe as an important factor, somewhat neutralizing the magnitude of the American influence, and encouraged it to intervene in the happenings of the regional system.[48] This involvement created a new environment saturated with international players and initiatives with the level, scope, and pace of its activity being influenced by the escalation in the field. Operation "Grapes of Wrath" (April 1996) stressed the complexity of the international environment that had been created. During this operation, the region became a "pilgrimage center" for European and American "negotiators," offering formulas for a cease-fire agreement.[49]

The escalation of the security situation in 1996, the establishment of an international supervision mechanism, and the upholding of elections in Israel and Lebanon focused the full attention of the regional and the international system, pushing the peace process, that had been stuck in one place during most of 1996, to the sidelines. Differences of approach and conflicts of interest between the United States and Europe caused many difficulties to the American effort to stabilize the security condition and establish a mechanism that would restrain Hezbollah. In the framework of the efforts to achieve the aforementioned objectives, the United States was functioned on several channels, simultaneously:

A. Facing the Lebanese government, it exercised direct pressure in the peace talks, in the Lebanese-American conference, and in the supervisory committee for the implementation of the agreement of understanding and for the increase of Lebanon's economic support. The American activity was meant to encourage the government of Lebanon to disarm the movement or at least to restrain it.

B. Facing Syria, the United States exercised direct pressure in the talks on the Israeli-Syrian channel and on the joint channel. At the beginning, the United States demanded that Syria disarm the movement and withdraw its troops from Lebanon, but later, the American position became eroded, and it asked Syria to act to restrain Hezbollah. Through the Syrian channel, the United States hoped to create the conditions that would allow the Lebanese government to disarm Hezbollah. Furthermore, Syria provided the gateway through which the Iranian support and the movement's means of warfare were arrived. Shutting down this vital channel of supply would raise difficulties as far as Hezbollah's ability to create crisis situations at a high frequency was concerned.

C. Facing Hezbollah, the American pressure was divided into two parts. The first part was mainly declarative and consisted of including the movement in the list of the terrorist organizations, and the second part was essentially operative and included freezing movement-related assets in the United States, closing down the movement's U.S.-based channels of funding (charity associations), including high echelons of the movement in the FBI's most wanted list, conducting surveillance of the networks of the movement's activists and supporters worldwide, and arresting Hezbollah's activists and supporters in the United States.

The American Activity to Restrain Hezbollah Facing the Lebanese Government

As the peace process moved forward, the United States realized that Hezbollah was a factor disrupting its advancement in the desired direction. The movement did everything in its power to sabotage its proper course by initiating an escalation during important, deciding junctions of the process. Naim Qassem explicitly declared that the movement's activities "bear a continuous nature and are correlated with the political conditions surrounding the negotiations, because we reject any form of compromise to begin with."[50] Therefore, the United States invested efforts in neutralizing Hezbollah's ability to influence the process by using all the operative and diplomatic means it could possibly recruit.[51]

On the eve of the peace talks (May–October 1991), al-Mousawi was requested to refer to the American initiative. His expressions on this matter clarified Hezbollah's clear-cut approach to this initiative, which was regarded as extremely dangerous for it. Al-Mousawi claimed that the initiative could cause the downfall of "the Islamic nation" and that the Muslim forces must be unified in order to cope with the danger.[52] He rejected out of hand rumors that the movement was forced to stop its activities following American pressure on the Lebanese government and emphasized that, facing the America initiative and the danger awaiting the movement, it would respond "by escalating the activity in the framework of the Jihad."[53]

The Lebanese, both willingly or due to Syrian pressures, rejected the American demands to disarm the movement and intertwined it in one package, along with the Israeli withdrawal from Lebanese territory. In February 1992, Lebanese prime minister Omar Karamé claimed that "Israel makes up excuses in order to create tension in the South and set new facts in the field in order to take advantage of this in the negotiations."[54] Senior government officials, all along the 1990s, blamed Israel for the creation of a deliberate escalation in southern Lebanon as part of its negotiation strategy in an attempt to pressurize Lebanon. They claimed that "as long as Lebanon remains under Israeli occupation, no one should weaken the resistance or disarm it from its weapons."[55]

The Peace Process as an Instrument for Creating the Conditions for the Disarmament of Hezbollah—a Failed Attempt

The peace process created the best political opportunity, as far as Israel and the United States were concerned, to eliminate Hezbollah as an armed, independent terrorist entity operating from Lebanon.[56] Hezbollah identified the threat and acted to thwart it by escalating the terrorist attacks every time the talks progressed, recruiting Iran to maintain the movement's interests and exercising indirect pressure upon Syria so that it wouldn't surrender to the demands of the United States. In November 1992, on the backdrop of the escalating situation in southern Lebanon, Nasrallah called upon the Lebanese government "to quit these hopeless talks" and stressed that the movement did not intend to change its policy and that "we mustn't surrender . . . to the threat of the US ambassador to Lebanon, which was being passed down from President to President, and from place to place."[57]

In August 1994, Qassem said that the American-Israeli policy of eliminating the movement had failed. The reasons for that, in his opinion, were a sharp increase in the support of the public opinion and the adoption of the resistance strategies by the Lebanese government.[58]

In the framework of its struggle to win over the Lebanese public opinion, Hezbollah took advantage of every opportunity it had in order to negatively present the United States and to emphasize its part in hurting the Muslims. So, for example, after the death of al-Mousawi, Nasrallah blamed the United States for being responsible for "all of the acts of massacre performed by Israel."[59] In May 1992, he attacked the American position by saying, "The Big Satan [this refers to the US—in origin] calling for the movement's disarmament is doing so, to prepare the atmosphere so that the Zionist enemy may continue perpetrating its crimes, and increase its attacks against the people."[60]

He warned the Lebanese government of an imbalanced chain of American pressures and claimed that the American demand from the Lebanese government to disarm the movement and to declare it a terrorist organization was just the beginning of the road.[61] According to him, the United States was "responsible for the Israeli aggression and therefore it would naturally try to eliminate any factor disrupting the American and the Israeli plans in the region."[62] In April 1993, after the U.S. elections and the visit of American secretary of state, Warren Christopher to the area, the head of Hezbollah's political wing, Hussein Khalil, said that, as far as the movement was concerned, there was no difference between the present American government and the previous one, because the new government was also marketing the Israeli plan.[63]

Fadlallah also expressed himself on issues concerning the relations with the United States and the peace process throughout the 1990s. He warned the Arab countries of the dangerous influences of the United States and called on the Arabs not to participate in the Madrid Conference. He called upon the Muslims to unite under Iran's leadership and to commence a battle against the American world domination. In order to do so, he claimed that they must recruit their own inner resources and conduct the long-term struggle in order to "turn the American era into an Islamic era in which one could implement the sovereignty of Islam all over the world."[64] In June 1992, Fadlallah stated that the purpose of the American policy toward Hezbollah was to limit the steps of the resistance by upsetting the Lebanese public opinion's support of the movement. In his opinion, "In the long run, the US is planning to launch an attack to eliminate the resistance in Lebanon."[65] In another interview during the same month, he said that diplomatic, economic, and political pressures by the Western countries, headed by the United States, were crushing Lebanon. These countries were aiming to shock Lebanon's political and economic system in order to force it to soften its positions concerning the peace talks and its approach toward the resistance activities. Fadlallah blamed the United States of taking a one-sided stand regarding the Middle-Eastern conflict, of "pampering" Israel, and of maintaining its military supremacy in the region.[66]

Hezbollah's success in the elections for parliament (1992) reinforced the movement's position in the Lebanese system and allowed it to claim that it was a legitimate Lebanese movement with a wide basis of popular support. In August

1992, Nasrallah emphasized this fact by saying that, among the reasons that caused the participation of Hezbollah in the elections, there was the desire "to show the West that they were not dealing with a small group or with some local organization."[67] At the end of the election year, he revealed that the United States, which at first opposed Hezbollah's participation in the elections, demanded that the Lebanese government expel Hezbollah's delegates from the parliament. He regarded this as a part of the American plan to stop the movement's activities.[68] Qassem predicted that the United States would not succeed in stabilizing a new world order because the Muslims in the world would object to this. He added that "in the election campaign [in Lebanon] everyone elected the Hezbollah and its delegates in order to tell the US, that we all provide the weapon along with the resistance."[69]

In February 1995, during the Islamic Revolution's anniversary celebrations, Nasrallah committed that his movement would continue acting in the way of the Jihad and the resistance and that "the US can do whatever it wants but there is no doubt that it won't be able to deny us of this faith, this commitment and this vision." He also said that the United States "would not be able to place fear in our hearts, no matter what steps it takes or decisions it makes. We are telling the US and Israel . . . that we all long to die as martyrs so you have no way to us."[70] In an announcement published by the movement in June 1995, in the midst of the preparations for another round of talks in the United States, it was said that the successful attack carried out by the movement recently was the movement's answer to the pressures of the Israeli and the American governments. It was also said that all the talk about the movement intending to stop the resistance was nothing more than "American and Zionist false heart wishes because the gun is . . . the only option for liberation" and that the movement did not need recognition from any factor, even if "it regards itself as influential."[71] The demand made by Robert Pelletreau, the U.S. assistant secretary of state for Near Eastern Affairs, of the Lebanese government to fight terrorism and disarm the movement was rejected by Fadlallah, who declared that "we will not obey America like slaves, and we will use all of our might in order to protect ourselves and will continue opposing the Lebanese government, the existence of Israel and the American hegemony."[72] In December 1995, during a meeting between the U.S. ambassador to Lebanon and President Hrawi, the ambassador raised the need to restrain Hezbollah. Hrawi responded to this by repeating the familiar Lebanese position and stressing the right to resist the Israeli occupation.[73]

The Grapes of Wrath events (April 1996) and the diplomatic efforts to settle the crisis placed Hezbollah, once again, at the center of international interest. However, just as before, the cease-fire negotiations were not conducted directly with it, but through Syria and Lebanon and also indirectly through Iran. But all this did not bother the movement to influence the course of things while efficiently navigating between its two patrons, Syria and Iran. The crisis provided, as far as Syria and Iran were concerned, an opportunity to minimize the influence of the United States on the regional system, and they aspired to incorporate the Europeans in the negotiations and within the international supervision mechanism. On April 20, in the midst of diplomatic contacts in Damascus to stabilize the crisis, Nasrallah's political advisor, Sheikh Hussein Khalil stated that a delegation on behalf of Hezbollah, which had conferred with the Syrian president, rejected the participation of the United States "in a committee that would ensure a ceasefire in Lebanon." Instead, he offered to establish a committee that would include Syria and Iran as members, alongside Russia, France, and Italy.[74]

From the perspective of the Hezbollah, the "Agreement of Understanding" was regarded as an important victory. Its basic demands were fulfilled; the land resistance activities against the IDF were accepted internationally; and the American attempt to correlate between the agreement and the renewal of the talks were rejected by Syria and Lebanon.[75] Fadlallah's response to this was "it [Hezbollah] has been excluded from the terrorism circles and shifted to the circle of armed groups, whose fight against the Israeli soldier was being interpreted as self defense."[76]

The escalation in the field, the elections in Israel and in Lebanon, and the discussion on the establishment of a supervisory body diverted the attention from the peace process, which had been halted in place all along 1996. So, from Hezbollah's point of view, the influence of the United States on the movement during this year was even lesser than it was during 1995. Hezbollah emerged reinforced in the Lebanese and regional arena as a result of Operation Grapes of Wrath and the peace process, which seemed like it was about to achieve its goals, had been halted. The governments of Lebanon and Syria rejected any initiative to disarm the movement, even during the hardest days of Operation Grapes of Wrath, while the Americans had to get used to the increasing European involvement in the Middle-Eastern peace process.[77]

This condition encouraged Nasrallah to continue his attack on the United States and to push the Europeans into increasing their involvement. Nasrallah accused the United States of sharing Israel's decision to launch Operation Grapes of Wrath while exploiting the atmosphere created following the 1996 "Sharm Summit" and using the discussions concerning the assembling of the supervisory committee to limit Hezbollah's steps. He stressed that Hezbollah could not be militarily eliminated and that it would persist its activity with determination, until its goals were achieved.[78]

Nasrallah's declarations were accompanied by activities. During the discussions concerning the roles of the supervisory committee, the movement was carried out terrorist attacks against the IDF in the areas of the security zone, to the dismay of the Americans. Nicholas Burns, the American State Department's spokesman admitted that the Understanding did not limit the activities of Hezbollah within the security zone area, but he did accuse Hezbollah of initiating a deliberate escalation and claimed that it was responsible for most of the breaches of the Agreement.[79] In October 1997, the American government published a list of terrorist organizations, which included Hezbollah. Hezbollah responded quickly and rejected out of hand its inclusion in the list, as well as the existence of a network of its supporters abroad. It claimed that the American decision derived from a political commitment that did not reflect reality, from dictatorship, and from aggressive intentions and that it was threatening Lebanese citizens abroad. At the same time, the movement addressed the government of Lebanon, demanded its support, and a response to the manner of the American announcement.[80]

Although these means didn't influence Hezbollah, Syria and the Lebanese government declared that they regarded the resistance as a legitimate right as long as the IDF was in operation on Lebanese territory. The American ambassador to Lebanon, who had been called upon to clarify the decision, claimed that the inclusion of Hezbollah in the list of terrorist organizations was based on the terrorist attacks it had carried out against Americans, including the attack on the American embassy and the assault on the American forces in Beirut and the kidnapping of hostages. He stated that the activities against the IDF in Lebanon were not included in the category of terrorist attacks. [81]

In August 1998, a Lebanese journalist revealed that, in a discussion conducted in the American Foreign Ministry, in the presence of the intended U.S. ambassador to Lebanon, David Satterfield, a dispute occurred between the participants in regard to Hezbollah's abilities and status in the regional and internal arena. Richard Norton, a senior researcher, well versed in the Lebanese political scene, claimed that Hezbollah was a political party with widespread popular support, which knew that the stopping of its military activity was just a question of time. On the other hand, Marius Deeb, also a senior researcher, was in a minority and claimed that the support of the movement was minimized and that it was not expected to change the characteristics of its military activity, because it was established upon violence.[82]

In fact, the objective the United States was hoping to achieve through the peace process and, later on, through the supervisory committee was the disarmament of Hezbollah or at least it's restraining, and this goal was partially achieved. The escalation in the field continued. The committee was ineffective and its decisions were not enforced. In December 1998, on the backdrop of yet another escalation, a Lebanese newspaper quoted Western sources in Paris, which claimed that the American warning policy was inefficient and that "the present situation in southern Lebanon is one which has been repeating itself a thousand times." The peace talks were also caught in a dead end and had to be halted. They were replaced by the Israeli initiative of a unilateral withdrawal from Lebanon, which was carried out in May 2000.[83]

On the sideline, we may note that the American demand to disarm the movement did not receive wide support from the Lebanese public opinion as well. Even figures who had objected to Hezbollah being an armed movement, such as the Shiite Mufti Kabalan, went publicly against the American intervention in Lebanon's internal affairs.[84] Qassem accused the United States of dominating the world and of intervening in the internal affairs of the Arab countries and offered to coordinate an Arab effort to ward off the American threat.[85]

The U.S. Funding of Lebanon's Rehabilitation—Further Means for Exercising Indirect Pressure upon Hezbollah—Another Failed Attempt

In December 1996, a fund-raising event took place in Washington for the rehabilitation of Lebanon. At the same time, the United States declared its intention to increase its aid to Lebanon to a sum of twelve million dollars in 1997. This event announced the increasing American involvement in Lebanon's rehabilitation.[86] The change in the American policy permeated into the consciousness of the Lebanese political system in 1998. During late 1998, Hezbollah's senior officials were troubled by the United States's new method of activity, which they described as a "friendlier and warmer approach towards the internal components of the Lebanese system." This method was intended, in their opinion, to allow the United States to expand its hold of Lebanon. Factors in Hezbollah claimed that the statements of the U.S. ambassador to Lebanon were like "serving honey dipped in poison." A Lebanese commentator estimated that the American economic aid to Lebanon would be translated into a political price that the Lebanese government would be forced to pay in the future.[87]

Concerned over these developments, Nasrallah said that "the purpose of the American activity is to penetrate Lebanon for the second time and intervene in matters of the state institutions, the government's policy and internal Lebanese affairs" and that the United States was preparing the groundwork for exercising pressure on political and economical levels in order to bully Lebanon into a separate agreement. Thus, he called upon the government to "follow the American presence and moves in Lebanon from an approach of concern, caution and precision" and even convened with Walid Junblatt to discuss the subject. At the same time, Nasrallah attacked the United States and accused it of carrying out activities of espionage and terrorism in Lebanon. According to his claim, the American ambassador was meeting Lebanese ministers and investigating them regarding "their in-office occupations." Lebanese sources knew enough to say that the movement's fear increased in light of the development of closer relations between the United States and Iran and the identification of the American determination to promote the peace process.[88]

Yet, this policy also did not succeed in creating the conditions required for the isolation and the disarmament of Hezbollah; its activities against the IDF forces in Lebanon continued in the same pattern until Israel's unilateral withdrawal from Lebanon in May 2000 on.

The Mutual Lebanese-American Committee as a Means of Disarming Hezbollah—Another Fallacious Attempt

In late 1994, in the midst of the peace talks, a Lebanese-American mutual committee was established in order to discuss the cancellation of the prohibition imposed by the United States upon its airplanes landing at the Beirut airport and upon the arrival of Americans in Lebanon.[89] The committee was used by the United States, just as the Syrians and Hezbollah had feared would happen, to pressurize the Lebanese government to disarm the movement. In January 1995, on the eve of the convening of the committee, *Al-Watan al-Arabi* published that the American committee included Robert Pelletreau, assistant U.S. secretary of state for Near Eastern Affairs; the head of the counterterrorism department of the state department; and a delegate from the department of justice, a team that tells of its fields of occupations. The reporter, who relied upon an American diplomatic source, stated that the United States would not suffice with local changes at the airport and would present demands for essential changes in Hezbollah to the extent of disarming it.[90] Hezbollah and the Syrians shared a mutual position on this matter. Thus, they exercised extreme pressure on the government from within the parliament and outside of it so that it wouldn't surrender to the American demands in the committee and wouldn't even allow the raising of the subject of Hezbollah upon the daily agenda. On the eve of the committee's convention, the Lebanese government notified that the talks would be minimized to the security regulations at the Beirut airport and its close vicinity.[91] After the commencement of the discussions, rumors were spread, that the United States had demanded the expulsion of Hezbollah's leaders from Beirut. Qassem, who had been asked to reply on this matter, said that "all of these talks about the expulsion of the Hezbollah's leaders from Lebanon are absurd and nonsense . . . this is an arrogant and illogical suggestion and I don't think that anyone responded to it."[92] During the same month, Fadlallah said that the United States was exercising pressure on Lebanon in an attempt to freeze the activity of the Islamic Resistance and to disarm it, among other things, under the claim that "this endangers Americans traveling to Lebanon . . . "[93]

At the same time, President Clinton ordered the freezing of the assets and bank accounts of the Lebanese and Palestinian Islamic organizations in the United States, including those of Hezbollah, in order to limit the movement's steps and shut down part of the funding resources of its activity. At about the same time, a decision was accepted at the NATO headquarters to prepare for action against the threat of the Islamic terrorist movements. These decisions angered the movement greatly. Its leaders regarded this as a declaration of "a World War against Islam." They called upon the Muslims to wage an "economic war against all American products."[94] Several days later, Nasrallah responded in a similar manner and added that these decisions would never have been accepted if Hezbollah was a weak movement.[95]

In April 1995, the Lebanese minister of defense, Muhsin Dalul, accused the United States of trying to isolate Lebanon and separate the Syrian and the Lebanese course. He said that the United States was "punishing" the Lebanese government for rejecting its demands and that the American representatives "do not visit us nor meet with us."[96] In May 1995, the Lebanese media published that the United States was behind the noninclusion of Hezbollah delegates in the Lebanese government. This knowledge, along with the widespread rumor that the United States was dissatisfied with the presence of the movement's activists in parliament, was perceived by the movement as a deliberate activity by the United States, intending to push it away from Lebanon's centers of influence. The movement's senior officials related to this, but stated that the decision to refrain from joining the government was accepted without any connection to the American pressure exercised upon the prime minister.[97]

A month later (June 1995), toward the expected conference of the Lebanese-American committee, the government of Lebanon convened in order to discuss the American demands placed on its table. These demands included legislating a war against terrorism law as first step against terror, signing the international treaties that concerned these matters, arresting people suspected of murdering Americans, and expelling suspects from the Beirut airport area.[98] In July 1995, it was published that, according to an American source, there was a possibility that the armies of Lebanon and Syria would disarm Hezbollah in the near future.[99]

In reality, the American attempt, in this channel, to limit Hezbollah's steps was also deemed not very successful. In return for the American announcement of July 1997 concerning the cancellation of the prohibited entry of U.S. citizens into Lebanon, the country was forced to confirm the antiterrorism law and to sign the international treaty dealing with terrorism, while the rest of the demands that concerned the Hezbollah, were rejected out of hand. The movement regarded this as a victory and declared that it would act in the parliament to prevent the acceptance of the law against terrorism that the government had approved in February 1997 and that it would not provide guarantees to any factor, but continue its policy as before.[100] In May 1998, on the basis of reports concerning a possible thawing of the Iran-U.S. relations, a Hezbollah senior official said that, although his movement was interested in improving its image in the West and its connections with the United States, this matter would not be on the agenda as long as the United States supported Israel.[101]

The Attempts to Cause the Movement's Disarmament via Syria

At a testimony carried out by Dr. Flynt Leverett in October 2003, in front of the United States's foreign relations committee at the Senate, on the subject of the U.S. policy toward Syria, he said that, ever since Madrid 1991, the work program upon which the American foreign policy toward Syria was established claimed that, as a part of any peace agreement, Syria should disarm Hezbollah.[102] This saying explained the logic behind the massive pressure exercised by the United States upon Syria during the 1990s. In this case as well, the more time went by, the more the ability of the United States to pressure Syria was eroded.

The Syrians, with more consistency and determination than its Lebanese puppet, rejected out of hand the American demand under the claim that the resistance was the legitimate right of the Lebanese.[103] The American demand of Syria to withdraw its forces from Lebanon also did not reach the stage of application in the field until after the murder of Hariri, which was attributed to Syria, on February 2005. It is worthwhile to mention that this demand was perceived by Hezbollah as another American move that was supposed to weaken and isolate it to an extent that would call for its disarmament.[104]

In July 1993, the Lebanese media advertised that the American Senate accepted a decision calling for the withdrawal of the Syrian forces from Lebanon and of Hezbollah from southern Lebanon. The Lebanese system responded with anger to the publishing of the form of the American decision. President Hrawi rejected the U.S. demand for a Syrian withdrawal under the claim that Syria's presence was still highly necessary for Lebanon. The Hezbollah movement published an opinion attacking the United States for its belligerent intervention in Lebanon's internal affairs and its demand for a Syrian withdrawal. The expression of opinion further emphasized that the movement would continue carrying out its policy despite the decisions of the Senate.[105]

This policy of the movement caused an escalation in southern Lebanon, which imposed difficulties upon the peace talks and diverted them from their planned course. The movement took the credit for this.[106] In February 1994, Fadlallah said that the United States was striving to get closer to the movement and, at the same time, to isolate it in an attempt to eliminate its entity as a movement. He assumed that, as of that point in time, "The US cannot eliminate the Islamic movement, which is deeply rooted among the Islamic nation," and therefore, he predicted that the American pressure would actually achieve the opposite result and increase the sympathy toward the movement.[107]

The escalation of the security condition threatened to destroy the peace process, on one hand, and on the other hand, it provided the United States with plenty of opportunities to demand that Syria and Lebanon disarm the movement. These demands were rejected by Syria and Lebanon, despite the heavy damages caused to the Lebanese system.[108]

Yet, the peace process presented further challenges for Syria. It realized that, in order to achieve its objectives in the Syrian-Israeli channel, meaning an Israeli withdrawal from the Golan Heights, it must make a payment in the Lebanese arena. Thus, it accepted decisions, in coordination with Iran and Lebanon, in regard to Hezbollah's future. So, for instance, the newspapers published that, on the eve of Assad's meeting with the U.S. President, Syria and Iran worked to find formulas that both of them could agree upon concerning the issues to be raised at the peace talks.[109] In May 1995, the newspaper *Al-Ousbou' Al-Arabi* published that Syrian foreign minister Farouk al-Sharaa visited Tehran with an idea of solving the issue of Hezbollah. It was also said that the visit was held following an American initiative that included a suggestion to conduct essential structural changes in Hezbollah, including neutralizing the movement's extreme radical fringes and reinforcing the pragmatic camp. According to the newspaper, Iran, which objected to the peace process, rejected the suggestion out of hand.[110] A month later (June 1995), the newspaper *Al-Shark al-Awsat* reported that Syria was interested in finding a formula to disarm Hezbollah that would appease Iran.[111]

The Lebanese newspaper *Magazine* also advertised that, on the visit of Pelletreau, the assistant U.S. secretary of state for Near Eastern Affairs to the area (June 1995), an agreement of principles was signed concerning the disarming of Hezbollah. Mohammed Raad, a parliament delegate on behalf of Hezbollah, who asked about the agreement, claiming that this was a political matter and that Syria and Lebanon could voice their opinions on this matter. Yet, the movement was the one that would accept decisions concerning its military future.[112] On June 30, 1995, Hezbollah's senior officials were summoned to a meeting with Khaddam in Damascus to discuss Hezbollah's future at the age after the singing of the peace agreement.[113]

The renewal of the negotiations on the Syrian-Israeli channel and the American negotiations during the last months of 1995 aroused concern among Hezbollah. Its leaders realized that a breakthrough could influence the future and status of the movement in the Lebanese arena, closely monitoring what was going on. Delegations on its behalf met with Syrian high officials in order to receive clarifications in regard to the Syrian plans, as well as with high officials in Iran, in order to make plans to thwart moves that could damage the movement. In the field, the movement increased its activity in order to create deliberate escalations that would damage the atmosphere of the peace talks.[114] In October 1995, Nasrallah claimed that "the American regime accepted a decision to kill us, conquer our lands and kill our women and children."[115]

A renewed wave of escalated violence during the months of November and December 1995 turned the tables once again for the United States and it demanded that Syria activate its influence on Hezbollah and restrain it. The spokesman of the American state department declared that "we will push Syria to use its influence in order to restrain the violence, end the bloodshed, and stabilize the situation in order to increase the chances for peace in Lebanon." At the same time, American Secretary of State Warren Christopher spoke to his Syrian counterpart and demanded that he act in order to stop the firing of Katyusha rockets toward the territory of Israel.[116]

In December 1995, Syrian foreign minister, Farouk al-Sharaa, declared that, if a relaxation of the situation would be achieved in southern Lebanon and Israel would withdraw from there, this would mean that the resistance "has achieved its goals." At the same time, it was reported that the vice president of Iran intended to visit Syria in order to receive clarifications on the directions of development in the Syrian-Israeli channel.[117] During the same month, Nabil Kaouk declared that the American pressure and the peace talks "could not make Hezbollah deviate from its struggle against the Zionist occupiers."[118]

In March 1996, the United States tried once more to stop the deterioration of the situation and demanded that Syria use its influence on Hezbollah to relax the situation. U.S. presidential press secretary Michael McCurry said that, at the same time, the United States was pushing Israel to show moderation.[119] However, the American efforts to prevent the worsening of the violence failed. In April 1996, Israel commenced the operation Grapes of Wrath. The United States accused Hezbollah of being responsible for the outbreak of the violence. During the operation and afterward, the United States continued its efforts to find a formula that would allow the ending of the crisis. For this purpose, it conducted direct contacts with Syria, Lebanon, and Israel and indirect contacts with Iran.[120] When the United States realized that the contacts were futile, it raised the level of handling the crisis, and American secretary of state Christopher was sent to the Middle East. Upon his arrival in Damascus on April 19, he said that "there are still certain difficulties and quite a way to go through . . . I predict harsh discussions during the next 24 or 48 hours."[121] On April 20, a particularly busy day of discussions, the Syrian capital, Damascus, simultaneously hosted the American secretary of state, the Russian foreign minister, the French foreign minister, and the Iranian foreign minister. They conducted discussions and negotiations between themselves and with the Syrian and the Lebanese prime ministers and the Hezbollah delegates, each operating to promote his or her own interest in the system that was being created.[122] The influx of international players made it difficult for the United States to reach an agreement and allowed Syria, Lebanon, and Iran to maneuver between the various initiatives suggested and to present further conditions. On April 21, Christopher stated that "Syria has great influence on Hezbollah and on Lebanon . . . it holds the key to closing the peace circle in the region." At the same time, he attacked Iran's involvement and claimed that it was "the enemy of the peace process. This is a terrorist country."[123]

In the Agreement of Understanding achieved and in the supervisory committee, Syria played a major role facing the international system and Hezbollah. It withstood the pressures of the United States, which demanded the restrain of the movement and ensured the integration of the European system in the regional process as a counterweight to the United States. In addition, it managed to achieve the international approval of the movement's activities against the IDF forces in Lebanon. This fact and the structure of the supervisory committee, which also included France, helped Syria reject the U.S. pressures each time an escalation took in the southern Lebanon as a result of Hezbollah's activities.

The dead end that the peace talks in the Syrian-Israeli channel encountered and the discussions concerning the Israeli initiative for a unilateral withdrawal made the American pressures exercised upon Syria devoid of any true purpose. Until Israel's withdrawal in May 2000, the American moves in the Syrian channel could not restrain Hezbollah. Even after the withdrawal of the IDF from Lebanon, the movement continued to develop its military infrastructure in southern Lebanon under Iranian and Syrian backup and support and constructed an array of land missiles of various types, Katyushas and rocket launchers, in order to threaten Israeli territory. The movement put this ability to use during the Second Lebanon War (July August 2006), when thousands of rockets and missiles were fired toward civilian population in Israel.

Summary

The international system had a marginal influence on Hezbollah's directions of development. The players of this system found it difficult to establish an activity policy due to disagreements in relation to defining Hezbollah as a terrorist organization. In fact, the United States was the only one that strove, from the 1980s on, to eliminate the movement as a terrorist entity. Europe, which increased its involvement in the Middle-Eastern system during the second half of the 1990s, actually made it hard for the United States to achieve its objectives. During the course of over two decades, the United States acted in order to create the conditions that could cause the movement's disarmament and its termination. The chances to achieve this were slim to begin with. During the early 1980s, the international system, including the United States, had difficulties identifying the groups and organizations that were operating under Hezbollah's custody and damaging them. During the second half of the 1980s, the international activity, mainly the American one, bore the nature of brokerage. During this period, the Lebanese militias including Hezbollah, strengthened their status and power in the internal arena at the expense of the regimental system, which was on the verge of collapsing. During the 1990s, several opportunities to disarm Hezbollah were created. But even then, the United States could not manage to achieve its goals. Furthermore, it ceased being a single player influencing the regional system and was forced to consider the positions of other international players.

With the downfall of the peace process during the late 1990s, most of the efforts of the international system were invested into solving crisis conditions in Lebanon. Even the unilateral withdrawal of the IDF could not create the conditions that would allow disarming the movement. In March 2005, a decision of including Hezbollah in the list of terrorist organizations was accepted in the European Parliament. This decision, which is yet to be practically expressed, could be the first step toward an effort of the international system to create the conditions that could restrain Hezbollah and disarm it.

In September 2004, decision 1559 was accepted by the security council of the UN, which called to respect Lebanon's sovereignty, end the Syrian presence, and disarm the militias. The clause regarding the disarmament of the militias was not realized due to Hezbollah's objection and the fear of the Lebanese government of the predicted price of fulfilling this clause of the decision.[124]

In August 2006, decision 1701 was accepted by the security council of the UN, leading to the end of the Second Lebanon War. The decision imposed an embargo upon weapon shipments for Hezbollah and determined that the entry of weapons into Lebanon without the consent of the Lebanese government was prohibited. The decision also called for the full implementation of decision 1559, which included disarming the militias. In this case, Syria, Iran, and the movement chose to ignore the decision of the security council and invested efforts into rearming the movement after the Second Lebanon War.

The declarations of the senior officials of the movement, the UN secretary general, and Israel, alongside the seizure of some of the warfare shipments to Hezbollah in 2007 show that, during that period,, immense means of warfare were smuggled into Lebanon for Hezbollah, mostly through Syria, and that Hezbollah's array of missiles and rockets actually increased in comparison with the movement's condition before the Second Lebanon War. Furthermore, the movement rejected the call to disarm.[125]

Hezbollah between the IDF's Withdrawal from Lebanon in May 2000 and the Second Lebanon War in July 2006

Introduction

On July 12, 2006, Hezbollah activists attacked an IDF patrol by the northern border of Israel and kidnapped two soldiers, Ehud Goldwasser and Eldad Regev. The kidnapping of the soldiers was the factor that caused the Second Lebanon War between Israel and Hezbollah. Israel's objectives in the war, driving Hezbollah out of southern Lebanon and removing the threat of missile launches toward Israel, were not fully achieved. Profound public criticism concerning the functioning of the IDF and of the government on the eve of the war and during it, led to the establishment of an investigation committee headed by Judge Winograd, to changes in the military's high command, and to shocks at the political level. On the other hand, Hezbollah suffered significant damage to its operational infrastructure and manpower and prepared to restore its ranks and position in Lebanon, as well as in the political and operative fields.

The Second Lebanon War broke out about six years after the IDF's withdrawal from southern Lebanon. During these years, several significant events occurred, including the outbreak of the al-Aksa Intifada (October 2000), the terrorist attacks in the United States (September 11, 2001), the war in Iraq from 2003, and the Syrian withdrawal from Lebanon in April 2005. These strategic events influenced and still influence Lebanon and Hezbollah, directly and indirectly. The movement was forced to establish its policy, facing the changing reality, and to cope with internal and external pressures aimed at disarming it.

Hezbollah and the Lebanese System—Mutual Influences Resulting in the Withdrawal of the IDF (2000)

Israel's withdrawal from Lebanon in May 2000 without an agreement created a new reality. The main issues that the movement was forced to deal with were the continued maintenance and development of its military array, the resistance, and the blocking of any attempt to disarm it. The claim that Hezbollah used in order to justify the resistance and its activity during the period before the withdrawal had become obsolete. Nasrallah was forced to formulate new arguments in order to justify the necessity of the armed resistance after the withdrawal and to market them within the community and the Lebanese system.

The discussion concerning the movement's condition after the Israeli withdrawal began many months before the withdrawal and continued after the Second Lebanon War. Will the movement continue fighting against Israel after the withdrawal, and if so, in which pattern? And should the movement disarm itself? These questions were at the heart of the Lebanese public and political discourse. Hezbollah held a consistent line of propaganda, claiming that its relations with Israel had nothing to do with the political circumstances and that even if Israel did withdraw its forces Hezbollah would continue regarding it as an illegitimate entity that must disappear. The nature of coping with Israel after its withdrawal was defined vaguely and in ambiguous terms, from which it turned out that the struggle against Israel could attain various forms until the proper opportunity for its annihilation should come along.[1] Alongside the vague statements, the movement's leadership emphasized the connection between the resistance policy and the Israeli withdrawal and its effectiveness compared to the unsuccessful attempt in the diplomatic channel. The Israeli withdrawal proved, as far as Hezbollah was concerned, that the policy it used against Israel was correct and that one must not surrender to the demand to disarm it.[2]

The expressions of the movement's high echelons, on the eve of the withdrawal, also concerned the nature of the relations if a peace agreement was signed between Lebanon and Israel. In this case, Nasrallah clarified that his movement would act to thwart commercial relations and normalization with Israel and would support the Palestinians in their struggle for the liberation of Jerusalem.[3] On the other hand, high echelons among the Shiite community in Lebanon, including Sheikh Muhammad Mahdi Shams al-Din and Nabih Berri, thought that Hezbollah must disarm itself, just like the other groups.[4]

The basic tension that the movement was situated in, from the beginning of the 1990s, worsened after the withdrawal. On one hand, there was the fighting against Israel until its annihilation, (a vision whose fulfillment didn't seem near) and on the other hand, there was the possibility of using the victory to promote the turning of Lebanon into an Islamic republic (a goal that the movement had been striving to accomplish ever since its establishment, and after the IDF's withdrawal, this was perceived as fulfilled, as far as it was concerned). This tension and the understanding that its basis of support for continuing its activity against Israel in the previous pattern had become minimized led Nasrallah to choose his typical "walking on the brink" strategy. He formulated new claims to justify the continued existence of the resistance, minimized the scope of the direct activities against Israel, expanded the indirect activity via the Palestinian terrorist organizations, and defined new rules of game against Israel. This position was supported by the Syrian president Bashar al-Assad, who sided with leaving the weapons of the resistance as they were as long as the Arab-Israeli conflict was still unresolved.[5]

The withdrawal of the IDF from Lebanon in May 2000, without an agreement, was eventually perceived, in the eyes of the players of the Lebanese and the regional system, as the victory of Hezbollah's strategy. The resistance model was studied by the Palestinian terrorist organizations and applied against Israel in Gaza and in the West Bank. The influence of the use of violence upon the public opinion in Israel and upon the decision makers was well used and studied during the same year by Yasser Arafat, who had chosen to resort to violence (October 2000—the al-Aksa Intifada) as the preferred means of achieving concessions from Israel.

The question of withdrawal from Lebanon without an agreement also came up in the testimony of Ehud Barak before the Winograd Committee. Barak revealed that, in March 2000, it was clear to the Israeli government that the withdrawal from Lebanon would be unilateral, without an agreement with Syria and Lebanon. He emphasized that the government decided to carry out the withdrawal on the basis of the Security Council's resolution number 425 and the backup and coordination of the United Nations (UN).[6]

The Struggle in the Internal Lebanese Arena Concerning the Continuation of the Resistance—the Shebaa Farms as a Case Study

The unilateral withdrawal of the IDF, without an agreement, permitted Hezbollah to claim that the demand to disarm was irrelevant because the role of the resistance was yet to be concluded, as long as Israel still held Lebanese lands. The claim that Israel was holding Lebanese lands was not exclusive to just Hezbollah. In April 2000, the government of Lebanon demanded that Israel retreat from the Shebaa Farms. Israel rejected the demand, claiming that the Shebaa Farms were originally Syrian territory. The UN backed Israel's position. Despite this, Lebanon continued demanding the right to apply the Lebanese sovereignty upon the farms. Several days before the withdrawal, Hezbollah fired toward the farms and declared its intention to continue the resistance activity in this sector.[7]

From then on, Hezbollah worked diligently under the orchestration of Nasrallah in order to internalize the need to liberate the Shebaa Farms into Lebanese hands.[8] Israel's rejection of the Lebanese demand provided a reason for Hezbollah to continue the resistance activity in the region even after the withdrawal. The Syrians supported this effort and applied a strategy of "holding the stick at both ends." They declared that the farms were Lebanese and, by doing so, provided Hezbollah with a reason to continue its activity; on the other hand, they refrained from determining whether the farms were under Lebanese sovereignty. In reality, from the withdrawal to the Second Lebanon War in July 2006, the Hezbollah activists carried out dozens of attacks against the IDF in the Shebaa Farms sector.

Maintaining the Shebaa Farms reason was important to Nasrallah. He stressed the need to liberate them and emphasized that his movement would continue fighting in order to achieve this goal. He rejected out of hand a compromise, according to which, the farms would be temporarily transferred to the custody of international forces. The only solution, as far as he was concerned, was complete Israeli withdrawal. He further claimed that the task of protecting Lebanon from Israeli aggression was imposed upon the resistance, and therefore, it must remain armed.[9]

The status of the farms was also raised in the discussions of the Lebanese National Dialogue Forum in 2006. In these discussions, the participants concluded that the farms belonged to Lebanon and that the government of Lebanon should address the UN with a demand to confirm its sovereignty over the farms.[10]

After the Second Lebanon War, a UN team was sent to examine the matter of the farms once more. This team was of the opinion that the Lebanese claims concerning the Shebaa Farms were valid and legal and recommended the reopening of the discussion on this subject. Israel objected to the proposal and demanded to discuss the subject of the farms only in the framework of an all-inclusive arrangement; Lebanon's and Syria's suggestions to transfer the territory to the custody of the UN were also rejected.[11]

During the Ashura parade in Beirut (January 2007), Nasrallah called for the establishment of a united national front for the liberation of the Shebaa Farms. He demanded that the government should enforce its sovereignty over all its territory, including the farms.[12] One month later, Walid Junblatt related to this matter. He held the opinion that the farms were in Syrian territory. According to him, a Syrian request, backed up by an official document instructing to transfer the farms to Lebanese ownership, could lead to a quick and simple solution of the problem. As for Hezbollah, he emphasized that the movement was looking for a reason to continue the resistance and found one, and even if this issue was resolved, Hezbollah would find another reason to continue the resistance.[13]

Tracking Hezbollah's expressions, from the years after the withdrawal of the IDF, shows that the issue of the farms was but one of the issues the movement used to reject its disarmament. Hezbollah made it clear that even if the problem of the Shebaa Farms was resolved, there were other controversial areas and topics in dispute between Israel and Lebanon, such as the seven villages within Israel's territory by Kibbutz Manara, the infiltration of Israeli planes into Lebanon's airspace, and the release of Lebanese prisoners. It seemed as if the movement's strategy in these fields had proved itself. Even after the Second Lebanon War, the Lebanese government did not have the power and ability to disarm Hezbollah or even to actively prevent its rearmament.[14]

The Internal Argument in Lebanon Concerning the Disarming of Hezbollah

The withdrawal of the IDF in May 2000 opened a new era in Lebanon and in the reciprocal relations between the regional players. The area that was under the control of the IDF was evacuated; the South Lebanon Army (SLA) headed by General Lahad fell apart. The withdrawal without an agreement with Syria and Lebanon did not oblige either of them to take the required steps. Israel expected, on the count of the Security Council's resolution 425 and the Ta'if Agreement, that the Lebanese government would realize its sovereignty over the territory by sending the Lebanese Army, restoring the activity of the governmental institutes in the area, and disarming Hezbollah. These issues were discussed many times during the peace talks throughout the 1990s.

In fact, the Lebanese government refrained from sending its army to southern Lebanon, and Hezbollah took over the vacuum that was created. Hezbollah's penetration into the field did not encounter any difficulties. Most of the inhabitants in the area were Shiites, and the rest were afraid of the movement's strength. The opening note for Hezbollah's gaining control over southern Lebanon was given in Nasrallah's victory speech, nicknamed the "Spider's Web Speech," in the Shiite town of Bint Jbeil."[15]

The movement's share in the withdrawal of the IDF was highlighted by its spokesmen during the election campaign for parliament that was conducted in Lebanon in 2000. The success was immediately translated into reinforcing the faction's power in the Lebanese parliament from ten representatives in the former parliament, which included seven Hezbollah leaders and three partners, to twelve representatives in the new parliament, out of which nine were Hezbollah people and three were partners.[16]

In June 2000, after the Israeli withdrawal and before the election campaign, Nasrallah clarified the main points of his policy in the Lebanese arena. He declared that Hezbollah was an Islamic movement while simultaneously acting as a Lebanese national party. He called for national unity, for supporting the resistance, and for investing an effort for releasing Lebanese prisoners imprisoned in Israel. Nasrallah emphasized that his movement would defend its victory and invest an effort, in the foreseeable future, into developing the deprived and faltering areas of Lebanon according to a national perspective. He added that Lebanon did not need to give Israel security guarantees and that the latter should remain concerned until the liberation of the Shebaa Farms. Nasrallah also related to the matter of the weapon of resistance. He estimated that Israel and the United States would invest efforts to cause the movement's disarmament and said that he was getting ready for such a possibility. He reassured the Lebanese that he would not use the resistance weapon in the Lebanese arena and that it was intended for the protection of the state security. He added that a discussion on the subject of disarming the movement would be held only once it was made clear that the country no longer required the resistance weapon.[17]

The discussion concerning the disarming the movement heightened during late 2004, following the Security Council's resolution, which called for the withdrawal of the foreign forces from Lebanon and for disarming the militias. Disputes among factors in the opposition in relation to this question and the commitment of the Lebanese government to the resistance rendered the discussion concerning this matter ineffective.

The camp of those calling to disarm the movement according to the UN resolutions included people from the opposition, such as Gebran Tueni, the editor of the daily *Al-Nahar*, and Amine Pierre Gemayel, the former president of Lebanon. The latter claimed that the government must fulfill its responsibility and sovereignty and establish Lebanon's defense upon the army, rather than upon the resistance.

On the one hand, Lebanese columnists who joined the call to disarm the movement claimed that the Hezbollah was conducting a Syrian-Iranian policy that was damaging Lebanon. On the other hand, the Lebanese government and senior Lebanese officials rejected the claim to disarm the movement. The government adopted Hezbollah's line and declared it to be the "resistance party" and a partner in defending Lebanon. It clarified that the discussion on this matter should be carried out in cooperation with Hezbollah and without pressure or international intervention. This position was also shared by Berri and Junblatt. Hezbollah, on its side, rejected the UN resolution and announced that this was a foreign intervention in Lebanon's internal affairs and that it did not concern the movement and that Hezbollah would object to any attempt to disarm it.[18]

Attempts to disarm the movement continued all along that period, until the second Lebanon War and afterwards. The use of a uniform propagandist line claiming that the role of the resistance was not over yet, in accordance with Syrian and Iranian support of continuing the resistance and alongside the basic weakness of the Lebanese political system, which refrained, even after the Syrian withdrawal (2005), from decisively handling the realization of the UN resolution, played into Hezbollah's hands. The movement was not disarmed.[19]

In fact, it doubled and tripled its military capabilities in comparison to the 1990s and built a wide-scoped military array, using Syrian-Iranian support, which included thousands of Katyusha rockets, missiles, and advanced antitank missiles that served the movement in the Second Lebanon War. This array, which was significantly damaged during the Second Lebanon War, was restored without any serious effort, on the part of Lebanon's government, to thwart the rearmament of Hezbollah.[20]

Hezbollah and the Political System in Lebanon

Israel's withdrawal from Lebanon worsened the intersectarian tension and mainly the tension between Hezbollah and the Lebanese government. The government's abstention from applying its sovereignty over southern Lebanon and Hezbollah's entry into the field turned southern Lebanon, within a short period of time, into another enclave under the control of Hezbollah. The movement's control in the field was expressed by the scope of its civilian, political, and military activity.

In July 2001, Naim Qassem claimed that the Israeli demand that Lebanon send the army to southern Lebanon was intended to serve Israel's security and jeopardize the safety of Lebanon's residents. All that Israel hoped was that the Lebanese Army would restrain Hezbollah. Therefore, in his words, it was a good thing that the Lebanese government decided against sending its army to southern Lebanon. Qassem stressed that the public order in southern Lebanon was being enforced by the state, which strengthened the presence and activity of the security mechanisms in the area.[21]

Hezbollah's independent activity in Lebanon and in the regional arena embarrassed the Lebanese government and reflected upon the relations of the movement with the government of Lebanon all along the period. The Lebanese government was required to operate to disarm the movement and to face accusations from Israel and the United States concerning the movement's involvement with terrorism. The government's official position was to continue its support of Hezbollah and the need for resistance at the Shebaa Farms sector, minimizing the importance of the movement's involvement in the regional arena and rejecting the accusations concerning the movement's armament and the involvement of the Revolutionary Guard Corps. Answers in this spirit were also conveyed in an official letter to the UN from the Lebanese government in February 2002.[22] In May 2002, the Israeli media published that Hezbollah was continuing to arm itself after the IDF's withdrawal from Lebanon and that it had about 1000 Katyusha rockets of various types. It further mentioned that the weapons in the movement's possession were of better quality than those the movement had beforehand.[23]

Despite the Lebanese government's outward support of Hezbollah and the need to continue the resistance, the relations between the two were tense and were characterized by ups and downs all along that period. Hezbollah's involvement in the regional arena tattooed the basis of the government's claim concerning the "Lebaneseness" of the resistance and exposed it to criticism and to internal and external pressures.[24] In the public debate that was raised in Lebanon from time to time, on the background of the Hezbollah's overindependent activity, the Lebanese government was required to fulfill its responsibility of restraining the movement and sending the army to southern Lebanon.[25] In May 2002, a Hezbollah senior official said that his movement's relations with the government were reasonable and that the movement's criticism of the government was matter-of-fact and concerned promoting the interests of the Lebanese public.[26]

The support that the movement gained from the direction of the Lebanese prime minister, Salim al-Huss, an obvious pro-Syrian, during the years 1998–2000, was lost with the victory of Rafik Al-Hariri, Hezbollah's old rival, who went back to serve as the Lebanese prime minister in September 2000. On the one hand, during the era of al-Huss as prime minister and of Emile Lahoud as president, Hezbollah gained the backing of the political system and wide support of the resistance activity.[27] On the other hand, with Hariri's return to the prime ministerial chamber, the twisted web of relations that characterized the Hariri–Nasrallah relations during his previous tenure as the Lebanese prime minister, between the years 1992 and 1998, was launched once again. Hariri's daily political agenda that called for the establishment of peace between the Arab world and Israel was in complete contradiction to Hezbollah's objectives. Hariri was dissatisfied, to say the very least, from the movement's conduct after the IDF's withdrawal from Lebanon; as far as he was concerned, it was damaging the efforts of rehabilitating Lebanon, its economy, and its international image.[28]

Altogether, Hariri refrained from taking far-fetched steps regarding Hezbollah, including disarming it, owing to his awareness of the movement's popularity among the members of the Shiite community and in parts of the Lebanese society, its military strength, and the Syrian objection. The government headed by Hariri displayed support of Hezbollah, toward the outside, and rejected the calls to disarm it.[29]

In October 2004, Hariri and his government resigned as a protest against the crude Syrian intervention in the orders of the regime in Lebanon and the extension of the tenure of President Lahoud to a third term. In February 2005, he was killed in a car bombing in Beirut, and an accusing finger was pointed at Syria. A popular and extensive protest and international pressure lead to the Syrian withdrawal from Lebanon in April 2005, as well as the resignation of the Lebanese government and the creation of a new balance of power between Syria's support-ers and objectors in Lebanon.

The withdrawal of the Syrian forces from Lebanon (April 2005) created a new reality that was characterized by a competition for positions of power between the regional players in the Lebanese system. The Syrian withdrawal was accompa-nied by increased international involvement in the Lebanese system and the formulation of a new political order. In the internal Lebanese system that was being formulated, three players or blocs operated alongside each other.

The first player was the "March 14th Forces," a Christian Sunni-Druze coalition under the leadership of Saad Hariri and Fouad Siniora, which included the Sunni group, most of the Druze group headed by Junblatt, and parts of the Christian camp headed by Samir Jaja and Amin Jumail. This coalition was pro-Western in essence and was supported by Sunni countries such as Saudi Arabia, Egypt, and Jordan.

The second player comprised the camp of the allies of Syria and Iran, which included the Shiite sect, members of Hezbollah and Amal, and parts of the Christian camp under the leadership of Michel Aoun and Lahoud. This camp was supported by Syria and Iran. The third player was the global Jihad organizations, and at least one of them, "Fatah al-Islam," was also supported by Syria.

In May 2005, the elections for parliament were held in Lebanon, in which the anti-Syrian camp headed by al-Hariri received 72 out of 128 parliament seats. Hezbollah and the Amal movements received thirty-five seats, of which Hezbollah's faction, Al-Wafa, received fifteen seats. Sunni leader, Siniora, who assembled the government, gained sweeping support in the parliament. With his entrance into position, Siniora started handling two essential subjects: first, promoting the investigation of the murder of Hariri, and second, determining the question of the Hezbollah movement and its status in the Lebanese arena.[30]

The composition of the Siniora government (2005) reflected the Shiite group's rise to power in the Lebanese arena and mainly the Hezbollah's rise to power. This was the first government in which two ministers participated on behalf of Hezbollah, and within it, the Shiite ministers from Amal and Hezbollah acted as one bloc. Hezbollah's entry into the government provoked an internal dispute within the movement. Those who supported joining the government claimed that a need was created to be in the junction of decision making during this period in order to maintain the interests of the resistance and to prevent any international initiative to force the Lebanese government to disarm the movement.[31]

From then on, the movement's activists worked diligently in collaboration with Amal to thwart and impose difficulties upon the government's decisions on issues that concerned the investigation of the murder of Hariri and the imple-mentation of resolution 1559. In December 2005, on the background of the government's decision to summon the UN to investigate the murder, the five Shiite members retired from the government and created a political crisis that made it difficult for the government to conduct the state affairs.[32]

The issues that were on the government's daily agenda, upon its election, obliged the establishment of an appropriate and agreed-upon forum. The forum that was established under the initiative of the chairman of the parliament, Berri, was called the "National Dialogue Forum." Senior representatives from all the groups in Lebanon participated in this forum. The Shiite sect was represented by Nasrallah and Berri. Facing them were al-Hariri, Siniora, Junblatt, and the Christians. The discussions of the National Dialogue Forum concerned the disarmament of Hezbollah, the application of the government's sovereignty over all Lebanese territory, and the Syrian involvement in Lebanon. Actually, the forum's discussions were ineffective; Hezbollah was not disarmed, and it continued initiating activities to promote its objectives against Israel and in the regional arena, including attempts to kidnap IDF soldiers and supporting Palestinian terrorism and activities in the area of the Shebaa Farms.[33]

The Lebanese government refrained from worsening its relations with Hezbollah even after Security Council resolution 1559, which called for the disarmament of the militias.[34] The government's position exposed it to harsh criticism from oppositional factors, considering it responsible for the strengthening of Hezbollah. The loudest critic was Gebran Tueni, a Christian Lebanese parliament member and the general manager of the Lebanese newspaper *Al-Nahar*. In a series of articles he published in the newspaper and in the speeches he delivered over the years since the Israeli withdrawal, he called for the disarmament of Hezbollah and demanded that the government take responsibility, enforce its sovereignty, and run the country. He claimed that Hezbollah was applying an independent policy within Lebanon, serving the interests of Syria and Iran. Tueni's criticism was not well accepted by Syria and its allies in Lebanon, and he was murdered in Beirut in December 2005.[35]

The murder of Tueni exacerbated the crisis between Hezbollah and the Lebanese government. In the meeting after the murder, the government decided, by a majority vote, to officially request the UN to send an international investigating committee to investigate the murder of Hariri, a decision that was disputed and rejected by Syria and its allies. Following the government's decision, five ministers from Hezbollah and Amal suspended themselves from participating in the government's meetings.[36]

Tueni was not the only one who regarded Hezbollah as an entity endangering Lebanon. Arab and Lebanese journalists and commentators also identified the movement's threat patterns in all the years of its activity in Lebanon; some of them were not very impressed by Nasrallah's declarations about his movement's integration in the Lebanese political system and by it joining the Lebanese government. So, for instance, after the Second Lebanon war (2006), Dr. Shaker al-Nabulsi, a Jordanian-American liberal, warned of Hezbollah's intention to establish an Islamic republic in Lebanon in the form of the Islamic Shia republic in Iran.[37]

The Second Lebanon War exposed the full intensity of the charged relations between Hezbollah and the March 14th Bloc. The March 14th Leaders accused Hezbollah of dragging Lebanon into an unnecessary war and of serving the Syrian and Iranian interests. There were those who regarded the resistance weapon as a threat to Lebanon. It was further claimed that Hezbollah's balance of deterrence was a failure and that the existence of weapons in the hands of the movement was no guarantee for the safety of Lebanon. The March 14th Camp tried to exploit the results of the war and Hezbollah's relative weakness to push the government to reinforce its policy and sovereignty over Lebanon. So, for instance, in the closing announcement of a convention held on 7 September 2006, the organizers emphasized that only the sovereign government should defend its citizens and that it won't stand for any external or internal intervention in its matters. The notification also called for the implementation of the international resolutions concerning Lebanon, with an emphasis on 1701, which dealt, among other things, with the issue of disarming Hezbollah. The notification stated that "one must end [the condition of] multiplicity of weapons [existing in Lebanon] and to stress that the army of Lebanon and the authorized legitimate security institutions have the exclusive right to defend Lebanon."[38]

Hezbollah and its allies did not remain indebted. In the rally of the "Divine Victory" organized by Hezbollah in August 2006, Nasrallah declared that the Siniora government could not continue running the country, and for this purpose, a government of national unity must be established to defend, rehabilitate, and unite Lebanon. The Lebanese government was accused of corruption and treason. At the same time, the movement and its allies threatened to bring down the current government. The March 14th Camp rejected Hezbollah's demand of establishing a government of national unity.[39]

Even these moves, taken by the government and its supporters, did not succeed in achieving the objective of either disarming the movement or forcing it to conduct itself according to the policy guidelines of the Lebanese government. Hezbollah continued applying its independent policy in Lebanon, arming and preparing itself for another round of violence, while its senior officials refused to proclaim publicly its completion of armament and its reaching of a renewed balance of deterrence facing Israel, one that was even more effective and qualitative than the previous one. At the beginning of November 2007, in proximity to the timing of a wide-scale drill carried out by the IDF in the Galilee area, Hezbollah revealed that it also upheld a drill that lasted three days in southern Lebanon. Thousands of activists from all the movement's units took part in the drill under the supervision of Nasrallah. It was set in a defensive layout simulating an IDF attack in Lebanon. Revealing it in the current timing was intended to convey a message of deterrence to Israel and to all the movement's objectors in Lebanon, according to which the movement restored its abilities and became ready to handle an Israeli attack.[40]

Hezbollah and the Regional System—Reciprocal Influences since the IDF's Withdrawal

The reciprocal relations between the players of the regional system, from the year 2000 on, were influenced by the aforementioned regional and international procedures and events. The most important of these, as far as we are concerned, were the death of Syrian president Hafez al-Assad (June 2000), the outbreak of the al-Aksa Intifada (October 2000), the terrorist attacks in the United States (September 2001), the war in Iraq from 2003, and the Syrian withdrawal from Lebanon in April 2005.

The death of President Assad and the rise into power of Bashar al-Assad in Syria was good for Hezbollah. Unlike his father, Bashar al-Assad maintained personal relations with Nasrallah and regarded Hezbollah as a strategic partner and not just as a tool to fulfill the Syrian interests. In his time, Syria began providing advanced means of warfare to the movement, including 220 mm and 302 mm rockets and advanced antitank missiles. Bashar al-Assad substantiated the movement's continuance of activity concerning the Shebaa Farms. After the September 11 terrorist attacks, the United States takeover of Iraq, and Syria's demarcation as one of the countries in the "axis of evil," Syria began gradually losing its hold in Lebanon. The inexperienced Bashar al-Assad had trouble facing the regional and the international pressure and the ever-rising voices calling for a Syrian withdrawal on the grounds of the Ta'if Agreement. In April 2005, after the murder of Hariri, one of the leaders of the opposition to the Syrian policy in Lebanon, an unprecedented popular wave of protest swept throughout Lebanon, and the Syrian president had to order the withdrawal of the Syrian forces from Lebanon.[41]

From then on, the Syrian influence upon the Lebanese system was carried out through the Syrian intelligence mechanisms and Syria's allies in Lebanon (Amal, Hezbollah, and pro-Syrian organizations). Syria operated to create such chaos in the Lebanese system that would allow it to reenter its forces into Lebanon. In this framework, Syria resorted to the policy of political assassinations. Its mercenaries assassinated many figures that objected to the Syrian presence in Lebanon during that period, including parliament members, senior journalists, ministers, and senior officials in the Lebanese system. Syria encouraged and supported the activity of global Jihad organizations in Lebanon, such as the "Fatah al-Islam" organization as a means of increasing the disquiet and insecurity in the country. The political crises since the Syrian withdrawal, in which Amal and Hezbollah were involved, also served the Syrian interest of maintaining a condition of political instability in Lebanon and preventing the Lebanese government from expanding its relations with the international system.[42] Altogether, Syria's weakness in the international system and the withdrawal of its forces from Lebanon increased Hezbollah's freedom of operation in the Lebanese arena and decreased Syria's ability to enforce its will upon the movement whenever its activity contradicted the Syrian interests.

The Israeli policy facing Hezbollah in the years between the IDF's withdrawal from Lebanon and the Second Lebanon War was mainly a policy of retaliation in the military field and of initiation at a diplomatic level. On the eve of its withdrawal from Lebanon, Israel determined the rules of the game facing the Lebanese system on the statement of the Israeli prime minister at the time, Barak, who imposed the responsibility for keeping the peace on the Lebanese side of the border upon the governments of Lebanon and Syria. Barak determined that an offensive activity of Hezbollah would entail an offensive Israeli retaliation against the Lebanese regime and/or Syrian targets. The Israeli statement was a clear message of deterrence to the governments of Lebanon and of Syria.[43]

In reality, the Israeli deterrence was not applied. Israel's minor reaction in the particularly significant event of the kidnapping of two IDF soldiers by Hezbollah at the Mount Dov sector (October 2000) did not match the regime of deterrence that Israel wished to establish facing the movement, and it operated like a boomerang against Israel. From then on, a leveled worsening took place in

Hezbollah's nature of activity along the border. After Arik Sharon's election to the post of prime minister on March 2001 and after a series of incidents, Sharon ordered an attack on a Syrian radar destination at the Beqaa valley in June 2001 and, by this, to design new rules of game facing Hezbollah. The attack aspired to convey a warning message to Syria to restrain the activities of Hezbollah. As a response, and out of a desire to convey its own message of deterrence, Hezbollah fired toward IDF outposts at Mount Dov and published an announcement saying that its activists had destroyed an Israeli radar.[44]

With the Israeli withdrawal from Lebanon, the movement started reorganizing its activity in Lebanon with the support of the Revolutionary Guard Corps. Lebanon was divided into military zones that included control headquarters, fortified sites, intelligence positions, and logistic sites. In this framework, fortified and camouflaged sites were constructed, in which various types of rocket and missile launchers were positioned. Fortified positions were built along the border with Israel for purposes of assembling intelligence and displaying presence. At the same time, a system of defense from a possible Israeli invasion was built, which included mining the possible penetration routes, equipping itself with improved antitank missiles, and establishing deterrence toward Israel.

On the strategic military level, Hezbollah equipped itself with mid-range missiles, whose span of ranges covered most of Israel's territory; land-sea missiles that had been activated during the Second Lebanon War against an Israeli vessel; and unmanned aerial vehicles (UAVs) that were equipped with explosives and launched toward Israel. Southern Lebanon and south Beirut became military enclaves controlled by Hezbollah, in which most military arrays were established and the Beqaa valley area became the movement's training and logistic center.[45]

The construction of the military array, which was conducted without an actual interruption from the side of the Lebanese government as well as from Israel, provided for Hezbollah the basis upon which the movement's deterrence against Israel was established. This array allowed the movement to portray itself as the "Protector of the South" from possible Israeli aggression. The more the military array was established, the more the movement's leadership made declarations concerning its responsibility toward maintaining the security of the Lebanese citizens and continuing the resistance. The resistance was presented as fulfilling the strategic role, alongside the Lebanese Army, of defending the country. This strategic line of propaganda used by the movement allowed it to reject the internal and the external pressures to disarm itself.[46]

Along with building its military array, Hezbollah started to carry out regular operational activities against the IDF along the borderline with Israel. Most of the activity was at the Mount Dov sector and the Shebaa Farms area, an activity space in which the movement operated in an initiated manner, but not only. During the period from the withdrawal of the IDF to the Second Lebanon War, Hezbollah carried out several activities in order to kidnap IDF soldiers for the purposes of bargaining, out of which two were successful (October 2000 and July 2006). In addition to that, it carried out dozens of firing activities and placed explosive devices along the border and near IDF posts and patrols. In one case, in May 2006, Hezbollah fired Katsyusha rockets toward Israel's territory. Yet, it did not refrain from allowing Palestinian organizations, by acquiescence, to fire Katyusha rockets toward Israel from the areas under its control, as long as it served its purposes.

The movement was also behind the terrorist attack of the Islamic Jihad Organization on March 2002 along the highway between Shlomi and Matzuba, in which six Israelis were killed. The terrorist activists infiltrated from Lebanon's territory.[47]

In May 2006, during the celebrations of five years to the IDF's withdrawal from Lebanon and in light of the Lebanese national dialogue that was also dealing with the question of disarming the movement, Nasrallah delivered a speech emphasizing the importance of the resistance and the need for the movement to remain armed. He claimed that Israel was an enemy country and that national defense must be established in order to face its strategic aggression, and that it should include the entire Lebanese society. Facing this threat, he offered to integrate Hezbollah into Lebanon's strategy of defense because, according to him, the movement had the operational ability and the experience, allowing it to create a balance of deterrence against Israel. In the same declaration, he specified some of his movement's military abilities and claimed that the movement had missiles that could cause damage in the depths of Israel and had sufficient operational ability to liberate the Shebaa Farms. In the same speech, Nasrallah pledged to return the Lebanese prisoners imprisoned in Israel "very soon."[48]

The Hezbollah-Iran relations were influenced by the formation of the power relations in the Iranian political system, the image of the Iranian president, and the relationship between Iran and Syria. The Iranian president Mohammad Khatami (1997–2005) suggested that the movement would invest more in the population and in the political arena, out of an assumption that the maintenance and development of the abilities of the resistance would become less important in the future.[49] His substitute, Mahmoud Ahmadinejad, led a line of radicalization and invested in the armament of Hezbollah, an investment whose results were well apparent during and after the Second Lebanon War. The Syrian withdrawal from Lebanon in 2005 left Iran as the only country with military presence on Lebanese soil. The absence of Syrian forces in Lebanon allowed Hezbollah and the Iranians a wider maneuvering space in order to consolidate Hezbollah's military strength and ability and turn it into the strongest military force in Lebanon.

The Syria-Iran relations during Bashar al-Assad's term and the Syrian-Iranian strategic alliance alongside the strategic change in Syria's approach toward Hezbollah only made work easier for the Iranians, who were striving to upgrade Hezbollah's military activities to a level of an Iranian division.[50]

The Revolutionary Guards' "Al Quds Force" was behind the building of Hezbollah's new military array. This force operated in Lebanon as a primal Iranian arm for the application of the Iranian policy in the struggle against Israel via a regional headquarters nicknamed the "Lebanese Corps" and the upholding of reciprocal relations with Syria. In this framework, Iran transferred means of warfare in large quantities to the hands of Hezbollah in Lebanon through Syria. The Hezbollah activists underwent training and military practices in the training camps of the Al Quds Force in Lebanon and Iran. In southern Lebanon, a defense line was built under Iranian supervision with the characteristics of an Iranian division. The Al Quds Force took an active role in the Second Lebanon War, alongside with Hezbollah, was integrated into the movement's commanding bodies, and even handled the restoration of the movement after the war.[51]

In the August 2007 article by Dr. Shaker al-Nabulsi in the Iranian newspaper *Al-Sharq* warning the establishment of an Islamic republic under Hezbollah's leadership in Lebanon, the author quotes segments from an interview with Ali Akbar Mohtashami-Pur, the former Iranian ambassador to Syria and Lebanon. Mohtashami-Pur, one of the founders of the Hezbollah movement during the 1980s, summarized the essence of the connection between Hezbollah and Iran on the background of the Second Lebanon War in three sentences: "Hezbollah is part of the regime in Iran; Hezbollah is an elementary factor in the Iranian security and military establishment; the connection between Hezbollah and Iran is much greater that the connection of a revolutionary regime with a party or a revolutionary organization outside of the borders of its country."[52] A similar description was published in *Al-Sharq Al-Awsat* in May 2006. The newspaper quoted an Iranian figure who told a group of Western statesmen in London that Iran attributed great importance to Hezbollah and that the organization "is one of the elements of our strategic security. It serves as an Iranian front line of defense against Israel. We do not agree that it needs to be disarmed . . . "[53]

Hezbollah had always been an important component in Iran's strategy and in its map of interests in the Middle East in particular. It provided for it an arm for the fulfillment of the Iranian interests facing Israel and served as an example for the success of the policy of exporting the revolution. By virtue of this fact, the Iranians continued to invest millions of dollars in the establishment of the movement and in its restoration even after the Second Lebanon War. Hezbollah provided another pipeline for the promotion of the Iranian interests in the Middle East and especially its policy against Israel. Upon the Israeli withdrawal from Lebanon, Hezbollah, under Iranian encouragement, opened a new channel of warfare against Israel via the Palestinian organizations from the territory of Lebanon to the West Bank area, the Gaza Strip area, and among the Israeli Arabs.

Hezbollah deepened its connections with the Palestinian terrorist organizations as a complementary move to achieving the goal of liberating Jerusalem and as a means of creating pressure upon Israel and thwarting agreements and procedures in the Israel–Palestinian Authority channel. The al-Aksa Intifada provided a good opportunity for Hezbollah and Iran to expand their influence in this arena. In June 2000, Nasrallah announced that he would continue objecting to any plan for normalizing the relations with Israel and that he would encourage and support the development of the resistance among the Palestinians as well.[54] Sweeping support of the Palestinians was heard all along the period from the movement's high echelons. Iran and Hezbollah's support of the Palestinians included funding terrorist bombings, training and guiding activists to carry out terrorist attacks, transferring operational knowledge, providing propagandist support through the movement's means of media, and smuggling means of warfare into the territories of the Palestinian Authority and the Gaza Strip through land and sea.[55]

To conclude, the processes in the regional system from the IDF's withdrawal played into the hands of Hezbollah. It coped better with the internal and the regional pressure attempting to disarm it, took over southern Lebanon, and built a wide-scale military array with Iranian guidance and support and Syria's blessings and without an actual interruption from either Israel or the government of Lebanon. At the same time, it increased its involvement in the Palestinian struggle by supporting, financing, smuggling means of warfare, providing operational knowledge, and encouraging terror activists to carry out terrorist attacks in Israel and further the means of achieving the goal of liberating Jerusalem and thwarting peace agreements and regional procedures.

Hezbollah and the International System—Reciprocal Influences since the IDF's Withdrawal (2000)

The problematic character of the international system's relations with Hezbollah and in the ability of this system to enforce arrangements upon the movement was revealed in its full severity during the visit of the UN General Secretary Kofi Annan to the headquarters of Nasrallah in Beirut, after Israel's withdrawal and through his handshake with Nasrallah. The handshake provides the acknowledgment of the international system of the movement's legitimacy and thwarts international cooperation for the disarmament of the movement and for the neutralization of its terrorist activity worldwide. This duality in the relations of the international system allowed Hezbollah the relative freedom of operation to recruit and to construct networks of collaborators and activists in Lebanon and in the international arena. The European Parliament's decision from 2005 to define Hezbollah as a terrorist organization was an important step in the European arena, yet it unfortunately did not oblige the countries of the European Union.[56]

The September 11 terrorist attacks aroused the reexamination of the terrorism threat in the international system. A number of countries even expanded the authorities of the security and intelligence agencies dealing with the thwarting of terrorism. In the Middle East, a new strategic situation was created following Syria's inclusion in the "axis of evil" and the American takeover of Iraq. The demand on Syria was to stop its support of terrorism and to withdraw its forces from Lebanon. The joint diplomatic effort of the United States and France after the murder of Hariri, the Lebanese prime minister, lead to a Security Council resolution (1559 from 2 September 2004) calling for Syria's withdrawal from Lebanon and for the disarmament of the militias, including Hezbollah. In April 2005, the Syrian forces withdrew from Lebanon.[57] Hezbollah, on its part, rejected the decision as irrelevant.[58]

The question of defining Hezbollah as a terrorist organization was up for a renewed discussion in the international arena after the September 11 terrorist attacks and following the diplomatic efforts of the United States and Israel to include the movement in the regional and the country lists of the terrorist organizations, yet this effort also did not gain sweeping success. During this time, only three more countries added Hezbollah to their list of terrorist organizations: Canada in 2002, Australia in 2003, and Holland in 2004.[59]

The European Parliament, which was also dealing with the issue of including Hezbollah in this list in 2005, accepted a decision according to which Hezbollah was a terrorist organization; yet beyond its declarative dimension, this decision did not oblige the countries in the European Union to take any actual steps against the movement's activists or to suspend contacts with it as long as there was no decision to do so from the level of the leaders of the European Union. Such a decision was not expected to be taken in the near future. Britain, for example, handled the question of including Hezbollah in the list of terrorist organizations that it published in 2000 and decided only to include in this list the movement's military arm, which operates outside Lebanese territory.[60]

The noninclusion of Hezbollah in the list of terrorist organizations in the international arena, not even in the European arena, continued to play into the hands of the movement and allowed it more easily to face the UN resolutions and the pressures from the United States and Israel, which acted to promote the matter of disarming the movement on the grounds of the UN resolutions from before the Second Lebanon War and afterward. In September 2002, U.S. assistant secretary of state Richard Lee Armitage stated that in the framework of the U.S. campaign against terrorism it shall also act against Hezbollah when the time is right. He added that Hezbollah "might be the A-team of terrorism and al-Qaeda the B-team."[61]

The struggle that the United States led against the funding of terrorism was partially applied on Hezbollah as well. In this case, the movement's funding components were defined as terrorism-supporting entities. The United States outlawed companies, funds, and institutes involved in funding activity for the movement, froze its assets in the United States, and acted to minimize its range of activity in the international arena. The Iranian Revolutionary Guard Corps were also defined by the United States as a terroristic entity. The revealing of some of the activities of the movement's networks at the Tri-Border area in South America and west Africa and the findings of the investigation of the terrorist attacks in Argentina testify to the scope of Hezbollah's financing infrastructure and its level of importance to the movement.[62]

The Israeli-American effort to isolate the movement, disarm it, and minimize its income resources was only partially successful. Hezbollah was well aware of the pressure that was expected following the September 11 events and was well prepared to handle the American-Israeli initiatives in the European and in the Lebanese arenas. The European countries refrained from declaring Hezbollah a "terrorist organization" and were not quick to cooperate with the United States on this matter. The government of Lebanon, on its side, backed up Hezbollah facing the outside pressure.[63]

In July 2005, Condoleezza Rice visited the Middle East, including Lebanon, where she met the new prime minister, Siniora, and Lebanese senior officials. During her visit, Rice demanded that the Lebanese government declare its commitment to apply resolution 1559. Siniora responded that Lebanon respected the UN's decisions, yet the matter of disarming the movement required a great deal of patience and would be discussed in the framework of a Lebanese internal dialogue. Hezbollah, on its side, denounced the American intervention in Lebanon's internal affairs.[64]

In an interview given to the TV channel Al-Arabia on September 2, 2005, Nasrallah referred to the demands of the international community from the Lebanese government to disarm the movement. He explained that, as per the principle guiding the movement, the resistance is a response to the Israeli aggression. Therefore, the role of the resistance would be concluded only withthe end of Israeli aggression. On the basis of this principle, Nasrallah claimed that he was willing to debate this with the international community. He announced that he would not accept American guarantees for an Israeli withdrawal from the Shebaa Farms. According to his claim, the international community did not have the ability to handle threats against Lebanon, and thus, there was no use in granting international guarantees for Lebanon's safety. In his words, Lebanon was facing Israeli aggression, expressed, among other things, by the occupation of the Shebaa Farms, the infiltration of Lebanon's airspace, and the retention of Lebanese prisoners. The answer to this aggression was the existence of the resistance alongside the army of Lebanon. This was the only formula, as far as he was concerned, to ensure Lebanon's safety.[65]

The international involvement in the occurrences in Lebanon through the UN was gradually expanded after the Israeli withdrawal and the murder of Hariri. The reappearance of the political murder cases in Lebanon and the crises they created placed Lebanon and its ability to handle the internal violence and the armed factors operating within it in the limelight of the international arena. Following this condition, the UN launched messengers and mediators in order to examine possible solutions in accordance with the investigators who were dealing with finding the murderers of Hariri.[66] This involvement also continued during and after the Second Lebanon War. Security Council resolution 1701 dealt with the cease-fire agreement with the entry of multinational forces (MNFs) into southern Lebanon and with the disarming of Hezbollah.

Despite the UN resolutions and the presence of its forces in Lebanon, the movement managed to restore its military abilities after the Second Lebanon War and to smuggle into Lebanon thousands of missiles and advanced means of warfare of various types. In 2007 and following the capture of some of the movement's shipments of means of warfare by the army of Lebanon, Nasrallah publicly declared the movement's effort to restore the military array and that he was even proud of achieving a balance of deterrence against Israel, once again, and even beyond.[67]

To conclude, Hezbollah was wise in exploiting the period after the IDF's withdrawal for intensification, organizing its ranks, and establishing control over Lebanon with Syrian and Iranian support. It continued its double-face policy of activity in the political arena, including within the Lebanese government, as well as outside the political arena, in order to promote its interests against Israel and against the Shiite and the Lebanese public opinion. A weak Lebanese government that bowed before Syria, alongside a strategic alliance between Syria and Iran, benefited the Hezbollah, which established its ranks in the Lebanese arena and became, after the Syrian withdrawal, the most significant military force in Lebanon. Lebanese fear of dealing with the question of disarming the movement and having the Lebanese government being controlled by Syria were some of the reasons for the Lebanese government's outward support of the resistance, even when this did not go along with Lebanon's interests.

In this complex state of affairs, it was only a question of time before the outbreak of another round of violence between Israel and Lebanon. This round of violence (the Second Lebanon War) also didn't create the conditions for disarming Hezbollah, and the mutual efforts of Israel and the United States could not make the international system join in creating international pressure upon Hezbollah by defining it as a terrorist organization. This fact allowed the movement to continue establishing its military abilities as well as its political strength at the same time.

10

Summary and Conclusions

Hezbollah was born out of the heat of the resistance battle . . . on June of '82. Following the Israeli invasion, people from various regions have convened and established the founding authority. They also have outlined the organization's activity guidelines . . . .The most eminent one was Abbas al-Musawi . . . .This was a Lebanese decision taken by young Lebanese people . . . and as for the role of Syria and Iran, this came up during a later stage."[1]

Al-Wasat, (18 March 1996)

This is how Nasrallah chose, in 1996, to present the movement's process of establishment while stressing the fact that the initiative was taken by the Lebanese Ulema.

The Hezbollah movement is a product of the environment in which it operates and of the interactions and the reciprocal relations between the players surrounding it. Hezbollah is a Lebanese Shiite movement with an affinity and a deep connection to the Iranian system, yet it was founded as the result of the development of social and political procedures in the Lebanese system in general and among the Shia sect in particular. The chaos that characterized the inter-Lebanese system from the mid-1970s allowed the growth of Hezbollah as a revolutionary social movement and permitted its violent and uncontrolled activity. The movement's consolidation and expansion during the 1980s was made possible due to the continuance of the chaotic condition in Lebanon and in the regional system, the fact of it being a source of attraction for the young Shiites, and the availability of resources for its activity.

As the movement expanded and became institutionalized, it turned more sensitive to the procedures and influences of the internal and the regional systems. It changed its activity policy from uncontrolled violence and from terrorist attacks as the leading strategy to controlled violence and guerrilla warfare and commenced a dialogue with the Lebanese political system. The change in the inter-Lebanese activity environment following the Ta'if Accord and the central Lebanese regime's establishment upon and under Syrian custody and support caused changes in the movement's activity patterns and its institutionalization. It showed a great deal of pragmatism and integrated into the restoring Lebanese system, while accepting this system's rules of game.

On the regional and the international fronts, the movement used a controlled policy that integrated guerrilla warfare and terrorist attacks while taking into account "profit and loss" considerations. Israel's withdrawal from Lebanon in May 2000 and its activities ever since have reinforced Hezbollah's status in

Lebanon and across the Arab world, and it had become a role model for the Palestinian terrorist organizations.

The development of Hezbollah was influenced by the reciprocal relations between the state and society, by the social, cultural, economic, and internal political conditions, and by the regional and the international systems. These systems differed as far as their level of influence upon the movement's development was concerned. Their scope of influence derived from their proximity to the movement and from the means of pressure they could exercise upon it. Sophisticated navigation by the movement's leadership between the players of the various systems and the ability of adjustment to the changing conditions allowed the movement to survive as a part of the restoring Lebanese system while continuing to simultaneously uphold presence and activity in the Lebanese political arena, alongside independent activity outside the limits of the institutionalized Lebanese system.

The movement's success, survival, and expansion, despite the efforts of its rivals, opponents, and competitors, are based upon two basic elements:

A. *The regulative element* is the ability to build an effective activity capability leaning on internal and external resources composed of efficient and hierarchical organization, military capability, funding, and the enforcement of organizational authority.

B. *The legitimacy element*, leaning on the organizational discourse, includes within itself dogmatic justifications for strategic changes carried out by the movement, the appropriation of Lebanese national responsibility, partial adjustment (if only seemingly), and willingness to operate in the framework of the existent Lebanese political system as an exception of evaluations of the situation, sensitivities to changes, and the influences of the sectarian public opinion.

The movement was founded at the height of an inter-Lebanese crisis as a revolutionary Shia movement with a universal Islamic vision, which acted under the banner of three central objectives: the implementation of the Islamic law in Lebanon as part of a worldwide Islamic revolution, the expulsion of the foreign forces from Lebanon, and the liberation of Jerusalem.

From the mid-1980s on, it has turned into a major player in the sectarian system. The violence that it carried out yielded immediate results and granted it the support and sympathy of the Shia population. Hezbollah regarded the Shia sect as a major and necessary component for achieving the goal of implementing an Islamic regime in Lebanon. Hezbollah's desire to establish its status as a popular movement has influenced its moves and policy. Its leaders renounced any connection to activities that damaged its image and the establishment of its position and even changed the movement's policy of activity every now and then.

The procedures and the changes in the Shiite community and in the inter-Lebanese and regional systems from the late 1980s on, alongside the beginning of the peace process in the Middle East, influenced the Hezbollah movement. It underwent a change from a movement with a revolutionary character and a universal Islamic vision, whose objectives were defined in a total manner in the long run, to a pragmatic movement with an Islamic-Lebanese identity and local objectives defined in the short range. The goal of establishing an Islamic state in Lebanon by overthrowing the regime via a revolutionary act was dimmed, and instead, the movement decided to operate in the framework of the existent political system in order to achieve its goals in a gradual manner. It sent its delegates to the parliament; expanded its organizational, social, and economic infrastructure; and increased the scope of its resistance activity against Israel. The resistance to Israel was presented as a legitimate guerrilla activity against an occupying army, thus gaining consensus and support of the Lebanese public opinion, which even helped the movement greatly in promoting its objectives in the sectarian and the Lebanese arena.

Hezbollah's decision to integrate into the Lebanese political system was the result of an evaluation of the situation that took into account the advantages, disadvantages, and the cost of the joining predicted from this move. The "control of the street," or in other words, the control of the sectarian public opinion was and remained the real reason for the struggles that the movement conducted by violence as well as by competition, ranging from dialogue to restrained struggle.

Hezbollah's striving for an escalation in its relations with the Amal movement in April 1988 reflected its (erroneous in retrospect) confidence in regard to the scope and the stability of the Lebanese Shia population's support. The end of the war allowed it to invest its resources in promoting its status in regard to the sectarian public opinion and to expand its popular infrastructure toward the predicted confrontation over the power centers and influence within the community and over the right to represent it, facing the Lebanese system.

The importance of the sect in Hezbollah's entirety of considerations increased even more from the stage in which the Lebanese political system commenced the first steps of implementing the Ta'if Accord and decided to hold elections for the parliament. Thus, the real struggle was over the sectarian public opinion, the one that was supposed to make a difference in the ballot box. For this purpose, the movement used all the means available at its disposal, from conducting public opinion polls and recruiting rhetoric to toning down the radical Islamic approach and the adopting a comprehensive political discourse that could be catchy for the Lebanese general public.

Its impressive success in the elections for parliament helped it to establish its image as a movement being restored, yet at the same time presenting it with a combined challenge to prove to its Islamic adherents that the price it had to pay on the way to the parliament was merely a matter of semantics and that the movement hadn't abandoned its ideological doctrine and the method of the resistance. As far as the sectarian public opinion, it was forced to provide proof and clarification concerning the level of truth of its pragmatic image, as well as in regard to the essence of its relations with the Lebanese state, against the background of its special bond with Iran.

One way or another, Hezbollah was aware of the changes in the Lebanese system as an exception to the development of high sensitivity to the sectarian public opinion, a system of reciprocal relations and mutual influences has developed between the movement and the sect, which continued expanding as long as the movement underwent institutionalization and internalized the activity patterns typical to the Lebanese system.

Hezbollah's leadership was wise enough to internalize, at least seemingly, the intersectarian and the Lebanese procedures that took place toward the end of the civil war in Lebanon and to formulate a political agenda that would be in accord with the restoring Lebanese system. The change, which was backed up by an all-encompassing propagandist activity, was meant to establish the movement's position within the sect and the Lebanese system as well as to exploit the tools and the existing means at the disposal of the institutional system in order to promote the movement's objectives and to increase the exposure of the Islamic message. Yet, the change concerned a cost, which the radical margins found to be too high. It obliged the movement to abandon its pan-Islamic, extrainstitutional revolutionary approach and to operate within the confines of the Lebanese political system. Hezbollah assumed that, during the final trimester of the 1990s, it had managed to convince the sectarian public opinion of the sincerity of its moves and of its new image. It operated in order to translate this into political power and to prepare the groundwork for activity in the era after Israel's withdrawal from Lebanon.

It is hard to determine whether Hezbollah managed to persuade its various publics that it was truly undergoing a process of change and to what extent and whether the sophisticated propaganda and the endless repetition of its messages in the various channels of the media indeed achieved their objectives. Yet, without disputing the importance of the sectarian public opinion in the eyes of the movement's leadership, to which it mainly addressed its messages, it conducted an ongoing and an often-violent struggle against the Amal movement over its support, and as a result of its understanding of the frame of mind among it, Hezbollah examined its policy and activities.

A supportive sectarian public opinion was necessary for the movement's existence and even more from the 1990s, as of the point in which it had positioned itself under the voters' judgment. For this reason, its moves in the Lebanese political arena were intended, in many cases, to serve its objectives in the intersectarian arena and to establish its status as a patriotic popular movement acting in order to promote and improve the condition of the deprived ones from among the members of the Shia sect while simultaneously conducting its war against Israel.

The inter-Lebanese system also influenced Hezbollah's trend of development as a movement. The chaos that characterized the political system, from the mid-1970s to the early 1990s, created an optimal activity environment for the movement's growth and provided it with ample political opportunities to expand and to promote its interests. During the 1980s and the 1990s, the Lebanese regime was under the shadow of either powerful regional players that "conducted" the Lebanese system or the players influencing it.

During the early 1990s, Syria turned into the most influential factor in the Lebanese regime; it established its position as the "de facto landlord" of Lebanon, and the regime's activities in regard to Hezbollah were carried out in accordance with the Syrian interests. The Lebanese regime operated within this system of restraints and dynamic changes in order to limit the movement's steps, to "domesticate" it, and to "subordinate" its policy to that of the government.

The implementation of the Ta'if Accord caused a strategic change in the Lebanese regime's policy and nature of activity, which influenced Hezbollah as well. It had to adjust itself to the restoring system, yet it did not "align" itself like the other power factors; nonetheless, it continued developing its military abilities and conducting a war of attrition against Israel. This "independence" provided a source of conflicts and struggles between the movement and the Lebanese regime, and the waves of violence and escalation disrupted the everyday life in Lebanon and mainly the regime's plans for promoting its own moves. The movement's "skating on thin ice" policy promoted it in the field of the resistance, yet created conflicts between it and the government in the inter-Lebanese field. The regime's decisiveness concerning internal issues formulated the limits of "right and wrong" in this arena, and the movement was forced to operate within their framework.

The Lebanese government didn't succeed in "bending" the movement's policy and forcing it to consider the national interests. In the absence of the ability to achieve this, against the background of internal and external restraints, the government conducted a flexible policy of supporting the activities of the resistance on the one hand, at least declaratively, and of acting to limit its steps as much as possible on the other hand. It prevented Hezbollah's entry into the administrative system and distanced it from involvement and influence upon the regional system of relations. As far as it was concerned, in critical locations such as Beirut it operated decisively in order to enforce its authority, while in southern Lebanon and eastward, in the Beqaa valley, it refrained from fully implementing its sovereignty and from a direct confrontation with the movement and allowed it to operate against Israel. The change of personnel in the Lebanese government during the late 1990s improved the movement's position in the political system, and its activities gained more and more sympathy in the government as well. In fact, the government did not disarm the movement even after the IDF's withdrawal from Lebanon.

The inability to "domesticate" Hezbollah probably derived from a combination of the following factors: the absence of efficient governmental influence mechanisms (political, economic, and military) against the movement; the government's unwillingness to confront the movement (due to public opinion pressures and the fear of deterioration of the situation in Lebanon); Syrian dominance in determining the Lebanese internal and foreign policy; and the deep involvement of the regional system's players in the occurrences in Lebanon.

The existence of a regional system with a great many players and conflicts, which most of the time saw basic differences of interest between them in regard to the Lebanese system in general and Hezbollah in particular, caused a relatively decreased level of influence by the system over the movement in relation to the strengths and abilities of its players. Each player in the system operated in order to promote its own interests and neutralize those of the other players. During periods or points in which a consensus of opinion existed between two regional players, they managed, not without an effort, to influence the movement's directions of development and to enforce somewhat of an authority upon it.

One way or another, the regional players' contradicting trends of influence and the existence of constraints that limited their activity against the movement allowed the movement to navigate its way in a winding path between its patrons and its rivals in accordance with its needs and policies, which were not always attuned with the desires of all the players of the regional system. The movement made it clear to everyone that, above all, it had its independent policy, and it operates according to it, consistently and decisively.

The international system had the most marginal influence upon the movement's trends of development. The players of this system had difficulties establishing a joint policy of activity due to differences of opinion in regard to defining Hezbollah as a terrorist organization. In practice, the United States was the only one that strove, from the 1980s onward, to eliminate the movement as a terroristic entity. Europe, which increased its involvement in the Middle-Eastern system during the second half of the 1990s, in fact made it difficult for the United States to achieve its objectives.

The 2010 model of Hezbollah is one of a pragmatic terrorist organization that is far more dangerous than that of the revolutionary Hezbollah of the 1980s. In fact, the movement hasn't abandoned its goals, but has changed its pace of application. It operates simultaneously within the Lebanese political system and outside it, a fact that grants it an activity range in both arenas. Hezbollah of 2010 leads the Lebanese opposition and has a veto capability on the government's decisions. This gives Hezbollah the power to block any decision that could harm its interests. The movement's pragmatic appearance had deceived and continues to deceive researchers and players in the international system. The movement's entry into the Lebanese political system was perceived by many as a first and important step pinpointing moderation and a change of the extreme ideological hardliner. Hezbollah even carried out a series of activities in order to emphasize the change that it had seemingly undergone. It has been investing, and still invests, from the early 1990s, significant efforts into blurring its pan-Islamic terroristic image while simultaneously building an image of a legitimate Lebanese organization fighting against an occupying army. During the 1990s, it minimized the scope of its terroristic activities against Western targets in Lebanon and abroad and executed strictly "qualitative" and confidential activities of terrorism while refraining from accepting responsibility for their performance and denying any connection to activity and operations.

Hezbollah's entry into the Lebanese parliament enforced its claim that it was a legitimate Lebanese movement, operating within the political framework and according to its rules, and that it had changed its radical revolutionary activity policy of the 1980s. Hezbollah managed to "convince" players within the Lebanese system and those of the international community that its activity was focused on the social-political arena in Lebanon and on the protection of the state from Israeli aggression.

However, an in-depth examination of the movement's activity, its institutes, and its manner of conduct in the regional and in the international arena, a very different picture is revealed from that which the movement is trying to market. The Shura Council, the body that runs the movement, is in charge of its military terrorist activity on one hand and of its social-political activity on the other hand. Imad Mughniyeh (killed in February 2008) served in this council and was also in charge of the movement's secret terrorist wing in Lebanon and abroad. Furthermore, "slips" of the heads of the movement, from time to time, have revealed their true attitudes. So, for example, in January 2002, in contradiction to the declarative line that emphasizes the movement's social-political arm and diminishes the military wing, Muhammad Funaysh, one of the movement's delegates in the parliament, stated that "one mustn't separate between the Hezbollah's military wing and its political wing."[2] The concept of an Islamic state in Lebanon was not archived, and it would surface whenever the right political opportunity came up.

Hezbollah is constantly developing and expanding, and during the last two decades, it managed to establish an infrastructure for an international network of terrorism in over forty countries, which it activates in a centralized manner via the Shura Council and the Jihad Council headed by Nasrallah and Mughniyeh. However, after the demise of Mughniyeh in 2008, his successors took over. This international terrorist network, whose cells have already carried out terrorist attacks and attempted attacks from the 1990s onward, is considered to be the most organized terrorist network in the world and presents a threat to the interests of the United States and those of the Western countries that have defined Hezbollah as a terrorist movement.

The terrorist network established by the movement abroad is used for tasks of gathering intelligence and damaging Israeli, Jewish, and Western targets abroad, for acquiring and smuggling means of warfare, and as a source for the financing of the movement's activities.

The movement went on initiating terrorist activities against Israel by launching missiles aimed at civilian settlements in Israel even after the IDF's withdrawal from Lebanon (May 2000) and during the Second Lebanon War (July 2006). At the same time, it trained, financed, and operated Palestinian terrorist groups and organizations to carry out terrorist attacks in order to thwart any progress in the relations between Israel and the Palestinian Authority. Hezbollah is also active in the recruitment and activation of Israeli Arabs for the execution of terrorist attacks. Ever since the end of the Second Lebanon War (August 2006), Hezbollah has been working laboriously with the large-scale support of Syria and Iran to restore its military arrays, which were damaged during the war and to establish an advanced and wide-scoped operational infrastructure with characteristics similar to those of the military deployment of a sovereign army. This infrastructure is more developed than what it had been during the outbreak of the Second Lebanon War, and it includes various types of missiles, with ranges that can cover a significant share of Israel's territory; advanced antitank missiles; and military knowledge concerning their operation.

Hezbollah is also active and involved in the Iraqi arena; it not only leads the media campaign against the American involvement in Iraq, but also finances fundamentalist Iraqi Shia elements. Besides, it has established a secret infrastructure in Iraq, and its activists, in collaboration with Iranian and domestic elements, are involved in terrorist attacks against American targets in the country.

To conclude, Hezbollah is not a state player and it cannot create an actual threat as far as the existence of one of the players in the international arena is concerned, yet it remains potentially dangerous. The movement is well aware of its limited power and thus it has navigated and still navigates between the various players with caution. Altogether, it hasn't hesitated to confront its patrons or its opponents and to exhibit a great level of independence, even when its leaders thought that giving up its position was in contradiction with its policy and the activity principles guiding it. In fact, the movement managed to survive all of the crises and even to restore its relations with its patrons and with the Lebanese public opinion in general and with the Shiite one in particular. Nasrallah, the leader of the movement since 1992, adopted a policy of "skating on thin ice" in his relations with the Lebanese and the regional systems and made the best out of both worlds in which the movement operates. He played the inter-Lebanese political game and acted in order to diminish the Lebanese fear of the idea of implementing the Sharia law in the country. This political activity is part of the characteristics of an activity adopted by the movement, separating the religious Shia thinking based on the principle of the reign of the religious scholar and of pan-Islamism from the daily practice of activity in the framework of the existent system in order to achieve the movement's objectives. This separation allows the movement to operate simultaneously within the political system and to continue developing the Shia thought without one bothering the other.

Epilogue

Hezbollah between the Second Lebanon War 2006 and the Second Unity Government 2009

General

The Seventh Hezbollah Conference discussions took place in November 2009.[1] At the conclusion of the conference, a few days before the approval of the new government at the Lebanese parliament, Nasrallah published his movement's new political manifesto. The document discussed the movement's principles, its viewpoint and its relationship with the Lebanese, and the regional and international systems in which and around which it operates.

On the internal Lebanese level, the manifesto details the movement's political aim of integrating into the Lebanese political system but hides its true long-term goal—the Islamization of Lebanon and the establishment of an Islamic republic from within the political system. The document further clarifies that the issue of disarming the "Resistance" is not on the table and that it will continue its activities to defend Lebanon until it is liberated.[2]

On the regional level, Hezbollah has remained consistent in its position toward Israel. It denies any acknowledgment of the legitimacy of the existence of Israel as a country in the region or any concession over the Palestinian land. The liberation of Jerusalem is an Islamic mission and Hezbollah aims to participate in Islamic Palestinian efforts to achieve this objective. The political manifesto mentions the movement's excellent relations with Iran and Syria, but emphasizes the fact that Hezbollah is a Lebanese movement operating within the Lebanese political system.[3]

On the international level, the United States is perceived as "enemy number one" and as the leader of global terrorism; the struggle against the United States is expected to be long and hard and will continue into future generations as well.

An analysis of the document illustrates how the movement's political thought has developed while still maintaining the radical principles and ideologies expressed in its constitution document of 1985 (the "open letter"). Nasrallah refrains from expressly referring to the movement's ideological tenants and from the question regarding the nature of its relationship with Iran, claiming the document deals with Hezbollah's political agenda and not with religious ideological issues.

Hezbollah's political manifesto constituted the basis for its entry into the second National Unity Government in November 2009 and brings the movement one step closer to its objective, as presented in the open letter in 1985, of turning Lebanon into an Islamic republic.[4] This chapter will discuss Hezbollah's activities that aimed at obtaining this objective between 2006 and 2009, as well as the main processes affecting the movement throughout this period.

Hezbollah and the Lebanese System between the Second Lebanon War (2006) and the Second Unity Government (2009)

The question of Hezbollah's position in the Lebanese system and the establishment of an international tribunal for the investigation of Hariri's murder were the main tasks of the Lebanese prime minister, Fuad Siniora, who was elected in 2005 in order to establish the government on behalf of the anti-Syrian camp. Siniora's government declared its support of the "Resistance", and, for the first time, it included two ministers from Hezbollah. A pro-Syrian president, an opposition growing in strength, the structure of the government system, and Lebanon's multiethnic nature made it difficult for Siniora to achieve real progress in realizing the goals he set for himself.

In December 2005, following the government's decision to invite the UN to investigate Hariri's murder, five Shiite ministers (two from Hezbollah and three from Amal) suspended their participation in the government's sessions. The tenuous relationship between the opposition and the government continued during 2006. The Second Lebanon War (July 2006) only aggravated the controversy and tension between the two camps.[5]

The Second Lebanon War took Hezbollah by surprise. Nasrallah admitted that he had misjudged the intensity of Israel's response to the abduction of the two IDF soldiers. The war hurt the movement's operational infrastructure and its standing in the Lebanese political arena. The movement's deterrence strategy, which it once took pride in, had failed.[6] The reason behind the existence of the "Resistance" for the defense of Lebanon alongside the Lebanese Army made headlines again within internal Lebanese dialogue, as well as in international circles. Again, as before, the Lebanese government was asked to disarm the militias, implying the inclusion of Hezbollah as well.

The Security Council's Resolution No. 1701, received on August 11, 2006, enabled the conclusion of the Second Lebanon War following 34 days of battle. The Council called to put an end to the fighting and for the retreat of the IDF forces from Lebanon. The Lebanese government was asked to enforce its sovereignty and authority over all of Lebanon. The Council approved an increase in UN forces, calling for 15,000 soldiers to be deployed in southern Lebanon. Among other things, the Council called on the international community to provide humanitarian and economic aid to Lebanon. On the subject of disarming the militias, it was decided that the UN Secretary General would formulate suggestions for the implementation of the Taif Accord and Resolution 1559, including disarmament, as well as investigate disputed issues such as the Shebaa Farms dispute. The Lebanese government was asked to work to prevent weapons smuggling by increasing security measures along the country's borders. On a grander scale, the Security Council called on all countries to work to prevent the sale or supply of weapons to individuals or organizations in Lebanon, as well as the provision of any technical aid or training in these fields without the authorization of the Lebanese government.[7]

Hezbollah's series of achievements were cut short by the Second Lebanon War. The war forced its leaders to act quickly to rehabilitate Hezbollah's image and status, first and foremost among the movement's members and the Shiites, but also in the inter-Lebanese arena. Some of the urgent issues on Hezbollah's agenda following the war included rehabilitating damaged civil and organizational infrastructure; continuing "Resistance" activity; and maintaining freedom of action, including in areas where the Lebanese Army and the Multi-National Forces were deployed.

The first step in rehabilitating the movement's image was launching a public relations campaign aimed at establishing the idea that Hezbollah achieved "a divine victory" in the war, thanks to its fighters firm standing despite Israel's numerical and technological superiority. Iran's and Syria's support of this propaganda line, along with public criticism in Israel of the way military and political campaigns were managed during the war, helped the movement establish the myth of divine victory among its public.[8]

On the civil level, the movement acted vigorously to help war victims, clearing ruins and rebuilding damaged buildings and infrastructure in Beirut and southern Lebanon. In the year following the war, the movement invested—with Iranian aid—hundreds of millions of dollars in rebuilding civilian infrastructure in Lebanon. Hezbollah made sure to document and publicize these activities through media networks—part of its campaign to earn points in the struggle to again win over the support of the Lebanese public in general and Shiites in particular.[9]

On the political level, the movement faced possible erosion in its status. It feared the Lebanese government would try to restrict the movement's activities and/or disarm it due to public criticism, the outcome of the war, and/or external pressure. The line adopted by Nasrallah was to demand the establishment of a national unity government. He threatened to topple the existing government if his demand was not accepted. Furthermore, as in previous instances, he stressed that the movement would not use force to achieve political goals but would rather operate within a democratic framework by bringing its supporters to the streets. Apparently, Nasrallah assumed that a unity government would enable the opposition to foil resolutions that could harm the movement's interests or that of its patrons.[10] It seems that this was also the American assessment. On November 1, 2006, the White House press secretary made an unusual announcement to the press, expressing U.S. concern over the existence of a combined Syrian-Iranian-Hezbollah plan to topple Siniora's government. The White House also revealed that there were indications that this move effectively would allow Syria to try to block Lebanon's endorsement of the establishment of the international tribunal meant to investigate Hariri's murder. Syria, of course, dismissed the American accusations.[11]

In November 2006, five Shiite ministers resigned from the Lebanese government, citing as grounds for their resignation the failure to add another representative to the government from the "Free Patriotic Movement (FPM)" party, belonging to the opposition. Some believed that this was merely part of a Syrian move to foil the establishment of the international tribunal for the investigation of Hariri's murder, to topple Siniora's government, and to establish a national unity government. In a speech given by Nasrallah to thousands of his supporters after these resignations, two conflicting messages stood out. One was that he did not fear a civil war, and the other was a promise to maintain stability in Lebanon. He again rejected the government's legitimacy and called it to resign. The Lebanese President, Emil Lahud, informed the UN Secretary General that he did not approve of the government's decision regarding the international tribunal and therefore called it illegitimate and claimed it did not oblige Lebanon.[12]

On the operational level, the movement continued implementing its independent policy, which included rebuilding the military array damaged during the war; formulating an action strategy based on the lessons drawn from the war; and recruiting new activists and training them in camps in Lebanon and Iran. In addition, the weaknesses revealed during the war were addressed, such as intelligence leaks,[13] the conduct of the commanders, and the deployment of communications and intelligence networks.[14] The movement also prepared the operational array for its missions, based on lessons derived from the war. Among other activities, it carried out systemic exercises and received advanced weaponry in large quantities.[15] This activity was carried out despite the presence of the Lebanese Army and the Multi-National Forces in the south. The Lebanese government—whether intentionally, by "turning a blind eye," or unintentionally, due to its inability to cope—enabled the movement's rearmament. In February and June 2007, the Lebanese Army intercepted trucks loaded with weapons for Hezbollah, but this was merely "a drop in the ocean."[16]

This activity was the pretext for declarations made by senior Hezbollah members, generally claiming that Hezbollah had reestablished the balance of deterrence against Israel, and it was better and more effective than before.[17] The UN Secretary General's report on Resolution 1701 (2007) cited Israeli sources claiming that Hezbollah had recovered its power, tripled the number of land-sea missiles in its possession, and equipped itself with new missiles capable of hitting targets south of Tel-Aviv.[18] In November 2007, around the time of the IDF's extensive exercise maneuvers in the north of Israel, Hezbollah revealed that the movement had carried out a three-day exercise with many participants in the south of Lebanon. The exercise was carried out under Nasrallah's supervision, in a defensive line-up simulating an IDF attack on Lebanon. Hezbollah's decision to reveal the exercise activities at that time was meant to send a message of determent to Israel and to those opposing the movement in Lebanon, showing how the movement had regenerated its capabilities and its readiness to face an Israeli attack.[19]

In April 2010, various sources reported the arrival of Syrian Scud missiles to Hezbollah.[20] With such missiles in the movement's possession, Hezbollah is better able to attack the heart of Israel. There is no dispute that in the years following the Second Lebanon War, the movement has improved its weapons arsenal both in terms of quantity and quality. These weapons originate out of Iran and Syria. They were smuggled or brought into Lebanon in the years following Second Lebanon War.[21]

The rivalry and tension between the government and the pro-Syrian camp headed by Hezbollah reached new heights in November 2007 with the conclusion of Lebanese President Emil Lahud's term in office. The inability to reach an accord on an accepted candidate dragged Lebanon into a severe constitutional crisis and further paralyzed the government's ability to run the country. The government's attempts to find a candidate with a chance to get elected by a parliamentary majority were rebuffed time after time by the pro-Syrian opposition. The Shiite Parliament chairman, Nabia Beri, Nasrallah's partner in creating the political crisis, refrained 19 times from convening the parliament to elect a new president. The crisis ended in May 2008, not before the eruption of a wave of violence in Lebanon, which ended in a settlement of the political situation through external intervention from the Arab world and with the signing of the Doha Accord by all of the parties.[22]

The Doha Accord benefits Hezbollah; the movement's demand for the right of veto at the Cabinet was fulfilled. Siniora's government ended its term right after the election of Michel Sulaiman as president. In its place, Siniora received a mandate to establish a national unity government, as demanded by Hezbollah, with 30 presiding ministers, 11 of which are ministers from the pro-Syrian camp, 16 from the anti-Syrian coalition, and 3 ministers that are to be appointed by the president (who is also pro-Syrian). The Lebanese government was required to declare its support of the "Resistance." It was further agreed that the elections law would be changed. This was expected to provide Hezbollah with an advantage in the 2009 elections for parliament.[23]

In July 2008, Siniora declared the establishment of a National Unity Government in accordance with the principles of the Doha Accord; the Unity Government declared its support of the "Resistance." In August 2008, the parliament ratified the government's establishment and its platform. This signaled the end of 22 months of political crisis that began with the resignation of the five Shiite ministers in November 2006. Hezbollah, which left Siniora's government with a door slam, returned as the great victor of the Doha Accord in July 2008.[24]

The Doha Accord is another example of the inability or unwillingness of the Lebanese government to deal with Hezbollah. It is a reminder that the use of violence is worthwhile for achieving political goals. Lebanon, which has been in a state of "cold civil war" for several years, experiences eruptions of violence from time to time, including political assassinations, explosives detonations, and mass demonstrations. This "state of affairs" is affected, among other factors, by the intervention of regional players Syria, Iran, and Israel, whether by encouraging and supporting Hezbollah's activity or by diplomatic and military attempts (the Second Lebanon War) to eliminate the movement as a terrorist entity or bring about its disarmament.

From Hezbollah's entry into the political arena in 1992 and since the IDF's retreat from Lebanon, Nasrallah has promised over and over to his Lebanese listeners that the movement's weapons are not directed against internal Lebanese targets but rather externally against Israel. He has assured them that his movement will operate within the framework of the rules of the Lebanese political arena and will refrain from using violence in this arena.[25] These declarations do not correspond with the events that occurred in May 2008, however.

Two decisions made by the Lebanese government in May 2008 caused Nasrallah to send the movement's activists to the streets: one, the declaration that an independent communication network the movement founded was illegal; and two, the dismissal of the head of Airport Security Services who cooperated with Hezbollah. The Hezbollah activists attacked anti-Syrian coalition (Sunni) targets, neighborhoods, and installations in Beirut, and took over the neighborhoods in the western part of the city.[26] The violent clashes threatened to ignite an all out civil war and the incidents spread to other areas of Lebanon. Dozens of casualties, Hezbollah's takeover of central areas in western Beirut, and Sunni and Christian inability to retaliate clarified once again to all the Lebanese and regional players who had the real power in Lebanon.[27]

The Lebanese Army, answering to the government, refrained from interfering in the incidents and imposing order. Only after five days of battles and dozens of casualties the army increased its patrols in Beirut. It did not, however, physically interfere by removing Hezbollah roadblocks or enforcing the government's decisions.[28] The Lebanese Army's conduct is further testimony to the government's weakness and its inability to enforce its resolutions.

The conflict in Lebanon greatly bothered the Sunni axis in the Middle East supporting Siniora's government. The Lebanese model is a microcosm of sorts of the regional system, in constant tension in respect to the Iranian power gain. The eruption of a civil war in Lebanon would affect other countries in the region. As such, these countries took quick steps to contain and stop the events immediately, even at the cost of far-reaching concessions of Hezbollah's demands. In fact, the Doha Accord founded the mechanism that enabled the return of the Lebanese system to a path of temporary stability, until the eruption of the next crisis.

Elections for the Lebanese parliament were held in July 2009, with Hezbollah and its allies preparing and expecting a government revolution within the Lebanese system. In actuality, the coalition (the March 14th Camp) headed by Hariri maintained its power and won the parliamentary elections with a majority of 71 seats versus 57 seats for the opposition.[29] This fact did not fundamentally change the balance of power in Lebanon. Hariri had difficulty forming a government and had to settle for the model of a joint national unity government with the opposition. In November 2009, after several months of discussions, Hariri's new government was presented to the parliament. In this government, too, similar to Siniora's national unity government, Hezbollah used its military and political power as leverage to secure the movement's interests. As a result, Hariri's national unity government includes 30 ministers, 15 of which are coalition ministers, 10 of which belong to the opposition headed by Hezbollah (out of which three are members of the movement), and five of which are independent ministers appointed by the president, Michel Sulaiman (pro-Syrian)—a combination that enables Hezbollah to veto government resolutions. Another achievement for the movement was the government's declaration of its continuing support of the "Resistance" and its decision to refrain from disarming the movement.[30]

In summary, the opposition headed by Hezbollah did not gain majority in the parliamentary elections but it did base its power within the Lebanese political system. It advanced one step closer to its objective of taking over the government of Lebanon. The steps taken by the Druze leader Walid Gunblat, who is well versed in the ins and outs of Lebanese politics, in order to develop a dialogue with Hezbollah and the Syrians only strengthened Hezbollah's status; even though

Hezbollah has not won the elections, there is no question of whether it is perceived as a major player in the Lebanese arena, both due to its military power and the political power that it has accumulated over the past years.[31]

Hezbollah in the Regional and International Theater

In November 2009, the Lebanese Parliament ratified the guidelines of the Second Unity Government. Regarding the core issues related to Hezbollah's and the opposition's standing, the government succumbed (like previous governments) to Hezbollah's demands. It declared its support for the "Resistance," including it as a component in Lebanon's security strategy alongside the Lebanese Army. It refrained from cooperating in the realization of the Security Council resolutions regarding the disarming of the movement.[32] This move, along with the ongoing erosion of Israeli and American efforts to classify Hezbollah as a terrorist organization in the international arena, are further proof of the difficulty the international system has in influencing the conduct of nongovernmental players such as Hezbollah.

However, it should be emphasized that the results of the Second Lebanon War, Israel's messages of deterrence, Syrian and Iranian interests, and the effects of the Lebanese system and interests of the movement all influenced the movement's conduct in the years following the Second Lebanon War. It refrained from escalating its activity along Israel's northern border.[33] The most prominent manifestation of this policy was in the course of the Cast Lead Operation—Israel's campaign against the Hamas movement in Gaza in 2008–2009. Hamas expected Hezbollah to open a front in the north against Israel, but beyond statements of support and attempts to encourage Muslim followers (mainly from Egypt) to act against their rulers who supported the Israeli operation through their silence, Hezbollah refrained from taking action from within Lebanon.[34]

In February 2008, Imad Mughniyeh, head of Hezbollah's Jihad Council and the person responsible for building the movement's power and planning terrorist attacks, was assassinated in Damascus. His assassination was a significant loss to the movement and an injury to its prestige. Hezbollah blamed Israel and declared that its retaliation would not be limited to the regional theater. In a speech given by Nasrallah to commemorate Hezbollah's Day of the Martyr in February 2010, he emphasized that there were many opportunities to carry out a retaliatory attack for Imad Mughniyeh's assassination but stated that the movement had decided not to carry it out. He added that Hezbollah would choose its targets, the time, the place and the appropriate response for Imad Mughniyeh's assassination.[35]

Information accumulated in the two years following Mughniyeh's assassination sheds light on the system of operational cooperation between Hezbollah and Iran in executing terrorist attacks abroad and on the existence of a Hezbollah operational infrastructure abroad, including in Muslim countries. The movement uses this infrastructure to carry out activities of various types, starting with funding activities through crime, drug trafficking, and weapons smuggling in South America, the United States and West Africa, for example, to operational support activities, like the establishment of terrorist networks and training activities, as conducted in Egypt, Yemen, and Iraq. In addition, the movement invests efforts in recruiting activists to gather intelligence on Israel and/or for the execution of terrorist attacks. The recruitment is done along the border with Israel, on European soil or in other places outside the Middle East.[36] The following information indicates Hezbollah's behavioral pattern in the regional and international theater.

The activity in the Iraqi theater: the past years have revealed how Iran has been involved via the Revolutionary Guards-Al-Quds Force and with Hezbollah in helping local Shiite organizations that oppose the American presence in Iraq. Iran has likewise provided operational knowledge, training, weapons, etc.[37] From the information published on the subject, Hezbollah's 3800/2800 unit operates in this theater.[38]

The aid to the Houthi in Yemen: since 2004, a violent struggle has raged between the Shiite Al-Houthi group in Yemen and the Yemenite government. In March 2009, in an interview with the London *Al-Hayat* newspaper, the Yemeni President Ali Abdullah Salih accused Hezbollah of extensively helping the Houthi rebels in training and in the transfer of information on the assembly of bombs in Yemen and Lebanon.[39] Iran is also accused of providing military and logistical aid to the Houthi, but rejects these accusations.[40]

The establishment of a terrorist infrastructure in Egypt: in April 2009, Security Forces in Egypt exposed a 49-member terrorist network, operating on Egyptian soil on behalf of Lebanese Hezbollah. The network included Lebanese, Syrians, Palestinians, and Sudanese. Its objectives included the training, instruction, execution, and perpetration of terrorist attacks using Palestinians against Israel. The investigation further exposed the network's intention to carry out three terrorist attacks against tourist targets in Egypt: Taba, Nueba, and Dahab, where many Israeli tourists visit. The investigation revealed that Hezbollah operates in Egypt but also in other countries surrounding Israel, including Jordan. During his interrogation, the network's leader said that Muhammad Qablan (head of the Hezbollah 1800 unit) handled him directly from the organization's headquarters in Lebanon. Egypt accused Iran and Hezbollah of attempting to undermine stability in Egypt.[41]

The exposure of Hezbollah's network in Azerbaijan: in 2008, Azerbaijan's government security forces arrested a unit including two Lebanese Hezbollah activists and four Azeris. The unit was connected to the Iranian Revolutionary Guard. It is known that the unit helped prepare for the execution of a terrorist attack at the Israeli embassy in Baku, as well as a Russian radar station. The unit members were also charged with espionage, drug trafficking, and gun smuggling.[42]

The exposure of a Hezbollah unit in Turkey: in September 2009, it was reported that Turkish officials arrested terrorist operatives tied with Hezbollah and Iran, who were planning on executing a terrorist attack against Israeli and American targets in Turkey. According to the information, the network planned on carrying out the attack in retaliation for Imad Mughniyeh's assassination.[43]

Involvement in international crime: Hezbollah was also involved in two cases of weapons smuggling from the United States into Lebanon during 2009. In recent years, the connection between the movement's activists/supporters and the drug cartels in South America has grown stronger. Several drug smuggling networks exposed in past years in the United States, South America, West Africa,

Europe, and Israel shed light on the depth of Hezbollah's involvement in drug trafficking. This involvement enables the movement to increase its income sources while at the same time constitutes a logistical and operational platform for the movement's activities abroad.

Rebuilding Hezbollah's operational and civil infrastructure in the Lebanese arena and maintaining its ongoing activity in the regional and international arena were made possible through the wide range of support and aid the movement received from its Iranian and Syrian patrons. The U.S. Department of State's Country Reports on Terrorism (2008) reveal that during 2008, Hezbollah received financial aid in the scope of 200 million dollars from Iran.[44] This aid apparently does not include Iranian investments in the training of the movement's activists through the Al-Quds Force, the rebuilding of its operational systems and its rearmament with advanced weaponry.

Hezbollah is perceived as an asset in the Syrian-Iranian strategic alliance. As such, the two countries are working at building the movement's status in the Lebanese arena both by arming it with advanced weapons in preparation for a possible conflict with Israel, and by integrating it in discussions for the formulation of a joint policy pertaining to the processes in the regional arena.[45] For example, Nasrallah was invited to Damascus in February 2010 for talks during Ahmadinejad's visit to the Syrian capital, following predictions of a possible outbreak of a regional war. At the end of the discussions, the movement's magazine, *Al-Intikad*, published a statement that a war against Israel is a reasonable possibility.[46]

In conclusion, the manifesto of the Second Unity Government (November 2009) aptly expresses how Hezbollah is coming closer to achieving its goal of taking over the Lebanese political system from within, as a preliminary step to the Islamization of Lebanon in the long run.[47] Iran and Syria's substantial support with weapons and funding—which are helping to turn Hezbollah into a military force and a strong economic player in Lebanon—enabled the movement to leverage this power into political power. In the regional arena, the movement's restrained policy is influenced by the lessons from the Second Lebanon War and by Iran and the movement's interests. The lack of international cooperation in disarming the movement according to the UN Security Council's resolutions, and the lack of enforcement of significant sanctions against the movement's weapon suppliers—Iran and Syria—provide Hezbollah with the freedom of action needed to take over the Lebanese political system.

Notes

Preface

1. Zvi Mazal "Did Lebanon join the axis of evil?" *The Jerusalem Center for Public Affairs,* 10 December 2009, http://www.jcpa.org.il/Templates/showpage.asp?FID=650&DBID=1&LNGID=2&TMID=99&IID=23698

Chapter 1

1. Doug McAdam and David A. Snow, *Social Movements* (Roxbury, 1997), Introduction.
2. J. McCarthy and M. N. Zald, "Resource Mobilization and Social Movements: A Partial Theory," *American Journal of Sociology* 82, no. 6 (May 1977): 1217–18.
3. Ibid.
4. McAdam and Snow, *Social Movements,* Introduction.
5. Ibid., 379.
6. H. Blumer, "Collective Behavior," in *Review of Sociology: Analysis of a Decade,* ed. J. B. Gittler (New York, 1957). See also T. R. Gurr, *Why Men Rebel* (Princeton, NJ: Princeton University Press, 1970); Denton E. Morrison, "Some Notes toward Theory on Relative Deprivation, Social Movements, and Social Change," in *Collective Behavior and Social Movements,* ed. Louis E. Genevie, (Itasca, IL: Peacock, 1978), 202–9.
7. John G. Meshunim, *Sociology* (Tel Aviv: Tel Aviv University Press, 1999), 620–21. W. Komhauser is the researcher most identified with this approach.
8. Ibid., 621–22.
9. Charles Tilly, *From Mobilization to Revolution* (Reading, MA: Addison Wesley, 1978); McCarthy and Zald, "Resource Mobilization and Social Movements." Among the school of management resources, it is worth emphasizing Lewis Killian, "Organization, Rationality and Spontaneity in the Civil Rights Movement," *American Journal of Sociology* 49 (1984): 770–83; and David S. Meyer and Nancy Whittier, "Social Movement Spillover," in *Social Movements,* ed. Doug McAdam and David A. Snow (Roxbury, 1997).
10. Gideon Sjoberg, "The Pre-Industrial City," *American Journal of Sociology* 60, no. 5 (March 1955): 438–45; M. Stein, *The Eclipse of Community* (New York: Harper & Row, 1964).
11. Ibid., 459–60.
12. Theda Skocpol, *Social Revolutions in the Modern World* (Cambridge University Press, 1994).
13. Doug McAdam and David A. Snow, "Conditions of Conduciveness: Political Opportunities," in *Social Movements,* ed. Doug McAdam and David A. Snow (Roxbury, 1997), 34–35.
14. Sidney Tarrow, *Power in Movement—Social Movements and Contentious Politics* (Cambridge University Press, Second Edition, 1998), 73–76.
15. Doug McAdam and David A. Snow, "Conditions of Organization: Facilitative Contexts," in *Social Movements,* ed. Doug McAdam and David A. Snow (Roxbury, 1997), 80.

16. Aldon D. Morris, "Black Southern Student Sit-in Movement: An Analysis of Internal Organization," in *Social Movements*, ed. Doug McAdam and David A. Snow, (Roxbury, 1997), 90.
17. Ibid., 91.
18. Ibid., 97–98, 107–9.
19. Ibid., 107–9.
20. Neil Smelser, *The Theory of Collective Behavior* (New York: Free Press, 1963), 17.
21. Karl Wolfgang Deutsch, "Social Mobilization and Political Development," *American Political Science Review* 55, (September 1961): 493–514.
22. William A. Gamson, *The Strategy of Social Protest* (Illinois: Dorsey Press, 1975), 15.
23. Tilly, *From Mobilization to Revolution*, 7, 69.
24. Gamson, *Strategy of Social Protest*, 14–27.
25. J. N. Urney and Kathleen Tierney, "Relative Deprivation and Social Movements: A Critical Look at Twenty Years of Theory and Research," *Sociological Quarterly* 23 (1982): 36.
26. David A. Snow, Louis A. Zurcher, and Jr. Sheldon Ekland-Olson, "Social Networks and Social Movements: A Micro Structural Approach to Differential Recruitment," in *Social Movements*, ed. Doug McAdam and David A. Snow (Roxbury, 1997), 123–26.
27. Pamela Oliver, "If You Don't Do It, Nobody Else Will, Active and Token Contributors to Local Collective Action," *American Sociology Review* 49 (1984): 604.
28. Snow, Zurcher, and Ekland-Olson, "Social Networks and Social Movements," 149–56.
29. Dirk Oegema and Bert Klandermans, "Why Social Movement Sympathizers Don't Participate: Erosion and Nonconversion of Support," *American Sociological Review* 59 (1994): 703–4.
30. Ibid., 704–5, 718–22.
31. Tarrow, *Power in Movement*, 80–81.
32. T. R. Gurr, *Why Men Rebel*, 238.
33. Jenkins J. Craig and Charles Perrow, "Insurgency of The Powerless Farm Worker Movement (1946–1972)," *American Sociological Review* 42 (1977): 251.
34. Pamela Oliver, "Rewards and Punishments as Selective Incentives for Collective Action: Theoretical Investigations," *American Journal of Sociology* 85, no. 6 (1980).
35. Hanspeter Kriesi, Ruud Koopman, Jan Willen Duyvendak, and Macro G. Giuni, "New Social Movement and Political Opportunities in Western Europe," in *Social Movements*, ed. Doug McAdam and David A. Snow (Roxbury, 1997), 55.
36. Karl-Dieter Opp and Wolfgang Rohel, "Repression, Micromobilization and Political Protest," *Social Forces* 69 (University of North Carolina Press, 1990): 521–47.
37. Doug McAdam and David A. Snow, "Interpretive Factors: Framing Process," in *Social Movements*, ed. Doug McAdam and David A. Snow (Roxbury, 1997), 232, 248–50.
38. Ibid., 238.
39. Ibid., 242.
40. Ibid., 245.
41. Stephen Ellingson, "Understanding the Dialectic of Discourse and Collective Action: Public Debate and Rioting in Antebellum Cincinnati," in *Social Movements*, ed. Doug McAdam and David A. Snow (Roxbury, 1997), 269.
42. Ibid., 277–78.
43. Doug McAdam and David A. Snow, "Movement Careers: Extra Movement Dynamics," in *Social Movements*, ed. Doug McAdam and David A. Snow (Roxbury, 1997), 365.
44. Tarrow, *Power in Movement*, 328–30.
45. Doug McAdam, "Tactical Innovation and the Pace of Insurgency," in *Social Movements*, ed. Doug McAdam and David A. Snow (Roxbury, 1997), 340.
46. William A. Gamson, "The Success of the Unruly," in *Social Movements*, ed. Doug McAdam and David A. Snow (Roxbury, 1997), 361.

47. Doug McAdam, and David A. Snow, "Movement Careers: Extra Movement Dynamics," in *Social Movements,* ed. Doug McAdam and David A. Snow (Roxbury, 1997), 365–66.
48. Ibid., 366.
49. Doug McAdam, "Tactical Innovation," 340–41.
50. Ruud Koopman, "The Dynamics of Protest Waves; West Germany, 1965 to 1989," in Social *Movements,* ed. Doug McAdam and David A. Snow (Roxbury, 1997), 369–70.
51. Ibid., 374–75.
52. Ibid., 374.
53. Ibid., 380–81.
54. Ibid., 379–80.
55. Ibid., 380–81.
56. Christian Smith, "Correcting a Curious Neglect, or Bringing Religion Back In," in *Disruptive Religion: The Force of Faith in Social Movement Activism,* ed. Christian Smith (New York: Routledge, 1996), 5–6.
57. Ibid., 11.
58. Ibid., 11–12.
59. Ibid., 13–17.
60. Ibid., 18.
61. Susan Olzak and Joan Nagel, "Introduction, Competitive Ethnic Relations: An Overview," in *Competitive Ethnic Relations,* ed. Susan Olzak and Joan Nagel (London: Academic Press, 1986), 4.
62. Joan Nagel, "The Political Construction of Ethnicity," in *Competitive Ethnic Relations,* ed. Susan Olzak and Joan Nagel (London: Academic Press, 1986), 94, 97–98. See also Olzak and Nagel, "Introduction, Competitive Ethnic Relations," 7–8.
63. Olzak and Nagel, "Introduction, Competitive Ethnic Relations," 3.
64. A summary of the approaches of Tilly, 1978; Mauss, 1975; and Blurner, 1969 in Meshunim, *Sociology.*
65. Max Weber, *On Charisma and Establishing Institutions* (Jerusalem: Hebrew University, 1980). And also James C. Scott, "Protest and Profanation: Agrarian Revolt and the Little Tradition," Part 1, *Theory and Society* 4, no. 1 (1977): 21–38; James C. Scott, "Protest and Profanation: Agrarian Revolt and the Little Tradition," Part 2, *Theory and Society* 4, no. 2 (1977), 211–45 See also about the existence and development of institutions in Michel Foucault, *Discipline and Punish: The Birth of the Prison* (London: Penguin, 1991).

Chapter 2

1. General Intelligence and Security Service, "From Dawa to Jihad: The Various Threats from Radical Islam to the Democratic Legal Order," http://www.minbzk.nl/contents/pages/42345/fromdawatojihad.pdf (accessed December 2004); Nazih Ayubi, *Political Islam, Religion and Politics in the Arab World* (London: Routledge, 1991), 18–26.
2. Emmanuel Sivan, *The Zealots of Islam* (Tel Aviv: Am Oved, 1986), 122–24; Naim Qassem, *Hezbollah—Al-Manhag Al-Tajriba Al-Mustakbal* (Beirut: Dar Al Hadi, 2002), 44–56; Mustansir Mir, "Jihad in Islam," in *The Jihad and Its Times,* ed. Hadia Dajani-Shakeel and Ronald A. Messier (Ann Arbor: University of Michigan Press, 1991); Richard Bonney, *Jihad: From Qur'an to Bin Laden* (New York: Palgrave Macmillan, 2004), 1–14; Gilles Kepel, *Jihad: The Trail of Political Islam* (Cambridge, MA: Harvard University Press, 2002); and David Cook, *Understanding Jihad* (University of California Press, 2005).
3. Bonney, *Jihad,* 154–55.
4. *Al Shark El Awsat,* 21 December 2001.
5. *Al Shark El Awsat,* 19 July 2003.
6. *Al Quds Alarabi,* 4 April 2003.

7. Shaul Mishal and Avraham Sela, *Time of Hammas, Violence, and Compromise* (Yediot Ahronot and Hemed Books, 1999), 48–52.

8. Samuel Huntington, "The Clash of Civilizations," *Foreign Affairs* (Summer, 1993).

9. This category includes the leaders of the discourse and the philosophy of the Shiite and Sunni radical Islam.

10. The leader of this group is John L. Esposito; John L. Esposito, *Islam and Politics* (New York: Syracuse University Press, 1991); John L. Esposito, *The Islamic Threat: Myth or Reality?* (New York, 1995); John L. Esposito and John O. Voll, *Islam and Democracy* (New York: Oxford University Press, 1996).

11. Some of this group's members are Pipes Daniel, "Political Islam Is a Threat on the West," In *Islam: Opposing Viewpoints,* ed. Poul A. Winter (San Diego, CA: Greenhaven, 1995)., See also Huntington, "The Clash of Civilizations." Prof. Emmanuel Sivan sides with the positions of this group as well.

12. Martin E. Marty, "Comparing Fundamentalisms," *Contention: Debates in Society, Culture, Science* 4, no. 2 (1996): 19–39; Appelby R. Scott, ed., *Spokesmen for the Despised: Fundamentalist Leaders of the Middle East* (Chicago: University of Chicago Press, 1997).

13. Martin E. Marty and Scott Appleby, eds., "Fundamentalisms Observed," *Fundamentalism Project,* vol. 1 (Chicago: University of Chicago Press, 1991); "Fundamentalisms and Society: Reclaiming the Sciences, the Family and Education," *Fundamentalism Project,* vol. 2 (Chicago: University of Chicago Press, 1991); "Fundamentalisms and the State: Remaking Politics, Economics, and Militance," *Fundamentalism Project,* vol. 3 (Chicago: University of Chicago Press, 1991); "Accounting for Fundamentalisms: The Dynamic Character of Movements," *Fundamentalism Project,* vol. 4 (Chicago: University of Chicago Press, 1991); and "Fundamentalisms Comprehended," *Fundamentalism Project,* vol. 5 (Chicago: University of Chicago Press, 1991).

14. Ervand Abrahamian, *Khomenism: Essays on the Islamic Republic* (Berkeley: University of California Press, 1993). See also Fred Haliday, "The Iranian Revolution and Its Implications," *New Left Review* 166 (Nov/Dec, 1987): 29–37. See also Valentine M. Moghadam, *Modernizing Women: Gender and Social Change in the Middle East* (Boulder, CO: Lynne Rienner, 1993). See also Owen Roger, *State, Power and Politics in the Making of the Modern Middle East* (London and New York: Routledge, 1992).

15. Edmund Burk, "Islam and Social Movements: Methodological Reflections," in *Islam, Politics, and Social Movements,* ed. Edmund Burk and Ira M. Lapidus (London, 1988), 18–21.

16. Shaul Shai and Yoram Schweitzer, *Afghan "Alumni": The Globalization of Terror* (International Institute for Counter-Terrorism, Issue 6, September 2000), 2–4.

17. Mishal and Sela, *Time of Hammas,* 22.

18. Francois Burgat, "Ballot Boxes, Militaries and Islamic Movements," in *The Islamism Debate,* ed. Martin Kremer (Tel Aviv University, 1997), 41.

19. Ayubi, *Political Islam,* 70–72.

20. Graham E. Fuller, "Islamism in the Next Century," in *The Islamism Debate,* ed. Martin Kremer (Tel Aviv University: Moshe Dayan Center, 1997), 141–43.

21. Mishal and Sela, *Time of Hammas,* 23–24. Ayubi, *Political Islam,* 70–118.

22. Sivan, *The Zealots of Islam,* 9–14.

23. R. Hrair Dekmeijan, *Islam in Revolution: Fundamentalism in the Arab World* (New York: Syracuse University Press, 1995), 4–5; Ayubi, *Political Islam,* 72–87, 118–19.

24. Dekmeijan, *Islam in Revolution,* 4–8.

25. Sivan, *The Zealots of Islam,* 12–13, 24–26.

26. Ibid., 74–76; Kepel, *Jihad: The Trail of Political Islam,* 23–27.

27. Dekmeijan, *Islam in Revolution,* 25–27; Kepel, *Jihad: The Trail of Political Islam,* 62–65.

28. Dekmeijan, *Islam in Revolution,* 27; Kepel, *Jihad: The Trail of Political Islam,* 27–30.

29. Ayubi, *Political Islam,* 158–64; MEMRI—Middle East Media Research Institute, "Review the Sermon's in Saudi Arabia Mosques (part 3), 22 March 2002, http://www.memri.org.il/cgi-webaxy/sal/sal.pl (accessed 9 May 2002).

30. Meir Hatina, *Islam in Modern Egypt,* Moshe Dayan Center for Middle Eastern and African Studies, (Tel Aviv: Tel Aviv University, Hakibbutz Hameuchad, 2000), 111; Oliver Roy, *The Failure of Political Islam* (Cambridge, MA: Harvard University Press, 1996), 53–56; Ayubi, *Political Islam,* 174–77; Kepel, *Jihad: The Trail of Political Islam,* 65–66.

31. Roy, *The Failure of Political Islam,* 48–53.

32. Ayubi, *Political Islam,* 160–67; Ali E. Hillal Dessouki, *Introduction, Islamic Resurgence in the Arab World* (New York, 1982), 22–25; and Sivan, *The Zealots of Islam,* 23.

33. Dekmeijan, *Islam in Revolution,* 85; Nachman Tal, *A Decade of Fundamentalism: The Egyptian and Jordanian Experience in Coping with Radical Islam* (Tel Aviv: Papirus, 1999).

34. Eyal Zisser, "The Muslim Brotherhood Movement in Syria: Between Acceptance and Struggle," in *Islam and Democracy in the Arab World,* ed. Meir Litvak (Tel Aviv: Tel Aviv University, Dayan Center, Hakibbutz Hameuchad, 1998), 96–120.

35. Esposito and Voll, *Islam and Democracy,* 9–10.

36. Dekmeijan, *Islam in Revolution,* 65, 223–49.

37. Ibid., 68.

38. Sivan, *The Zealots of Islam,* 96–98; Kepel, *Jihad: The Trail of Political Islam,* 84–86.

39. Asher Sesar, "The Muslim Brothers in Jordan: Coexistence and Controlled Conflict," in *Islam and Democracy in the Arab World,* ed. Meir Litvak (Tel Aviv: Tel Aviv University, The Dayan Center, Hakibbutz Hameuchad, 1998), 123–46; Yadlin Rivka, "Can Two Walk Together, Except They Be Agreed: Democracy and Islam in Egypt," in *Islam and Democracy in the Arab World,* ed. Meir Litvak (Tel Aviv: Tel Aviv University, The Dayan Center, Hakibbutz Hameuchad, 1998), 72–95.

40. Mishal and Sela, *Time of Hammas,* 47–54; Roy, *The Failure of Political Islam,* 41–42.

41. Mishal and Sela, *Time of Hammas,* 23–25.

42. Ibid., 25–27. Meir Litvak, ed., *Islam and Democracy in the Arab World,* (Tel Aviv: Tel Aviv University, Dayan Center, Hakibbutz Hameuchad, 1998), 9–10.

43. Rivka, "Can Two Walk Together," 72–95; Hatina, *Islam in Modern Egypt,* 38–42.

44. Roy, *The Failure of Political Islam,* 75–88.

45. Kepel, *Jihad: The Trail of Political Islam,* 3–42.

46. D. MacDonnell, *Theories of Discourse: An Introduction* (Oxford: Blackwell, 1986); Jennifer Milliken, "The Study of Discourse in International Relations: A Critique of Research and Methods," *European Journal of International Relations* 5, no. 2 (1999): 225–54; Stuart Hall, ed., *Representation: Cultural Representations and Signifying Practices* (London: Sage, 1997); M. Foucault, *Discipline and Punish* (Harmondsworth, UK: Penguin, 1984).

47. Ira M. Lapidus, "Islamic Political Movements: Patterns of Historical Change," in *Islam Politics and Social Movements,* ed. Edmund Burk and Ira M. Lapidus (Berkeley: University of California Press, 1985), 7–16.

48. Shapira Shimon, "Shiite Radicalism in Lebanon," (master's thesis, Tel Aviv University, 1987), 6–7, 34–35.

49. Furman Arie, "Individual and Society in the Philosophy of Contemporary Islam Faithful," in *Islam and Democracy in the Arab World,* ed. Meir Litvak (Tel Aviv: Tel Aviv University, The Dayan Center, Hakibbutz Hameuchad, 1998), 65.

50. Bonney, *Jihad: From Qur'an to Bin Laden,* 211–15.

51. Ayubi, *Political Islam*, 130–34. 52. Sivan, *The Zealots of Islam*, 139; Kepel, *Jihad: The Trail of Political Islam*, 43–60.

53. Ayubi, *Political Islam*, 134–45.

54. Kepel, *Jihad: The Trail of Political Islam*, 61–64.

55. Mishal and Sela, *Time of Hammas*, 14–21.

56. Sivan, *The Zealots of Islam*, 92–96; Kepel, *Jihad: The Trail of Political Islam*, 24–42.

57. Ahmed S. Mussalli, "Modern Islamic Fundamentalist Discourses on Civil Society, Pluralism and Democracy," in *Civil Society In the Middle East*, ed. Augustus Richard Norton (Leiden, New York: 1995), 93–94.

58. Amir Tahiri, "*The Spirit of Allah: Khomeini and the Islamic Revolution*," trans. Shamir Ami (Tel Aviv: Am Oved, 1987), 179; Kepel, *Jihad: The Trail of Political Islam*, 36–42; Ayubi, *Political Islam*, 146–47.

59. Ibid., 133–35, 146; Kepel, *Jihad: The Trail of Political Islam*, 106–22.

60. An interview with Naim Qassem, *Al-Diar*, 1 November 1995; Bonney, *Jihad: From Qur'an to Bin Laden*, 293–304. 61. Tahiri, *The Spirit of Allah*, 219–20.

62. Kepel, *Jihad: The Trail of Political Islam*, 118–35.

Chapter 3

1. The "Lebanese National Salvation Front" included the leaders of the strong militias, including the leader of the Phalanges Bashir Gemayel, Sunni prime minister Shafik Wazzan, Amal movement's secretary general Nabih Berri, and other figures.

2. Wadah Sharara, *Dawlat Hizb Allah, Lubnan mujtami'an Islamiyyan* (Beirut, 1998), 118–19; Isan Al-A'zi, *Hezbollah: Min Alhilm Alideology Ila Wakai'a Alsiasia* (Beirut, 1998), 21–23.

3. Ayla Hammond Schbley, "Resurgent Religious Terrorism: A Study of Some of the Lebanese Shi'a Contemporary Terrorism," *Terrorism* 12 (1989): 213–15.

4. Juan R. I. Cole and Nikki R. Keddie, ed., *Shi'ism and Social Protest* (New Haven and London: Yale University Press, 1986), 1–29; Augustus Richard Norton, *Amal and the Shi'a Struggle for the Soul of Lebanon* (Austin, TX: 1987), 15.

5. Norton, *Amal and the Shi'a Struggle*, 72; Juan and Keddie, *Shi'ism and Social Protest*, 1–29

6. Shimon Shapira, "The Shiite Radicalism in Lebanon" (master's thesis, Tel-Aviv university, 1987), 2–4.

7. Fouad Ajami, *The Hidden Imam*, Hebrew version (Tel-Aviv: Am Oved, 1986), 66–69.

8. Helena Cobban, "The Growth of Shi'i Power in Lebanon and Its Implications for the Future," in *Shi'ism and Social Protest*, ed. Juan R. I. Cole and Nikki R. Keddie (New Haven and London: Yale University Press, 1986), 138–43.

9. Ajami, 70.

10. Shapira, "The Shiite Radicalism in Lebanon," 18–19.

11. Joseph Olmert, "The Shi'is and the Lebanese State," in *Shi'ism, Resistance, and Revolution*, ed. Martin Kramer (Boulder, CO: Westview, 1987), 194–200; Ajami, 68–80.

12. Ajami, 81–94, 105–107.

13. Ibid., 29–50; Martin Kramer, *Fadlallah Hezbollah's Compass* (University of Tel Aviv, Moshe Dayan Center, 1997), 12–19.

14. Shimon Shapira, *Hezbollah between Iran and Lebanon*, (Hakibbutz Hameuchad, 2000), 11.

15. Wadah Sharara, *Dawlat Hizb Allah, Lubnan mujtami'an Islamiyyan* (Beirut, 1996), 42, 56–58, 64.

16. Ajami, 110–11, 116–19, 130.
17. Ibid., 145–56.
18. Ibid., 163–68.
19. Salim Nasar, "Roots of the Shi'i Movement," *Merip Reports*15, no.5 (June 1985): 11; Sharara, *Dawlat Hizb Allah, Lubnan mujtami'an Islamiyyan*, 180–89.
20. Norton, *Amal and the Shi'a Struggle for the Soul of Lebanon*, 35–38.
21. Sharara, *Dawlat Hizb Allah, Lubnan mujtami'an Islamiyyan*, 74–79.
22. Norton, *Amal and the Shi'a Struggle for the Soul of Lebanon*, 6–7, 14–17; Ajami, 1986, 218.
23. Ajami, 218–19.
24. Norton, *Amal and the Shi'a Struggle for the Soul of Lebanon*, 29–32.
25. Ibid., 43–44.
26. Ibid., 39–46; Ajami, 202.
27. Ajami, 97, 111–13.
28. Shapira, 8–9.
29. Ibid., 11–12; Norton, *Amal and the Shi'a Struggle,* 77–79.
30. Shapira, 12.
31. Norton, *Amal and the Shi'a Struggle,* 44–45; Shapira: 12.
32. Shapira, 17.
33. Norton, *Amal and the Shi'a Struggle,* 46–48.
34. Ajami, 198–203.
35. Kramer, *Fadlallah Hezbollah's Compass,* 24–25.
36. Augustus Richard Norton, "The Origins and Resurgence of Amal," in *Shi'ism, Resistance, and Revolution,* ed. Martin Kremer (Boulder, CO: Westview, 1987), 203–17.
37. Ibid., 49–52.
38. Ibid., 55–56.
39. Ibid., 56–57; Sharara, 109–11.
40. Ajami, 221–23; Norton, "Origins and Resurgence," 213–14.
41. Shimon Shapira, "The Iranian Policy in Lebanon between the Years 1959–1989" (PhD thesis, Tel Aviv University, 1994), 179–82.
42. Ibid., 60–65.
43. Magnus Ranstrop, *Hizb'allah in Lebanon: The Politics of the Western Hostage Crisis* (London: Macmillan, 1997), 26. Sharara, 108–09.
44. Al Azi, *Hezbollah,* 21–25.
45. Sharara, 13–19; Ranstrop, *Hizb'allah in Lebanon,* 27–28.
46. *Al-Diar,* 6 November 1990.
47. Sharara, 134, 154–55, 162–65; Shapira, "Iranian Policy in Lebanon," 137–39.
48. Shapira, "Iranian Policy in Lebanon," 113–20; Sharara, : 196–97.
49. Ranstrop, *Hizb'allah in Lebanon,* 35–36.
50. Shapira, "Iranian Policy in Lebanon," 120–21. Augustus Richard Norton, "Shi'ism and Social Protest in Lebanon," in *Shi'ism and Social Protest,* ed. Juan. R. I. Cole and Nikki R. Keddie (New Haven and London: Yale University Press, 1986), 172.
51. Al Azi, *Hezbollah,* 21–25; Sharara, 1996: 1–8.
52. *Al-'Ahd,* 19 October 1987. Ranstrop, *Hizb'allah in Lebanon,* 65.
53. Shapira, "Iranian Policy in Lebanon," 132. *El Watan,* 26 October 1984.
54. Kramer, *Fadlallah Hezbolla's Compass,* 32–35.
55. Shapira, "Iranian Policy in Lebanon," 132–34; Sharara, 195–98.
56. Kramer, *Fadlallah Hezbolla's Compass,* 33–34.
57. Ibid., 32–35.   Shapira, "Iranian Policy in Lebanon," 131.
58. Judith Palmer Harik, "The Public and the Social Services of the Lebanese Militias," (Oxford: Center for Lebanese Studies, September 1994), 24.

59. Shapira, "Iranian Policy in Lebanon," 137–39.

60. Al-Azi, *Hezbollah*, 53–63.

61. Clinton Bailey, "Lebanon's Shi'its after the 1982 War," in *Shi'ism, Resistance, and Revolution*, ed. Martin Kramer (Boulder: CO: Westview, 1987), 219–36; Nizar Hamzeh, "Islamism in Lebanon: A Guide," *MERIA Journal*1, no.3 (September 1997).

62. *Al Nahar Al Arabi*, 31 August 1987.

63. Norton, *Amal and the Shi'a Struggle*, 100; *Al-Watan Al-Arabi*, 26 October 1984; *Al Nahar Al Arabi*, 31 August 1987.

64. Judith Palmer Harik, "Between Islam and the System: Sources and Implications of Popular Support for Lebanon's Hizballah," *Journal of Conflict Resolution* 40, no. 1 (March 1996): 50–51.

65. Augustus R. Norton, "Shi'ism and Social Protest," 173; Radio Phalange, 24 March 1986.

66. *Ad-Dustour*, 4 May 1986; *Monday Morning*, 30 March 1987; *Al-Watan Al- Arabi*, 19 October 1987; Al-*Massira*, 19 September, 1987; Al- *Taleea Al Arabia*, 16 March 1987.

67. Shapira, "Iranian Policy in Lebanon," 200–01.

68. *Taleea Al Arabia*, 16 March 1987.

69. *Al-Mustaqbal*, 22 March 1986; *Kayhan*, 19 August 1986; *Al-Khaleej*, 1 March 1987; *Al-Massira*, 19 September 1987; *Al-Nahar Al-Arabi*, 28 April 1987.

70. Ranstrop, *Hizb'allah in Lebanon*, 37–38. Sharara, 455–56; *Al-Khaleej*, 1 March 1987; *Al-Safir*, 25 October 1987; Radio Voice of Islam, 25 February 1987.

71. *Al-Nahar Al-Arabi*, 28 April 1987.

72. AFP, 20 September 1987; *Al-Nahar*, 29 August 1987.

73. *Al-Nahar*, 14 March 1987; *La Revue du Liban*, 31 March 1987; *Al-Ahd*, 21 March 1987.

74. *Al-Taleea Al Arabia*, 16 March 198; *Al-Nahar*, 4 March 1987; Radio Liban Libre, 8 March 1987; Harik, "Public and Social Services," 25; Ranstrop, *Hizb'allah in Lebanon*, 35.

75. Martin Kramer, *The Islamism Debate* (Tel Aviv University, 1997), 36–38; Edgar O'Ballance, *Islamic Fundamentalist Terrorism 1979–95: The Iranian Connection* (New York: University Press, 1997), 64–68; AP, 5 October 1984; *Al-Majallah*, 10 December 1983, *Al-Ahd*, 14 November, 1986.

76. O'Ballance, *Islamic Fundamentalist Terrorism*, 71–72.

77. *Maariv*, 24 February 1984.

78. Norton, *Amal and the Shi'a Struggle*, 112–14.

79. Ibid., 173.

80. Ibid., 106; *Al-Nahar Al-Arabi*, 31 August 1987; *Al-Sharaa*, 16 June 1986.

81. Norton, "Shi'ism and Social Protest," 175–76. Helena Cobban, "Growth of Shi'i Power in Lebanon," 151–52; *Maariv*, 21 January 1985, 17 February 1985, and 14 March 1985; Hamzeh, "Lebanon's Hizbullah: from Islamic Revolution to Parliamentary Accommodation," *Third World Quarterly* 14, no.2 (1993): 322; An interview of Nabih Berri with the Iranian news agency, Dayan Institute files: 11.6.87/843/010.

82. Ranstrop, *Hizb'allah in Lebanon*, 65; Sharara, 344.

83. Hamzeh, "Lebanon's Hizbullah," 323; Hala Jaber, *Hezbolla: Born with a Vengeance* (Columbia University Press, 1997), 29–30.

84. Ranstrop, *Hizb'allah in Lebanon*, 66–67; *Al-Ahd*, 19 October 1987.

85. *Al-Wahhda Al-Islamia*, 4 December 1987.

86. *Al-Ahd*, 2 May 1987; *Al-Nahar*, 13 August 1987; *Al-Wahhda Al-Islamia*, 4 December 1987.

87. AFP, 20 September 1987.

88. *Al-Alem*, 16 May 1987.

89. Ibid.

90. *Al-Ahd*, 19 October 1987.
91. Jaber, *Hezbollah*, 32–34; *Nouveau Magazine*, 5 December 1987; *Al-Sharaa*, 23 November 1987.
92. Radio Phalange, 7 September 1987.
93. Kramer, *Islamic Debate*, 64–66; Ranstrop, *Hizb'allah in Lebanon*, 63; Radio Beirut, 26 January 1987; *Al Majallah*, 20 November 1985; *Al-Nahar al_Arabi*, 1 July 1987; *Al-Mustaqbal*, 22 March 1986 .
94. *Al Qabas*, 31 August 1985; *Al-Nahar*, 7 July 1985.
95. Ranstrop, *Hizb'allah in Lebanon*, 94–96; see also: O'Ballance, *Islamic Fundamentalist Terrorism*, 82–89.
96. *Nouveau Magazine*, 25 July 1987; *Al-Nahar*, 7 July 1985; http://www.washington-report.org/backissues/052785/850527008.html
97. Ranstrop, *Hizb'allah in Lebanon*, 1.
98. Shapira, "Iranian Policy in Lebanon," 197; Kramer, *Islamic Debate*, 64–68; *Monday Morning*, 4 May 1987; *Al-Nahar*, 24 August 1987.
99. AFP, 24 March 1987; *La Revue Du Liban*, 7–14 March 1987; AFP, 1 July 1987. *Kayhan*, 23 May 1987; *Al-Nahar Al-Arabi*, 21 December 1987; *Al-Nahar*, 12 August 1987.
100. Ranstrop, *Hizb'allah in Lebanon*, 35–36; Jaber, *Hezbollah*, 29–33.
101. Harik, "Public and Social Services," 22; *Al-Amal*, 2 October 1987.
102. Kramer, *Islamic Debate*, 26–27, 61; Harik, "Public and Social Services," 25–26.
103. *Al-Ahd*, 17 February 1987.
104. *Al-Ahd*, 1 August 1989; Hamzeh, "Lebanon's Hizbullah," 329; *Al-Amal*, 2 October 1987; Sharara, 343.
105. *Al-Ahd*, 10 October 1987.
106. *Al-Safir*, 4 October 1987; *Al-Haqiqa*, 4 September 1987.
107. *Al-Safir*, 24 September 1987; *Al-Massira*, 19 September 1987; *Al-Nahar Al- Arabi*, 12 October 1987.
108. *Al-Nahar*, 13 October 1987.
109. Sharara, *Dawlat Hizb Allah, Lubnan mujtami'an Islamiyyan*, 203–05, 233–34; AFP, 3 March 1997.
110. Sharara, *Dawlat Hizb Allah, Lubnan mujtami'an Islamiyyan*, 241–46; Jaber, *Hezbolla*, 42.
111. AP, 31 July 1988.

Chapter 4

1. Nizar Hamzeh, "Lebanon's Hizbullah: from Islamic Revolution to Parliamentary Accommodation," *Third World Quarterly* 14, no. 2 (London: April 1993): 321–37. *Al-Safir*, 15 November 1997.
2. Magnus Ranstrop, *Hizb'allah Political and Military Strategy in the 1990s—from Revolutionary Dogma to Lebanonization?* (Oxford: British Middle East Studies Association Conference, 1997). Eyal Zisser, "Hizballah in Lebanon at the Crossroads," in *Religious Radicalism in the Greater Middle East*, ed. Bruce Maddy-Weitzman and Efraim Inbar (Frank Cass, 1997). Augustus Richard Norton, "Hizballah: From Radicalism to Pragmatism," *Middle East Policy* 5, no. 4 (January 1998): 151.
3. AFP, 22 October 1988. *AP*, 12 May 1988. *Al-Sharaa*, 30 May 1988. *Al-Diyar*, 1 June 1988. Phalangists' Radio, 7 June 1988, 18 July 1988. Martin Kramer, "Sacrifice and Fratricide in Shiite Lebanon," in *Violence and the Sacred in the Modern World*, ed. Mark Juergensmeyer (London: Frank Cass, 1992), 30–35.
4. Middle East News Agency, 13 August 1988. AFP, 13 August 1988 and 1 September 1988. Free Voice of Lebanon Radio, 11 September 1988, 29 November 1998. Voice of

the Motherland Radio, 24 October 1998. Voice of Islam Radio, 1 October 1990. Naim Qassem, *Hezbollah—Al-Manhag Al-Tajriba Al-Mustakbal* (2002), 147–50.

5. *Al-Sabah-Al-Hir*, 13 October 1989. *Al-Shark Al-Awsat*, 16 April 1996.
6. *Al-Sabah-Al-Hir*, 13 October 1989. *Al-Shark Al-Awsat*, 16 April 1996.
7. *Al-Sharaa*, 25 April 1988. *Al-Hawdat*, 15 April 1988.
8. Voice of Lebanon Radio, 24 August 1988.
9. *Al-Sharaa*, 25 April 1988. *Al-Hawdat*, 15 April 1988. Phalangists' Radio, 24 May 1988. AFP, 9 September 1988.
10. *Al-Kifah Al-Arabi*, 18 July 1988. Voice of the Nation Radio, 17 June 1988. *Al-'Ahd*, 16 February 1999.
11. *Al-Sharaa*, 25 April 1988. *Al-Hawdat*, 15 April 1988.
12. *Al-Hakika*, 21 May 1988. Beirut Radio, 24 May 1988. Phalangists' Radio, 24 May 1988.
13. Free Voice of Lebanon Radio, 10 October 1988. AFP, 5 May 1988. Voice of Islam Radio, 31 October 1988. AFP, 30 October 1988. AP, 30 October 1988.
14. AFP, 31 July 1988.
15. Monte Carlo Radio, 12 May 1988. Free Voice of Lebanon Radio, 12 May 1988.
16. Free Voice of Lebanon Radio, 12 May 1988. AFP, 7 May 1988. Monte Carlo Radio, 13 May 1988. Voice of the Nation Radio, 22 May 1988.
17. *Al-Tusdur*, 23 May 1988. Phalangists' Radio, 17 August 1988. Free Voice of Lebanon Radio, 17 July 1988.
18. AP, 12 May 1988. Phalangists' Radio, 12 May 1988. Voice of the Motherland Radio, 24 October 1988. Voice of the Nation Radio, 20 December 1988.
19. Beirut Radio, 29 May 1988. AFP, 29 May 1988. *Al-Kifah Al-Arabi*, 18 July 1988.
20. *Al-Anwar*, 3 July 1988.
21. Islamic Republic News Agency (IRNA), 6 June 1988. Kuwaiti News Agency, 16 June 1988. Al-Ahd, 17 June 1988. Al-Diyar, 29 June 1988. *Al-Anwar*, 3 July 1988. *Al-Sharaa*, 12 December 1988. *Al-Kifah Al-Arabi*, 1 August 1988. *Al-Khalij*, 29 June 1988.
22. AFP, 30 October 1988, 9 September 1988, 18 October 1988. Teheran Radio, 22 August 1988.
23. Free Voice of Lebanon Radio, 22 October 1988. Voice of the Nation Radio, 29 November 1988, 21 December 1988. Phalangists' Radio, 29 November 1988. Beirut Radio, 29 November 1988, 21 December 1988.
24. AP, 30 October 1988. AFP, 30 October 1988.
25. *Al-Nahar*, 12 December 1988.
26. Phalangists'Radio, 9 January 1989.
27. Beirut Radio, 3 January 1989. Free Voice of Lebanon Radio, 5 January 1989, 10 January 1989, 13 January 1989. AFP, 4 January 1989, 5 January 1989, 10 January 1989, 13 January 1989. Voice of the Nation Radio, 10 January 1989. Qassem, *Hezbollah*, 150.
28. Phalangists' Radio, 3 January 1989, 4 January 1989, 24 January 1989. AFP, 3 January 1989, 4 January 1989; Kuwaiti News Agency, 24 January 1989. Radio Damascus, 24 January 1989.
29. Kuwaiti News Agency, 30 January 1989. Radio Monte Carlo, 30 January 1989.
30. Phalangists' Radio, 31 January 1989; Voice of the Nation Radio, 13 February 1989, 4 July 1989. Damascus Radio, 15 February 1989; Voice of the Motherland Radio, 15 February 1989. *Al-Hakika*, 4 April 1989. AFP, 16 February 1989, 31 December 1989. Reuters, 5 December 1989, 29 December 1989.
31. *Al-'Ahd*, 16 February 1990. *Al-Nahar*, 6 January 1990; AP, 8 July 1990; *Reuters*, 8 July 1990.
32. Iranian Television, 2 March 1990.
33. *Al-Anwar*, 7 September 1990.

34. *Nouveau Magazine* (Lebanon), 13 October 1990.
35. Phalangists' Radio, 9 September 1990. Voice of Islam Radio, 1 October 1990. Voice of the Nation Radio, 4 October 1990, 30 October 1990, 9 November 1990.
36. *Al-Sharaa,* 8 October 1990. Voice of the Nation Radio, 31 October 1990.
37. *Al-Anwar,* 9 November 1990, 10 November 1990, 14 November 1990. Voice of the Mountain Radio, 5 October 1990. *Al-Balad,* 20 October 1990. Reuters, 13 November 1990. AFP, 27 October 1990.
38. Voice of the Nation Radio, 9 November 1990. *Al-Rai Al-Yawm,* 26 July 1990.
39. Martin Kramer, *Hizbollah Vision of the West* (Washington, D.C.: Washington Institute for Near East Policy, policy paper no. 16, October 1989), 31–40.
40. *Al-Diyar,* 29 June 1988. Reuters, 14 January 1989, 21 January 1989.
41. *Nouveau Magazine* (Lebanon), 27 February 1988. Martin Kramer, ed., *The Islamism Debate* (Tel Aviv University, 1997), 73.
42. Kramer, *The Islamism Debate,* 74. Radio Monte Carlo, 31 May 1988.
43. *Al-Rai Al-Yawm,* 25 May 1988.
44. *Al-Khalij,* 29 June 1988.
45. Phalangists' Radio, 24 January 1989.
46. Voice of the Motherland Radio, 6 January 1990.
47. *Al-Anwar,* 10 November 1990.
48. *Al-Sabah Al-Hir,* 13 October 1989.
49. *Al-Nahar,* 6 January 1990.
50. *Al-'Ahd,* 16 February 1990.
51. *Al-Anwar,* 9 November 1990.
52. Free Voice of Lebanon Radio, 21 May 1988. *Al-Tusdur,* 4 April 1988.
53. *Al-Kifah Al-Arabi,* 18 July 1988.
54. *Al-Kabas,* 7 July 1988. *Al-Khalij,* 29 June 1988.
55. Beirut Radio, 21 December 1988.
56. Teheran Radio, 15 January 1989.
57. *Kul Al-Arab,* 20 March 1989.
58. AFP, July 17 1990. Al-Anwar, 12 September 1990. *Nouveau Magazine* (Lebanon), 13 October 1990. Al-Hayat, 16 February 1991. *Monday Morning* (Beirut), 18 March 1991.
59. *Al-Hayat,* 6 February 1991. Reuters, 19 April 1991. Free Voice of Lebanon Radio, 30 May 1991.
60. *Al-Shark Al-Awsat,* 4 April 1991. AFP, 20 April 1991, 27 October 1990.
61. *Al-Hawdat,* 7 December 1990, *Nouveau Magazine* (Lebanon), 12 January 1991. *Al-Balad,* 6 April 1991. *Reuters,* 20 December 1990. *Al-Sha'ala,* 1 June 1991.
62. *Al-Hayat,* 25 January 1991. *Al-Hawdat,* 7 December 1990. *Nouveau Magazine* (Lebanon), 12 January 1991. *Al-Sha'ala,* 1 June 1991.
63. Voice of the Nation Radio, 1 October 1991.
64. Voice of the Nation Radio, 26 May 1991, 16 July 1991. *Al-Masira,* 27 May 1991. *Al-Safir,* 22 May 1991.
65. *Al-Sha'ala,* 1 June 1991.
66. Voice of the Nation Radio, 26 May 1991. *Al-Sha'ala,* 1 June 1991.
67. *Al-Safir,* 22 May 1991. Radio Nur, 26 May 1991.
68. WTN, 2 June 1991.
69. Voice of the Nation Radio, 26 May 1991, 16 July 1991. *Al-Aalam (World's) Magazine,* Interview of secretary general of Hizbullah, His Eminence Sayyed Abbas al-Musawi, (RIP) Tehran (18 Safar 1412 A.H.), 28 August 1991, www.nasrollah.org/english/indexeng.htm
70. Voice of Islam Radio, 22 December 1991.
71. Voice of the Nation Radio, 27 May 1991.

72. Radio Nur, 6 June 1991. Voice of the Nation Radio, 16 July 1991.
73. Voice of the Mountain Radio, 29 October 1992.
74. Voice of the Nation Radio, 27 May 1991.
75. Voice of the Nation Radio, 27 May 1991, 16 July 1991.
76. Voice of the Nation Radio, 27 May 1991, 16 July 1991.
77. *Sawat Al-Kuwait,* 28 May 1991. Voice of the Nation Radio, 27 May 1991. Voice of Islam Radio, 27 May 1991. Radio Nur, 11 September 1991.
78. *Al-Shark Al-Awsat,* 21 November 1991.
79. *Al-Nahar,* 24 July 1991. Voice of Islam Radio, 23 July 1991, 6 September 1991. Reuters, 29 October 1991.
80. Radio Nur, 6 October 1991.
81. Radio Nur, 6 June 1991. Voice of the Nation Radio, 16 July 1991.
82. Voice of the Nation Radio, 28 February 1992.
83. Voice of the Motherland Radio, 2 October 1991.
84. Wadah Sharara, *Dawlat Hizb Allah, Lubnan mujtami'an Islamiyyan* (Beirut, 1996), 463.
85. AFP, 8 January 1992.
86. *Al-Hayat,* 12 March 1992.
87. Hassan Nasrallah was an activist in the Amal movement who switched to the Hezbollah. During Almosawi's term as secretary general, Nasrallah was responsible for finances and military issues in the Shura Council. Originally a hardliner, he adopted a more pragmatic line after his election as secretary general.
88. *Al-Hayat,* 12 March 1992.
89. Voice of the Nation Radio, 28 March 1992. Radio Nur, 16 February 1995. Carl Anthony Wege, "Hizbollah Organization," *Studies in Conflict and Terrorism* 17, (April–June 1994): 154–56.
90. Voice of the Nation Radio, 28 February 1992. Teheran Radio, 5 March 1992.
91. *Al-Hayat,* March 12 1992.
92. Voice of the Nation Radio, 28 February 1992.
93. IRNA, 4 March 1992. Ranstrop, *Hizb'allah Political and Military Strategy,* 19.
94. *Al-Manbar,* 1 August 1992.
95. *Teheran Times,* 28 February 1992.
96. *Al-Manbar,* 1 August 1992. Ayatollah Al-Sayed Muhammud Hussein Fadlallah, "An Islamic Perspective on the Lebanese Experience," *Middle East Insight* 6, no. 1 (1988): 19.
97. Voice of Islam Radio, 4 March 1992. Voice of the Nation Radio, 28 February 1992.
98. Voice of the Nation Radio, 28 February 1992, *Al-Hayat,* 12 March 1992. *Al-Manbar,* 1 August 1992.
99. Voice of the Nation Radio, 28 February 1992.
100. *Al-Hayat,* 12 March 1992.
101. Voice of the Nation Radio, 28 February 1992.
102. *Al-Hayat,* 12 March 1992.
103. *Al-Hayat,* 12 March 1992. Voice of the Nation Radio, 16 July 1991. AFP, 8 January 1992.
104. Voice of the Nation Radio, 26 May 1992.
105. Voice of the Nation Radio, 27 May 1991. *Al-Hayat,* 12 March 1992.
106. AFP, 8 January 1992. Hamzeh, "Lebanon's Hizbullah," 324.
107. *Al-Safir,* 14 November 1997.
108. Qassem, *Hezbollah,* 267–69.
109. Ibid., 270–73.

110. *Al-Balad,* 8 August 1992. Voice of the Nation Radio, 15 August 1992. Radio Nur, 28 August 1992.

111. *Al-'Ahd,* 7 August 1992. *Al-Anwar,* 10 July 1992. Radio Nur, 13 August 1992, 4 September 1992. Sharara, *Dawlat Hizb Allah, Lubnan mujtami'an Islamiyyan,* 470–71. Hamzeh, "Lebanon's Hizbullah," 330–34.

112. *Sunday Times,* 29 August 1992.

113. Ranstrop, *Hizb'allah Political and Military Strategy,* 12.

114. Judith Palmer Harik, "Between Islam and the System: Sources and Implications of Popular Support for Lebanon's Hizballah," *Journal of Conflict Resolution* 40, no. 1 (March 1996): 41–67.

115. Voice of the Nation Radio, 28 February 1992. IRNA, 4 March 1992. Hamzeh, "Lebanon's Hizbullah," 332. *Al-Safir,* 27 January 1997.

116. *Al-Safir,* 27 January 1997.

117. Radio Nur, 14 August 1992. *Al-Manbar,* 1 August 1992. Qassem, *Hezbollah,* 267–72.

118. Reuters, 21 August 1992.

119. Kramer, *The Islamism Debate,* 86–88.

120. *Al-Hayat,* 12 March 1992. Voice of the Nation Radio, 26 May 1992.

121. *Al-Diyar,* 17 June 1992. Qassem, *Hezbollah,* 272–74. AFP, 8 January 1992. Radio Nur, 28 February 1992.

122. *Al-'Ahd,* 3 August 1992. AFP, 13 September 1992.

123. *Tehran Times,* 29 August 1992.

124. AFP, 8 January 1992.

125. *Al-Balad,* 22 August 1992.

126. *Al-Manbar,* 1 August 1992. Radio Nur, 29 August 1992.

127. *Al-'Ahd,* 7 August 1992.

128. Voice of the Nation Radio, 28 October 1992.

129. *Al-Liwa,* 16 September 1992.

130. Qassem, *Hezbollah,* 269–74. *Al-Diyar,* 17 June 1992. *Al-Manar,* 25 July 1995. *Al-Iman,* 24 November 1995.

131. *Radio Nur,* 14 August 1992.

132. *Al-'Ahd,* 17 July 1992.

133. Reuters, 21 August 1992.

134. Radio Nur, 10 July 1992.

135. *Al-Anwar,* 10 July 1992.

136. *Al-'Ahd,* 3 August 1992.

137. Hassan Nasrallah, *Tehran Times,* 28 September 1992.

138. Radio Nur, 10 July 1992.

139. *Al-Balad,* 22 August 1992.

140. Qassem, *Hezbollah,* 389–98.

141. Radio Nur, 10 July 1992. *Al-Balad,* 8 August 1992. *Al-'Ahd,* 3 August 1992, 7 August 1992. *Al-Manbar,* 1 August 1992.

142. Radio Nur, 10 July 1992, 20 July 1992, 4 September 1992. *Al-Balad,* 8 August 1992.

143. Radio Nur, 10 July 1992.

144. Ibid.

145. Radio Nur, 28 August 1992, 4 September 1992. Beirut Radio, 4 September 1992. Harik, "Between Islam and the System," 45–51.

146. *Al-Sharaa,* 24 October 1992. Qassem, *Hezbollah,* 273–75. For comparative data on Lebanese election results from 1992 to 1996, see http://libanvote.com/lebanese9296/sect/Chiitesnext.html

Chapter 5

1. Mid-East News Service, 18 June 1996; 2 September 1996; 18 September 1996; *Nidaa Al-Watan,* 5 June 1997.
2. *Al-Sharaa,* 24 October 1994; *Al-Hiyat,* 10 February 1995; *Al-Aman,* 26 May 1995; 24 November 1995.
3. *Al-Safir,* 27 November 1995.
4. Naim Qassem, *Hezbollah—Al-Manhag Al-Tajriba Al-Mustakbal* (Beirut: Dar Al Hadi, 2002), 81–87; *Nidaa Al-Watan,* 7 July 1997.
5. *Al-Safir,* 28 January 1997.
6. LBC, 16 April 1996; *Al-Balad,* 20 February 1995.
7. *Al-Safir,* 27 January 1997; *Nidaa Al-Watan,* 19 January 1997; LBC, 5 March 1997; *Al-Ousbou' Al-Arabi,* 30 March 1997.
8. *Nidaa Al-Watan,* 19 January 1997.
9. *Al-liwaa,* 23 January 1997.
10. *Al-Safir,* 24 May 1993.
11. *Al-Diyar,* 29 June 1993, 13 July 1995; *Al-Balad,* 22 October 1994.
12. *Al-Hawadeth,* 19 October 1994.
13. *Al-Nahar,* 25 May 1995; *Al-Bayrak,* 23 May 1995; Mid-East News Service, 22 May 1995.
14. *Al-Talaat,* 29 November 1995.
15. *Al-Safir,* 8 May 1993; *Nidaa Al-Watan,* 7 July 1995; *Al-Sharaa,* 16 May 1995.
16. *Al-Hawadeth,* 1 May 1996; *Al-Hiyat,* 3 June 1993; *Al-Shu'la,* 1 June 1993; *Al-Diyar,* 29 June 1993.
17. *Al-Talaat,* 24 august 1993; Radio Nur, 26 June 1996; *Al-Diyar,* 28 June 1993.
18. Radio Nur, 16 February 1995; *Nidaa Al-Watan,* 7 July 1995.
19. *Al-Talaat,* 29 November 1995.
20. *Al-Balad,* 22 October 1994; *Al-Ousbou' Al-Arabi,* 31 March 1997.
21. *Al-Diyar,* 22 March 1993; CNN, 31 July 1993; Mid-East News Service, 13 May 1996, 16 May 1996.
22. Mid-East News Service, 13 October 1994; *Al-Balad,* 20 February 1995; Radio Voice of the People, 15 April 1995; Radio Beirut, 20 June 1995, 24 June 1995; *Al-Ahd,* 21 April 1995; Radio Nur, 10 December 1995.
23. *Al-Hawadeth,* 1 May 1993; *Al-Safir,* 24 May 1993; *Nidaa Al-Watan,* 10 September 1993; *Al-Sharq al-Awsat,* 28 December 1995.
24. *Al-Shu'la,* 11 June 1993; *Alawsat,* 2 May 1994; *Le Mond,* 21 February 1995; *Al-Musawwar,* 12 March 1999.
25. *Magazine,* 15 July 1994.
26. *Al-Diyar,* 29 June 1993; *Al-Balad,* 22 October 1994; LBC, 24 September 1995.
27. *Al-Balad,* 22 October 1994.
28. *Al-Nahar,* 3 July 1995. This is also the research approach of Amal Saad-Ghorayeb in her book *Hizbullah Politics and Religion* (London: Pluto, 2002). *Almassira,* 23 October 1995.
29. *Al-Safir,* 23 August 1997.
30. LBC, 5 March 1997; *Al-Safir,* 4 December 1995.
31. *Al-Manar,* 22 February 1994; Radio Free Lebanon, 12 January 1995; *Al-Ahd,* 16 July 1995; *Nidaa Al-Watan,* 7 July 1995.
32. *Al-Balad,* 22 October 1994; *Al-Manar,* 17 February 1996; Radio Nur, 17 April 1995.
33. Kuna (Kuwait News Agency), 6 March 1994; *Al-Safir,* 11 October 1994; *Al-Ahd,* 21 April 1995; Radio Nur, 18 July 1995; *Al-Manar,* 25 July 1995.
34. *Al-Balad,* 22 October 1994; *Al-Hiyat,* 15 April 1995; Radio Free Lebanon, 22 May 1995; *Al-Manar,* 25 July 1995.

35. *Al-Manar,* 25 July 1995; *Al-Safir,* 10 June 1996; *Al-Mashhad al-Siyasi,* 30 March 1997; *Al-Nahar,* 10 September 1998.
36. Radio Nur, 22 January 1995, 28 July 1995; Reuters, 22 January 1995; *Al-Manar,* 11 July 1996; Qassem, *Hezbollah,* 202–9.
37. *Al-Safir,* 22 July 1996; Mid-East News Service, 22 July 1996; *Al-Nahar,* 17 July 1996; Radio Nur, 21 July 1996, 22 July 1996, 23 July 1996, 30 July 1996; *Al-Sharaa,* 27 September 1996.
38. *Al-Talaat,* 24 August 1993.
39. The IDF operations "Accountability" and "Grapes of Wrath" were meant to create internal pressure within Lebanon and the Shiite community, bringing about the disarming of Hezbollah or the restraining of it. During the operations, heavy damages in property and lives were caused to the inhabitants of the south, who were forced to abandon their homes.
40. *Al-Diyar,* 26 June 1995; *Al-Ahd,* 20 October 1995.
41. *Al-Talaat,* 24 August 1993; *Al-Nahar,* 28 March 1994; *Al-Manar,* 5 May 1996.
42. LBC, 24 September 1995.
43. *Al-Nahar,* 3 July 1995.
44. *Al-Nahar,* 3 July 1995; METV, 14 March 1996; *Al-Manar,* 30 April 1996.
45. Radio Phalange, 28 October 1995; *Al-Balad,* 18 February 1995; Radio Voice of Islam, 4 July 1995; *Al-Aman,* 11 March 1994; *Al-Manar,* 2 February 1995.
46. METV, 24 August 1994; Qassem, *Hezbollah,* 158.
47. Mid-East News Service, 24 October 1994; *Al-Manar,* 24 October 1994.
48. Radio Nur, 16 February 1995, 28 July 1995.
49. *Al-Manar,* 26 February 1995.
50. *Al-Manar,* 5 April 1995.
51. Radio Nur, 26 March 1995; Radio Teheran, 18 June 1995.
52. Mid-East News Service, 3 April 1995; *Nidaa Al-Watan,* 4 May 1995; Radio Teheran, 7 April 1995; LBC, 5 May 1995; Radio Voice of Islam, 31 May 1995, 23 June 1995; *Al-Manar,* 1 June 1995; AFP, 23 June 1995; Radio Nur, 23 June 1995, 24 June 1995, 9 July 1995, 28 November 1995.
53. *Al-Nahar,* 3 July 1995.
54. *Al-Manar,* 20 July 1995; Radio Nur, 28 July 1995.
55. *Al-Ahd,* 25 October 1995.
56. Radio Nur, 21 March 1996.
57. Radio Nur, 30 March 1996.
58. Radio Nur, 9 April 1996.
59. Radio Nur, 28 July 1995.
60. AFP, 22 October 1995.
61. *Al-Manar,* 26 April 1996; Radio Nur, 30 December 1995.
62. *Al-Manar,* 30 April 1996; Radio Voice of Islam, 12 April 1996.
63. Operation "Grapes of Wrath" occurred in April 1996. Toward its end, an Israeli shell struck a center of civilian population in the Lebanese village of Qanaa, causing the death of dozens of civilians. The incident overclouded the achievements of the entire operation and caused international pressure upon Israel to end it immediately.
64. The Qanaa incident was exploited to serve as the propaganda of the movement and to portray Israel's aggression. *Al-Manar,* 15 April 1997, 30 April 1996; Mid-East News Service, 18 May 1996.
65. Radio Nur, 27 April 1996, 28 April 1996; *Al-Safir,* 1 May 1995; *Al-Manar,* 26 April 1996, 9 May 1996.
66. Radio Phalange, 25 May 1995; *Al-Safir,* 1 May 1996; AFP, 26 April 1996. Radio Nur, 26 April 1996.

67. *Al-Manar,* 5 May 1996; *Al-Safir,* 1 May 1996, 13 May 1996; *Al-Diyar,* 21 May 1996; Radio Voice of Islam, 28 May 1996; Radio Nur, 19 May 1996; Radio Voice of the People, 13 June 1996.
68. Radio Nur, 6 September 1996.
69. AFP, 4 July 1996; Radio Nur, 12 October 1996, 16 October 1996, 20 October 1996, 22 October 1996, 8 December 1996; Radio Damascus, 9 December 1996.
70. *Al-Diyar,* 11 December 1997; LBC, 5 March 1997; Radio Nur, 25 February 1997.
71. Radio Nur, 6 September 1996; *Financial Times,* 13 August 1996; *Al-Manar,* 19 February 1997.
72. *Al-Safir,* 13 May 1996, 14 October 1996; *Al-Sharq al-Awsat,* 8 November 1996.
73. Radio Voice of Islam, 14 December 1996; Radio Teheran, 16 December 1996; LBC, 5 March 1997; *Al-Alam,* 19 April 1997.
74. *Al-Safir,* 27 January 1997.
75. Radio Nur, 28 September 1997.
76. *Al-Safir,* 27 January 1997, 13 July 1997; Radio Nur, 21 February 1997, 11 April 1997; Radio Free Lebanon, 26 February 1997; Mid-East News Service, 13 July 1997; *Al-Nahar,* 20 August 1997.
77. *Al-Sharq al-Awsat,* 21 August 1997; Mid-East News Service, 25 August 1997; *Al-Diyar,* 14 September 1997; *Al-Manar,* 15 January 1998.
78. *Al-Manar,* 29 August 1997; Radio Nur, 21 August 1997.
79. *Alawsat,* 22 December 1997; Radio Al-Shark, 5 December 1997.
80. METV, 14 March 1996; *Nidaa Al-Watan,* 28 March 1995.
81. *Al-Talaat,* 24 August 1993; *Al-Ahd,* 22 October 1993; *Al-Aqsadi,* 1 September 1993; AFP, 7 November 1993; NTV, 14 March 1996; Radio Nur, 16 April 1996; *Al-Manar,* 27 April 1997.
82. Radio Nur, 28 July 1995.
83. AFP, 8 March 1994.
84. *Al-Sharaa,* 15 August 1994; *Al-Manar,* 17 April 1995.
85. *Al-Sharaa,* 24 October 1994; *Al-Safir,* 16 November 1994; AFP, 22 October 1995; Radio Nur, 31 January 1996.
86. Iranian Television, 14 October 1997; *Al-Ahd,* 9 November 1994, 20 January 1995. Radio Nur, 10 January 1996; *Al-Balad,* 22 February 1997.
87. AFP, 14 January 1995; *Le Mond,* 21 February 1995.
88. *Al-Shaab,* 28 April 1998; Radio Nur, 3 February 1996, 11 November 1997. *Al-Musawwar,* 12 March 1999; *Le Figaro,* 9 March 1998.
89. *Al-Sharaa,* 3 November 1995, 18 December 1995; *Guardian,* 1 August 1994; *Al-Diyar,* 16 April 1995; *Al-Sharq al-Awsat,* 30 May 1995; *Al-Watan Al-Arabi,* 22 September 1995; *Al-Hiyat,* 13 June 1995; *Al-Safir,* 27 November 1995.
90. *Al-liwaa,* 19 February 1997; *Al-Safir,* 27 January 1997; *Alawsat,* 22 December 1997.
91. *Al-Nahar,* 29 September 1997.
92. *Al-Safir,* 27 January 1997.
93. Radio Voice of the People, 18 June 1996.
94. Radio Nur, 3 November 1997.
95. *Al-Hiyat,* 13 July 1995; Mid-East News Service, 1 November 1994; *Al-Nahar,* 19 June 1995; *Al-Ousbou' Al-Arabi,* 26 June 1995.
96. *Al-Nahar,* 3 July 1995; AP, 3 August 1995.
97. *Almassira,* 6 May 1996; *Al-Hiyat,* 22 January 1996.
98. *Al-Safir,* 12 December 1995; *Al-Balad,* 16 December 1995; *Al-Sharaa,* 18 December 1995, 17 June 1996; *Al-Manar,* 5 May 1996.
99. *Al-Hiyat,* 28 August 1995; *Al-Anwar,* 2 November 1995; *Al-Safir,* 27 November 1995; *Al-Sharaa,* 18 November 1995; *Al-Manar,* 30 August 1997; *Al-Diyar,* 6 August 1998.

100. *Al-Hiyat*, 13 June 1995; *Al-Sharq al-Awsat*, 16 April 1996.
101. *Al-Safir*, 27 November 1995; *Al-Sharq al-Awsat*, 28 December 1995; *Al-Sharaa*, 11 March 1996; *Al-Nahar*, 24 November 1995; Radio Nur, 17 November 1995.
102. Radio Phalange, 28 October 1995; *Al-Safir*, 27 November 1995; NTV, 14 March 1996; *Al-Manar*, 17 February 1996.
103. *Al-Aman*, 24 November 1995.
104. *Al-Sharq al-Awsat*, 25 September 2003.
105. METV, 16 December 1997; *Al-Diyar*, 14 September 1997.
106. *Al-Sharaa*, 29 March 1998.
107. *Al-Sabil*, 30 May 1995; *Al-Nahar*, 9 November 1994; *Al-Watan Al-Arabi*, 17 February 1995; Radio Voice of Islam, 29 May 1995; *Al-Sharaa*, 5 June 1995; *Al-Safir*, 10 June 1996.
108. *International Herald Tribune*, 4 July 1995; *Monday Morning*, 15 May 1995.
109. *Al-Balad*, 22 October 1994; *Alawsat*, 11 March 1996; *Al-Diyar*, 27 November 1994; *Le Mond*, 21 February 1995.
110. *Al-Manar*, 5 May 1996; Mid-East News Service, 3 May 1996; *Al-Diyar*, 20 December 1996; *Al-liwaa*, 23 January 1997.
111. *Al-Safir*, 8 June 1995; *Al-Nahar*, 1 June 1995; *Al-Manar*, 9 May 1996.
112. *Al-Safir*, 8 June 1995; *Al-Sharaa*, 10 July 1995; *Al-Bayrak*, 17 May 1998.
113. Radio Nur, 11 November 1995, 6 September 1996; *Al-Manar*, 7 January 1995, 20 February 1995; AFP, 12 February 1995, 24 February 1995.
114. *Al-Ahd*, 13 February 1996; *Al-Diyar*, 6 July 1995; AFP, 18 February 1997.
115. *Al-Diyar*, 16 1995.
116. *Nidaa Al-Watan*, 6 March 1995, 13 March 1995; Kuna (Kuwait News Agency), 12 March 1995; Radio Beirut, 14 March 1995; AP, 14 March 1995; AFP, 15 March 1995; METV, 14 March 1995; *Al-Hiyat*, 13 June 1995; *Al-Sharaa*, 15 April 1996.
117. Radio Nur, 18 April 1997; LBC, 18 April 1997; *Al-Mashhad al-Siyasi*, 24 March 1997.
118. *Magazine*, 23 June 1995; *Al-Watan Al-Arabi*, 11 August 1995.
119. NTV, 14 March 1996; *Al-Musawwar*, 26 March 1996.
120. *Al-Manar*, 25 July 1995; *Al-Sharaa*, 30 March 1998.
121. *Al-Watan Al-Arabi*, 7 July 1995; *Nidaa Al-Watan*, 17 July 1995; *Al-Nahar*, 3 July 1995; *Al-Anwar*, 8 July 1995; *Al-Hiyat*, 23 June 1995.
122. *Al-Nahar*, 3 July 1995.
123. *Alawsat*, 22 December 1997.
124. *Al-Hiyat*, 13 June 1995; *Al-Ahd*, 9 June 1995; *Al-Ousbou' Al-Arabi*, 26 June 1995; *Al-Nahar*, 20 February 1996.
125. *Al-Sharaa*, 18 December 1995.
126. Radio Voice of Islam, 1 November 1995; *Al-Safir*, 27 November 1995; *Al-Nahar*, 15 November 1995.
127. *Al-Sharaa*, 14 August 1995; *Almassira*, 23 October 1995; *Al-Hiyat*, 28 August 1995; *Al-Diyar*, 6 September 1995; *Al-Bayrak*, 31 October 1995; *Al-Safir*, 27 November 1995, 4 December 1995, 12 December 1995, 10 June 1996; AFP, 25 August 1996.
128. *Al-Diyar*, 16 December 1995; *Al-Sharaa*, 18 December 1995, 15 April 1996.
129. Radio Nur, 6 May 1996, 4 July 1996; AFP, 25 August 1996; *Al-Safir*, 27 January 1997.
130. *Al-Safir*, 18 June 1996.
131. Radio Nur, 1 June 1996; Mid-East News Service, 28 June 1996.
132. *Al-liwaa*, 30 July 1996; AFP, 19 September 1996; *Al-Diyar*, 11 June 1996; Radio Nur, 13 August 1996, 28 August 1996, 6 September 1996.
133. Radio Nur, 6 September 1996; *Al-Manar*, 19 August 1996; Mid-East News Service, 21 August 1996, 2 September 1996.
134. Mid-East News Service, 28 August 1996, 3 September 1996, 4 September 1996, 8 September 1996; Radio Beirut, 28 August 1996; *Al-Sharq al-Awsat*, 18 March 1997.

135. Mid-East News Service, 6 September 1996, 10 September 1996, 18 September 1996. *Al-Safir,* 27 January 1997.

136. Olive Roy, *The Failure of Political Islam* (Cambridge, MA: Harvard University Press, 1996), 75–88.

137. *Al-Sharq al-Awsat,* 18 March 1997, 17 November 1997; *Al-Diyar,* 12 June 1995; Radio Nur, 22 April 1997; *Al-Kifah al-Arabi,* 24 November 1997; *Al-Alam,* 21 February 1998.

138. Radio Nur, 28 July 1995, 22 April 1997; *Al-Sharq al-Awsat,* 9 November 1997.

139. *Al-Balad,* 5 April 1997.

140. *Al-Safir,* 5 January 1998; *Al-Nahar,* 24 April 1998; Radio Voice of the People, 15 July 1997; *Al-Sharq al-Awsat,* 13 May 1998; Radio Phalange, 17 May 1998; *Al-Watan Al-Arabi,* 17 July 1998; *Nidaa Al-Watan,* 4 May 1998; Radio Free Lebanon, 3 June 1998.

141. *Al-Bayrak,* 30 April 1998; *Nidaa Al-Watan,* 4 May 1998; Radio Nur, 22 May 1998; *Al-Nahar,* 8 December 1998; *Al-Sharaa,* 8 June 1998.

142. *Al-Nahar,* 22 October 1998; *Al-Balad,* 30 May 1998; *Al-Ahd,* 29 May 1998; Radio Nur, 20 June 1998; *Al-Sharq al-Awsat,* 21 August 1998.

143. *Al-Balad,* 6 April 1991.

144. *Al-Sharaa,* 14 August 1995; *Al-Nahar,* 17 February 1996.

145. AFP, 13 September 1992.

146. *Al-Aman,* 20 October 1995; *Al-Safir,* 27 November 1995.

147. Radio Nur, 6 September 1996; *Al-Safir,* 18 June 1996.

148. METV, 24 August 1992; Radio Nur, 3 June 1996; *Al-Safir,* 10 June 1996.

149. *Al-Manar,* 25 July 1995; *Al-Safir,* 10 June 1996.

150. *Al-Safir,* 30 April 1996.

151. *Al-liwaa,* 19 February 1997.

152. Radio Voice of the People, 15 July 1998; *Al-Musawwar,* 12 March 1999.

153. *Al-Safir,* 15 November 1997.

154. *Al-Siyassa Al-Dawliya,* 6 February 1995; *Al-Nahar,* 22 April 1995, 25 May 1995; Radio Phalange, 4 May 1996.

155. *Al-Sharq al-Awsat,* 1 March 1998.

156. *Magazine,* 23 June 1995.

157. *Al-Ousbou' Al-Arabi,* 26 June 1995.

158. *Almassira,* 23 October 1995; *Al-Hiyat,* 6 May 1996; Radio Nur, 7 February 1997; METV, 5 March 1997; AFP, 13 February 1997; *Al-Hakeka,* 5 June 1987; *Al-Ahd,* 5 September 1987; *Nouveau Magazine,* 1 February 1987.

159. AP, 16 October 1997; Radio Nur, 26 October 1997; *Al-Watan Al-Arabi,* 17 October 1997; *Al-Sharq al-Awsat,* 12 October 1997.

160. *Al-Safir,* 4 December 1995; *Radio Nur,* 22 April 1996.

161. *Al-Sharaa,* 13 October 1997; Radio Voice of the People, 15 July 1998; Reuters, 13 May 1988; Radio Free Lebanon, 12 May 1988.

162. *Al-Safir,* 9 January 1997.

163. *Al-Safir,* 18 June 1996; *Alawsat,* 22 December 1997.

164. *Al-Hiyat,* 1 April 1997; *Al-Ahd,* 4 April 1997. "An Open Letter," *Jerusalem Quarterly* 48 (Fall 1988): 111–16; Radio Nur, 1 April 1997, 14 April 1997; *Al-Kifah al-Arabi,* 17 April 1997.

165. *Al-Kifah al-Arabi,* 17 August 1997; *Al-Safir,* 19 August 1997; *Al-Diyar,* 19 August 1997; *Al-Mmanr,* 30 August 1997.

166. *Al-Manar,* 21 September 1997; *Al-Safir,* 22 September 1997.

167. *Al-Balad,* September 1997; Radio Nur, 29 September 1997; *Al-Nahar,* 29 September 1997; Iranian Television, 14 October 1997; *Al-Hiyat,* 16 October 1997; *Al-Safir,*

18 October 1997; *Al-Sharaa*, 3 November 1997; METV, 16 December 1997; *Al-Sharq al-Awsat*, 12 December 1997.

168. *Al-Ahd*, 21 December 1997.

169. *Al-Ahd*, 21 November 1997.

170. Radio Nur, 3 November 1997, 26 November 1997, 22 December 1998; *Al-Safir*, 5 November 1997; *Al-Balad*, 22 November 1997; METV, 16 December 1997; Qassem, *Hezbollah*, 177–79.

171. *Al-Sharaa*, 28 July 1994; *Nidaa Al-Watan*, 5 June 1997; Qassem, *Hezbollah*, 179–81.

172. *Alawsat*, 29 May 1995; *Al-Safir*, 8 May 1993; *Al-Sharaa*, 16 May 1995; *Al-Mashhad al-Siyasi*, 30 March 1997.

173. *Al-Hiyat*, 28 July 1995.

174. *Al-Hiyat*, 23 June 1995; Radio Nur, 8 June 1995; AP, 5 August 1995.

175. *Al-Hiyat*, 23 June 1995; *Al-Aman*, 20 October 1995; *Al-Diyar*, 3 February 1997.

176. *Al-Watan Al-Arabi*, 13 September 1996; *Al-Diyar*, 3 February 1997.

177. *Kuna (Kuwait News Agency)*, 4 July 1997; *Al-Sharaa*, 28 July 1997; *Al-Nahar*, 21 July 1997; Radio Phalange, 26 July 1997; *Al-Safir*, 16 July 1997, 11 August 1997; *Al-Diyar*, 14 June 1997, 24 July 1997.

178. Radio Phalange, 26 July 1996, *Al-Nahar*, 21 July 1997, 11 November 1997; *Nidaa Al-Watan*, 5 June 1997.

179. AP, 4 July 1997; AFP, 4 July 1997; *Al-Safir*, 10 July 1997; Radio Nur, 10 July 1997; *Al-Ahram*, 26 July 1997; *Al-Kifah al-Arabi*, 11 August 1997; *Magazine*, 8 August 1997.

180. *Al-Hiyat*, 6 July 1997, 11 November 1997; *Al-Nahar*, 5 July 1997, 21 July 1997; *Al-Diyar*, 12 July 1997; Radio Monte Carlo, 7 August 1997; *Al-Safir*, 13 August 1997; *Beirut Times*, 1 October 1997; *Al-Bayrak*, 15 November 1997; *Al-Sharq al-Awsat*, 16 December 1997.

181. *Nidaa Al-Watan*, 22 December 1997.

182. AFP, 25 January 1998; Kuna (Kuwait News Agency), 25 January 1998; Radio Free Lebanon, 25 January 1998; Radio Phalange, 26 January 1998; *Al-Sharq al-Awsat*, 25 September 2003.

183. *Al-Sharq al-Awsat*, 8 February 1998; METV, 5 February 1998; *Independent*, 5 February 1998; *Al-Watan Al-Arabi*, 17 July 1998; *Al-Sharq al-Awsat*, 21 August 1998.

184. Gary C. Gambill and Ziad K. Abdelnour, "Hezbollah: Between Tehran and Damascus," *Middle East Intelligence Bulletin* 4, no. 2 (February 2002). http://www.meib.org/articles/0202_l1.htm; *Al-Watan Al-Arabi*, 3 December 1999; *Al-Sharq al-Awsat*, 25 September 2003; *Al-Nahar*, 1 July 2000.

185. *Al-Sharaa*, 14 July 1997, 28 July 1997, 11 August 1997, 13 October 1997; *Nidaa Al-Watan*, 4 July 1997, 11 August 1997; *Al-liwaa*, 25 November 1997; *Al-Mmanr*, 30 August 1997; *Al-Diyar*, 14 September 1997; METV, 16 December 1997.

186. *Al-Watan Al-Arabi*, 17 July 1998.

187. *Al-Mmanr*, 30 August 1997.

188. Magnus Ranstrop, *Hizb'allah in Lebanon: The Politics of the Western Hostage Crisis* (Oxford: British Middle East Studies Association Conference, 1997), 24; Eyal Zisser, "Hizballah in Lebanon at the Crossroads," *Terrorism and Political Violence* 8, no.2, (London: Summer 1996): 104–8.

Chapter 6

1. *Al-Nahar al-Arabi Wa al-Duwali*, 1 July 1985.

2. *Al-Hawadeth*, 4 October 1987.

3. Hassan Krayem, "The Lebanese Civil War and the Taif Agreement," http://almashriq.hiof.no/ddc/projects/pspa/conflict-resolution.html

4. Barak Oren, *The Lebanese State and its Institutions : From Disintegration to Reconstruction, the Army as a Case Study,* Hebrew version (Jerusalem University, 2000), 309–12.

5. Fouad Ajami, *The Hidden Imam,* Hebrew version (Tel-Aviv: Am Oved, 1986), 141–45; Augustus Richard Norton, *Amal and the Shi'a Struggle for the Soul of Lebanon* (Austin, 1987), 46–48.

6. Naba'a is an Armenian quarter on the outskirts of Beirut, in which Shiite immigrants from southern Lebanon had been settling ever since the 1940s along with Palestinian refugees. The Christians laid a siege on the quarter in order to eliminate the Palestinian presence there. The Shiites found themselves between the devil and the deep sea, being forcefully involved in the war of others. An agreement between Mussa Sadr and the Christians permitted the expulsion of the Shiites from the quarter. Kramer, *The Islamism Debate,* 24–25; Ajami, *The Hidden Imam,* 198–99. Norton, *Amal and the Shi'a Struggle,* 207. Augustus R. Norton, "Political Violence and Shi'a Factionalism in Lebanon" *Middle East Insight* 3, no. 2 (1983): 18. Shimon Shapira, *Imam Musa Alsadr, the Generator of the Shiite Movement in Lebanon* (Tel Aviv University, 1986), 20–22. Shimon Shapira, "The Iranian Policy in Lebanon between 1959–1989, Hebrew version (PhD thesis, Tel Aviv University, 1994), 179–82. *Al-Nahar al-Arabi Wa al-Duwali,* 1 July 1985.

7. Martin Kramer, ed., *The Islamism Debate* (Tel Aviv University, 1997), 31–33. Yosef Ulmert, "The Shiites in Lebanon: From Marginal Sect to Major Factor," in *Revolution and Protest in the Shiite Islam,* ed. Martin Kramer (Tel Aviv University, 1985), 126–29. *Monday Morning,* 27 April 1981. Omri Amir, "The Rise of a Secular Leader in the Shiite Sect in Lebanon: The Way of Nabih Berri between the Years 1978–1992" (master's thesis, Tel-Aviv University, October 1995), 48–50.

8. Wadah Sharara, *Dawlat Hizb Allah, Lubnan mujtami'an Islamiyyan* (Beirut, 1996), 342.

9. Ulmert, "The Shiites in Lebanon," 132–34. Barak, 2000: 283–88.

10. *Kul al-Arab,* political file, 23 May 1984, http://www.lp.gov.lb/Presidency/nouwab.htm. M Daniel Nassif, "Nabih Berri Lebanease Parliament Speaker," *Middle East Intelligence Bulletin* 2, no. 1, (December 2000).

11. Shimon Shapira, "The Iranian Policy in Lebanon between the Years 1959–1989" (PhD thesis, Tel Aviv University, 1994), 135–38.

12. Magnus Ranstrop, *Hizb'allah in Lebanon: The Politics of the Western Hostage Crisis* (London: Macmillan, 1997), 34–36. Naim Qassem, *Hezbollah—Al-Manhag Al-Tajriba Al-Mustakbal* (Beirut: Dar Al Hadi, 2002), 133–37. *Al-Safir,* 10 June 1996. Sharara, *Dawlat Hizb Allah,* 343.

13. Shapira, "The Iranian Policy in Lebanon," 140–42.

14. *Al-Balad,* 22 October 1994.

15. *Al-Amal,* 11 May 1984, 20 May 1984. Radio Phalange, 27 June, 1984. Voice of Free Lebanon Radio, 6 August 1984.

16. *Al-Nahar al-Arabi Wa al-Duwali,* 1 July 1985. *Al-Qabas,* 31 August 1985. Radio Phalange, 8 July 1987.

17. *Al-Amal,* 11 May 1984, 20 May 1984. Radio Phalange, 27 June 1984. Voice of Free Lebanon Radio, 6 August 1984.

18. *Al-Qabas,* 31 August 1985. *Kayhan,* 19 August 1986.

19. *Al-Mustaqbal,* 22 March 1986.

20. *Nouveau Magazine,* 27 February 1988.

21. *Al-Mustaqbal,* 22 March 1986. Radio Monte-Carlo, 13 May 1988.

22. *Al-Nahar al-Arabi Wa al-Duwali,* 1 July 1985. *La Revue du Liban,* 14 March 1987.

23. *Al-Sharaa,* 30 May 1988.

24. *Kayhan,* 19 August 1986.
25. Voice of Free Lebanon Radio, 24 July 1987. *Nouveau Magazine,* 25 July 1987. *Al-Ahd,* 5 September 1987.
26. *Al-Ahd,* 30 August 1987. *Al-Anwar,* 11 July 1988.
27. *Saba'a AlKair,* 13 October 1989.
28. *Al-Khaleej,* 1 March 1987. *Al-Nahar,* 24 August 1987. *Al-Nahar al-Arabi Wa al-Duwali,* 30 August 1987. *Al-Ittihad,* 9 March 1987. *Al-Nahar,* 30 January 1988. *Al-Mustaqbal,* 22 March 1986.
29. *Al-Ahd,* 24 February 1989.
30. *Al-Ahd,* 5 September 1987. *Al-Qabas,* 23 July 1986.
31. *Al-Nahar al-Arabi Wa al-Duwali,* 14 October 1985. 24 August 1987. *Al Taleea al Arabia,* 13 January 1986. *Al-Bayrak,* 16 October 1986. *Al-Ittihad,* 6 April 1986.
32. *Al-Nahar,* 24 February 1987. Voice of the Resistance Radio, 9 March 1987. Radio Phalange, 9 March 1987. AFP, 8 March 1987. Radio Damascus, 1 June 1988.
33. Radio Nur, 4 November 1989.
34. William W. Harris, "Lebanon," in *Middle East Contemporary Survey,* vol. 12, ed. Haim Shaked and Ami Ayalon (Boulder, CO: Westview, 1988), 630–31. *Al-Sharaa,* 20 July 1987. *Al-Nahar al-Arabi Wa al-Duwali,* 24 July 1987. *Al-Ittihad,* 10 March 1987.
35. *Al-Ousbou' Al-Arabi,* 17 November 1986. *Nouveau Magazine,* 10 February 1987. *Al-Nahar,* 31 March 1987. *Al-Safir,* 16 April 1986.
36. *Al-Ahd,* 30 August 1987. See also *Al-Nahar al-Arabi Wa al-Duwali,* December 1987. Qassem, *Hezbollah,* 113.
37. *Al-Qabas,* 23 July 1986. *Nouveau Magazine,* 10 February 1987. *Al-Ahd,* 30 August, 1987. *Al-Nahar,* 3 January 1988.
38. *La Revue du Liban,* 14 March 1987.
39. AP, 15 February 1987. AFP, 8 March 1997. *Kayhan,* 28 May 1987. *Al-Safir,* 14 May 1987. *Al-Majallah,* 15 July 1987. *Nahar al-Arabi Wa al-Duwali,* 11 August 1987. *Al-Ahd,* 30 August 1987. *Al-Dustour,* 30 November 1987. *Al-Nahar,* 30 January 1988.
40. William W. Harris, "Lebanon," in *Middle East Contemporary Survey,* vol. 13, ed. Haim Shaked and Ami Ayalon (Boulder, CO: Westview, 1991), 524.
41. Augustus Richard Norton, "Lebanon after Tawif: Is the Civil War Over?" *Middle East Journal* 45, no. 3 (Summer 1991): 456–73.
42. Ibid., 467–69. Reuters, 21 December 1990.
43. Reuters, 19 April 1991. AP, 29 April 1991. Al-Nahar, 18 May 2003.
44. William B. Harris, "Lebanon," in *Middle East Contemporary Survey,* vol. 16, ed. Ami Ayalon (Boulder, CO: Westview, 1996).
45. Qassem, *Hezbollah,* 267–73.
46. *Al-Diyar,* 30 March 1991. *Al-Shu'la,* 1 June 1991. Qassem, *Hezbollah,* 152–54.
47. *Al-Balad,* 6 April 1991. Qassem, *Hezbollah,* 152–53. *Al-Safir,* 22 May 1991. Radio Nur, 26 May 1991. *Al-Shu'la,* 1 June 1991. *Al-Hayat,* 12 March 1992.
48. Voice of the Mountain Radio, 29 October 1992. Voice of the People Radio, 16 July 1991.
49. *Al-Balad,* 20 October 1990. AFP, 7 October 1990. *Al-Sharaa,* 8 July 1991. *Al-Diyar,* 30 March 1991. Voice of the People Radio, 27 May 1991. Radio Nur, 6 June 1991. *Al-Balad,* 6 April 1991. Reuters, 18 April, 1991. Qassem, *Hezbollah,* 155–56.
50. *Al-Nahar,* 8 October 1992.
51. Barak, 2000: 396. *Nidaa Al-Watan,* 10 March 1993.
52. *Nidaa Al-Watan,* 1 October 1993.
53. Voice of the People Radio, 28 February 1992.
54. *Nidaa Al-Watan,* 22 June 1993. *Al-Safir,* 11 June 1993.

55. Voice of the People Radio, 20 September 1993. Voice of Islam Radio, 20 September 1993. Radio Monte Carlo, 13 September 1993. Radio Nur, 18 September 1993. *Al-Wasat,* 11 October 1993. Qassem, *Hezbollah,* 163–65.

56. *Al-Shark al-Awsat,* 7 October 1993. Voice of Islam Radio, 16 September 1993. Voice of the People Radio, 16 September 1993. Radio Mont Liban, 20 September 1993. Radio Nur, 24 October 1993.

57. *Al-Nahar,* 29 September 1993, Radio Nur, 24 October 1993, 9 November 1993.

58. Radio Nur, 19 December 1993, 28 July, 1995. *Al-Wasat,* 11 October 1993, 2 May 1994.

59. *Al-Safir,* 24 February 1994. Mid-East News Service, 1 April 1993, 3 September 1996. *Al-Hayat,* 16 March 1994. AFP, 22 July 1995. *Al-Balad,* 29 July 1995. *Al-Wasat,* 11 March 1996. *Al-Manar,* 3 September 1996.

60. *Al-Safir,* 26 March 1994. Iranian Television, 30 March 1994. *Al-Wasat,* 2 May 1994. LBC, 17 September 1996.

61. LBC, 20 March 1996. *Al-Sharaa,* 11 March 1996.

62. Qassem, *Hezbollah,* 279–84.

63. *Al-Balad,* 27 July 1994. *Al-Shark al-Awsat,* 28 December 1995.

64. *Al-Safir,* 11 October 1994. *Al-Hawadeth,* 19 October 1994. *Al-Sharaa,* 31 October 1994.

65. *Al-Balad,* 22 October 1994. *Al-Diyar,* 24 November 1994.

66. Radio Free Lebanon, 22 May 1995. *Al-Ousbou' Al-Arabi,* 28 May 1995. Mid-East News Service, 22 May 1995. 25 May 1995. *Al-Anwar,* 30 May 1995.

67. *Al-Nahar,* 25 May 1995.

68. *Al-Ahd,* 9 June 1995. Radio Nur, 31 May 1995, 6 June 1995. Voice of the People Radio, 18 June 1995.

69. *Al-Majallah,* 11 June 1995. *Al-Ousbou' Al-Arabi,* 26 June 1995.

70. *Al-Nahar,* 17 May 1995. *Al-Safir,* 18 May 1995. *Al-Diyar,* 13 July 1995. Radio Nur, 28 July 1995. *Al-Shark al-Awsat,* 28 December 1995. AFP, 27 October 1995. *Al-Manar,* 25 July 1995. *Al-Sharaa,* 15 April 1996. *Al-Wasat,* 15 March 1996.

71. *Al-Manar,* 28 September 1995. *Al-Safir,* 30 September 1995. *Al-Watan Al-Arabi,* 29 September 1995. *Al-Balad,* 21 October 1995. *Al-Massira,* 23 October 1995. *Al-Hayat,* 21 October 1995. *Al-Anwar,* 2 November 1995.

72. *Al-Aman,* 24 November 1995.

73. *Al-Sharaa,* 15 April 1996. LBC, 16 December 1997.

74. *Al-Diyar,* 23 October 1996, 9 November 1996, 20 December 1996. *Nidaa Al-Watan,* 26 October 1996. *Al-Shark al-Awsat,* 14 October 1996.

75. *Al-Balad,* 30 November 1996. *Al-Shark al-Awsat,* 18 March 1997.

76. *Al-Diyar,* 14 September 1997.

77. *Nidaa Al-Watan,* 4 August 1998. *Al-Nahar,* 11 November 1998. Radio Nur, 28 November 1998, 1 December, 1998. *Al-Ahd,* 4 December 1998. *Al-Manar,* 6 December 1998. Qassem, *Hezbollah,* 279–84.

78. *Daily Star,* 12 December 1998. Radio Nur, 15 December 1998, 21 December 1998. LBC, 14 December 1998. *Al-Hayat,* 19 December 1998. Radio Phalange, 15 December 1998.

79. *Al-Mustaqbal,* 12 August 1999.

80. *Al-Diyar,* 23 October 1998. *Al-Nahar,* 22 October 1998. *Al-Sharaa,* 23 November 1998.

81. AFP, 24 October 1997. LBC, 23 July 1996. *Al-Shark al-Awsat,* 8 February 1998.

82. Gary C. Gambill and Ziad K. Abdelnour, "Hezbollah: between Tehran and Damascus," *Middle East Intelligence Bulletin* 4, no. 2 (February 2002), http://www.meib.org/articles/0202_l1.htm. *Al-Watan Al-Arabi,* 3 December 1999.

83. *Al-Diyar,* 5 December 1992.

84. Voice of the People Radio, 28 September 1993.
85. *Al-Safir,* 9 December 1992. *Al-Hawadeth,* 1 May 1993.
86. *Al-Balad,* 23 October 1994. *Al-Diyar,* 24 November 1994.
87. *Al-Siyassa Al-Dawliya,* 6 February 1995.
88. *Al-Hayat,* 1 April 1997. *Al-Ahd,* 4 April 1997. Qassem, *Hezbollah,* 114.
89. *Al-Manar,* 21 September 1997. Qassem, *Hezbollah,* 174, 176.
90. *Al-Shu'la,* 1 June 1991. Radio Nur, 6 June 1991. WTN Television, 2 June 1991. Radio Nur, 17 February 1993.
91. Radio Nur, 6 June 1991.
92. Voice of the Mountain Radio, 1 October 1991. Voice of Islam Radio, 11 November 1992.
93. Radio Nur, 6 June 1991. *Al-Kifah al-Arabi,* 18 January 1993.
94. Radio Nur, 28 August 1992. Voice of the People Radio, 28 October 1992. *Rose al-Yousef Magazine,* 2 November 1992.
95. *Al-Nahar,* 15 September 1992. *Al-Ahd,* 7 August 1992. *Al-Sharq,* 9 November 1992.
96. *Al-Manar,* 25 July 1995.
97. *Al-Hayat,* 12 March 1992. *Tehran Times,* 29 August 1992. *Al-Nahar,* 29 January 1992.
98. *Al-Nahar,* 29 January 1992. Voice of the Mountain Radio, 28 October 1992.
99. LBC, 20 February 1992. BBC Radio, 4 June 1992. AFP, 22 February 1992, 26 May 1992.
100. *Al-Hayat,* 24 May 1992. Mid-East News Service, 7 June 1992. Radio Free Lebanon, 11 November 1992. *Al-Sharq,* 9 November 1992.
101. Voice of Arab Lebanon Radio, 11 November 1992. Voice of Free Lebanon Radio, 11 November 1992. Voice of the Mountain Radio, 12 November 1992.
102. Voice of the Homeland Radio, 12 November 1992. Voice of Islam Radio, 19 November 1992. Mid-East News Service, 14 November 1992. Radio Nur, 11 November 1992. AP, 14 November 1992.
103. *Al-Hayat,* 15 November 1992.
104. *Al-Hayat,* 15 November 1992. *Al-Diyar,* 16 November 1992.
105. LBC, 28 November 1992.
106. AFP, 26 May 1992.
107. Radio Phalange, 27 December 1992.
108. *Al-Sharq,* 9 November 1992.
109. *Al-Shark al-Awsat,* 14 October 1993. *Nidaa Al-Watan,* 1 October 1995.
110. *Al-Hayat,* 28 October 1994. *Al-Diyar,* 28 October 1994. *Al-Sharaa,* 31 October 1994. *Al-Hayat,* 4 October 1994. *Al-Balad,* 18 February 1995. *Nidaa Al-Watan,* 19 June 1995.
111. *Al-Hayat,* 5 January 1994. *Al-Wasat,* 6 October 1994. AFP, 8 December 1994. *Al-Diyar,* 20 February 1994. Radio Nur, 1 December 1994, *Nidaa Al-Watan,* 17 July 1995. *Al-Wasat,* 27 February 1995.
112. Radio Phalange, 28 October 1995. *Almassira,* 23 October 1995. Voice of Islam Radio, 1 November 1995. *Al-Safir,* 27 November 1995. AFP, 30 January 1997.
113. *Al-Balad,* 8 November 1997. Radio Nur, 11 November 1997. Radio Nur, 15 February 1998.
114. Jordanian Television, 23 September 1997. *Al-Watan al-Arabi,* 22 May 1998.
115. CNN, 31 July 1993; *Al-Diyar,* 22 March 1993. BBC Radio, 24 April 1993. *Al-Safir,* 8 May 1993.
116. Mid-East News Service, 30 July 1993.
117. Radio Nur, 31 July 1993. AFP, 1 August 1993. *Al-Hayat,* 31 July 1993.
118. Etalaat, 10 September 1993. Radio Monte Carlo, 1 August 1993. *Al-Manar,* 22 February 1994. *Al-Aman,* 11 March 1994. Barak, 2000: p. 396. *Al-Nahar,* 18 February 1994. *Al-Safir,* 26 February 1994. *Al-Siyassa Al-Dawliya,* 2 March 1994.
119. Etalaat, 10 September 1993.

120. Ibid. *Al-Aman,* 11 March 1994. Radio Nur, 12 March 1994. Radio Monte Carlo, 1 August 1993.
121. Etalaat, 10 November 1993. *Al-Nahar,* 18 February 1994. AFP, 8 March 1994. Mid-East News Service, 5 April 1994. Voice of Free Lebanon Radio, 9 March 1994. *Al-Aman,* 11 March 1994. Radio Nur, 14 December 1994.
122. Radio Monte Carlo, 3 June 1994. AFP, 3 June 1994. Mid-East News Service, 5 June 1994. *Al-Nahar,* 9 June 1994. *Monday Morning,* 6 June 1994. Radio Nur, 3 August 1994. Radio Nur, 9 June 1994. *Al-Sharaa,* 15 August 1994.
123. *Al-Ahd,* 12 August 1994. Voice of the People Radio, 9 August 1994.
124. *Filastin al-Muslima,* 1 October 1994. Radio Nur, 20 February 1995.
125. AFP, 2 July 1995. *Al-Diyar,* 26 June 1995. *Al-Bayrak,* 1 December 1995. *Al-Balad,* 31 December 1995. *Al-Wasat,* 11 March 1996.
126. *Nidaa Al-Watan,* 7 July 1995. *Al-Hayat,* 12 July 1995.
127. Mid-East News Service, 23 June 1996. *Al-Shark al-Awsat,* 22 March 1996.
128. LBC, 20 March 1996. Mid-East News Service, 6 March 1996. Beirut Radio, 6 March 1996. Radio Nur, 28 March 1996.
129. LBC, 14 April 1996. Voice of Islam Radio, 5 April 1996. *Al-Nahar,* 16 April 1996.
130. CNN, 19 April 1996.
131. BBC, 19 April 1996.
132. *Al-Safir,* 31 May 1996. *Nidaa Al-Watan,*17 June 1996.
133. *Al-Safir,* 31 May 1996, 27 January 1997. *Nidaa Al-Watan,* 17 June 1996, 17 January 1997. *Al-Manar,* 5 May 1996. Mid-East News Service, 28 May 1996, 29 May 1996. Radio Phalange, 25 May 1996. LBC, 28 May 1996. Radio Nur, 30 May 1996, 6 September 1996, 13 September 1996. Qassem, *Hezbollah,* 287–88.
134. *Al-Safir,* 30 April 1996. Radio Phalange, 4 May 1996, 25 May 1996.
135. LBC, 14 April 1996. CNN, 27 April 1996. Radio Phalange, 25 April 1996. *Al-Hayat,* 22 April 1996.
136. Beirut Radio, 30 April 1996.
137. Radio Phalange, 25 May 1996. *Independent, 7* May 1996. Voice of Islam Radio, 28 May 1996. *Al-Shark al-Awsat,* 27 May 1996. Voice of the People Radio, 13 June 1996. *Al-Manar,* 5 May 1996, 11 June 1996. Radio Nur, 19 May 1996.
138. Radio Tehran, 10 May 1996. Irna, 10 May 1996. LBC, 22 May 1996. AFP, 23 May 1996.
139. Mid-East News Service, 28 May 1996. Al-Manar, 6 June 1996.
140. Voice of Free Lebanon Radio, 18 October 1996, 19 October 1996. Radio Nur, 20 October 1996, 14 December 1996. *Al-Safir,* 14 October 1996; 10 December 1996. *Al-Shark al-Awsat,* 8 November 1996. AFP, 13 December 1996, 14 December 1996. *Al-Diyar,* 20 December 1996.
141. Radio Nur, 29 August 1996. LBC, 13 November 1996, 21 December 1996. *Al-Balad,* 16 November 1996. *Al-Nahar,* 1 January 1997.
142. *Al-Diyar,* 25 April 1997. *Al-Manar,* 30 August 1997.
143. Radio Nur, 10 November 1996. *Al-Ahd,* 18 October 1996. *Al-Balad,* 19 October 1996.
144. *Al-Liawaa,* 23 January 1997. *Al-Diyar,* 25 April 1997.
145. Radio Nur, 29 August 1996, 16 February 1997. Mid-East News Service, 15 December 1996.
146. Radio Nur, 25 February 1997. *Nidaa Al-Watan,* 17 January 1997. *Al-Balad,* Lebanon, 5 April 1997.
147. Radio Nur, 24 July 1997.
148. Radio Nur, April 25 1997, 29 April 1997, 30 April 1997, 8 July 1997. *Daily Star,* 17 July 1997. Iranian Television, 7 August 1997. Radio Al-Sharq, 25 April 1997.
149. *Al-Balad,* 26 July 1997. BBC, 8 August 1997. *Al-Safir,* 29 April 1997. *Al-Diyar,* 14 September 1997.

150. *Al-Shark al-Awsat,* 20 August 1997. *Al-Nahar,* 20 August 1997.
151. Radio Nur, 8 August 1997, 11 August 1997. *Al-Safir,* 13 August 1997. *Al-Diyar,* 16 August 1997.
152. Al-Jazeera TV, 24 February 1999.
153. LBC, 24 February 1999.
154. *Al-Massar,* 15 March 1999. AFP, 15 March 1999.
155. *Al-Mustaqbal,* 12 August 1999.
156. Alalam, 21 February 1998.
157. An article, written by the head editor of the *Al-Nahar* newspaper, Gebran Tueni, on 29 May 2003.

Chapter 7

1. Avraham Sela, *The Decline of the Arab-Israeli Conflict* (State University of New York Press, 1998), 9–15.
2. Asa'd Abu khalil, "Syria and the Shiites: Al-Asad's Policy in Lebanon," *Third World Quarterly* 12, no. 2 (April 1990); Shimon Shapira, *Hezbollah between Iran and Lebanon* (Hakibbutz Hameuchad, 2000), 9–10, 51–52; Magnus Ranstrop, *Hizb'allah in Lebanon: The Politics of the Western Hostage Crisis,* (London: Macmillan, 1997), 111.
3. Shapira, *Hezbollah between Iran and Lebanon,* 53–76; Augustus Richard Norton, *Amal and the Shi'a Struggle for the Soul of Lebanon* (Austin, 1987), 53, 56–58.
4. Reuben Avi-Ran, "Syria and the Christian Camp in Lebanon 1975–1978 from Cooperation to Violent Confrontation," (Shiloach Institute for the Study of the Middle-East and Africa: Tel-Aviv University, May 1980); Sela, *Decline of the Arab-Israeli Conflict,* 179–83; Maoz Moshe, *Israel Syria the End of the Conflict?* Hebrew version (Maariv Library, 1996), 146–48, 159.
5. AbuKhalil, "Syria and the Shiites," 1–20.
6. Wadah Sharara, *Dawlat Hizb Allah, Lubnan mujtami'an Islamiyyan* (Beirut, 1996), 108–09; Ranstrop, *Hizb'allah in Lebanon,* 25–26; Shapira, *Hezbollah between Iran and Lebanon,* 77.
7. Shapira, *Hezbollah between Iran and Lebanon,* 79–86.
8. Ibid., 86–88; Isan Al-Azi, *Hezbollah :Min Alhilm Alideology Ila Wakai'a Alsiasia* (Beirut, 1998) 13–19; David Menshari, *A Decade of War and Revolution* (Tel Aviv: Kibbutz Me'uhad, 1988), 216–21; Magnus Ranstrop, *Hizb'allah in Lebanon: The Politics of the Western Hostage Crisis* (London: Macmillan, 1997) 34, 114.
9. Edgar O'Ballance, *Islamic Fundamentalist Terrorism 1979–95: The Iranian Connection* (New York: New York University Press, 1997), 41–42; Hala Jaber, *Hezbollah: Born with a Vengeance* (Columbia University Press, 1997), 107–12; Sharara, 253–54; Patrick Seale, *Asad: The Struggle for the Middle East* (Berkely, CA / Los Angeles, 1988), 394–95; Ranstrop, *Hizb'allah in Lebanon,* 34, 114.
10. Sharara, 337; *Stern,* 4 August 1988.
11. Norton, *Amal and the Shi'a Struggle,* 43–44, 46, 49–52, 66–67, 85–86.
12. Sela, *Decline of the Arab-Israeli Conflict,* 252–54.
13. Uri Sagi, *Lights in the Mist* (Yediot Aharonot, 1998), 97–98; Ayre Naor, *Government in a War: The Israel's Government Functioning during the Lebanon War* (1982), Lahav, 1986. (Hebrew version), 29–42, 50–52.
14. Baily Clinton, "Lebanon Shi'is after the 1982 War," in *Shi'sm Resistance and Revolution,* ed. Martin Kramer (Boulder, CO: Westview, 1987), 230.
15. Sela, *Decline of the Arab-Israeli Conflict,* 252–54.

16. Eyal Zisser, *Asad's Syria at a Crossroads* (Tel Aviv: Hkibutz Hameuad, 1999), 152. Ayre Naor, *Government in a War,* 150–64; Maoz, *Israel Syria the End of the Conflict?* 157–61.

17. Maoz, *Israel Syria the End of the Conflict?* 166–68.

18. Ranstrop, *Hizb'allah in Lebanon,* 34–35; Shapira, Hezbollah between Iran and Lebanon, 106–07.

19. Ibid., 33; AbuKhalil, "Syria and the Shiites," 14; Jaber, *Hezbollah: Born with a Vengeance,* 47–49; *Al-Nahar al-Arabi Wa al-Duwali,* 21 December 1987.

20. *Al-Ahd,* 4 April 1987, 19 October 1987; *Al-Hakikah,* 4 September 1987.

21. *Alawsat,* 25 October 1993.

22. Shaul Shay, *Terror in the Name of the Imam: Twenty Years of Shiite' Terror,* Hebrew version (Mifalot, IDC, Herzelia, 2001), 72–74; O'Ballance, *Islamic Fundamentalist Terrorism,* 77–78; *Ma'ariv,* 23 October 1983.

23. Ranstrop, *Hizb'allah in Lebanon,* 53. AbuKhalil, "Syria and the Shiites," 13–15.

24. AP, 11 March 1996; *Al-Ousbou' Al-Arabi,* 30 March 1997.

25. Haim Shaked and Daniel Dishon, ed., *Middle East Contemporary Survey* 8 (1983–1984), 546–54; Baily, 225–27.

26. Ibid., 564; Ranstrop, *Hizb'allah in Lebanon,* 66–67.

27. Jehudit Barsky, "The Struggle Is Now Worldwide: Hizballah and Iranian-Sponsored Terrorism," (Anti-Defamation League [ADL], 1995), 35–39; *Al-Qabas,* 31 July 1985; Ranstrop, *Hizb'allah in Lebanon,* 68–71, 91–93; Shay, 141–44; *Al-Khaleej,* 27 July 1987.

28. *Al-Amal,* 20 May 1984.

29. Norton, *Amal and the Shi'a Struggle,* 101; Radio Phalange, 20 May 1984, 10 June 1984, 27 June 1984, 23 August 1984, 2 September 1984, 8 September 1984, 18 September 1984; *Al-Amal,* 20 May 1984; Voice of Lebanon Radio, 6 August 1984, 6 September 1984.

30. *Al-Majallah,* 20 November 1985; Jaber, *Hezbollah: Born with a Vengeance,* 105; AP, 1 July 1985. *Al-Nahar,* 7 July 1985; *Al-Ousbou' Al-Arabi,* 16 December 1985.

31. *Al Taleea al Arabia,* 20 May 1985, 13 January 1986; Voice of the Homeland Radio, 3 October 1985; *Al-Qabas,* 23 July 1986; *Al-Dustor,* 10 March 1986, 1 September 1986; *Almassira,* 30 August 1986; Radio Phalange, 24 March 1986; *Alittihad,* 4 April 1986; *Le Point,* 8 April 1986; AFP, 1 May 1986; *Al-Safir,* 16 April 1986; *Al-Bayrak,* 16 October 1986; *Al-Watan al-Arabi,* 30 May 1986, 3 July 1986.

32. *Al-Dustor,* 1 September 1986; *Almassira,* 30 August 1986; Voice of Lebanon Radio, 9 September 1986; *Al-Anwar,* 15 September 1986; AFP, 6 November 1986, 28 October 1986.

33. *Kayhan,* 19 August 1986, 18 May 1987; Voice of Free Lebanon Radio, 1 August 1986; *Al-Ousbou' Al-Arabi,* 11 August 1986.

34. Yehudit Barsky, "The Struggle is Now Worldwide: Hizballah and Iranian- Sponsored Terrorism"(*Anti-Defamation League* [ADL], 1995), 41–42; AFP, 23 January 1987.

35. *Al-Watan al-Arabi,* 12 March 1986; *Al-Qabas,* 23 July 1986.

36. *Nouveau Magazine,* 15 November 1986; *Kayhan,* 28 May 1987; *Al-Majallah,* 15 July 1987. Naim Qassem, *Hezbollah–Al-Manhag Al-Tajriba Al-Mustakbal* (Beirut: Dar Al Hadi, 2002), 156.

37. Voice of Islam Radio, 25 February 1987; *Al-Nahar,* 26 February 1987; Irna, 27 February 1987; *Alittihad,* 28 February 1987; Radio Tehran, 2 March 1987; *Al-Bayan,* 3 April 1987; *Kayhan,* 28 May 1987; *Al-Majallah,* 15 July 1987.

38. *La Revue du Liban,* 14 March 1987; *Alittihad,* 10 March 1987; *Al-Ahd,* 9 September 1987; *Al-Nahar,* 31 July 1987; Radio Tehran, 4 April 1987.

39. *Al-Ahd,* 17 February 1987; *Al-Nahar,* 13 October 1987; *Al-Safir,* 4 October 1987; *Al-Dustor,* 4 April 1988; *Al-Nahar al-Arabi Wa al-Duwali,* 23 December 1987; *Sunday Times,* 6 August 1989.

40. *Al-Safir*, 30 June 1987; AFP, 21 June 1987, 29 June 1987, 1 July 1987; *Al-Nahar*, 24 June 1987; *Al-Qabas*, 29 June 1987, 16 July 1987; Voice of Free Lebanon Radio, 13 July 1987; *Al-Bayrak*, 3 July 1987; Barsky, 1995, 41; *Al-Sharaa*, 29 June 1987, 18 August 1987; Radio Monte Carlo, 19 August 1987; Radio Damascus, 18 August 1987.

41. *Al-Sharaa*, 9 March 1987, 13 April 1987; AFP, 1 July 1987.

42. Voice of the Homeland Radio, 10 March 1987; *Alyom Alsabaa*, 9 March 1987; *Al-Nahar*, 9 March 1987; *Al-Watan al-Arabi*, 22 March 1987.

43. Voice of Free Lebanon Radio, 2 April 1987, 4 April 1987; *Nouveau Magazine*, 12 August 1987.

44. AFP, 28 January 1988, 15 May 1988, 3 August 1988; *Stern*, 4 August 1988; *Al-Watan al-Arabi*, 12 Febraury 1988; AP, 23 May 1988; Radio Phalange, 27 May 1988. Voice of Islam Radio, 27 May 1988; *Alittihad*, 29 July 1988.

45. *Al-Khaleej*, 29 June 1988; AFP, 24 January 1989, 13 August 1988; Beirut Radio, 16 May 1988; Radio Damascus, January 25 1989; Voice of Islam Radio, 1 October 1990; Voice of the People Radio, 4 October 1990.

46. AP, 12 May 1988; *Alittihad*, 29 May 1988.

47. Radio Phalange, 15 May 1988; AFP, 27 May 1988, 9 January 1989, 13 January 1989, 24 January 1989, 30 January 1989, 13 March 1989; Irna, 6 June 1988; *Al-Ahd*, 17 June 1988; *Al-Kifah al-Arabi*, 18 July 1988; Radio Tehran, 23 January 1989; Radio Damascus, 25 January 1989; Reuters, 8 July 1989.

48. Shapira, *Hezbollah between Iran and Lebanon*, 182.

49. Nahman Shay, "Security 50," Alfa Communication Ma'ariv, 1998, September–July 1982; Mordechai Naor, *The Book of the Century: The Photographed History of the Land of Israel in the Twentieth Century* (Am Oved: Ministry of Defense, 1996), 444, 448, 450, 456.

50. Shaked and Dishon, *Middle East Contemporary Survey*, 545.

51. Norton, *Amal and the Shi'a Struggle*, 107–13; Baily, 231–32.

52. Ibid., 113–14, 118.

53. Ibid., 118; Qassem, *Hezbollah*, 65.

54. Ranstrop, *Hizb'allah in Lebanon*, 38–39, 66–67; *Al-Wahda al-Islamiya*, 4 December 1987; Qassem, *Hezbollah*, 123–38.

55. *Al-Ahd*, 19 October 1987.

56. *Al-Ahd*, 25 April 1987, 2 May 1987; *Al-Balad*, 23 October 1994.

57. *Al-Ahd*, 24 February 1989; *Al-Raya*, 30 July 1990; *Al-Shu'la*, 11 June 1993.

58. Radio Tehran, 28 July 1990; *Al-Sharaa*, 8 October 1990; *Al-Hawadeth*, 7 December 1990.

59. *Al-Nahar*, 26 September 1986.

60. *Al-Watan al-Arabi*, 26 September 1986.

61. Abu khalil, "Syria and the Shiites," 13–15.

62. Eyal Zisser, *Assad's Syria at a Crossroads* (Tel Aviv: Kibbutz Me'uhad, 1999), 65.

63. Maoz, *Israel Syria the End of the Conflict?* 176–226.

64. *Al-Ousbou' Al-Arabi*, 6 February 1995; *Al-Quds Radio*, 24 February 1995; *Al-Hayat*, 28 February 1995.

65. LBC, 5 March 1997. Zisser, *Assad's Syria*, 106–08; *Al-Ousbou' Al-Arabi* , 25 August 1997; *Nidaa Al-Watan*, 6 August 1997.

66. Zisser, *Assad's Syria*, 146; *Al-Shu'la*, 1 June 1991; *Al-Anwar*, 24 May 1991; Voice of the People Radio, 28 February 1992.

67. Radio Nur, 26 August, 1992; *Magazine*, 11 June 1993; *Al-Shark al-Awsat*, 5 May 1993; *Al-Sharq*, 9 November 1992; AFP, 8 December 1994; *Al-Hayat*, 23 June 1995.

68. LBC, 5 March 1997.

69. *Al-Sharaa*, 19 May 1997; *Al-Shu'la*, 1 June 1991; *Almassira*, 27 May 1991; Qassem, *Hezbollah*, 179–80.

70. Voice of the People Radio, 28 February 1992; *Al-Sharaa,* 19 May 1997; *Al-Hayat,* 23 June 1995, 21 October 1995.

71. Zisser, *Assad's Syria,* : 184–85; *Magazine,* 11 June 1993.

72. AFP, 3 October 1992; Radio Tehran, 5 October 1992.

73. *Al-Watan al-Arabi,* 9 June 1996; *Etalaat,* 24 August 1993; Radio Nur, 1 August 1993.

74. *Al-Sharq al-Awsat,* 7 October 1993; AFP, 19 April 1996.

75. Radio Tehran, 4 June 1994; *Al-Moharar,* 28 February 1994, 10 July 1997; *Al-Safir,* 18 October 1997.

76. *Al-Hayat,* 20 November 1993; *Al-Shark al-Awsat,* 19 November 1993; Radio Nur, 26 October 1993; AFP, 31 October 1993; *Irna,* 13 September 1993; LBC 24 September 1995; *Al-Watan al-Arabi,* 14 October 1997.

77. *Al-Kifah al-Arabi,* 8 February 1993; *Al-Hayat,* 21 October 1995, 22 April 1996; *Al-Balad,* 25 November 1995; *Al-Nahar,* 16 April 1996; *Alawsat,* 29 April 1996; LBC, 22 May 1996; Kuna (Kuwait News Agency), 22 May 1996.

78. *Al-Ahd,* 16 February 1990.

79. *Al-Watan al-Arabi,* 11 September 1992.

80. ACN Television, 20 November 1992; *Al-Shu'la,* 11 June 1993; Orbit Television, 23 May 1997; *Alarab Alyoum,* 21 March 1998; *Al-Diyar,* 10 June 1994.

81. *Alawsat,* 25 October 1993.

82. *La Revue du Liban,* 6 March 1993.

83. LBC, 24 August 1994; Radio Nur, 12 February 1995; *Al-Watan al-Arabi,* 9 June 1995; Voice of the People Radio, 13 June 1996; *Al-Shark al-Awsat,* 18 March 1997.

84. AFP, 22 February 1992; *Al-Hayat,* 5 March 1992; *Al-Shark al-Awsat,* 26 February 1992; Sawt al-Kuwait (Voice of Kuwait), 25 August 1992.

85. *Al-Sharq,* 8 June 1992; Reuters, 2 June 1992; AFP, 3 June 1992; *Sawt al-Kuwait,* 7 August 1992; *Al-Hayat,* 12 August 1992; *Al-Shark al-Awsat,* 7 October 1992, 16 October 1992; *Al-Sharuq,* 19 November 1992.

86. *Al-Safir,* 8 May 1993; *Al-Shark al-Awsat,* 7 October 1993, 19 November 1993; *Al-Dawliya,* 2 March 1994; AFP, 8 March 1994; *Al-Awsat,* 3 October 1994; *Al-Hayat,* 28 February 1995.

87. *Etalaat,* 24 August 1993; Radio Monte-Carlo, 28 July 1993; Mid-East News Service, 31 July 1993; Radio Tehran, 30 July 1993; Radio Monte-Carlo, 31 July 1993; AP 17 April 1996; Radio Nur, 27 April 1996; *Al-Balad,* 20 April 1996.

88. *Al-Ahd,* 31 July 1993; *Al-Diyar,* 28 October 1994.

89. Radio Phalange, 9 August 1994; Voice of the People Radio, 9 August 1994; Radio Nur, 9 August 1994; *Magazine,* 12 August 1994.

90. *Der Spiegel,* 16 January 1995; *Al-Watan al-Arabi,* 7 July 1995; AFP, 20 March 1996.

91. Radio Monte-Carlo, 8 January 1994, 25 June 1994; Mid-East News Service, 8 January 1994, 5 June 1994; Radio Tehran, 7 April 1994; *Al-Nahar,* 7 April 1994; *Al-Manar,* 24 October 1994; *Al-Hayat,* 1 October 1994.

92. *Al-Mustaqbal,* 30 June 1995; *Nidaa Al-Watan,* 27 June 1995; *Al-Watan al-Arabi,* 7 July 1995; Mid-East News Service, 5 July 1995.

93. *Al-Shark al-Awsat,* 25 June 1995; *Alawsat,* 3 July 1995; *Al-Nahar,* 30 June 1995.

94. AFP, 7 July 1995; *Nidaa Al-Watan,* 7 July 1995; *Al-Diyar,* 13 July 1995; *Al-Moharar,* 24 July 1995.

95. *Al-Nahar,* 3 July 1995; *Al-Manar,* 8 July 1995; Radio Nur, 16 October 1995; *Al-Aman,* 20 October 1995.

96. Mid-East News Service, 21 December 1995; Reuters, 20 December 1995; *Al-Shark al-Awsat,* 21 December 1995; *Al-Safir,* 21 December 1995.

97. AFP, 23 December 1995.

98. *Al-Safir,* 23 December 1995; *Al-Shark al-Awsat,* 28 December 1995; *Al-Hayat,* 23 March 1996; *Al-Shark al-Awsat,* 22 March 1996.

99. Kuna (Kuwait News Agency), 15 April 1996, 17 April 1996; *Al-Watan al-Arabi,* 12 January 1996; *Al-Nahar,* 16 April, 1996; *Al-Hayat,* 16 April 1996, 12 May 1996, 19 October 1996; *Newsweek,* 1 May 1996; Iranian Television, 21 April 1996; Qassem, *Hezbollah,* 170–71.

100. *Al-Shark al-Awsat,* 28 December 1995; AFP, 18 March 1996; *Al-Safir,* 10 June 1996.

101. Reuters, 16 April 1996.

102. CNN, 26 April 1996, 27 April 1996; *Al-Watan al-Arabi,* 25 October 1996.

103. *Al-Safir,* 1 July 1996; Mid-East News Service, 10 July 1996; SANA (Syrian Arab New Agency), 22 August 1997; *Al-Mushahid Assiyasi,* 30 March 1997; *Al-Nahar,* 10 July 1998.

104. *Al-Hayat,* 21 January 1997; Radio Nur, 8 January 1997; *Al-Ahd,* 24 January 1997; *Al-Diyar,* 3 February 1997; *Al-Safir,* 27 January 1997, 21 August 1997; *Foreign Report,* 6 February 1997; *Nidaa Al-Watan,* 6 August 1997.

105. *Salam,* 25 October 1998; *Nidaa Al-Watan,* 2 February 1998; Radio Nur, 28 November 1998; *Al-Ahd,* 4 December 1998; *Irna,* 30 November 1998.

106. Reuters, 14 October 1997; Iranian Television, 14 October 1997; *Irna,* 15 October 1997; *Al-Shark al-Awsat,* 14 October 1997, 17 October 1997; *Al-Diyar,* 16 October 1997; *Al-Hayat,* 16 October 1997; *Al-Safir,* 18 October 1997; *Al-Sharaa,* 17 November 1997; *Alarab Alyoum,* 21 March 1998.

107. *Al-Hayat,* 29 March 1998; Radio Nur, 30 March 1998; LBC 30 March 1998; *Irna,* 30 March 1998; *Al-Shark al-Awsat,* 8 February 1998; *Al-Watan al-Arabi,* 17 April 1998; *Al-Nahar,* 25 April 1998; *Nidaa Al-Watan,* 6 May 1998; *Al-Diyar,* 30 April 1998.

108. *Al-Hayat,* 14 May 1998, 20 May 1998.

109. *Al-Ahram,* 6 June 1998.

110. *Al-Shark al-Awsat,* 16 April 1996; *Al-Safir,* 17 April 1996.

111. LBC, 16 April 1996; BBC Television, 13 April 1996; *Al-Manar,* 5 May 1996.

112. Radio Nur, 14 August 1992, 19 February 1995; *Al-Sharq,* 9 November 1992; *Al-Hayat,* 12 March 1992; *Al-Watan al-Arabi,* 11 September 1992.

113. Voice of Free Lebanon Radio, 29 June 1993; *Al-Safir,* 27 August 1993; *Al-Diyar,* 22 March 1993; LBC, 21 February 1992, 17 April 1996; BBC, 4 June 1992.

114. WTN Television, 2 June 1991; *Al-Liawaa,* 10 August 1991.

115. *Al-Hawadeth,* 7 December 1990; *Al-Sharaa,* 8 July 1991; *Al-Nahar,* 24 July 1991, 28 March 1994; Radio Nur, 29 September 1991, 26 May 1992; Voice of Islam Radio, 6 June 1991; Voice of the Homeland Radio, 2 October 1991; Radio Tehran, 4 March 1992; *Al-Balad,* 30 May 1992.

116. Voice of the homeland Radio, 12 November 1992; Voice of Free Lebanon Radio, 11 November 1992; AP, 14 November 1992; Mid-East News Service, 14 November 1992; ACN Television, 18 November 1992; Voice of Islam Radio, 19 November 1992; *Alawsat,* 2 May 1994; *Al-Diyar,* 19 December 1995; Iranian Television, 14 October 1997; *Al-Safir,* 15 November 1997.

117. *Al-Safir,* 27 August 1993; Radio Nur, 1 August 1993, 2 August 1993; *Etalaat,* 24 August 1993; *Al-Manar,* 26 February 1995, 19 March 1996.

118. Radio Nur, 16 February 1995, 18 February 1995, 21 March 1996.

119. Radio Nur, 25 June 1995; *Al-Manar,* 8 July 1995; *Al-Ahd,* 20 October 1995.

120. *Almassira,* 23 October 1995.

121. Radio Nur, 10 November 1996.

122. LBC, 16 December 1997; *Alalam,* 21 February 1998.

123. AFP, 12 February 1995, 2 June 1994; Mid-East News Service, 5 June 1994; *Filastin al-Muslima,* 1 October 1994; Radio Nur, 14 December 1994; *Al-Manar,* 18 February 1996, 18 March 1996; *Nidaa Al-Watan,* 21 February 1997.

124. Voice of the People Radio, 18 June 1995.

125. *Al-Diyar,* 1 November 1995; Le Monde, 21 February 1995; *Magazine,* 15 July 1994; Kuna (Kuwait News Agency), 24 July 1994; LBC, 24 August 1994; *Al-Watan al-Arabi,* 26 December 1994; Mid-East News Service, 5 February 1995; *Nidaa Al-Watan,* 7 July 1995.

126. *Al-Nahar,* 22 December 1994; *Al-Hayat,* 13 June 1995; Radio Nur, 25 June 1995.

127. *Nidaa Al-Watan,* 11 January 1994; *Alawsat,* 3 October 1994.

128. AFP, 25 October 1995; Al-Safir, 20 November 1995; Mid-East News Service, 26 October 1995.

129. Radio Nur, 12 September 1993; *Al-Anwar,* 24 May 1993; *Al-Nahar,* 22 December 1992.

130. *Al-Manar,* 9 May 1996; *Al-Safir,* 27 January 1997; *Al-Liawaa,* 17 April 1997; Qassem, *Hezbollah,* 166–71.

131. Radio Nur, 2 May 1996, 10 November 1996, 31 December 1996, 13 April 1997; *Independent,* 11 June 1996; *Ha'aretz,* 11 June 1996; *Al-Sharaa,* 20 August 1997.

132. Radio Nur, 31 December 1996; *Al-Diyar,* 25 April 1997; *Al-Ahd,* 30 April 1997; *Al-Sharaa,* 27 April 1997.

133. *Al-Safir,* 27 January 1997.

134. Shay, 1998: A summary of the events of 1997. *Al-Manar,* 13 February 1997, 9 March 1997; Radio Nur, 16 February 1997, 25 February 1997, 11 April 1997; Iranian Television, 10 February 1997; CNN, 14 September 1997; Qassem, *Hezbollah,* 173; *Al-Diyar,* 14 February 1997.

135. *Al-Liawaa,* 24 September 1997.

136. *Al-Shark al-Awsat,* 18 March 1997; BBC Radio, 22 October 1997; Radio Nur, 18 January 1998, 15 February 1998; Al-Safir, 16 February 1998, 19 February 1998; *Al-Nahar,* 9 March 1998; *Al-Hayat,* 23 September 1998.

137. *Al-Manar,* 19 January 1998, 3 March 1998; Qassem, *Hezbollah,* 182–86.

138. *Ha'aretz,* 3 January 1999, 31 January 1999, 12 February 1999, 5 March 1999, 9 March 1999, 13 April 1999, 19 September 1999.

139. *Al-Diyar,* 28 June 1993.

140. Radio Nur, 24 October 1993; *Al-Nahar,* 22 December 1994.

141. *Alawsat,* 18 March 1996; Qassem, *Hezbollah,* 339–49.

Chapter 8

1. *Ma'ariv,* 11 March 2005. Nicholas Blanford, "Hizballah in the Firing Line," *Middle East Report Online,* 28 April 2003; "Notable Exception: Some European States are Unwilling to Label Hizballah a Terrorist Group," http://www.aipac.org/Notable Exception112904.htm.; Patrick Gooddenough, "Australian Muslim Leader praises Suicide Bombers," http://www.crosswalk.com/news/1247108.html

2. Sami G. Hajjar, "Hizballah: Terrorism, National liberation, or Menace?" www.911investigations.net/IMG/pdf/doc-1063.pdf

3. Clyde R. Mark, "Lebanon," Foreign Affairs, Defense, and Trade Division, Issues Brief for Congress (Congressional Research Service, Library of Congress, updated 23 April 2003).

4. Matthew Levitt, "Banning Hizballah activity in Canada," in Peacewatch/Policywatch Anthology 2003, Washington Institute for Near East Policy, 102–4.

5. http://www.ynetnews.com/articles/0,7340,L-3506586,00.html

6. Robert Satloff, "U.S. Policy toward Islamism: A Theoretical and Operational Overview," (Copyright 2000 by the Council on Foreign Relations,New York), 16–18; Rensselaer Lee and Raphael Perl, Foreign Affairs, Defense, and Trade Division, Issues

Brief for Congress, "Terrorism, the Future, and U.S. Foreign Policy," (Congressional Research Service, Library of Congress, updated 12.12.2002).

7. "IDF Intelligence Chief Views Hizballah-Syria Ties, PA Chaos, Saudi Stability," *Jerusalem Post*, 26 July 2004.

8. http://www.defenselink.mil/policy/speech/oct_8_02.html

9. http://www.intelligence.org.il/eng/bu/hizbullah/pb/app4.htm. http://www.fbi.gov/pressrel/pressrel01/khobar.pdf

10. "Hezbollah Had Plans to Attack US, Israeli Ships in Singapore" AFP, 9 June 2002; "Hezbollah Denies Plan to Attack US, Israeli Ships in Singapore," AFP, 10 June 2002.

11. Matthew Levitt, "Hezbollah: A Case Study of Global Reach," Washington Institute for Near East Policy.

12. "9/11 Commission Find Ties between Al-Qaeda and Iran," *Time Magazine,* 16 July 2004; 9/11 Commission Report, 86, 128.

13. "Terrorist and Organized Crime Groups in the Tri Border Area (TBA) of South America," Federal Research Division Library of the Congress Washington D.C., July 2003, 14–24.

14. Ibid., 19.

15. Ely Karmon, "Fight on all Fronts, Hizballah the War on Terror and the War in Iraq," Washington Institute Policy Focus, 2003, 11.

16. "Asian Organized Crime and Terrorist Activity in Canada, 1999–2000," Federal Research Division Library of the Congress Washington D.C. July 2003, 34.

17. Romanian Intelligence Report Cites Hizballah, Islamic Liberation Party Activity Bucharest Ziua in Romanian 13 Feb 02 p 7 ZIUA Wednesday, February 13, 2002.

18. http://fl1.findlaw.com/news.findlaw.com/hdocs/docs/terrorism/uskourani111903 ind.pdf; http://www.tkb.org/documents/Cases/USA_v_Hammoud_00-CR-00147_ (NC-W)_Superseding_Indictment_002.pdf

19. http://www.intelligence.org.il/eng/bu/hizbullah/chap_d.doc; Karmon "Fight on all Fronts," 8–11; Yehudit Barasky, "Hizballah the Party of God," AJC, May 2003.

20. "Terrorist and Organized Crime Groups in the Tri-Border Area (TBA) of South America," Federal Research Division, Library of Congress, July 2003.

21. *Ha'aretz,* 3 February 2005. http://www.intelligence.org.il/eng/bu/hizbullah/chap_d. doc.

22. http://www.intelligence.org.il/eng/bu/hizbullah/chap_d.doc

23. Karmon, "Fight on all Fronts;" http://www.aijac.org.au/resources/aijac-media/cr-age-020603.html; Colin Rubenstein, "Australia is Right to Ban Hezbolla, Here's Why," *Age,* 2 June 2003.

24. http://www.intelligence.org.il/eng/bu/hizbullah/chap_d.doc. *Al-Manar,* 30 June 2004.

25. Bernard Lewis, "The Revolt of Islam: When Did the Conflict with the West Start and How Could It End?" in *Following 11 September—Islam and the West between Confrontation and Reconciliation,* edited by Esther Webman (Tel Aviv: Moshe Dayan Center, 2002), 15–20; Shimon Shapira, *Hezbollah between Iran and Lebanon* (Hakibbutz Hameuchad, 2000), 114.

26. Eitan Gilboa, "The US and Israel—the Infrastructure of the Unique Relations," (Ministry of Defense, 1993), 132–38. "Letter to the Speaker of the House and the President Pro Tempore of the Senate on the Termination of United States Participation in the Multinational Force in Lebanon," 30 March 1984, http://www.reagan.utexas.edu/resource/speeches/1984/33084f.htm

27. "Open Letter from Hizballah to the Disinherited in Lebanon and the World," (Hizballah's manifesto), February 1985.

28. See http://www.pbs.org/wgbh/pages/frontline/shows/target/interviews/cowan.html

29. Mark, "Lebanon," 23 April 2003. See also "Statement by Deputy Press Secretary Speaks on the Situation in Lebanon," http://www.reagan.utexas.edu/resource/speeches/1983/81983b.htm
30. Mark, "Lebanon," 23 April 2003.
31. *Al-Majallah,* 18 December 1983.
32. http://www.pbs.org/wgbh/pages/frontline/shows/target/interviews/cowan.html. Gilboa, 1993: 132-138; Clyde R. Mark, "Lebanon," Foreign Affairs Defense, and Trade Division, CRS Issue Brief for Congress, 11 August 2003.
33. http://www.pbs.org/wgbh/pages/frontline/shows/target/interviews/cowan.html
34. Mark, "Lebanon," 23 April 2003.
35. *Al-Ahd,* 19 October 1987.
36. *Al-Nahar,* 29 May 1987.
37. AFP, 23 July 1987.
38. *Al-Ahd,* 5 September 1987.
39. Reuters, 13 March 1988.
40. AFP, 3 July 1990.
41. *Al-Dustor,* 4 April 1988. *Nouveau Magazine,* 27 February 1988.
42. AP, 31 July 1988.
43. Reuters, 3 August 1989. *Al-Nahar,* 3 August 1989.
44. National Security Review 19, White House, Washington, July 7, 1989, http://bushlibrary.tamu.edu/research/reviews.html; Mark, "Lebanon," 11 August 2003.
45. Voice of the Mountain Radio, 1 October 1991.
46. *Al-Hayat,* 24 May 1992. *Sawt al-Kuwait,* 23 April 1992. AFP , 23 June 1995. *Al-Safir,* 7 January 1995.
47. Lebanese Television VTN, 14 March 1996.
48. Kuna (Kuwait News Agency), 17 April 1996. Reuters, 17 April 1996. Lebanese Television, 17 April 1996. *Tishreen,* 3 June 1998.
49. Lebanese Television, 17 April 1996. AFP, 17 April 1996. AP, 17 April 1996. Reuters, 20 April 1996.
50. Radio Tehran, 8 April 1995.
51. Mid-East News Service, 19 September 1997. *Al-Nahar,* 17 September 1997.
52. Voice of the Homeland Radio, 27 May 1991. Radio Nur, 6 June 1991. *Al-Ahd,* 9 August 1991.
53. *Al-Nahar,* 17 October 1991. Radio Nur, 6 June 1991. Reuters, 29 October 1991.
54. LBC, 20 February 1992. BBC Radio, 4 June 1992.
55. *Al-Nahar,* 3 March 1992. Irna, 18 February 1993. Mid-East News Service, 13 October 1994.
56. Voice of the People Radio, 5 June 1992. *Almassira,* 22 July 1992.
57. Radio Nur, 11 November 1992.
58. Ibid., 14 August 1994.
59. Ibid., 18 February 1992.
60. Ibid., 26 May 1992. *Al-Shark al-Awsat,* 1 March 1998.
61. Ibid., 3 June 1992.
62. *Al-Manbar,* 1 August 1992.
63. Voice of the People Radio, 17 April 1993.
64. *Al-Sharq,* 30 June 1991. AP, 27 July 1991. *Al-Salam,* 28 July 1991.
65. *Al-Sharq,* 8 June 1992.
66. *Al-Anwar,* 11 May 1992.
67. *Tehran Times,* 29 August 1992.
68. *Al-Shorouk,* 19 November 1992.
69. Radio Nur, 17 February 1993.

70. Ibid., 12 February 1995.
71. Voice of Islam Radio, 19 June 1995. *Nidaa Al-Watan* 19 June 1995.
72. Voice of Islam Radio, 17 June 1995.
73. *Nidaa Al-Watan,* 23 December 1995. Radio Nur, 4 February 1996.
74. AFP, 20 April 1996. Reuters, 20 April 1996. Radio Monte-Carlo, 20 April 1996. Radio Al-Sharq, 20 April 1996. Iranian Television, 27 April 1997. Al-Jazeera, 27 April 2000.
75. CNN, 26 April 1996. Kuna (Kuwait News Agency), 9 August 1996. Radio Phalange, 28 April 1996.
76. Radio Phalange, 4 May 1996. Radio Nur, 28 April 1996, 30 July 1997.
77. CNN, 14 April 1996. *Al-Safir,* 17 April 1996. Lebanese Television, 17 April 1996. Kuna (Kuwait News Agency), 25 April 1996. Mid-East News Service, 3 August 1996. *Al-Safir,* 14 April 1998.
78. *Al-Manar,* 5 May 1996, 20 November 1996. Radio Nur, 20 November 1996, 9 January 1997. *Al-Diyar,* 14 September 1997.
79. Kuna (Kuwait News Agency), 20 May 1996.
80. *Al-Ahd,* 17 October 1997. Radio Nur, 9 October 1997. *Al-Safir,* 22 April 1998.
81. *Al-Safir,* 22 April 1998, 14 December 1998.
82. Ibid., 31 August 1998.
83. Mid-East News Service, 2 March 1997. Radio Nur, 13 April 1997, 8 August 1997. *Al-Bayrak,* 30 August 1997. *Al-Nahar,* 16 September 1997. *Monday Morning,* 19 January 1998. *Al-Watan al-Arabi,* 19 June 1998. *Al-Safir,* 30 November 1998.
84. *Monday Morning,* 12 October 1992.
85. *Al-Shaab,* 28 April 1998.
86. Mark, "Lebanon," 11 August 2003.
87. *Al-Safir,* 14 December 1998. *Al-liawaa,* 16 December 1998.
88. Orbit Television, 15 December 1998. *Al-Diyar,* 14 December 1998.
89. *Nidaa Al-Watan,* 31 December 1995. Radio Beirut, 28 December. Radio Nur, 1 January 1995.
90. *Al-Watan al-Arabi,* 27 January 1995. *Al-Shark al-Awsat,* 19 February 1995. *Al-Moharer,* 3 July 1995.
91. Mid-East News Service, 18 January 1995. *Al-Hayat,* 17 January 1995.
92. Radio Nur, 16 February 1995.
93. Ibid., 3 February 1995.
94. Ibid., 10 February 1995, 12 February 1995. *Al-Dawliya,* 6 February 1995. *Al-Balad,* 18 February 1995.
95. Radio Nur, 16 February 1995.
96. Voice of the People Radio, 15 April 1995. *Al-Hayat,* 18 June 1995.
97. Radio Tehran, 27 May 1995. *Al-Anwar,* 30 May 1995. *Al-Nahar,* 30 May 1995. *Al-Hayat,* 18 June 1995.
98. Mid-East News Service, 18 June 1996. Voice of Islam Radio, 16 June 1995.
99. *Al-Watan al-Arabi,* 7 July 1995.
100. Kuna (Kuwait News Agency), 26 June 1997. *Nidaa Al-Watan,* 4 August 1997. LBC, 21 July 1997. *Al-Siyassa,* 19 September 1997. Mark, "Lebanon," 11 August 2003.
101. AP, 12 May 1998. Al-Hayat, 14 May 1998. Radio Phalange, 20 June 1998.
102. Dr. Flynt Leverett, "Syria-U.S. Policy Directions," Saban Center for Middle East Policy, Brookings Institution in Washington, Testimony for Committee on Foreign Relation United States Senate, 30 October 2003, 1.
103. ACN Television,18 November 1992.
104. Mark, "Lebanon," 11 August 2003. Voice of the Mountain Radio, 21 March 1992. *Al-Hayat,* 24 February 1993, 10 February 1995.
105. *Al-Nahar,* 3 July 1993, 10 July 1993. 19 July 1993. *Al-Sharq,* 5 July 1993.

106. *Al-Nahar,* 22 December 1994.

107. *Kayhan,* 15 February 1994.

108. CNN, 31 July 1993. *Etalaat,* 24 August 1994. Radio al-Sharq, 10 August 1994. Reuters, 25 May 1994. Radio Monte Carlo, 25 June 1994.

109. *Al-Shark al-Awsat,* 19 November 1993. *Al-Bayrak,* 16 February 1993.

110. *Al-Ousbou' Al-Arabi,* 6 February 1995.

111. *Al-Shark al-Awsat,* 25 June 1995. *Al-Watan al-Arabi,* 7 July 1995.

112. *Magazine,* 23 June 1995. *Al-Diyar,* 26 June 1995. *Al-Manar,* 17 June. Radio Free Lebanon, 18 June 1995.

113. *Al-Nahar,* 30 June 1995.

114. *Al-Safir,* 23 December 1995.

115. Voice of the Phalange Radio, 28 October 1995.

116. Reuters, 16 October 1995, 28 November 1995. *Al-Hayat,* 30 November 1995. Radio Nur, 29 June 1995.

117. *Al-Hayat,* 24 December 1995.

118. Irna, 26 December 1995.

119. AFP, 20 March 1996. Voice of the People Radio, 22 March 1996.

120. Radio Phalange, 12 April 1994. Reuters, 12 March 1996.

121. BBC, 19 April 1996. CNN, 20 April 1996.

122. AFP, 20 April, 1996. Radio Monte Carlo, 20 April, 1996. Reuters, 20 April 1996. Radio al-Sharq, 20 April 1996.

123. AFP, 21 April 1996. Reuters, 22 April 1996. *Al-Dustor,* 27 August 1997. *Al-Bayrak,* 30 August 1997.

124. http://daccessdds.un.org/doc/UNDOC/GEN/N04/498/92/PDF/N0449892.pdf? OpenElement

125. http://domino.un.org/UNISPAL.NSF/9a798adbf322aff38525617b006d88d7/ 3e1d31ccd699df0c852571cb0052d40b!Open Document

Chapter 9

1. *Al-Hayat,* 21 February 2000; *Al-Istiklal,* 3 February 2000; *Ha'aretz,* 10 April 2000.

2. "Hassan Nasrallah," http://www.ynet.co.il/yaan/0,7340,L-344215-MzQ0MjE1Xzk4 MjY2Njg2XzE0ODY4NzIwMAeqeq-FreeYaan,00.html

3. *Al-Hayat,* 21 February 2000.

4. *Al-Ahram,* 14 February 2000, 15 February 2000.

5. *Al-Kuds,* 13 June 2000; quoted http://www.memri.org.il/memri/LoadArticlePage.asp? language=Hebrew&enttype=4&entid=868#_ftn1

6. The Winograd Committee, http://www.vaadatwino.org.il/statements.html#null; Security Council Endorses Secretary-General's Conclusion on Israeli Withdrawal from Lebanon as of 16 June, http://www.un.org/News/Press/docs/2000/20000618.sc6878. doc.html

7. Daniel Sobelman, "New Rules of the Game: Israel and Hizbollah after the Withdrawal from Lebanon" (Tel Aviv: Jaffee Center for Strategic Studies, Tel-Aviv University), http://www.tau.ac.il/jcss/memoranda/memo65.pdf

8. *Al-Safir,* 18 December 2000.

9. *Al-Ayyam,* 26 June 2000.

10. Dr. Reuven Erlich, "Raising the Issue of the Sheba'a Farms in the Proposed American-French Security Council Draft Resolution for Ending the Fighting: Background Information and Significance," http://www.terrorism-info.org.il/malam_multimedia/ English/eng_n/html/sheba_farms_e (accessed August 9, 2006); "Shebaa Farms: Are they

Lebanese or Syrian?". http://yalibnan.com/site/archives/2006/01/shebaa_farms_ar.php (accessed 29 January, 2006).

11. *Ha'aretz*, 19 October 2007.

12. "Nasrallah Calls for Liberating Lebanon's Shebaa Farms," http://yalibnan.com/site/archives/2007/01/nasrallah_calls_1.php (accessed January 30, 2007).

13. Walid Jumblatt, "The Most Fierce Liberal in Lebanon, http://yalibnan.com/site/archives/2007/02/walid_jumblatt.php (accessed February15, 2007).

14. Nahmias Roni, "Worry: Shebaa farm will be announced Lebanese and Israel will be demand to withdraw," http://www.ynet.co.il/articles/0,7340,L-3235890,00.html#n (accessed April 3, 2006); "The security council: Shebaa farms are part of Lebanon," http://www.ynet.co.il/articles/0,7340,L-3038622,00.html (accessed January 29, 2005).

15. Eyal Zisser, "The Return of Hizbullah," Middle East Quarterly (Fall 2002), http://www.meforum.org/article/499.; "Hassan Nasrallah," http://www.ynet.co.il/yaan/0,7340,L-344215-MzQ0MjE1Xzk4MjY2Njg2XzE0ODY4NzIwMAeqeq-FreeYaan,00.html

16. *Hurriyet*, 30 May, 2000.

17. *Al-Safir*, 28 Jun 2000.

18. "The public discourse about disarming Hezbollah," http://www.memri.org.il/cgi-webaxy/sal/sal.pl (accessed June 4, 2005).

19. *Al-Nahar*, August 10, 2005.

20. "Hezbollah leader Hassan Nasrallah publicly admits that his organization is rearming and secretly transporting arms to south Lebanon, in blatant violation of Security Council Resolution 1701," http://www.terrorism-info.org.il/malam_multimedia/English/eng_n/html/nasrallah_e20feb07.htm(accessed February 23, 2007).

21. *Al-Nahar*, 19 July 2001.

22. *Al-Nahar*, 27 February 2002.

23. *Ma'ariv*, Newspaper, 2 June 2002.

24. *Al-Nahar*, 14 March 2002.

25. *Al-Nahar*, 10 April 2002, 04 July 2002.

26. *Al-Zaman*, 29 May 2002.

27. Daniel Sobelman, "New Rules of the Game: Israel and Hizbollah after the withdrawal from Lebanon," (Tel Aviv: Jaffee Center for Strategic Studies, Tel-Aviv University, 2003), 47.

28. *Al-Hayat*, 21 July 2001; Gary C. Gambill and Ziad K. Abdelnour, "*Dossier: Rafiq Hariri Prime Minister of Lebanon*," 3, no.7 (July 2001), http://www.meib.org/articles/0107_ld1.htm; *Al-Nahar*, 22 February 2001; *Al-Safir*, 17 July 2001.

29. *Al-Safir*, 7 September 2002; *Al-Nahar*, 9 September 2002; Gary C. Gambill, "Dossier: Hassan Nasrallah Secretary-General of Hezbollah," 6, no.2/3 (February, March 2004), http://www.meib.org/articles/0402_ld.htm.

30. Ali Waqad, "Lebanon: Rafic Alhariri's government resigne," http://www.ynet.co.il/articles/0,7340,L-2992589,00.html (accessed October 20, 2004); Roei Nahmias, "Lebanon: The election for the parliament started," http://www.ynet.co.il/articles/0,7340,L-3091696,00.html; Ran Farhi, "Hezbollah and the Lebanese politics," http://www.omedia.co.il/Show_Article.asp?DynamicContentID=1635&MenuID=726&ThreadID=1014017 (accessed June 16, 2006).

31. *Al-Safir*, 11 June 2005; *Al-Nahar*, July 11, 2005.

32. Zevi Barel, "Syria's good soldier," http://www.haaretz.co.il/hasite/objects/pages/PrintArticle.jhtml?itemNo=812517 (accessed January 11, 2007); "Lebanon's New Government Line-Up (update)," http://www.lebanonwire.com/0705/05071901LINEUPLW.asp (accessed July 19, 2005).

33. Sela Yohai, "Saad Harriri: The Lebanon's hope," http://www.omedia.co.il/
Show_Article.asp?DynamicContentID=1701&MenuID=603 (accessed July 30, 2006).
34. "The public discourse about disarming Hezbollah," http://www.memri.org.il/cgi-webaxy/
sal/sal.pl
35. The editor of the Lebanese newspaper "al Nahar" attacks Hezbollah's activity in
Southern Lebanon, http://www.memri.org.il/cgi-webaxy/sal/sal.pl (accessed December
1, 2003); Shtern Yoav, "Lebanon accuse: Syria assassinated the member of the parliament," http://www.haaretz.co.il/hasite/pages/ShArtPE.jhtml?itemNo=790866 (accessed
December 13, 2005).
36. *Daily Star,* December 13, 2005.
37. http://www.elaph.com/ElaphWeb/ElaphWriter/2006/8/170391.htm. http://www.elaph.
com/ElaphWeb/ElaphWriter/2006/8/171932.htm
38. "Following the war: Lebanon in front of political crisis," http://www.memri.org.il/
cgi-webaxy/sal/sal.pl (accessed October 30, 2006).
39. Ibid.
40. "Hezbollah exposed the existence of big practice that was held in the beginning of
November for three day in southern Lebanon," http://www.terrorism-info.org.il/
malam_multimedia/Hebrew/heb_n/html/hezbollah_1107.htm (accessed November 8,
2007).
41. Col. (Ret.) Reuven Erlich, "The road to the second Lebanon war: the Lebanese scene in
the years 2000-2006," http://www.terrorism-info.org.il/malam_multimedia/English/
eng_n/html/lebanon_0_06e.htm (accessed October 30, 2007).
42. Mai Shidiak, "No one will hush me," Sela Yohai http://www.omedia.co.il/
Show_Article.asp?DynamicContentID=1518&MenuID=726 (accessed June 19, 2006).
43. *Ma'ariv,* 13 January 2001.
44. *Al-Safir,* 13 July 2001. Sobelman, "New Rules of the Game," 59–60.
45. *Ma'ariv,* 28 January 2001; Col. (Ret.) Reuven Erlich, "The road to the second Lebanon war:
the Lebanese scene in the years 2000–2006," http://www.terrorism-info.org.il/malam_
multimedia/English/eng_n/html/lebanon_0_06e.htm (accessed October 30, 2007).
46. Sobelman, "New Rules of the Game," 82–83.
47. "The terrorist's activities of Hezbollah along the Israeli Lebanon border since the withdrawal of IDF's forces from Lebanon" (May 2000), http://www.intelligence.org.il/
sp/6_04/si_7d_04.htm (accessed July 2004).
48. "Hezbollah leader Hassan Nasrallah boasts of the organization's ability to maintain
a balance of deterrence with Israel," http://www.terrorism-info.org.il/malam_
multimedia/English/eng_n/html/hezbollah_e0506.htm (accessed May 28, 2006).
49. *Al-Sharq al-Awsat,* 24 August 2002; *Al-Safir,* 13 July 2001.
50. "The strategic alliance between Syria and Iran: Economic and military aspects,"
http://www.memri.org.il/cgi-webaxy/sal/sal.pl (accessed August 3, 2007).
51. "Using the Quds Force of the Revolutionary Guards as the main tool to export the
revolution beyond the borders of Iran," http://www.terrorism-info.org.il/malam_
multimedia/English/eng_n/html/iran_e0307.htm (accessed April 2, 2007).
52. *"The liberal intellectual shaker alnabulsi alert from Shiite Islamic republic in Lebanon,"*
http://www.memri.org.il/cgi-webaxy/sal/sal.pl (accessed August 28, 2006).
53. *Al-Sharq Al-Awsat,* 11 May 2006.
54. *Al-Safir,* 28 June 2000.
55. *Al-Safir,* 27 April 2006; "Chapter 4: Hezbollah activity during 2006," http://www.
nsc.gov.il/NSCWeb/Docs/chapterd.pdf
56. *Al-Safir,* 21 June 2000.
57. http://daccessdds.un.org/doc/UNDOC/GEN/N04/498/92/PDF/N0449892.pdf?
OpenElement.

58. "Hezbollah does not intend to disarm," http://www.terrorism-info.org.il/malam_
multimedia/html/final/sp/heb_n/hezbollah_0905.htm
59. "Lebanon Country Brief: January 2008," http://www.dfat.gov.au/geo/lebanon/
country_brief.html; "Currently listed entities," http://www.ps-sp.gc.ca/prg/ns/le/
cle-en.asp#h20; Annual Report 2004: General intelligence and security service, p. 19,
http://www.fas.org/irp/world/netherlands/aivd2004-eng.pdf
60. *Al-Nahar,* 21 July 2002.
61. *Al-Nahar,* 9 September 2002.
62. *Al-Sharq al-Awsat,* 7 November 2001; "U.S. Cites Hizballah Member for Terrorist
Financing: Treasury Dept. designates two of Assad Barakat's companies, as well," http://
www.america.gov/st/washfile-english/2004/June/20040610145904ASrelliM0.3693354.
html (accessed 10 June, 2004); Country Reports on Terrorism, released by the Office
of the Coordinator for Counterterrorism, Chapter 3: State Sponsors of Terrorism
Overview http://www.state.gov/s/ct/rls/crt/2006/82728.htm (accessed April 30, 2007).
63. *Al-Safir,* 14 November 2001.
64. *Le-Monde,* 25, July 2005; LBC, 22 July 2005; *Al-Arabiyah,* 20 July 2005.
65. "Hezbollah does not intend to disarm," http://www.terrorism-info.org.il/malam_
multimedia/html/final/sp/heb_n/hezbollah_0905.htm.
66. *Al-Sharq al-Awsat,* 4 November, 2005, 7 December 2005; *Daily Star,* 19 November
2005.
67. "One year since the acceptance of UN Security Council Resolution 1701, which ended
the second Lebanon war: An interim report," http://www.terrorism-info.org.il/
malam_multimedia/English/eng_n/html/un1701_0807.htm, (accessed August 12, 2007).

Chapter 10

1. *Al-Wasat,* 18 March 1996.
2. *Al-Manar,* 18 January 2002.

Epilogue

1. "Hezbollah Adopts New Political Document to Be Announced in Days," *Al-Jazeera,* 20
November 2009, http://aljazeera.com/news/articles/34/Hezbollah_Adopts_New_
Political_Document_to_Be_Anno.html.
2. Ibid.
3. "Hezbollah Vows to Boost Arsenal," *Al-Jazeera,* 30 November 2009,
http://english.aljazeera.net/news/middleeast/2009/11/20091130161054587528.html.
4. "Nasrallah: Continue Arming to Fight Israel," *The Jerusalem Post,* 30 November 2009,
http://www.jpost.com/Home/Article.aspx?id=161859.
5. "Hezbollah Ministers Quit Cabinet," *BBC News,* 12 November 2006,
http://news.bbc.co.uk/2/hi/middle_east/6139730.stm.
6. Maj.-Gen. (res.) Yaakov Amidror, "Misreading the Second Lebanon War," *Jerusalem
Issue Brief,* Vol. 6, No. 16, Jerusalem Center for Public Affairs, 16 January 2007, http://
www.jcpa.org/JCPA/Templates/ShowPage.asp?DBID=1&LNGID=1&TMID=111&FI
D=283&PID=1844&IID=1485.
7. "Security Council Calls for End to Hostilities Between Hezbollah, Israel: Unanimously
Adopting Resolution 1701 (2006)," Department of Public Information, UN Security
Council, 11 August 2006, http://www.un.org/News/Press/docs/2006/sc8808.doc.htm.

8. "Nasrallah: Winograd Proves We Won," *The Jerusalem Post*, 31 January 2008, http://www.jpost.com/Home/Article.aspx?id=90641; "Nasrallah on the Anniversary of Hezbollah's Victory over Israel," *The Palestine Telegraph*, 17 August 2009, http://www.paltelegraph.com/world/middle-east/77-middle-east/1856-nasrallah-on-the-anniversary-of-hezbollahs-victory-over-israel.

9. Hezbollah's 'Jihad al-Bina' Defies U.S. Sanctions," *Naharnet*, 25 February 2007, http://www.naharnet.com/domino/tn/NewsDesk.nsf/Lebanon/49DB1D0CAE241BC DC225728D003C6C0F?OpenDocument.

10. David E. Sanger and Michael Slackman, "U.S. Reports Plot to Topple Beirut Leaders," *The New York Times*, 2 November 2006, http://www.nytimes.com/2006/11/02/ washington/02prexy.html.

11. Ibid.

12. Yoav Shtern, "Nasrallah: We Have No Reason to Fear a Brother's War," *Haaretz*, 15 November 2006, http://news.walla.co.il/?w=/22/1008122; "Profile: Fouad Siniora," *BBC News*, http://news.bbc.co.uk/2/hi/middle_east/4641865.stm.

13. Alex Sorin, "Lebanese Paper Publishes Details of 22 Recently Arrested 'Israeli spies,'" *The Jerusalem Post*, 30 July 2009, http://www.jpost.com/home/article.aspx?id=231.

14. "Terrorism from Lebanon—2007 Update," *Anti-Israeli Terrorism in 2007 and its Trends in 2008*, Israel Ministry of Foreign Affairs, 5 June 2008, http://www.mfa.gov.il/ MFA/Terrorism-+Obstacle+to+Peace/Terrorism+from+Lebanon-+Hizbullah/ Terrorism+from+Lebanon+-+2007+update.htm?DisplayMode=print.

15. Barak Ravid, "Report: Hezbollah carries out military drills in south Lebanon," *Haaretz*, 22 November 2008, http://www.haaretz.com/news/report-hezbollah-carries-out-military-drills-in-southlebanon-1.257945.

16. "Terrorism from Lebanon—2007 Update."

17. "Nasrallah's Deputy: Hezbollah Ready for New War," *The Jerusalem Post*, 5 May 2007, http://www.jpost.com/Home/Article.aspx?id=60270.

18. "Iran Arming Hezbollah Via Turkey," *CBN News*, 5 March 2008, http://www. cbn.com/CBNnews/333543.aspx; Barak Ravid, "Israel to the UN: Hezbollah has Tripled the Number of Land-Sea Missiles and Has Rehabilitated its Power North of the Litani," *Haaretz*, 1 November 2007, http://www.haaretz.co.il/hasite/pages/ShArt.jhtml? itemNo=918932&contrassID=1&subContrassID=0&sbSubContrassID=0; Yoav Shtern and Amos Harel, "Hezbollah We Shall Take Practical Steps Against IDF Flights in Lebanon," *Haaretz*, August 3, 2008, http://www.haaretz.co.il/hasite/spages/1007660. html.

19. http://www.terrorism-info.org.il/malam_multimedia/Hebrew/heb_n/html/hezbollah_1107.htm.

20. "Hezbollah Admits Receiving Syrian Scuds," *The Jerusalem Post*, 15 April 2010, http://www.jpost.com/MiddleEast/Article.aspx?id=173217; "Qassem: We Have the Right to Own All Sorts of Arms to Carry Out Our Obligations," *Naharnet*, 15 May 2010, http://www.naharnet.com/domino/tn/NewsDesk.nsf/Lebanon/ 953E6A520CEDF152C225772400346A8C?OpenDocument.

21. Amos Harel and Shlomo Shamir, "Barak to UN: Hezbollah Arms Target Israeli Civilians," *Haaretz*, 24 February 2010, http://www.haaretz.com/news/barak-to-un-hezbollah-arms-target-israeli-civilians-1.266260.

22. Reuters, "There May Be a Solution to the Crisis in Lebanon: The Chief of Staff Shall Be President," *Ynet News*, 2 December 2007, http://www.ynet.co.il/articles/0,7340, L-3478262, 00.html; Yoav Shtern and news agencies, "The Lebanese President: Hezbollah Forces Will Be Integrated in the Army. The parliament has approved the nomination of the Chief of Staff, Michel Sulaiman, as President. George Bush: I am certain Sulaiman will disarm Hezbollah," *Haaretz*, 25 May 2008, http://www.haaretz.co.il/hasite/spages/986792.html.

23. Yoav Shtern, "Lebanese Relieved as Standoff Ends," *Haaretz*, http://www.haaretz. co.il/hasite/pages/ShArtPE.jhtml?itemNo=985697; Associated Press, "Hezbollah Supporters Celebrate: Hezbollah to Get Veto Power in a New National Government," *Haaretz*, 21 May 2008, http://www.haaretz.com/news/lebanese-relieved-as-standoff-ends-hezbollah-supporters-celebrate-1.246256.
24. Roi Nahmias, "Hezbollah has Gained Veto in the Government and a Change in the Electoral Districts," *Ynet News*, 21 May 2008, http://www.ynet.co.il/articles/0,7340,L-3545985,00.html.
25. Associated Press and Jerusalem Post Staff, "Hezbollah has Right to Transfer Arms," *The Jerusalem Post*, 16 February 2007, http://www.jpost.com/Home/Article.aspx?id=51772.
26. "Nasrallah: Lebanese Government's Decision is 'Declaration of War'," *The Jerusalem Post*, 8 May 2008, http://www.jpost.com/Home/Article.aspx?id=100581.
27. Associated Press, "Lebanon: The Rival Factions Have Agreed on the Conclusion of the Conflict," *Ma'ariv*, 21 May 2008, http://www.nrg.co.il/online/1/ART1/736/434.html.
28. "Lebanon: Soldiers Deployed to Maintain Order," *Ma'ariv*, 13 May 2008, http://www.nrg.co.il/online/1/ART1/732/879.html; Associated Press, "Lebanon: The Violent Fire Exchanges in Tripoli Have Resumed," *Ma'ariv*, 12 May 2008, http://www.nrg.co.il/online/1/ART1/732/558.html.
29. "Republic of Lebanon, Legislative Elections of 7 June 2009," http://psephos.adam-carr.net/countries/l/lebanon/lebanon2009.txt; Associated Press and Jerusalem Post Staff, "Nasrallah Accepts Defeat in Elections," *The Jerusalem Post*, 8 June 2009, http://www.jpost.com/Home/Article.aspx?id=144760.
30. "Lebanese President Michel Suleiman Said the Government Cannot Ask Shiite Guerilla Group Hezbollah to Give up Its Arms at a Time of Heightened Israeli Tension and Before Agreement on a National Defense Strategy was Reached," *Reuters*, http://www.reuters.com/article/idUSTRE64715V20100508.
31. "Jumblatt, Nasrallah Met to Assess Damascus Visit," *Yalibnan*, 9 April 2010, http://www.yal-ibnan.com/2010/04/09/jumblatt-nasrallah-met-to-assess-damascus-visit/.
32. The political platform of the new Lebanese government reflects an attempt to find common ground between the political factions. It also demonstrates the limitations of Prime Minister Saad Hariri and his supporters in dealing with Hezbollah, which has reinforced its internal Lebanese legitimacy. *Intelligence and Terrorism Information Center*, 4 January 2010, http://www.terrorism-info.org.il/malam_multimedia/English/eng_n/html/lebanon_e003.htm.
33. "Terrorism from Lebanon—2007 Update."
34. Roee Nahmias, "Nasrallah: Egypt Accomplice in 'Gaza Crime'," *Ynet News*, 28 December 2008, http://www.ynetnews.com/articles/0,7340,L-3646081,00.html; Roee Nahmias, "Report: Egypt to Warn Israel of Hezbollah Attack," 28 December 2008, *Ynet News*, http://www. ynet.co.il/english/articles/0,7340,L-3647103,00.html.
35. Full text of H. E. Sayyed Nasrallah speech on Day of Martyred Leaders, http://english.moqawama.org/essaydetails.php?eid=10225&cid=214.
36. "Arrest of Hezbollah Agent from Kalansua," 6 Aug 2008, Israel Ministry of Foreign Affairs, http://www.mfa.gov.il/MFA/Terrorism-+Obstacle+to+Peace/Terrorism+from+Lebanon-+Hizbullah/Arrest%20of%20Hizbullah%20agent%20from%20Kalansua%206-Aug-2008.
37. "Chapter 3: State Sponsors of Terrorism," *Country Report on Terrorism 2008*, 30 August 2009, U.S. Department of State, http://www.state.gov/s/ct/rls/crt/2008/ 122436.htm.
38. "Hezbollah External Security Organization," Australian Government, http://www.nationalsecurity.gov.au/agd/www/nationalsecurity.nsf/AllDocs/7986D153 6C0FFD5FCA256FCD001BE859?OpenDocument.

39. "President of Yemen: The Hezbollah Organization is Supplying Military and Logistical Training to the Yemenite Al-Khawthi Group, which is Striving to Topple the Regime," *ICT's Jihadi Websites Monitoring Group Insights*, The Institute for Counter-Terrorism (Herzliya, Israel: August 2009), 5–6, http://www.ict.org.il/Portals/0/Internet% 20Monitoring%20Group/JWMG_Hezbollah_Yemen.pdf.

40. "Iran Denied Supporting the Houthi," *Moheet News*, http://www.moheet.com/ show_news.aspx?nid=292525&pg=1.

41. "Exposure of a Hezbollah Terrorist Network in Egypt, Summary and Characteristics," *ICT's Jihadi Websites Monitoring Group Insights*, The Institute for Counter-Terrorism (Herzliya, Israel: August 2009) http://www.ict.org.il/Portals/0/Internet% 20Monitoring%20Group/JWMG_Hezbollah_Egypt.pdf.

42. Anar Valiyev, "Alleged Iranian and Hezbollah Agents on Trial for Targeting Russian-Operated Radar Station in Azerbaijan," *Terrorism Monitor* 7 (20), Jamestown Foundation, 9 July 2009, http://www.jamestown.org/single/?no_cache=1&tx_ttnews% 5Btt_news%5D=35246&tx_ttnews%5BbackPid%5D=7&cHash=3e9587db9d; Yossi Melman, "Hezbollah, Iran Plotted Bombing of Israel Embassy in Azerbaijan," *Haaretz*, 31 May 2009.

43. Avi Issacharoff, "Turkish Forces Foil Hezbollah Attack on Israeli Target," *Haaretz*, 9 December 2009, http://www.haaretz.com/print-edition/news/turkish-forces-foil-hezbollah-attack-on-israeli-target-1.2529.

44. "Chapter 3: State Sponsors of Terrorism," *Country Report on Terrorism 2008*, U.S. Department of State, 30 August 2009, http://www.state.gov/s/ct/rls/crt/2008/ 122436.htm.

45. "Egypt: Nasrallah is Serving as an Iranian Agent in Lebanon," *The Jerusalem Post*, 30 January 2009, http://www.jpost.com/Home/Article.aspx?id=131204; "Israeli Officials: Iran Solidifies Grip on Hezbollah," *The Jerusalem Post*, 8 September 2008, http://www.jpost.com/Home/Article.aspx?id=113654.

46. David Schenker "Is Israel Facing War with Hezbollah and Syria?" *Middle East Strategic Information*, 12 April 2010, http://www.mesi.org.uk/ViewBlog.aspx?ArticleId=81.

47. Zvi Mazal, "Did Lebanon Join the Axis of Evil?" *The Jerusalem Center for Public Affairs*, 10 December 2009, http://www.jcpa.org.il/Templates/showpage.asp?FID=650& DBID=1&LNGID=2&TMID=99&IID=23698.

Bibliography

AbuKhalil, Asa'd. "Druze, Sunni, and Shiite Political Leadership in Present-Day Lebanon." *Arab Studies Quarterly* 7, no. 4 (Fall 1985): 28–58.

———. "Ideology and Practice of Hizballah in Lebanon: Islamization of Leninist Organizational Principles." *Middle Eastern Studies* 27, (July 1991): 390–403.

———. "Syria and the Shiites: Al-Asasd's Policy in Lebanon." *Third World Quarterly* 12, no. 2 (1990). Ajami, Fouad, "Lebanon and its Inheritors," *Foreign Affairs* 63 (Spring 1985). Al-A'zi, Isan. *Hezbollah :Min Alhilm Alideology Ila Wakai'a Alsiasia.* Beirut, 1998.

Al-Azmeh, Aziz. *Islam and Modernity's.* London: Verso, 1993.

Avi-Ran, Reuben. *Syrian Involvement in Lebanon (1975–1985).* Tel Aviv: Jaffee Center For Strategic Studies, 1986.

Ayubi, Nazih. *Political Islam, Religion and Politics in the Arab World.* London: Routledge, 1991.

Blumer, H. "Collective Behavior." In *Review of Sociology: Analysis of a Decade,* edited by J. B. Gittler. New York, 1957.

Burk, Edmund. "Islam and Social Movements: Methodological Reflections." In *Islam, Politics, and Social Movements,* edited by Edmund Burk and Ira M. Lapidus, 17–35. London, 1988.

Choueiri, Youssef M. *Islamic Fundamentalism.* London, 1990.

Cobban, Helena, "The Growth of Shi'i Power in Lebanon and Its Implications for the Future." In *Shi'ism and Social Protest,* edited by Juan R. I. Cole and Nikki R. Keddie, 137–55. London: Yale University Press, 1986.

Coughlin, Con. Hostage: The Complete Story of the Lebanon Captives. London: Little Brown, 1992.

Deeb, Marius. "Shia Movements in Lebanon: Their Formation, Ideology, Social Basis, and Links with Iran And Syria." *Third World Quarterly* 10, no. 2 (April 1988): 683–98.

Dekmeijan, R. Hrair. *Islam in Revolution: Fundamentalism in the Arab World.* New York: Syracuse University Press, 1995.

Donohue, John J., and John J. Esposito, eds., *Islam in Transition.* New York: Oxford University Press, 1982.

Eickelman, Dale F., and James Piscatori. "Social Theory in the Study of Muslim Societies." In *Muslim Travelers: Pilgrimage, Migration, and the Religious Imagination,* edited by Dale F. Eickelman, and James Piscatori. London: Routledge, 1990.

Esposito, Jhon L. *Islam and Politics.* New York: Syracuse University Press, 1991.

———. *The Islamic Threat.* New York, 1992.

———. *The Islamic Threat: Myth or Reality?* New York, 1995.

Esposito, Jhon L., and John O. Voll. *Islam and Democracy.* New York: Oxford University Press, 1996.

Fadlallah, Ayatollah Al Sayed Muhamammed Hussein. "Islam and Violence in Political Reality." *Middle East Insight* 4, no. 4 (1986).

———. "An Islamic Perspective on the Lebanese Experience." *Middle East Insight* 6, no. 1 (1988).

————. "The New World Order and the Middle East—an Islamic Perspective." *Middle East Insight* 8, no. 1 (1991).

Fisk, Robert. *Pity the Nation: Lebanon at War*. Oxford, 1992.

Gurr, T. R. *Why Men Rebel*. Princeton University Press, 1970.

Hajjar, Sami G. *Hizballah: Terrorism, National Liberation, or Menace?* US Army War College, Strategic Studies Institute, August 2003.

Hamzeh, Nizar. "Lebanon's Hizbullah: from Islamic Revolution to Parliamentary Accommodation." *Third World Quarterly* 14, no. 2 (April 1993): 321–37.

Harik, Judith Palmer. "Between Islam and the System: Sources and Implications of Popular Support for Lebanon's Hizballah." *Journal of Conflict Resolution* 40, no. 1 (March 1996): 41–67.

Hatina, Meir. *Islam in Modern Egypt*. Tel Aviv: Tel Aviv University, Hakibbutz, 2000.

Hiro, Dilip. *Fire and Embers—A History of the Lebanese Civil War*. London: Weidenfeld and Nicholson, 1993.

Hoffman, B. "Holy Terror—The Implication of Terrorism Motivated by Religious Imperative." Rand P-7834, 1993.

Hussain, Asaf. *Political Terrorism and the State in the Middle East*. London: Mansell, 1988.

Hussein, Agha J., and Ahmad S. Khalidi. *Syria and Iran: Rivalry and Cooperation*. London: Pinter Publishers and the Royal Institute of International Affairs, 1995.

Jaber, Hala. *Hezbollah: Born with a Vengeance*. Columbia University Press, 1997.

Jenkins, J. C. *Resource Mobilization Theory and the Study of Social Movements*. Annual Review of Sociology, 1983.

Juergensmeyer, Mark. "The Logic of Religious Violence." *Journal of Strategic Studies*10, no. 4 (1987): 172–93.

Karmon, Ely. *Fight on All Fronts: Hizballah the War on Terror and the War in Iraq*. The Washington Institute Policy Focus, 2003.

Kepel, Gilles. *Jihad: The Trail of Political Islam*. Cambridge, MA: Harvard University Press, 2002.

————. *Muslim Extremism in Egypt: The Prophet and Pharaoh*. Berkeley: University of California Press, 1985.

Kohlberg, Etan. "Western Studies of Shi'an Islam." In *Shi'ism Resistance and Revolution*, edited by Martin Kramer, 31–46. Boulder, CO: Westview, 1987.

Kramer, Martin, "Hizbollah the Calculus of Jihad." In *Arab Awakening and Islamic Revival*, edited by Martin Kramer, 209–30. London: Transaction, 1996.

————. *Hizbollah Vision of the West*. Washington: Washington Institute for Near East Policy, policy paper no.16, October 1989.

————. ed. *The Islamism Debate*. Tel Aviv University, 1997.

————. "Redeeming Jerusalem: The Pan-Islamic Premise of Hizballah." In *The Iranian Revolution and the Muslim World*, edited by David Menashari, 105–30. Boulder, CO: Westview, 1990.

Lapidus, Ira M. "Islamic Political Movements: Patterns of Historical Change." In *Islam Politics and Social Movements*, edited by Edmund Burk and Ira M. Lapidus, 3–35. Berkeley: University of California Press, 1985.

Litvak, Meir, ed. *Islam and Democracy in the Arab World*. Tel Aviv: Tel Aviv University, Hakibbutz Hameuchad, 1998.

Mallat, Chbili. *Shi'i Thought from Shout of Lebanon*. Oxford: Center for Lebanese Studies, 1988.

McAdam, D. *Political Process and the Development of Black Insurgency, 1930–1970*. Chicago University Press, 1982.

McAdam, Douga, and David A. Snow. *Social Movements*. Roxbury, 1997.

McCarthy, J., and M. N. Zald. "Resource Mobilization and Social Movements." *American Journal of Sociology* 82 (1977).

Menshari, David. *A Decade of War and Revolution*. Tel Aviv: Kibbutz Me'uhad, 1988.

Meshunim, John G. *Sociology*. Tel Aviv: Tel Aviv University Press, 1999.

Mir, Mustansir. "Jihad in Islam." In *The Jihad and its Times*, ed. Hadia Dajani-Shakeel and Ronald A. Messier. Ann Arbor: University of Michigan Press, 1991.

Mishal, Shaul, and Avraham Sela. *Time of Hammas, Violence, and Compromise*. Yediot Ahronot and Hemed Books, 1999.

Norton, Augustus Richard. *Amal and the Shi'a Struggle for the Soul of Lebanon*. Austin, 1987.

———. *Hiaballah of Lebanon: Extremists vs. Mundane Politics*. New York: Council of Foreign Relation, 1999.

———. "Hizballah: from Radicalism to Pragmatism." *Middle East* Policy 5, no. 4 (January, 1998): 147–58.

O'Ballance, Edgar. *Islamic Fundamentalist Terrorism 1979–95: The Iranian Connection*. New York: New York University Press, 1997.

Olmert, Josef. "Iranian-Syrian Relations: between Islam and Realpolitick." In *The Iranian Revolution and the Muslim World*, edited by David Menashari, 171–88. Boulder, CO: Westview, 1990.

O'Sullivan, Noël K., ed. *Terrorism and Revolution: The Origin of Modern Political Violence*. London: Harvester, 1986.

Piscatori, James, ed. *Islam in the Political Process*. Cambridge University Press, 1983.

———. *Islam in a World of Nations States*. London: Royal Institute of International Affairs, 1986.

Qassem, Naim. *Hezbollah – Al-Manhag Al-Tajriba Al-Mustakbal*. Beirut: Dar Al Hadi, 2002.

Ramazani, R. K. *Revolutionary Iran: Challenge and Response in the Middle East*. Baltimore: Johns Hopkins University Press, 1986.

Ranstrop, Magnus. *Hizb'allah in Lebanon: The Politics of the Western Hostage Crisis*. London: Macmillan, 1997.

———. *Hizb'allah Political and Military Strategy in the 1990s—from Revolutionary Dogma to Lebanonization?* Oxford: British Middle East Studies Association Conference, 1997.

———. "The Strategy and Tactics of Hizballah's Current 'Lebanonization Process.'" *Mediterranean Politics* 3, no. 1 (Summer 1998): 103–34.

Roy, Olivier. *The Failure of Political Islam*. Cambridge, MA: Harvard University Press, 1995.

Saad-Ghorayeb, Amal. *Hizbullah Politics and Religion*. London: Pluto, 2002.

Schbley, Ayla Hammond. "Resurgent Religious Terrorim: A Study of Some of the Lebanese Shia Contemporary Terrorism." *Terrorism* 12 (1989): 213–47.

Schiff, Ze'ev, and Yaa'ari Ehoud, *Israel's Lebanon War*. London, 1985.

Scott, James C. "Protest and Profanation: Agrarian Revolt and the Little Tradition." Part 1. *Theory and Society* 4, no. 1 (1977): 21–38.

———. "Protest and Profanation: Agrarian Revolt and the little Tradition." Part 2. *Theory and Society* 4, no. 2 (1977): 211–45.

Sela, Avraham. *The Decline of Arab-Israeli Conflict, Middle East Politics and the Quest for Regional Order*. State University of New York, 1998.

Shapira, Shimon. *Hezbollah between Iran and Lebanon*. Hakibbutz Hameuchad, 2000.

Sharara, Wadah. *Dawlat Hizb Allah, Lubnan mujtami'an Islamiyyan*. Beirut, 1996.

Sivan, Emmanuel. *The Zealots of Islam*. Tel Aviv: Am Oved, 1986.

Skocpol, Theda. *Social Revolutions in the Modern World*. Cambridge University Press, 1994.

Steinbruner, John D. *The Cybernetic Theory of Decision*. Princeton University Press, 1974.

Taheri, Amir. *Holy Terror: The Inside Story of Islamic Terrorism*. London: Sphere Books, 1987.

———. *The Spirit of Allah: Khomeini and the Islamic Revolution*. Translated by Shamir Ami. Tel Aviv: Am Oved, 1987.

Tilly, C. *From Mobilization to Revolution*. Reading, MA: Addion Wesley, 1978.

Turner, R. H., and L. M. Killian. *Collective Behavior*. Englewood Cliffs, NJ: Prentice Hall, 1972.

Vaziri, Haleh. "Iran Involvement in Lebanon: Polarization and Radicalization of Militant Islamic Movements." *Journal of South Asian and Middle Eastern Studies* 16, no. 2 (Winter 1992): 1–16.

Wright, Robin. *Scared Rage: The Wrath of Militant Islam*. New York: Simon and Schuster, 1985.

Zisser, Eyal. "Hizballah in Lebanon at the Crossroads." In *Religious Radicalism in the Greater Middle East,* edited by Bruce Maddy-Weitzman and Efraim Inbar, 90–110. London: Frank Cass, 1997.

———. "Hizballah: New Course or Continued Warfare?" *MERIA Journal* 4, no. 3 September 2000.

———. "Syria and the United States: Bad Habits Die Hard." *The Middle East Quarterly* 10, no. 3 (Summer 2003).

———. "Syrian Foreign Policy under Bashar al-Assad." *Jerusalem Issue Brife* 4, no. 2 (29 August 2004).

Index